Sociolegal Perspectives of Linguistic Minorities in Europe

The Basque Language, Education, and Media

by

Ihintza Palacin Mariscal

Basque Politics Series #27

Sociolegal Perspectives of Linguistic Minorities in Europe:

The Basque Language, Education, and Media

by

Ihintza Palacin Mariscal

University of Nevada, Reno

Center for Basque Studies

This book was published with generous financial support from the Basque Government.

Center for Basque Studies
University of Nevada, Reno
1664 North Virginia St,
Reno, Nevada 89557 usa
http://basque.unr.edu

Copyright © 2025 by the Center for Basque Studies and the University of Nevada, Reno
ISBN-13: 978-1-949805-84-0
EPUB ISBN: 978-1-967179-05-3
All rights reserved.

Library of Congress Cataloging-in-Publication Data

Names: Palacin Mariscal, Ihintza, author.
Title: Sociolegal perspectives of linguistic minorities in Europe : the Basque language, education and media / Ihintza Palacin Mariscal, PhD.
Description: [Reno] : [Center for Basque Studies Press], [2024] | Includes bibliographical references and index. | Summary: "This book addresses the legal framework and social embedding of the Basque language. As a minority language located between two European states (France and Spain) with different approach towards minority languages, the task of understanding the legal framework of the Basque language and its relationship with the community of speakers is challenging. In fact, this legal framework results in a vast array of legal rules for Basque speakers. This book examines the fundamental and linguistic rights of these minority language speakers (norm users), from international and European legal frameworks to national or regional ones. It carries out a comparative analysis between France and Spain, and between the three Basque regions to examine the legal framework. This doctrinal analysis is complemented by the study of key actors participating in the context and implementation of the legal norms regulating the Basque language. An emphasis is placed on the analysis of the relationship between the legal framework of the Basque language and the Basque society, applying a sociolegal methodology"-- Provided by publisher.
Identifiers: LCCN 2023045040 (print) | LCCN 2023045041 (ebook) | ISBN 9781949805840 (paperback) | ISBN 9781967179053 (epub)
Subjects: LCSH: Linguistic minorities--Legal status, laws, etc.--European Union countries. | Minorities--Legal status, laws, etc.--European Union countries. | Language policy--European Union countries. | Basque language. | Europen Union countries--Languages--Social aspects.
Classification: LCC KJE5146.L36 P35 2024 (print) | LCC KJE5146.L36 (ebook) | DDC 342.2408/73--dc23/eng/20240116
LC record available at https://lccn.loc.gov/2023045040
LC ebook record available at https://lccn.loc.gov/2023045041

Printed in the United States of America

Acknowledgments

First and foremost, I am extremely grateful to Bruno de Witte, whose expertise was invaluable from the beginning to the end of this process. Your knowledge was irreplaceable. I thank you for your guidance, encouragement, and your patient support.

Second, I would like to acknowledge Joxerramon Bengoetxea, who helped me sharpen my theoretical approach, and with whom I had the pleasure to experience firsthand what teaching in a university really means. Thank you for your support, the opportunities you gave me, and all the interesting conversations we had while sipping coffee during breaks.

I also thank Gábor Halmai and Xabier Arzoz. I was lucky to meet Halmai at the European University Institute (EUI), where we had many inspiring conversations and seminars, and Arzoz has been an invaluable resource from the very start of this journey. Both provided detailed feedback of my text and shared their time generously.

This project, of course, would not have been possible without my interviewees, who were such a tremendous help to me. Thank you for sharing your expertise and your experience with me. I can assure that your passion about the Basque language is contagious.

Finally, I thank everyone who has been part of this journey—bidelagunak—and the Center for Basque Studies for guiding me along this journey.

What a beautiful road we have traveled together! Eskerrik asko.

Contents

Introduction ix

Part I: General Legal Framework of the Basque Language 1

Chapter 1: International and European Legal Framework and the Basque Language 3
Chapter 2: French Law and the Basque Language 33
Chapter 3: Spanish Law and the Basque Language 59

Part II: Education and the Basque Language 85

Chapter 4: Legal Framework of the Basque Language in Education 89
Chapter 5: Context of the Basque Language and Education 125

Part III: The Basque Language and Media 183

Chapter 6: Legal Framework of Media and the Basque Language 189
Chapter 7: Context of Media and the Basque Language 225
Conclusion 263
Bibliography 275
Appendix 1: Legal Documents 285
Appendix 2: Interviews 287
About the Author 289

Introduction

The Basque language (*Euskara*)¹ is seldom mentioned in discussions on the linguistic diversity in Europe, yet it has been spoken for more than eight thousand years and is the only non-Indo-European language of Western Europe still in active use. Basque people enjoy highlighting the antiquity of their language, so much so that the word used in Basque to refer to the Basques—*Euskaldunak*—literally means "those who have/speak Basque."² Thus, it comes as no surprise that Basque people do not relish the idea of losing such an essential element of their identity.

Basque symbolizes resistance, resilience, and reinvention. Yet, this language, which flourished throughout history, has been declining to the point of being classified as vulnerable by the UNESCO *Atlas of the World's Languages in Danger*.³ The construction of nation-states, years of assimilation, and more recent sociopolitical conflicts have all contributed to the decline of this language, which was mainly spoken rather than written.⁴ However, from the first publication in the Basque language in 1545,⁵ the creation of the "unified Basque language" (*Euskara batua*) in 1968, and several linguistic policies that have started to emerge for its protection, Euskara has managed to maintain itself.

The sociopolitical landscape of the Basque Country (*Euskal Herria*) plays an important role in the health and politization of the Basque language, as well as the reality of Basque speakers.⁶ On the Atlantic side of the Pyrenean border, between France and Spain, the Basque Country is now politically divided into three parts: the Basque Autonomous Community (BAC) and Navarre in Spain, and the *Communauté d'Agglomération Pays Basque* in France. The latter is the administrative entity corresponding to the Northern Basque Country (*Iparralde*). In addition to the diversity of its territories, "the Basque Country reveals a great deal of internal heterogeneity in terms of history, demographics, socioeconomics, language, culture and ideology."⁷ Regarding their linguistic policies, the three administrative areas have made different choices, and their evolution has been different. The co-official status given to the Basque language in the BAC means that this language is an official language in the public administration, together with Spanish. The same applies in the parts of Navarre where Basque is co-official (the so-called "Basque-speaking area").[8] In contrast, in Iparralde, the official language of the administration remains French, showcasing a different approach. Yet, influenced by their linguistic, cultural, and historical common ground, these territories have also continued to foster relationships with each other by means of formal legal cooperation[9] and through informal practices of cooperation, in which public institutions, as well as companies, civil society, associations, and private individuals take part (as is the case, for instance, with *Euskaraldia*[10] and *Korrika*[11]).

Civil society is regularly active in the Basque Country. Some significant examples of this are, among others, the creation of immersive schools in Basque—*Ikastola* schools,[12] the creation of the "market of Durango" (*Durangoko azoka*) for showcasing Basque literature and music, or even the creation of the first daily newspaper in Basque—*Egunkaria*.[13]

Notably, the Basque diaspora, by virtue of its continuous connection with the Basques "back at home" and Basque institutions, is key to understanding Basque identity and culture. These diasporic communities are mainly in the United States of America and Argentina, where we can find Basque schools, higher education institutions with Basque studies programs, and even Basque folklore events.[14] The Basque sociopolitical context and the Basque diaspora are important elements when researching Euskara.

Another element must be added to this discussion: the border (*muga*). This line drawn between Spain and France goes beyond the sociopolitical aspect elaborated earlier. The border, a symbol of division between the French and Spanish legal systems, is merely a bridge when analyzed through the linguistic lens. Transborder cooperation is a key element when discussing the Basques, and even more when analyzing the Basque language.

Regarding the politization of the language (politization understood as its regulation by the law), we find the first appearance of Euskara in a legal text in 1349. An ordinance of Huesca in that year expressly prohibited the use of Basque (together with Arabic and Hebrew) in the affairs of the city.[15] This formulation appeared continuously in ordinances until the nineteenth century. Therefore, the first mention of the Basque language in law—that we know of—starts with the prohibition of its use! This could be said to have been a premonition of what was to come.

After the short interlude of the Second Spanish Republic, when Basque was recognized as an official language in Navarre and the BAC,[16] Franco's dark years saw the systematic persecution of the Basque language. Examples include people being detained and fined for using Basque (a group of women were detained in 1959 for teaching catechism in Basque); prohibiting names and their spellings in Basque (by order of the Ministry of Justice, May 18, 1938); prohibiting the use of Basque in public documents (as prescribed by the Decree of June 2, 1944); and prohibiting the Basque language in the printed press (through an Order from April 1, 1947).[17]

On the other side of the border, Basque—like other regional languages[18]—has been in ongoing competition with the "national" language. The construction of French as the "national" language started with the Ordinance of Villers Cotterêts of 1539. This text granted to the French language the status of administrative language, rather than Latin or regional languages, and French slowly conquered the national territory. The linguistic policy of France (French as the sole official language) helped in that conquest.[19] The 1789 French Revolution added another layer to the language of the nation, linking French to national identity and thereby emphasizing a monolingual nation-state to guarantee equality among citizens. Furthermore, the famous speeches of Bertrand Barère de Vieuzac and Abbé Grégoire in 1794 called for the "eradication of local languages and the exclusive adoption of the French language."[20] This led to new assimilation policies, notably in education and public administration. Even in the current Fifth Republic, President Pompidou claimed that there is "no space for regional languages and cultures in a France destined to mark Europe with its seal."[21]

The early stages of linguistic regulation regarding the Basque language show that Euskara has more often been the object of legal prohibition than of legal protection. As shown by the (now classic) book *El libro negro del Euskera* (The black book of the Basque language) by Joan Mari Torrealdai, collecting three hundred years of prohibition, restriction, or hostility toward the Basque language, these difficulties have persisted over time.[22]

Fast forwarding to today, the Spanish Constitution accepts "other languages of Spain" as official in the autonomous communities (in its Article 3) and thus, Basque is co-official in the BAC and Navarre,[23] contrasting with the previous dictatorial regime's persecution and assimilation system. In France, despite Basque not having any regional co-official status as in Spain, Article 75-1 of the Constitution considers the regional languages as belonging to the "patrimony of France," and in 2017 a new administrative unit was created that corresponds to the territory of Iparralde.[24] To add to this, the Basque language is placed in a multilevel structure, where both France and Spain are part of the European Union and the Council of Europe, whose legal systems, including the European Charter for Regional or Minority Languages (henceforth the Language Charter), are relevant for the case of the Basque language.[25]

The definitions provided by the Language Charter can be used as the starting point of this book since the Basque language is considered a regional or minority language. In fact, Article 1.a of the Language Charter offers a definition of this category.

> For the purposes of this Charter:
> a. "regional or minority languages" means languages that are:
> i. traditionally used within a given territory of a State by nationals of that State who form a group numerically smaller than the rest of the State's population; and
> ii. different from the official language(s) of that State; it does not include either dialects of the official language(s) of the State or the languages of migrants;

Since Euskara is a language "traditionally used within a given territory" and since Basque speakers form "a group numerically smaller than the rest of State's population," and since Euskara is "different from the official languages" of France and Spain, we can safely identify Euskara as being a regional or minority language. To support this claim, we can add the available sociolinguistic data to better understand the language's degree of vulnerability in all three administrative divisions of the Basque Country.

Today's landscape of the Basque language varies, depending on the territory we are examining. Using the data provided by the Sociolinguistic Survey of 2016,[26] in the whole of the three Basque administrations (the BAC, Navarre, and Iparralde), 28.4 percent of the inhabitants older than sixteen years are Basque speakers, 16.4 percent understand (but don't speak) Basque, and 55.2 percent do not speak or understand Basque. This sociolinguistic research also shows the difference between the three areas. In the BAC, 33.9 percent are Basque speakers,

Introduction

whereas in Navarre, this number drops to 12.9 percent. Iparralde falls in the middle, with 20.5 percent Basque speakers. This data is shown in figure 1 below:

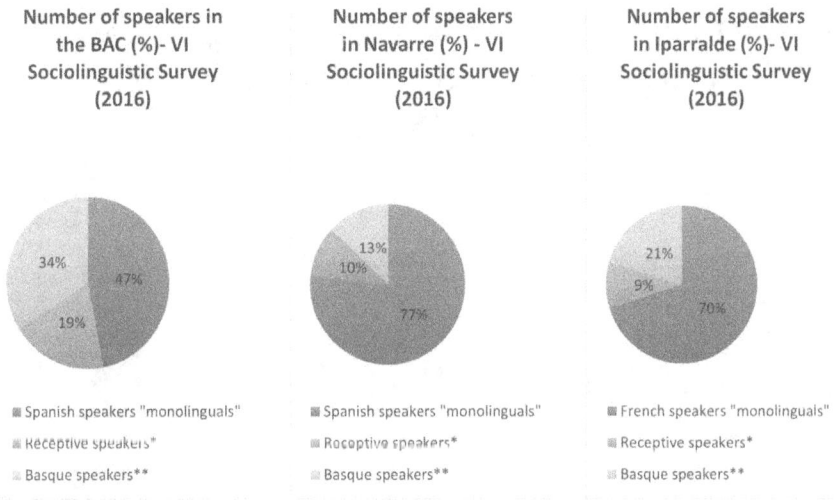

Figure 1. Language proficiency by region. The whole area of the Basque language, 2016 (%).[27]
(*) Receptive speakers: those who understand but do not speak Basque.
(**) Basque speakers: being Basque speakers does not mean they only speak this language. These speakers are at least almost exclusively bilinguals between Basque-Spanish or Basque-French. Also, note the Sociolinguistic Survey refers to the Spanish speakers or French speakers as "monolinguals," but this does not mean, despite not speaking Basque, these people cannot speak other languages. Therefore, the author considers this term is misleading.

Although at first glance these percentages might seem low, it is important to bear in mind the improvement made since the first sociolinguistic research in 1991. In fact, when the first sociolinguistic research appeared, the number of Basque speakers was only 22.3 percent in total. Comparing both surveys, the number of inhabitants who understand Basque has also risen (from 7.7 percent in 1991 to 16.4 percent in 2016). When analyzing this data, there is a corresponding decrease of monolingual Spanish/French speakers (from 70 percent in 1991, to 55.2 percent in 2016). Another thing to note is that the number of Basque speakers has grown in the BAC and Navarre but has decreased in Iparralde. Looking at the age groups of the sociolinguistic research, one can see that the largest number of Basque speakers (in all three areas joined together) are under the age of 35 (age groups of 16–24 and 25–34). The number of Basque speakers has also risen in the 35–49 age group. This is a tendency we can see over time in figure 2.

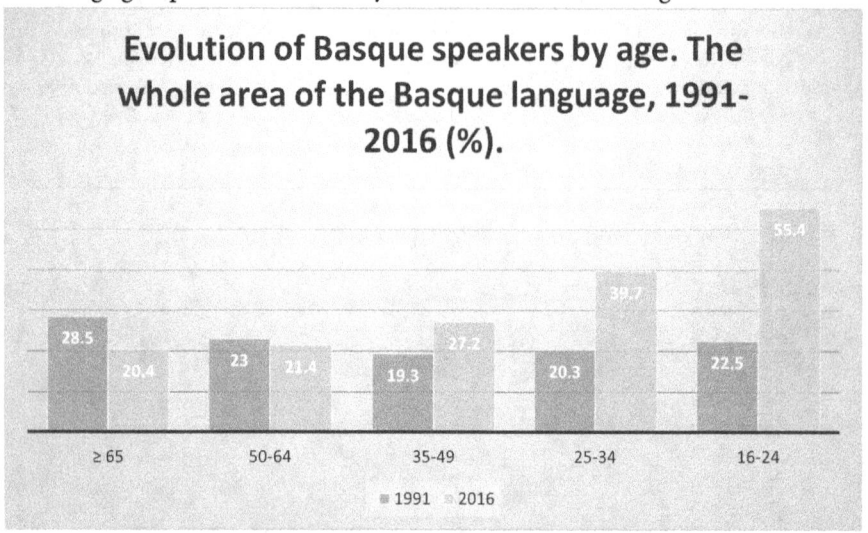

Figure 2. Evolution of Basque speakers by age.

This data helps us understand that the increase over time in the number of Basque speakers has happened through the younger generations. Yet, at the same time, what was once the largest group of speakers (the older generation) has been diminishing over the years. Regarding Iparralde, it is worth noting that the largest percentage of Basque speakers is still found among the oldest group, 65 and older.

If we focus on the level of *facility* or *fluency*[28] when speaking Basque, we see that 16 percent of Basques (in all regions combined) feel more comfortable speaking Basque than any other language. These are defined as Basque bilinguals. The highest percentage of Basque bilingual speakers remains the group of 65 and older in 2016 (42.2 percent), and the lowest percentage of Basque bilinguals is among the group of 35–49 (20.1 percent). If we compare the different Basque territories, we see that the lowest percentage of Basque bilingual speakers is in Iparralde (20.9 percent) while the largest is in the BAC (26.8 percent). In Navarre, 23.2 percent are Basque bilingual. "Balanced bilinguals"[29] represent 29.5 percent. The largest percentage of balanced bilinguals is located between 35 and 65 years old. By region, Iparralde has the highest percentage of balanced bilinguals with 37.6 percent, followed by the BAC (29.3 percent) and Navarre (25.7 percent). In figure 3, the Basque bilinguals are shown in light gray, the balanced bilinguals are in gray, and the non-Basque bilinguals are in black.[30] Unlike figure 1, figure 3 excludes the monolinguals to focus on the Basque speakers.

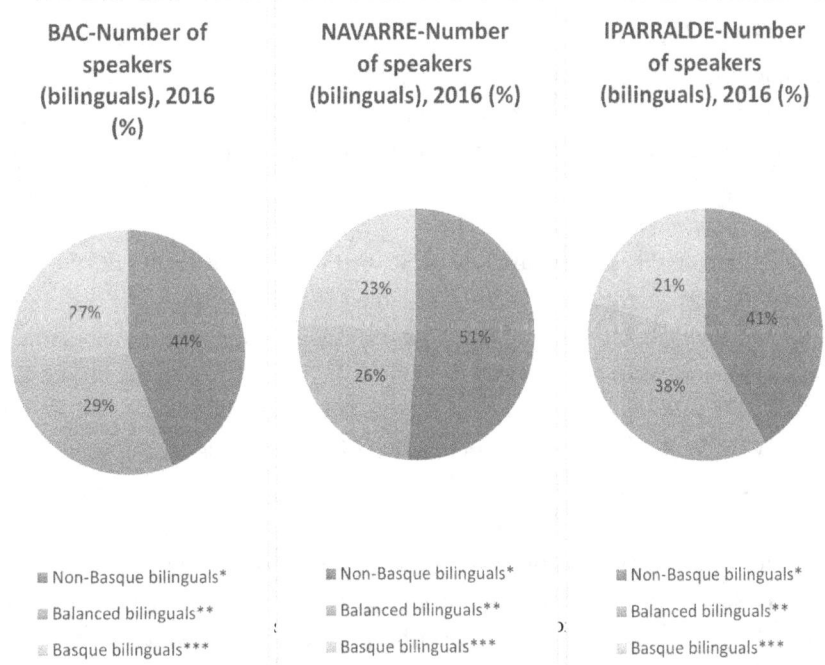

(*) When referring to a "non-Basque" language, the sociolinguistic report explains that this refers mainly to Spanish or French, but the report also highlights the new languages that are increasing their presence in the Basque territories, such as Romanian, Portuguese, Arabic, and Russian—and which, therefore, a non-Basque bilingual may speak.
(**) This refers to bilinguals who have the same level in both languages (Spanish and Basque, or French and Basque). In Basque: *elebidun orekatuak*.
(***) This refers to bilinguals who feel more fluent in Basque than in Spanish and/or French, despite being bilinguals in both languages.

Concluding this brief presentation of the book's main topic: The Basque language is a minority language that has struggled with restrictions and prohibitions by law but has managed to survive. The recent, more favorable legal norms still show differences between the three Basque administrative territories. And finally, the latest sociolinguistic data indicates that there is still a great deal of work to do for the improvement of the health of this minority language. This book will present the legal norms regulating the Basque language and, at the same time, will uncover the reality of the speakers beyond the norms.

Methodology

Considering the Basque language's struggles over the decades, and the commitment of Basque speakers toward the maintenance and survival of this language, this book will ask the following questions: How is the Basque language regulated by law in the three Basque administrations, and what is the relationship between this legal framework and the Basque society?

To answer these questions, a plural methodology is necessary. We must explore the legal framework (*the law*) regarding the Basque language, performing a doctrinal analysis, and we must combine this analysis with a contextual examination of this normative order (*the context*). This dual examination will enable us to understand two things: why the law has developed as it has (in the three territories), and how the legal rules are applied in practice—in other words, the "upstream" and "downstream" dimensions of the legal rules. The inquiry into the social context is instrumental in answering the question of how the Basque language is legally regulated, since to understand it, one needs to study the sociolegal context.

In doing so, we will adopt MacCormick's *norm giver* and *norm user* distinction.[31] Norm givers are those creating the norm (a parliament, for example) and norm users are the humans, the recipients of the norm. This offers a rich explanatory theoretical framework that considers a realist vision of the law, including the norm users in the equation. Other theoretical frameworks could have been contemplated for carrying out this research. The strictly positivist route would have been a good option to research the legal framework of the Basque language; yet, by only focusing on the positivist approach, we would miss the context in which this law lives. In the world of sociolegal theory, systems theory could have been useful in researching both the legal and the social systems of the Basque language. However, systems theory, despite recognizing that the law is in communication with society, fails to pay enough attention to norm users. In fact, the study of a legal order cannot be detached from the study of norm users: "The very fact of institutionalization of legislative power means that the results of exercise of that power may be statutory texts that are very imperfectly, if at all, observed as working norms from any norm-user's point of view."[32] The norm users are the actual recipients of rights and duties, and they end up defining the legal system.[33] Therefore, focusing on the norm users establishes a comprehensive framework for the analysis of the legal framework and social embedding of the Basque language.

As mentioned earlier, the Language Charter is of paramount importance when it comes to regional or minority languages in Europe. It is also relevant for this research, notably because of the approach to linguistic rights this Language Charter provides. The Language Charter does not merely list linguistic rights; it also contains areas in which these rights must be developed, highlighting the importance of the *implementation* of linguistic rights for the regional or minority languages. This research takes a similar approach, since it does not stop at the doctrinal analysis of the legal protection of the Basque language but goes beyond and examines the context in which these rights are intended to be implemented, thus providing a comprehensive understanding of the legal framework of the Basque language.

A key point for this study is the diversity of the legal regulation of Euskara. Indeed, this diversity calls for a comparative analysis of the domestic law of two states—France and Spain—including the regionally specific law applying in the BAC, Navarre, and Iparralde, within a European and international normative context. The regulation of the Basque language includes not only the legal rules themselves (the so-called "black letter law") but also the legal practice(s) regarding those rules. This means, following MacCormick's definition of law as being the "institutional normative order,"[34] that norm givers (institutions creating the law) are not only responsible for the legal regulation of the Basque language, but they also give meaning to the law.[35] Actually, norm givers are meant to create norms that meet the normative expectations and aspirations of society.[36] In doing so, they create norms with an idea in mind. For instance, by granting co-officiality to the Basque language, norm givers meet the normative expectations of the citizens who speak that language and want to obtain full linguistic rights.

The doctrinal dimension of this research will be divided into a general doctrinal analysis and the study of two specific areas of social life (education and media). The first area of social life studied in this research is immediately evident when reading the previous sociolinguistic data: The key for the creation of new speakers resides in the transmission of the language, mainly through the education system. The linguistic aspect is of central importance in education.[37] It is via schooling that pupils correctly learn languages and use them outside the private sphere of their families and homes. Furthermore, considering that the first language is not Basque for 79.5 percent of the population of the Basque Country,[38] the role of education has been, and still is, crucial for the survival of the language.

The second area of social life we will analyze is linked to access to the language as well as its transmission: media. Despite not being as discernible in the sociolinguistic data analyzed previously, accessing and producing media are crucial for minority languages. Broadcasting, written press, and new communication technologies play a pivotal role in transmitting a language, using a language, and giving a platform for voices in that language to be heard. Therefore, the choice of these two areas of social life lies in their importance for the survival and improvement of the Basque language. Both media and education are key for its transmission, the increase in number of speakers, and the creation of public spaces for its use. A study of the relevant context will accompany each doctrinal analysis. Focusing on the norm users and norm givers will help us, by targeting the key actors of social life, to reach a comprehensive understanding of how the law on the Basque language functions in the social reality, and why the law was written as such. Analyzing public and private actors of the general Basque legal order will enable us to draw a comprehensive and accurate picture of the law and context of Euskara.

This book examines the key actors for both areas of the analyzed social life. Actors are defined in this research as participants in the implementation of the legal norms on the Basque language. The category of actors includes both norm givers and norm users. For clarity, in this research, actors are divided into public and private, depending on whether the actors belong to public or private law. Thus, actors take a variety of shapes: from public institutions to private individuals in the form of parents (norm users), or from courts (norm givers) to newspapers, and so on. This book aims to analyze key actors—both public and private—in the areas of education and media. Sometimes these actors coincide, but not always. Further in this research we will reflect on the different shapes norm users take, as well as the sometimes-blurry division between norm givers and norm users.

To accurately interpret the social context of the legal order of the Basque language, selected interviews were conducted to better understand the situation in each one of the cases. The fact that the author is part of the Basque community, an insider, was helpful in gaining access to these actors, as well as in conducting the interviews in their chosen language, which was Basque.

Because the author is a Basque speaker and believes in the importance of preserving the Basque language and respecting linguistic rights, the approach of this book has been developed from that perspective. Nonetheless, the author has made every effort to provide an objective analysis. Also, and most importantly, this book sheds light on the enormous influence the legal order has on the everyday linguistic rights of Basque speakers and gives a contextualized account of the normative order of the Basque language.

Structure of the book

Part I will provide a doctrinal analysis of the legal framework of the Basque language in all three Basque administrative territories. This will consist of the examination of the international and European regimes toward regional or minority languages, paying special attention to their relevance for the Basque language. This part of the book will proceed to study the constitutional laws of France and Spain and their different approaches toward the Basque language, together with an exploration of the relevant case law. Part I also examines the general legislative texts, especially those adopted at the regional level in the case of Spain.

In part II we will explore the topic of education and the Basque language. Here, the analysis will provide both doctrinal and empirical research to present a contextualized view of the legal regulation of this domain. More specifically, this part will explore the different legal regulations of Euskara in education both at the national level in France and Spain, as well as within the three Basque administrations. This doctrinal examination will then be complemented with empirical studies of the role of public and private actors that are essential to understand bottom-up and top-down dimensions of the legal norms regulating education in Euskara.

Part III will examine the topic of media and the Basque language. This section will adopt a similar structure to that of part II: a doctrinal analysis of the law relating to the place of Basque in the media will be complemented with examples of public and private actors' roles that will explain why the law has developed the way it has and how the legal norms are applied in practice.

Finally, the conclusion will reflect on the links between the legal framework and the context regarding the legal regulation of the Basque language. We will discuss the similarities and differences between the areas of education and media, and between the three administrations of the Basque Country and their respective legal frameworks. This will help us showcase how the study of the social context has enriched the understanding of the legal rules on Euskara. We will give some recommendations based on the findings of this research, as well as provide ideas for future research directions.

Notes

1. Euskara (or Euskera) is the name of the Basque language in Basque. The author will use both "Basque" and "Euskara" interchangeably throughout the thesis.
2. Translated by the author.
3. Moseley, Atlas of the World's Languages in Danger.
4. The oral tradition is still alive with bertsolaritza (traditional oral sung poetry) and pastolara (a musical play).
5. Bernat Etxepare, Lingua vasconum primitiae, 1545. This book in Basque was published under a Latin title. It was followed by the first publication of the New Testament in Basque in 1571 by Joannes Leizarraga.
6. The Basque Country is often used as the equivalent of the Basque Autonomous Community (BAC), but in this book the Basque Country is understood as the combination of the three administrative divisions where Basque is spoken: the BAC, Navarre, and Iparralde (the Northern Basque Country, which is that part of the Basque Country to the north of the international frontier between Spain and France).
7. Azurmendi, Bachoc, and Zabaleta, "Reversing Language Shift: The Case of Basque," 238.
8. This issue will be discussed throughout the book, and the legal basis of this territorial division of co-officiality is discussed in part I, chapter 3.
9. See the latest language policy partnership agreement between institutions from the BAC, Navarre, and Iparralde in 2020: https://www.mintzaira.fr/fileadmin/documents/Aktualitateak/Eusko_Jaurlaritza_eta_Nafarroa/2020/3ko_

ituna_Annexe_2020_fr.pdf (Accessed July 20, 2021).
10 Euskaraldia is an initiative in all three Basque administrative territories with the aim of creating social conditions for speaking Basque, with the goal of increasing the social use of Basque. See https://euskaraldia.eus/es/ (Accessed April 29, 2021).
11 Korrika is an exhibition race held in the three Basque administrative territories to raise funds for the organization AEK (Alfabetatze Euskalduntze Koordinakuntza, Basque Literacy Coordination) that teaches Basque to adults. See https://korrika.eus/index.php/es/inicio (Accessed April 29, 2021).
12 Ikastola schools are analyzed in part II on education.
13 The newspaper Egunkaria is analyzed in part III on media.
14 Ikastola schools in the USA and Argentina; Basque traditional sports known as jai alai in the USA; the Center for Basque Studies at the University of Nevada, Reno; the Jaialdi festival of Basque culture and folklore in Boise, Idaho; and "Euskal Etxeak" around the world, to name a few.
15 Lacasta Estaun, "El Euskera en el alto Aragón," 141.
16 See part I, chapter 3.
17 Torrealdai, El libro negro del euskera.
18 The French label of "regional languages" to refer to these historical languages is controversial. The author addresses this appellation in part I, chapter 2.
19 Adrey, Discourse and struggle in minority language policy formation, 110.
20 Adrey, 115.
21 Translated by the author: "Il n'y a pas de place pour les langues et cultures régionales dans une France destinée à marquer l'Europe de son sceau," Georges Pompidou, April 14, 1972.
22 The collection of these examples and more are found in Torrealdai, El libro negro del euskera.
23 This will be elaborated further in part I, chapter 3.
24 See part I, chapter 2.
25 The relationship of the Language Charter and the Basque language will be discussed in chapter 1.
26 All the figures below are extracted from the 2016 Sociolinguistic Survey, published jointly by the Basque government, the Government of Navarre and the Public Office of the Basque Language. https://www.irekia.euskadi.eus/uploads/

attachments/9954/VI_INK_SOZLG-EH_eus.pdf?1499236557 (Accessed May 18, 2020). The translation of the information in the figures has been provided by the author. After the preparation of this book, the VII Sociolinguistic survey was published, showing similar tendencies.

27 The following figures are made and translated by the author using the data from the VI Sociolinguistic Survey.
28 In Basque: erraztasuna.
29 This refers to bilinguals who have the same level in both languages (Spanish and Basque, or French and Basque). In Basque: elebidun orekatuak.
30 When referring to a "non-Basque" language, the sociolinguistic report explains that this refers mainly to Spanish or French, but the report also highlights the new languages that are increasing their presence in the Basque territories, such as Romanian, Portuguese, Arabic, and Russian—and which, therefore, a non-Basque bilingual may speak.
31 MacCormick, "Institutional Normative Order: A Conception of Law"; MacCormick, Institutions of law.
32 MacCormick, Institutions of law, 71.
33 Bengoetxea, Neil MacCormick y la razón práctica institucional.
34 MacCormick, "Institutional Normative Order: A Conception of Law."
35 Bengoetxea, Neil MacCormick y la razón práctica institucional.
36 Bengoetxea, "Legal theory and sociology of law," 14.
37 Milian i Massana, Más sobre derechos lingüísticos, 117.
38 See the Sociolinguistic Survey of 2016. This data will be analyzed thoroughly in part II (particularly in chapter 5).

Part I

General Legal Framework of the Basque Language

This section will analyze the different regulations of the Basque language, at various levels. It will examine the international and European regulations (in chapter 1) as well as national and regional regulations in France (chapter 2) and in Spain (chapter 3), to provide a general understanding of the regulation of the Basque language by law.

1

International and European Legal Framework and the Basque Language

The protection of minorities in Europe started in the seventeenth and eighteenth centuries and, at first, protection was directed toward religious minorities. Territories often changed hands, and the inhabitants' religions changed with the rulers.[1] Later on, in the nineteenth century, Europe saw the rise of ethnic or cultural nationalism, as well as the golden age of "classical" international law. At the same time, the nineteenth century saw the development of language as the asset of nation-states, leading to the spread of control of the use of language(s) by the state.[2] After the sufferings of the Second World War, the second wave of protection of minorities blossomed with the creation of international tools for their protection.

When discussing international law and the Basque language, and by extension, the international law of linguistic minorities, we will shed light on the contemporary international framework of languages, and minority languages more precisely. Minority rights differ from general human rights in the sense that the latter concerns universal and individual rights, whereas the former concerns specific rights of each minority, including both individual and collective rights.[3] Also, minority rights can be considered as specific applications of the right to equality.[4] It is important to keep in mind that languages are woven into most international instruments. In other words, their protection is usually layered in between the protection of other elements.

Another element to remember when discussing the legal framework of the Basque language is the law of the European Union, France and Spain being both member states. Other European instruments precisely created for the protection of minorities and linguistic minorities are also essential for an understanding of the legal framework of the Basque language.

The Protection of (Minority) Languages through General Human Rights

As aptly summarized by Pons Parera, three paradigms of protection are applicable in the international legal framework of language rights: first, by creating linguistic rights or by the presence of linguistic content implicit in other rights; second, by protecting minorities (linguistic and national minorities in particular); and third, by protecting linguistic diversity.[5] These three paradigms are interactive, reinforcing or neutralizing each other. The paradigms are reflected, in various ways, in the international and European legal instruments for the protection of language rights. The United Nations (UN) has traditionally included linguistic rights under the protection of human rights,[6] while the United Nations Educational, Scientific and Cultural Organization (UNESCO) has covered the protection of linguistic and cultural diversity.[7] At the European level, the most comprehensive protective system in terms of language rights remains in the hands of the Council of Europe. This protection network consists of three elements: human rights,[8] the protection of minorities,[9] and the safeguarding of linguistic diversity.[10] Pons Parera also adds that the Organization for Security and Cooperation in Europe (OSCE) has intervened in language rights,[11] notably since the creation of the High Commissioner on National Minorities in 1992.[12] Yet, there is no binding universal multilateral treaty with the sole objective of protecting linguistic rights.

Key Areas of Protection of Languages in General Human Rights

The protection of linguistic rights in the international legal system appears in five main areas: the principle of nondiscrimination; freedom of expression; names; criminal procedure rights; and education. Yet, the key element for the protection of language rights under the international human rights framework is the principle of nondiscrimination.[13] The UN Human Rights Committee defines the term "discrimination" as "distinction, exclusion, restriction or preference which is based on any ground such as [. . .] language [. . .] and which has the purpose or effect of nullifying or impairing the recognition, enjoyment or exercise by all persons, on an equal footing, of all rights and freedoms."[14] Following this principle would mean the exclusion of "all discriminatory treatment which implies the denial or deprivation of rights from using a specific language."[15] The principle of nondiscrimination does not confer linguistic rights or offer protection of languages per se, but is rather a protection linked to the exercise of the other rights recognized by international treaties. Although the principle of nondiscrimination implies the need for equal treatment among individuals, it does not aim to protect differentiated identities. Therefore, Pons Parera defines the principle of nondiscrimination as a "case of a minimum threshold, opposable against those actions or displays that stigmatize or give unfavorable treatment to certain people or groups due to the use or defense of a language."[16] As a matter of fact, "the common theme is the maintenance of principles of antidiscrimination and noninterference so that linguistic minorities can enjoy linguistic freedom in the private sphere,"[17] and noninterference is not the same as the state actively promoting multilingualism.

Alongside the principle of nondiscrimination, the protection of language rights is woven into the principle of freedom of expression[18] and the right to hold opinions.[19] The right of freedom of expression not only refers to the message but also to the language in which it is expressed:[20]

> It [is] impossible to ignore the fact that freedom of expression normally takes on its meaning when the individual is placed in a certain social context. The impediment by the authorities of the use of a certain language in a framework of collective exercising of the freedom of expression will normally fall on the exercising of rights.[21]

Therefore, despite the fact that the use of a language (or more than one) can be limited by a constitutional text, constrictive linguistic interventions are accepted as long as they meet the conditions required on the limits to freedom of expression, notably when it comes to the private use of the language.[22] The case of freedom of expression also shows linguistic limitations are kept mainly to the public sphere.[23] It must be noted, however, this can be extended to situations with private media, or private conversations. Hence, the international legal system on human rights understands the protection of linguistic rights both in public and private areas, notably under the banner of freedom of expression. For instance, Article 2.1[24] of the UN Declaration on the Rights of Persons Belonging to National or Ethnic, Religious and Linguistic Minorities claims the right of minorities to "use their own language in *private and public*."[25] This UN Declaration, paired with the Framework Convention for the Protection of National Minorities on the right of freedom of expression,[26] supports the view that the international legal system protects language rights both in public and private settings.

Another element linked to private life and its linguistic content under the human rights law is the right to choose a name.[27] In fact, the linguistic content of this right stretches the "traditional" understanding of it—the "traditional" purpose being the identification of a person, with some legal restrictions accepted in the name of public interest.[28] The linguistic layer of this right is the right of the parents to choose the name of their child in a language that is not the official language of the state.[29] This right of the parents regarding their child's name is still contested, notably in France.[30]

When discussing the language rights in the international human rights legal system, one must not forget criminal procedure rights.[31] Under international law, a person who is arrested or accused of a crime must be informed of the reasons for the arrest and the nature and cause of the accusations against this person in a language that she or he understands. Also, the person must be offered the free assistance of an interpreter if they cannot understand the official language.

Finally, education is another area where the international human rights legal system provides room for language rights. The general principle is in the Convention on the Rights of the Child of 1989, where the child's "cultural identity, language and values"[32] should be respected. This "discredits the homogenizing linguistic-school policies and models, which ignore or underestimate the child's language."[33] Yet, despite the CRC's Article 30 protecting minorities,[34] and notably linguistic minorities, positive obligations for the states remain somewhat vague and general.[35]

European Convention of Human Rights and the European Court of Human Rights

The European Convention of Human Rights (ECHR) and the European Court of Human Rights (ECtHR)[36] were not expressly created with the protection of minorities in mind. The goal of this European human rights protection system is, according to its Preamble, to secure "the universal and effective recognition and observance of [human rights]"[37] in order to pursue the aim of the Council of Europe, which is "the achievement of greater unity between its members."[38] Hence, the overall goal of the ECHR is the "maintenance and further realization of Human Rights and Fundamental Freedoms."[39] The ECHR was created to protect human rights in general, and the explicit protection of minorities is included in other Council of Europe instruments that will be examined later in this chapter.[40] Also, it is important to note the ECHR does not include group rights. The ECHR was created as a regional instrument to provide fundamental and human rights protection to individuals. This means, in the text of the ECHR, that linguistic minorities are not expressly mentioned. However, the ECHR "counters and prevents discrimination or degrading treatment toward individuals who belong to particular linguistic groups. It is thus an important contributor to the maintenance of the rights of linguistic minorities, even if those rights are mostly confined to the private sphere and are essentially a prohibition of discrimination."[41]

The ECHR sanctions the breach of minority language speakers' human rights but does not actively encourage the promotion or development of linguistic minorities. Despite not being a specific instrument of linguistic minority protection, the ECHR does protect individuals, as members of minority groups. Indeed, the case law of the ECtHR provides us with some examples where minorities have been protected using the ECHR text.

The ECtHR interprets Articles 8, 9, and 11 in a "group related sense."[42] For instance, in *Sidiropoulos v. Greece*,[43] the ECtHR stated that "mention of the consciousness of belonging to a minority and the preservation and development of a minority's culture could not be said to constitute a threat to 'democratic society.'"[44] Another key case regarding the protection of minorities by the ECtHR is that of *Chapman v. United Kingdom*,[45] since the Strasbourg Court recognized that there is a positive obligation for the states, under Article 8 of the ECHR to "facilitate the Gypsy way of life."[46] In fact, the ECtHR considers "the vulnerable position of Gypsies as a minority means that some special consideration should be given to their needs and their different lifestyle."[47]

The ECtHR has delivered landmark decisions about the protection of minorities, yet the protection of linguistic minority rights remains scarce. In 1968, the *Belgian linguistic case*[48] showed the traditional approach of the ECtHR to linguistic rights. This case had to do with Articles 8 and 14 of the ECHR. The ECtHR claimed Article 2 of Protocol 1 does not grant a right to education in one's own language. This case clearly had to do with the linguistic rights of a linguistic minority, but the Strasbourg Court was rather restrictive about language rights in relation to educational rights of these French-speaking minorities. However, the ECHR and the interpretation of the ECtHR offer some room for the protection of linguistic minorities,[49] outside of the above-mentioned case law, notably via the freedom of expression in Article 10. This will be explored further in part III, which focuses on media.

International Protection of Minorities and Minority Languages

International law also offers specific protection for minorities and minority languages. These are worth exploring for the example of the Basque language. Article 27 of the International Covenant on Civil and Political Rights is essential for minority protection on the international scene. The analysis will continue at the European level with the European Charter for Regional or Minority Languages, and the Framework Convention for the Protection of National Minorities.

Article 27 of the International Covenant on Civil and Political Rights

The aftermath of the Second World War brought a new era of minority rights protection, notably with the International Covenant on Civil and Political Rights (ICCPR). Since we are going to focus on language rights and linguistic minorities, we will shift our focus to Article 27 of the ICCPR:

> In those States in which ethnic, religious or *linguistic minorities* exist, persons belonging to such minorities shall not be denied the right, in community with the other members of their group, to enjoy their own culture, to profess and practice their own religion, or *to use their own language.*[50]

Despite being written in negative terms, Article 27 does recognize the existence of a right. In addition, it must be noted that Article 27 of the ICCPR contains the obligation for the states to *take positive measures of protection*[51] for the promotion of the linguistic and culture identity of the minority.[52] In fact, according to the Human Rights Committee, this right is granted to "individuals belonging to minority groups and which is distinct from, and additional to, all the other rights which, as individuals in common with everyone else, they are already entitled to enjoy under the Covenant."[53] Article 27 imposes specific obligations on state parties for the protection of these rights, notably linguistic rights.[54] Furthermore, the presence of minorities for the purposes of the application of Article 27 does not depend on the recognition by the state of them, and "the applicability of the protective measures set out is general in all those states in which minorities exist."[55] This might have been one of the reasons why the French state submitted a reservation to Article 27 of the ICCPR,[56] resulting in the Basques and the Basque language not being protected under Article 27 in France. Euskara is, however, protected under this article in Spain. Thus, despite Article 27 seeming to grant a comprehensive protection to minorities, "the opening phrase [. . .] almost invites states to declare that they have no minorities, but only France has recorded an 'official statement to that effect.' "[57] The example of Article 27 of the ICCPR and the reservation of France show the issue of the international legal system regarding the Basque language: The protection by the human rights legal system depends on the willingness of a state to protect its minorities.

Even where a democratic system is coupled with a rule-of-law society, this in itself is not sufficient guarantee against majoritarian abuse or dominance. After all, the laws that guide the institutions of such a state are themselves the product of a majoritarian decision-making process. Hence, human and minority rights are still seen as a necessary defense against the otherwise all-powerful state.[58]

Therefore, despite being limited, the international legal system is necessary for the protection of minorities and minority languages. Luckily for the Basque language, European law provides for an extension of this protection.

The European Charter for Regional or Minority Languages (the Language Charter)

When studying the European legal framework of the Basque language, one must inevitably address the Language Charter. Both Spain and France signed this treaty, which means that it could play a role in the protection of the Basque language in both countries. However, as is widely known, France has not ratified the Language Charter. Thus, only Spain has legal obligations.

The Language Charter is a convention adopted within the framework of the Council of Europe, and it is the only binding document (to date) expressly dealing with minority languages. It emerged from the aim of the Council of Europe to adopt treaties for "the maintenance and further realisation of human rights and fundamental freedoms."[59] The Council of Europe, thus, decided to create a document for the protection of linguistic minorities. This Language Charter used cultural heritage as the starting point of its scope of protection; this means, instead of protecting linguistic minorities as groups, it protects regional or minority languages as cultural pillars. This treaty[60] has been ratified by twenty-five states, and eight states signed but did not ratify the Language Charter (June 2020).[61]

The Language Charter is an unusual document. On the one hand, it is based on state obligations instead of individual or collective rights; on the other, it is a binding treaty with a non-binding monitoring mechanism.[62] The charter was created to respond to a variety of situations: No regional or minority language has the exact same issues or faces the same reality. Therefore, the Language Charter included obligations of promotion, suggesting "the need for a proactive interpretation and implementation of the obligations under the charter."[63] Any state that signs and ratifies this text is obliged to slow the decline of the protected regional or minority language and to promote it. This would imply that states have an active role to play in the promotion of a minority language. Yet, the Language Charter leaves discretion to signatory states to provide a list of the languages they want to protect. Indeed, states define, interpret, and apply the Language Charter with wide flexibility. This flexibility is one of the recurrent criticisms of the charter. Regarding this controversy, Gwynedd Parry emphasizes: "It potentially leaves minority language policy at the mercy of political expediency."[64]

Knowing that some states might fear that joining the charter would jeopardize their own national majoritarian language, its drafters had the coexistence of languages in mind, namely, the fostering of language diversity. To achieve this, the Language Charter's four foundations are: Linguistic diversity is essential to the European cultural heritage. Linguistic diversity has to be specially backed. Diversity does not imply policies of linguistic segregation. And finally, support offered by the charter maintains the unity and territorial integrity of signatory states.[65] Therefore, the Language Charter does not conceive languages in antagonistic terms but rather adopts a multilingual approach.

Adding to the peculiarity of the Language Charter, we note that this treaty does not grant political rights to linguistic minority groups. With the aim of reassuring the states that join the charter, the treaty contains some provisions on this matter. For instance, Article 5 affirms that the Language Charter does not seek to affect the territorial or political integrity of the signatory states by promoting the rights of linguistic minorities. In fact, the Language Charter is, in this sense, "depoliticized": it does not grant any rights for linguistic minorities to challenge state authority. The underlying aim of the Language Charter is clearly to promote diversity in equality. In other words, the charter does not divide citizens of a state but rather emphasizes equality among them, supporting the idea of a multilingual state. It is worth mentioning again that France did not ratify the Language Charter, controversially considering that this text was against the principles of unicity[66] and equality of the French Republic.[67]

The Language Charter as a Language Rights Treaty

In addition to offering the tools for multilingual cohabitation, the Language Charter underscores several linguistic rights. By proclaiming "the right to use a regional or minority language in private and public life is an inalienable right,"[68] the Language Charter protects both the language and its speakers. It has been argued that this charter embodies a culturalist approach to the protection of regional or minority languages.[69] Yet, I believe that this approach does not entirely suit the reality of the scope of protection of this text. A language is not merely a cultural element. Indeed, as a language is meant to be transmitted—it is an act—the protection of this cultural element implies a protection of the individuals who speak it, the individuals who teach it, the institutions where it is taught, the newspapers that provide information and news in this language, and the policies that grant access to justice in this language. The focus of the Language Charter on regional or minority languages themselves brings no "explicit rights for the users" of these languages.[70] This point is invoked, for instance, in the Language Charter's explanatory report.[71] Thus, the Language Charter protects different actors and institutions surrounding regional or minority languages, but it does not affect "the legal regime of persons belonging to minorities."[72]

The Language Charter contains a long list of articles (twenty-three) devoted to the shaping of the protection and development of regional or minority languages. Before providing further explanations on the rights contained in the Language Charter and its structure, we must understand precisely how this text defines a regional or minority language. As a reminder,[73] Article 1.a of the Language Charter defines a regional or minority language as:

  i. traditionally used within a given territory of a State by nationals of that State who form a group numerically smaller than the rest of the State's population; and
  ii. different from the official language(s) of that State; it does not include either dialects of the official language(s) of the State or the languages of migrants;

Following this definition of regional or minority languages, the Language Charter excludes "new" languages that appear in Europe because of migration or globalization. Also provided by Article 1 (sections b and c) are explanations of "territory" and "non-territorial languages."

  b. "territory in which the regional or minority language is used" means the geographical area in which the said language is the mode of expression of a number of people justifying the adoption of the various protective and promotional measures provided for in this Charter;
  c. "non-territorial languages" means languages used by nationals of the State which differ from the languages or languages used by the rest of the State's population but which, although traditionally used within the territory of the State, cannot be identified with a particular area thereof.

Here, the Language Charter again stresses the distinction between the regional or minority languages and the languages of immigrants with its reference to languages "traditionally used." Therefore, we could say that the Language Charter uses history as a starting point.[74] History is, first, used to validate the status of protection. Second, historical reparation is sought through protection of regional or minority languages recognized under the Language Charter. The use of history as a starting point is explained by the nature of regional or minority languages protected by the Language Charter. Indeed, there is no doubt that most (or all) of these languages have been subject to repression, imposition, or assimilation.

The Structure of the Language Charter

The Language Charter contains five parts, each one with a specific purpose. Part I contains general provisions such as definitions (Article 1), existing regimes of protection, and existing obligations. Part II contains only one article, Article 7,[75] which, however, is a lengthy explanation of the objectives and principles of the Charter and also sets standards of conduct. Part III (Articles 8 to 14) offers a list of measures to promote the use of regional or minority languages in public life. This list functions as an *à la carte* system, where the signatory state decides which provisions will suit its current situation. These provisions are grouped under different categories: education (Article 8), judicial authorities (Article 9), administrative authorities and public services (Article 10), media (Article 11), cultural activities and facilities (Article 12), economic and social life (Article 13), and transfrontier exchanges (Article 14). Part IV contains Articles 15 to 17, relating to the application of the Language Charter. Part V contains the final provisions of the charter in Articles 18 to 23.

The main particularity of the Language Charter resides in the above-mentioned Part III. The signatory states are required to apply a minimum of thirty five of the rights listed here, following the *à la carte* system, in which states have some freedom in choosing their obligations.[76] This system was created to encourage states to comply with the integral Language Charter gradually and to adapt to the diverse linguistic landscape of Europe. This system has, however, been criticized.[77]

Article 7 of the Language Charter provides the objectives and principles of the treaty. According to Dunbar, Article 7 is the most important provision in the Language Charter, as it applies to all the regional or minority languages of the signatory states.[78] In fact, Part II applies to all the regional or minority languages, in contrast to Part III, which applies only to the regional or minority languages designated by the signatory state. This means that Article 7 applies to all the languages under the definition of "non-territorial languages" offered by the Language Charter. Part III contains precise rules, whereas Article 7 contains the broad objectives of the Language Charter. The importance of Article 7 also lies, therefore, in its content. According to Article 7.1: "the Parties shall base their policies, legislation and practice on the following objectives and principles," after which nine objectives and principles are listed (Article 7.1.a to 7.1.i), offering a broad framework to the signatory states. Woehrling points out that "the principles are precise and place considerable demands on states which are serious about putting them into practice,"[79] showing that Article 7 is policy-oriented and does not share Part III's limitations.

Finally, it must be noted that, although there is no judicial enforcement mechanism of the Language Charter, there is a monitoring system to assess how effectively the Charter is implemented in each of the signatory states.

The Monitoring Mechanism of the Language Charter

Not only is the form and purpose of this European language treaty unique, but so is its implementation mechanism. The Language Charter does not offer a judicial or quasi-judicial mechanism. There is also no possibility, for individuals or states, to lodge any complaints. The implementation mode of the Language Charter is a state-reporting system provided in Part IV of the charter. This system entitles the Committee of Experts to evaluate the implementation of the charter by a signatory state and to write a report to the Committee of Ministers of the Council of Europe. As de Beco explains, the decision behind the choice of this implementation mechanism is political. He considers that states were "unwilling to submit their policies, legislation and practice with respect to regional or minority languages to judicial or quasi-judicial oversight."[80] Therefore, the Language Charter contains a monitoring mechanism to assess how the text is implemented in the signatory state, with the Committee of Ministers having the authority to submit recommendations.[81] According to Article 15.1 of the Language Charter, signatory states must present their first report "within the year following the entry into force of the Language Charter with respect to the Party concerned, the other reports at three-yearly intervals after the first report." This monitoring mechanism is under the authority of the Committee of Experts (Article 17 of the Charter). Each member state sends one expert to form the Committee of Experts. It must be noted, however, that even if the experts are appointed by states, they do not fulfill the role of representatives of the state. They are appointed for six years and are eligible for reappointment. To become a member of the Committee of Experts, their "high integrity" must be taken into consideration, to guarantee the free exercise of their function. These experts are from different fields, but lawyers and linguists tend to predominate.[82] There is no requirement for experts to speak one of the regional or minority languages present in their state. Also, members of the

Committee of Experts are not allowed to vote when there is a matter concerning a periodical report of the state in which they were elected.

The control by the monitoring mechanism operates in the following terms: Each state signatory to the charter must submit reports periodically to the Secretary General.[83] In these reports, they must explain the policies and actions they have established to meet their obligations under the Language Charter. During the monitoring mechanism, the Committee of Experts has the following roles: It examines the report provided by the state; if there is any doubt regarding the text of the report, it sends questions to the state party. It visits the state to meet the authorities, NGOs (nongovernmental organizations), and any competent body that might be useful to assess the application of the Language Charter. It assesses other information provided by associations or bodies in the signatory state who have an interest in the correct application of the Language Charter. Finally, it adopts an evaluation report (5) that includes recommendations—if necessary—to the Committee of Ministers, which will make additional recommendations to address the apropos state party.[84]

The last phase of the monitoring report involves, therefore, the Committee of Ministers. Once the report of the Committee of Experts has reached the Committee of Ministers, the latter can decide to make recommendations to the state. The state will, in theory, take action to comply with the Language Charter more effectively by aligning its policies, legislation, or practice with the text. Even if the Committee of Ministers is the organ responsible for submitting recommendations to states, the "detailed work of monitoring" is the responsibility of the Committee of Experts.[85] Indeed, the "output" of the Committee of Experts brings a rich amount of information regarding the landscape of minority and regional languages in Europe. In addition, the Council of Europe may decide to take the further step of organizing a Language Charter Implementation Roundtable in the state.

The Language Charter, Spain, and the Basque Language

Article 3(3) of the Constitution of 1978 already protected regional or minority languages in Spain,[86] and the adoption of the Language Charter reinforces this protection. Spain signed the Language Charter on November 5, 1992, ratified it in February 2001, and in 2005, the initial monitoring cycle ended.

The political division of Spain into seventeen autonomous communities contributes to a welcoming attitude toward the protection of regional or minority languages. In fact, the devolution of constitutional power to the different autonomous communities plays a fundamental role in linguistic minority protection in Spain.[87] In the autonomous communities, when the Statute of Autonomy (*Estatuto de Autonomía*) recognizes it, co-official languages can be found. When signing the Language Charter, in addition to the protection offered by Part II to all regional or minority languages existing within the state,[88] Spain extended the protection of the Language Charter to the six autonomous communities that contain a co-official language. These autonomous communities are the Balearic Islands, Catalonia, the BAC, Galicia, Navarre, and Valencia. Therefore, the protection of the Language Charter mainly applies in the borders defined by the political division of Spain. The two autonomous communities that confer the co-official status to the Basque language are the BAC and Navarre. To date,[89] Spain has submitted five reports in the monitoring mechanism procedure (2002, 2007, 2010, 2014, and 2018). Regarding the Basque language, however, despite having signed the Language Charter in 1999, France did not ratify this document,[90] leaving the protection of the Basque language incomplete.

Framework Convention for the Protection of National Minorities

Regarding minority rights, the European legal system also includes the Framework Convention for the Protection of National Minorities (Framework Convention). Despite this instrument not being applicable to the Basque language by the approach taken by Spain,[91] it merits our attention.

This convention was a great step forward for the protection of minorities in Europe: It was "clearly a result of the impressive renaissance of international efforts to safeguard the rights of persons belonging to national minorities."[92] In fact, the Framework Convention (1995) adds another layer of protection to the international human rights law. This is highlighted by Article 1: "The rights of persons belonging to those minorities forms an integral part of the protection of human rights." Although it is not the only instrument that was created for the protection of minorities by the Council of Europe, it is the most comprehensive document in the field. Hofmann adds to this: "Its [the Framework Convention's] particular relevance derives from the fact that it is the first legally binding, multilateral treaty to address the protection of national minorities in general."[93] For the first time, the Framework Convention switched the focus to minority rights in general in the European space and was "destined to carry much of the burden of putting into effect minority rights in European space for the foreseeable future."[94] Yet, the Framework Convention does not provide a definition of what a "national minority" means in the text of the convention.[95] The broad approach to minorities in general and lack of definition of its main object of protection (national minorities) could have rendered it a "façade treaty," falling short regarding the improvement of the situation for minorities. However, as rightly noted by De Witte:

> Although the Framework Convention was criticized and derided at the time of its adoption as being little more than a window-dressing operation, it has gained in authority and efficacy due to the dynamic monitoring practice of its advisory committee and the willingness of a number of states to "play the game."[96]

Regarding the structure, the Framework Convention contains a preamble and thirty-two articles for implementing the treaty. Section I contains general principles, Section II contains the tools for implementing the treaty, and Section III contains principles on the interpretation of the Framework Convention. Section IV outlines the monitoring mechanism, and Section V welcomes the states not belonging to the Council of Europe to join the treaty with an invitation from the Committee of Ministers. This treaty protects minorities via key principles in Section II such as (among others) nondiscrimination, promotion of effective equality, freedom of assembly, freedom of religion, and the right to learn and to be instructed in the minority language.

Regarding linguistic minorities, the Framework Convention takes a broad sample of situations in which minority languages should be protected: Article 10(1) recognizes the right to use these languages in public and private life, Article 14(1) has to do with the right to learn the minority language, and Article 14(2) recognizes the right to be taught in one's minority language. However, despite the Framework Convention being positive in the sense that it offers protection for minority languages, it has been criticized because of its nonspecific language—which weakens its ability to protect minorities.[97] In any case, the clauses about minority language protection give rise to an "intense dialogue" between the governments and the Framework Convention's Advisory Committee, pushing for a "more generous interpretation" of the obligations of the states under this treaty.[98]

The impact of this treaty on the Basque language admittedly is limited. Spain signed the Framework Convention on February 1, 1995, and it was ratified on July 20, 1995. The Basque language is co-official in the BAC and Navarre, and thus, the contributions of the Framework Convention would be limited. Yet, Pons Parera makes an interesting point.[99]

The Basque minority located in the non-Basque-speaking area of Navarre could draw some benefits from the Framework Convention if they are identified as recipients of its protection. Still, Spain's approach to the Framework Convention was to include only the Roma community in its scope of protection, while acknowledging at the same time that this community does not constitute a national minority.[100]

Interestingly, the Advisory Committee on the Framework Convention during its first Opinion[101] in 2003 on the first cycle of Monitoring[102] of the implementation of this convention asked the Spanish government for an explanation of the language content on "peoples of Spain" or "nationalities" that appear in the Preamble and Article 2 of the Constitution.[103] Spain, using the lack of definition of "national minorities" in the Framework Convention, shifted the discourse from "peoples of Spain" and "nationalities" to a discussion on the division of Spain into autonomous communities, and stressed their inclusion in the "Spanish nation."[104] Spain highlighted the autonomous communities as unities having historical, cultural, and linguistic ties, but not having significant ethnic components.[105] By using the lack of definition of national minorities and shifting the discourse to the autonomous communities, Spain avoided applying the Framework Convention to minorities other than the Roma community.

Another country that could have used the Framework Convention to protect its national and linguistic minorities is France, notably in the case of Basque. Yet, France did not sign the Framework Convention. It should be highlighted that France, Andorra, Monaco, and Turkey remain the only countries of the Council of Europe that have neither signed nor ratified the Framework Convention.[106]

To summarize both minority rights instruments of the Council of Europe—the Language Charter and the Framework Convention—it is clear that both treaties have been essential for the development of a "common European understanding of the legal protection of regional and minority languages."[107] However, both treaties have their limits. Regarding the Basque language, the first limit is, evidently, the lack of ratification of the Language Charter and lack of signature of the Framework Convention by France. This constitutes, unquestionably, a serious impediment for the protection of (linguistic) minorities in France. Nonetheless, this should not be interpreted as France not having duties toward its minorities. France is still under the international human rights legal framework and thus should abide by the principle of nondiscrimination and the minimum standards on minorities discussed previously in this chapter. Second, because the Basque minority is not protected by the Framework Convention in Spain, the entire weight of responsibility for its protection falls on the Language Charter (regarding the Council of Europe's legal system).[108] Last, the third main limit for the Basque language lies in the division of Spain into autonomous communities. In fact, the effective application of the Language Charter rights depends on the autonomous communities, which hold co-official languages. In the case of Basque, the BAC and Navarre are the administrations putting into practice the rights contained in the Language Charter. This results in challenges when an autonomous community performs a linguistic division within its territory (like in Navarre) or when the application of a certain right depends on the central administration (such as language rights related to justice), for instance.[109] However, despite these limits, the Language Charter remains relevant for the improvement of linguistic rights of Basque speakers. Civil society, regional administrations, and speakers themselves refer to the Language Charter often as a point of reference for effective linguistic rights.

European Union Law and the Basque Language

When it comes to language rights within European Union (EU) law, a variety of concepts come into play, starting with the official and working languages of the EU. The main three linguistic rights expressly guaranteed by EU law are: the right to use any official languages of the EU in relation to its institutions,[110] the nondiscrimination on grounds of language,[111] and the right to interpretation and translation in criminal proceedings.[112] In addition, other EU norms protecting cultural diversity, linguistic diversity, and nondiscrimination must be examined. Yet, since this book focuses on the Basque language, all these elements need to be evaluated from the regional or minority language perspective.

There are now twenty-four official languages and working languages in the EU.[113] Yet, this number does not include the regional or minority languages of the member states. In fact, currently, two-thirds of the languages spoken in member states today have no institutional recognition in EU law.[114] The language that is official in the entire territory of the member state or the language that is official in the central institutions of the member state is the one granted official and working language status.[115] This results in languages such as Basque (official in parts of Spain) not being considered an official and working language of the EU institutions.

Anyone analyzing the EU law would immediately notice that little has been done to protect regional or minority languages. Among other reasons, this is because of the lack of EU competences in matters of linguistic policy. As a matter of fact, the EU can only act in the domains and for the purposes for which the EU treaties allow it to act.[116] There are, however, two supporting competences of the EU—in Article 6 of the Treaty on the Functioning of the European Union (TFEU)—that relate to linguistic matters: education (Article 6.e) and culture (Article 6.c). In addition, since language is intertwined with other areas or competences, the EU could adopt linguistic measures through the regulation of other fields. Nevertheless, the reality remains, the EU legal framework does not form a strong infrastructure for the protection of regional or minority languages.

Looking into the rules, it is worth mentioning that linguistic diversity seems to hold a special place in EU law, as shown by Article 3, paragraph 3 of the Treaty on European Union (TEU)[117] and Article 22 of the European Union Charter of Fundamental Rights, a provision dealing with cultural, religious, and linguistic diversity.[118] If we look further, we can find elements mentioning multilingualism or multiculturalism as a value to be protected within the EU in other forms. For instance, Article 165 of the TFEU aims to develop the cultural and linguistic diversity in education,[119] and Article 167 of the TFEU protects "national and regional diversity" and the "diversity of cultures."[120] Finally, there is Article 21 of the Charter of Fundamental Rights of the EU, which prohibits discrimination on grounds of language, as was previously noted in this chapter. This right has not entered EU law with the inclusion of Article 21 in the charter, but is rather inherent to the principle of equality, one of the unwritten fundamental principles of the EU and frequently used by European Courts.[121]

Focusing on Article 22 of the Charter of Fundamental Rights, we discover it does not translate easily into concrete minority protection standards.[122] Despite the progress the proclamation of linguistic rights entails, this principle does not guarantee equality between citizens' mother tongues. De Witte argues that the main reason for this inequality is the protection by Article 22 that applies to the national languages of the member states and not to the regional languages, nor to the languages of migrant communities.[123] In any case, under Article 22, "the emphasis is largely on preventing discrimination rather than on conferring any rights to speakers of minority languages."[124] Furthermore, whereas the EU is required to respect the national identities of member states and their linguistic diversity, the EU "feels uneasy about imposing a similar requirement concerning respect for subnational identities or for minorities."[125] Therefore, the duty to respect linguistic diversity is not clear when it comes to respecting regional or minority languages: first, deducing concrete duties from the general statement of Article 22 seems difficult; and second, the EU has limited competences to carry out policies of promoting linguistic diversity.

Despite having tools available at the EU level for the protection of linguistic minorities and the Basque language, "the legal status of national minorities (including their language rights) is one of the few remaining policy areas in which the role of the European Union continues to remain minimal and almost inexistent."[126] In fact, the EU does not seem to play a role in standard-setting regarding minority rights. Regarding minorities in general, and their linguistic rights in particular, the rule of thumb seems to be to rely on the documents provided by the Council of Europe (the Language Charter and the Framework Convention mainly) for setting the scene concerning their rights, and to leave the remaining protection and developments to member states. This is extremely problematic, notably in the case of states such as France, which consistently claim there are no minorities in their territories and, therefore, they should not take part in the protection of minority rights in their countries.[127] Yet, France is quick to forget it is tied by international law and its system of international human rights protection that sets a minimum standard, notably on the grounds of nondiscrimination discussed earlier.

The international and European legal systems regarding the Basque language show the intricacies of minority rights protection and the complications of language rights protection. Regarding Euskara, international law establishes a set of principles and minimum standard protection, with a distinction between the approach of France and of Spain. The same difference in approach appears at the European level, notably with the Framework Convention and the Language Charter. Despite international and European laws being useful for our analysis of the Basque language, the key to understanding the legal protection of this language is at the national level. The next step, therefore, is analyzing the constitutional legal framework of the Basque language both in France and in Spain.

Notes

1 Weller, *The rights of minorities in Europe*, 29.
2 Woehrling, "Droit des personnes, droit des minorités, droit des langues: les différentes techniques juridiques de protection de l'expression linguistique," 217.
3 Woehrling, 223.
4 Woehrling (223) notes that this approach was taken by the Permanent Court of International Justice in its Advisory Opinion No. 26 of 1935.
5 Pons Parera, "International Legislation and the Basque Language," 75.
6 The International Covenant on Civil and Political Rights of 1966 (ICCPR), and the International Covenant on Economic, Social and Cultural Rights of 1966 (ICESCR).
7 Declaration on the Rights of Persons Belonging to National or Ethnic, Religious and Linguistic Minorities of 1992.
8 European Convention on Human Rights, 1950 (ECHR).
9 Framework Convention for the Protection of National Minorities, 1995 (FCPNM).
10 European Charter for Regional or Minority Languages, 1992 (ECRML).
11 Pons Parera, "International Legislation and the Basque Language," 76.
12 The Hague Recommendations Regarding the Educational Rights of National Minorities, 1996, and the Oslo Recommendations on the Linguistic Rights of National Minorities, 1998.
13 Article 2.1 of the Universal Declaration of Human Rights (UDHR), Article

2.1 of the International Covenant on Civil and Political Rights (ICCPR), and Article 14 of the European Convention on Human Rights (ECHR).

14 Human Rights Committee General Comment Number 18: Nondiscrimination. 10 November 1989, paragraph 7. https://www.refworld.org/docid/453883fa8.html (Accessed July 1, 2020)
15 Pons Parera, "International Legislation and the Basque Language," 77. As we will see later in chapter 2, this is not the definition of nondiscrimination adopted by the French state regarding linguistic rights.
16 Pons Parera, 78.
17 Parry, "History, Human Rights and Multilingual Citizenship: Conceptualising the European Charter for Regional or Minority Languages," 330.
18 We are going to explore this further in relation to the case of the Basque language in part III.
19 Article 19 ICCPR and Article 10 ECHR.
20 See part III, chapter 6.
21 Pons Parera, "International Legislation and the Basque Language," 79 80.
22 Article 17 ICCPR and Article 8 ECHR protect private and family life, home, privacy, and correspondence. Indeed, in the private sphere, freedom of expression is less limited.
    Pons Parera (ibid.) gives an example where courts have prevented public authorities from conditioning the language used by the individual in his or her private sphere. Indeed, the Spanish Constitutional Court in its decision 201/1997, of November 25, decided the right to family privacy found in Article 18 of the Spanish Constitution protected the inmate in a penitentiary institution to use the Basque language in communications with his or her family. The linguistic freedom of the inmate had to be respected.
23 Human Rights Committee, *Ballantyne, Davidson, McIntyre v. Canada*, of March 31, 1993, considers Article 19 of the ICCPR applicable to language on commercial signs. More specifically, it requires that the limitations be established by law, that they pursue any of the objectives listed in Article 19.3. a and b of the ICCPR, and that they are necessary to achieve the legitimate purpose established (in this case, to protect the rights of the French minority in Canada, it is not necessary to prohibit commercial signs in English).
24 UN Declaration on Minorities, Article 2.1: "Persons belonging to national or

ethnic, religious and linguistic minorities (hereinafter referred to as persons belonging to minorities) have the right to enjoy their own culture, to profess and practise their own religion, and to use their own language, in private and in public, freely and without interference or any form of discrimination."

25 Emphasis added by the author. https://www.ohchr.org/Documents/Issues/Minorities/Booklet_Minorities_English.pdf (Accessed May 22, 2020).

26 See Articles 9.1, 10.1, 11.2, and 11.3 of the Framework Convention. FCPNM will be examined later in this chapter.

27 Article 24.2 ICCPR and Article 7 CRC (Convention on the Rights of the Child).

28 Pons Parera, "International Legislation and the Basque Language," 79.

29 In the case *Johansson v. Finland*, September 6, 2007, the parents wanted to name their son "Axl Mick" and were rejected by the Register. The European Court of Human Rights (ECtHR) observed the violation of Article 8. The ECtHR, decided "the preservation of a national name practice may be considered part and parcel of that aim and therefore in the public interest" insofar as the name does not harm the child and "had already gained acceptance in Finland, and it has not been contended that this has had any negative consequences for the preservation of the cultural and linguistic identity of Finland."

30 For instance, see the Fañch case, summarized in the discussion about French law and the Basque language in chapter 2. Also, regarding the Basque language, it must be mentioned during Franco's dictatorship, citizens, notably the Basques, were forced to translate their names into Spanish.

31 Article 9 UDHR; Arts. 9.2 and 14.3 ICCPR; Article 5.2 and Article 6.3, sections a and e, ECHR.

32 Article 29.1.c.

33 Pons Parera, "International Legislation and the Basque Language," 80.

34 France has a reservation on this Article 30. This will be explored further in part II.

35 The Language Charter, however, provides clear measures to ensure the protection of regional or minority languages in education. This will be analyzed later in this chapter.

36 The author will refer to the ECtHR as the Strasbourg Court interchangeably.

37 Preamble of the ECHR.

38 Ibid.

39 Ibid.

40 This chapter will examine the Framework Convention for the Protection of National Minorities and the European Charter for Regional or Minority Languages.
41 Parry, "History, Human Rights and Multilingual Citizenship: Conceptualising the European Charter for Regional or Minority Languages," 344.
42 Marko, "Constitutional recognition of ethnic difference—towards an emerging European minimum standard?" 29.
43 ECtHR, July 10, 1998, *Sidiropoulos and Others v. Greece.*
44 Ibid., paragraph 41.
45 ECtHR, January 18, 2001, *Chapman v. United Kingdom.*
46 Ibid., paragraph 96. Text emphasized in italics by the author:
"Nonetheless, although the fact of belonging to a minority with a traditional lifestyle different from that of the majority does not confer an immunity from general laws intended to safeguard the assets of the community as a whole, such as the environment, it may have an incidence on the manner in which such laws are to be implemented. As intimated in *Buckley*, the vulnerable position of Gypsies as a minority means that some special consideration should be given to their needs and their different lifestyle both in the relevant regulatory planning framework and in reaching decisions in particular cases (judgment cited above, 1292-95, §§ 76, 80 and 84). To this extent, *there is thus a positive obligation imposed on the Contracting States by virtue of Article 8 to facilitate the Gypsy way of life.*"
47 Ibid., paragraph 96.
48 *Case relating to certain aspects of the laws on the use of languages in education in Belgium v. Belgium,* July 23, 1968.
49 See the analysis of case law in part III.
50 Emphasis in italics added by the author.
51 In the Human Rights Committee's words (see Human Rights Committee General Comment Number 23, on Article 27, April 8, 1994, paragraph 6.1, 6.2). This is a controverted issue. Indeed, the reading of the provision does not support such a conclusion, and many legal scholars don't share that opinion. Even those who advocate it recognize that states have absolute leeway as to the scope and content of the positive measures to be adopted.
52 Pons Parera, "International Legislation and the Basque Language," 82.
53 Human Rights Committee General Comment Number 23, on Article 27, April 8, 1994, paragraph 1.

54 Ibid., paragraph 9.
55 Pons Parera, "International Legislation and the Basque Language," 82.
56 "In the light of article 2 of the Constitution of the French Republic, the French Government declares that article 27 is not applicable so far as the Republic is concerned." https://treaties.un.org/Pages/ViewDetails.aspx?src=TREATY&mtdsg_no=IV-4&chapter=4&clang=_en#EndDec (Accessed May 20, 2020).
57 Thornberry and Estébanez, *Minority Rights in Europe*, 14.
58 Weller, *The rights of minorities in Europe*, 611.
59 Article 1.b of the Statute of the Council of Europe (Accessed February 5, 2021): https://rm.coe.int/CoERMPublicCommonSearchServices/DisplayDCTMContent?documentId=0900001680306052.
60 Even if for some treaties adopted by the Council of Europe, as is the case for the Language Charter, the term "treaty" does not appear in the title, they are part of the definition of international treaties, governed by the Vienna Convention on the Law of Treaties. Once the negotiations about a treaty end successfully, the Committee of Ministers adopts the text and it is opened for signature (for member states, but it can also be opened to nonmember states and organizations, via invitation by the Committee of Ministers). Another point to take into consideration is the explanatory reports that are published for most conventions by the Committee of Ministers. These explanatory reports are written by the Committee of Experts drafting each treaty and are adopted by the Committee of Ministers together with the treaty.
61 Azerbaijan, France, Iceland, Italy, Malta, Moldova, Russia, and the Former Yugoslav Republic of Macedonia.
62 See explanation on the monitoring mechanism below.
63 De Varennes, "Language protection and the European Charter for Regional or Minority Languages: Quo vadis?" 33.
64 Parry, "History, Human Rights and Multilingual Citizenship: Conceptualising the European Charter for Regional or Minority Languages," 338.
65 Thornberry and Estébanez, *Minority Rights in Europe*, 140.
66 Term used in the English version of the decision of the French Constitutional Council.
67 This refers to the decision of the Constitutional Council in 1999, discussed in

chapter 2.
68 See Preamble of the Language Charter. The term "right" does not appear very often in the text of the Language Charter, but Article 6 on information states: "The Parties undertake to see to it that the authorities, organisations and persons concerned are informed of *the rights and duties* established by this Charter," and Article 9.1.a.ii on judicial authorities states: "The Parties undertake [. . .] in criminal proceedings [. . .] to guarantee the accused *the right to use* his/her regional or minority language" (emphasis added by the author). Nevertheless, it is clear the Language Charter provides rights to regional or minority language speakers.
69 For instance, Woehrling, "Introduction."
70 Dunbar, "6. The Committee of Experts of the European Charter for Regional or Minority Languages (The CECL)," 152.
71 Explanatory Report, paragraph 11.
72 Article 4 of the Language Charter: "The provisions of this Charter shall not affect any more favourable provisions concerning the status of regional or minority languages, or the legal regime of persons belonging to minorities which may exist in a Party or are provided for by relevant bilateral or multilateral international agreements."
73 Article 1 of the Language Charter has already been mentioned in the introduction.
74 See Parry, "History, Human Rights and Multilingual Citizenship: Conceptualising the European Charter for Regional or Minority Languages," 336.
75 See appendix 1.
76 De Witte, "Linguistic minorities in Western Europe: Expansion of rights without (much) litigation?" 35.
77 As explained by De Varennes, "Language protection and the European Charter for Regional or Minority Languages: Quo vadis?" 29.
78 Dunbar, "Article 7. Objectives and principles."
79 Woehrling, *The European Charter for Regional or Minority Languages*, 103.
80 de Beco, *Human Rights Monitoring Mechanisms of the Council of Europe*, 155.
81 This monitoring mechanism was reinforced in November 2018. The states are now required to inform on the implementation of recommendations identified by the Committee of Experts in its evaluation report as being for immediate action. See https://search.coe.int/cm/Pages/result_details.aspx?ObjectId=-09000016808f22ea (Accessed June 24, 2021).

82 Dunbar, "6. The Committee of Experts of the European Charter for Regional or Minority Languages (the CECL)," 156-57.
83 After the 2018 reform, the monitoring cycles are every five years; and every two and a half years, states must submit an evaluation report on the implementation of measures of immediate action. Another change brought by that reform is that experts can only be reappointed once.
84 These additional recommendations are not binding.
85 Dunbar, "6. The Committee of Experts of the European Charter for Regional or Minority Languages (the CECL)," 156.
86 The Spanish Constitution and the protection of the Basque language in Spain will be analyzed in chapter 3.
87 Explained in chapter 3.
88 Spain's declaration made on the ratification of the Language Charter shows Spain considers itself obliged regarding the languages that are not official but merely recognized and protected in certain autonomous communities (Aragon, Castile and Leon, and Asturias).
89 June 2021.
90 Explained in chapter 2.
91 See below, in chapter 3.
92 Hofmann, "The Framework Convention for the Protection of National Minorities: An Introduction," 1.
93 Hofmann, 3.
94 Thornberry and Estébanez, *Minority Rights in Europe*, 115.
95 See Hofmann, "The Framework Convention for the Protection of National Minorities: An Introduction," 16.
96 De Witte, "Introduction: Exploring a Central Pillar of the European Minority Rights System."
97 Parry, "History, Human Rights and Multilingual Citizenship: Conceptualising the European Charter for Regional or Minority Languages," 332.
98 De Witte, "Linguistic minorities in Western Europe: Expansion of rights without (much) litigation?" 36.
99 Pons Parera, "International Legislation and the Basque Language," 84.
100 Ruiz Vieytez, "Minorías, nacionalidades y minorías nacionales. La problemática aplicación en España del Convenio marco para la protección de las minorías

Nacionales del Consejo de Europa" .202.

101 https://rm.coe.int/CoERMPublicCommonSearchServices/DisplayDCTMContent?documentId=090000168008bcee (Accessed July 22, 2024).

102 See all the different monitoring cycles of the implementation of the Framework Convention by Spain: https://www.coe.int/en/web/minorities/spain (Accessed July 22, 2024).

103 The Spanish Constitution and its language rights content will be analyzed in chapter 3.

104 Pons Parera, "International Legislation and the Basque Language," 84.
See Spain's Comments on the Opinion of the Advisory Committee: https://rm.coe.int/CoERMPublicCommonSearchServices/DisplayDCTMContent?documentId=090000168008c974 (Accessed July 22, 2024).

105 Ibid. 4, paragraph 5.10: "The populations of the various Autonomous Communities have in common the existence of historical-cultural and linguistic links, but there are no significant ethnic components."

106 For the full list, see https://www.coe.int/en/web/minorities/etats-partie (Accessed June 12, 2020).

107 De Witte, "Linguistic minorities in Western Europe: Expansion of rights without (much) litigation?" 36.

108 The Framework Convention would reinforce the existing protection of the Basque language.

109 For education and media, these limits will be further developed in parts II and III.

110 As it appears in Article 20.2.d of the TFEU (Treaty on the Functioning of the European Union):
"2. Citizens of the Union shall enjoy the rights and be subjects to the duties provided for in the Treaties. They shall have, inter alia:
[...]
d) the right to petition the European Parliament, to apply to the European Ombudsman, and to address the institutions and advisory bodies of the Union in any of the Treaty languages and to obtain a reply in the same language."
These linguistic rights are thoroughly explained by Bruno de Witte in "Language Rights and the Work of the European Union" (2018).

111 As it appears in Article 21 of the European Union Charter of Fundamental Rights on Non-discrimination (emphasis added by the author):
"1. *Any discrimination based on* any ground such as sex, race, colour, ethnic or social origin, genetic features, *language*, religion or belief, political or any other opinion, membership of a national minority, property, birth, disability, age or sexual orientation *shall be prohibited.*
2. Within the scope of application of the Treaty establishing the European Community and of the Treaty on European Union, and without prejudice to the special provisions of those Treaties, any discrimination on grounds of nationality shall be prohibited."

112 See the Directive 2010/64 of October 20, 2010, Official Journal of the EU 2010, L 280/1. Discussed in De Witte, "Language Rights and the Work of the European Union."

113 See https://european-union.europa.eu/principles-countries-history/languages_en (Accessed April 10, 2024).

114 Milian i Massana, "Recognition of the Basque language in EU law: A Pending issue?" 95.

115 Except for Lëtzeburgesch. See Milian i Massana, "Recognition of the Basque language in EU law," 96.

116 Exclusive and shared competences are listed in Articles 3 and 4 of the TFEU, respectively.

117 Article 3, paragraph 3 of the Treaty on European Union (emphasized by the author):
"[The Union] shall respect its rich cultural and *linguistic diversity*, and shall ensure that Europe's cultural heritage is safeguarded and enhanced."

118 Article 22 of the EU Charter of Fundamental Rights: "The Union shall respect cultural, religious and linguistic diversity."

119 Article 165 of the TFEU. See appendix 1.

120 Article 167 of the TFEU. See appendix 1.

121 De Witte, "The protection of linguistic diversity through provisions of the EU Charter other than Article 22," 180.

122 De Witte, "The Constitutional Resources for an EU Minority Protection Policy," 115.

123 De Witte, "The protection of linguistic diversity through provisions of the EU

Charter other than Article 22," 178.
124 Parry, "History, Human Rights and Multilingual Citizenship: Conceptualising the European Charter for Regional or Minority Languages," 332.
125 Arzoz, "The protection of linguistic diversity through Article 22 of the Charter of Fundamental Rights," 146.
126 De Witte, "Language Rights and the Work of the European Union," 221.
127 See Gilbert and Keane, "Equality versus fraternity? Rethinking France and its minorities."

2

French Law and the Basque Language

The Basque language is categorized in French law as a "regional language."[1] The French legal system uses this term to designate "historical" or "traditional" languages spoken in France, confining them to specific regions. In this respect, French law understands the Basque language as a regional matter and does not categorize it as having the same value as French, a language understood as the language all French citizens share. The term "regional language" already contains a value judgment and a categorization of the languages of France. And yet, regional languages may be considered in a fortunate situation, since they are at least included in the French legal system, and therefore somehow protected. In a multicultural and multilingual country such as France, "old" and "new" minorities and their issues are hidden behind a French conception of equality between citizens, one that equates equality with unity.

These issues need further study; understanding them is essential for comprehending the French general legal framework on the Basque language. The two main parts that must be discussed are the French Constitution and key French laws.

The French Constitution and the Basque Language

In France, the historical linguistic minorities, under the name of "regional languages," do obtain a certain degree of protection. However, the norm that still prevails is the prohibition of positive action. To understand French constitutional law and the Basque language, it is important to grasp the French constitutional heritage on language matters. That analysis will be followed by a thorough examination of the two key articles of the Constitution that regulate languages used in France, namely Article 2 and Article 75-1.

The French Constitutional Heritage and Regional Languages

To discuss French constitutional law, one must also consider the constitutional block. The Constitution of 1958 is completed by a collection of texts known as the "constitutional block." This implies that, while considering the rights and duties under the Constitution, one should also look at the block contained in the Preamble: The Declaration of the Rights of Man and of the Citizen of 1789; the Preamble of the Constitution of 1946; and the Charter for the Environment (*Charte de l'environnement*) of 2004. The term "constitutional block" describes the totality of the constitutional rules, as well as unwritten norms with constitutional value,[2] such as freedom of expression.[3]

When discussing the legal heritage or the constitutional tradition in France, we must consider the weight of the principles brought by the French Revolution.[4] Indeed, this event marked the consecration of popular sovereignty and national sovereignty in opposition to royal sovereignty. In other words, "in the French model the nation is built upon the *demos* with the *ethnos* receding to the point of becoming almost invisible."[5] This shift in the legal territory of France was brought about by the ideology of the *Révolutionnaires*; with the well-known input of Emmanuel Sieyès in *Qu'est-ce que le Tiers-État?* (1789),[6] the nation becomes the source of power.

This approach to the French nation with the well-known principles of "*liberté, égalité, fraternité*" (freedom, equality, fraternity) already creates an obstacle to a regime of protection of minority or regional languages in France. Moreover, the Constitution of 1958 carries the weight of the revolutionary heritage of individualism and rejection of any reference—even the smallest—to particularism:[7] "The French model is thoroughly individualistic and leaves no room at the constitutional level for recognitions or deployment of group or national identity."[8] Therefore, the current approach to the French nation, present in the Constitution, has been rather consistent since 1789. Yet, regarding the indivisibility of the Republic—the notion now present in Article 1 of the Constitution—is not a product of the French Revolution, but rather was already present under the *Ancien* Régime.[9] This notion of unity is an excellent example of challenges posed to the protection of minorities in France by its constitutional heritage, as shown by the Constitutional Council's (*Conseil Constitutionnel*) decision on the statute of the territorial unit of Corsica.[10] In that case, the *Sages* decided that the mention of "the Corsican people, a component of the French people" was unconstitutional "as the Constitution recognizes only the French people."[11]

The notion of the indivisibility of the Republic and of the French nation is not the only obstacle to the recognition of minority rights in France. Rouland brilliantly elaborates on the legal tradition in France and the issue of minorities.[12] He argues that the French legal system failed to "manage the heterogeneity," via the Constitutional Council affirming the superiority of indivisibility over plurality. Inevitably, following the parliamentary regimes of the Third and the Fourth Republics, the Constitution of the Fifth Republic remained within this revolutionary tradition.

As already shown above by the Corsican example, the relationship between the French Constitution and minorities is tense. It is even argued in traditional French scholarship that minorities as such have no place in France since all citizens are bound by the principle of equality. This entails the nonrecognition of cultural or group rights and the difficult (non)conciliation of positive action and equality in France. However, does the Republican model really fit French society in the twenty-first century? One could argue the French Republican model has never reflected the multicultural reality of France. What scholars and politicians usually call the Republican model is a mere artificial intellectual construction of a distorted reality created in the eighteenth century. The notion of equality is one of these constructions.

Equality in the French constitutional model, as it appears in Article 1 of the Declaration of the Rights of Man and of the Citizen of 1789, is understood as citizen being "born" and remaining "free and equal in rights." The Constitutional Council rigidly interprets this principle. On this matter, Levade underscores how the principle of equality represents an irreversible revolutionary acquirement.[13] The tricky part of the notion of equality, as understood by the revolutionaries, is that it has always been directly linked with the theory of the national sovereignty. This makes the act of identifying any other group in the French nation impossible since it would imply the negation of the equality, showing the failure of the pursued ideal (the revolutionary approach to the French nation). Nonetheless, this equality is only construed around the institution of the state. This means that the French construction of equality results in the nonrecognition of any minority or disadvantaged group.[14]

The importance of the French language in the creation of the nation as understood by the *Révolutionnaires*, creators of the French Constitution, is unquestionable. However, as Debbasch points out, they did not explicitly mention the national language.[15] In his opinion, the revolutionaries "gave more importance to the universality of rights than to the universality of language."[16] Yet, when creating the first constitution in 1791 (also the first constitution consecrating the French nation), the text was written in the common language: French. Two centuries before a French constitution proclaimed French as the language of the nation, the *Révolutionnaires* made French the language of the Republic. They did so by imposing the principle of a single French law,[17] that was applicable to the entire national territory, in opposition to customary laws that were still present in the country.[18] The revolutionary logic regarding linguistic policies is simply a country where the citizen speak a one and only language—a rather idealistic project, considering that the majority of the population at that time did not speak French.[19] This logic entailed a succession of laws and policies regarding linguistic standardization. The main targeted area was education (see part II), but other areas were also affected. The decree of July 20, 1794, imposes the exclusive use of French in public and private acts, by sanctioning the violation of this decree with six months of imprisonment.[20] Enlightenment and Jacobin principles,[21] therefore, do not leave room for scenarios wherein minority languages would have an official status.[22]

Given the revolutionary heritage and the constitutional tradition regarding minorities, French nation, and equality, it comes as no surprise that the question of minority languages creates headaches in France. Again, this shows the problematic French construction of the notion of equality, since in France it is believed there are seventy-five regional or minority languages in total:[23]

> Traditionally, France has been against minority rights. French authorities have consistently rejected the use of the term "minorities" and have banned any form of special measures for national, racial, ethnic, religious, or linguistic groups.[24]

This rejection of minority rights and the concept of minorities in general remains a big issue, in which narrowly understood constitutional principles do not properly address the multicultural reality of France. The term "uniformity" in the context of the French nation is oxymoronic. Fluxes in migration, years of colonization, internal diversity (coming from historic minorities), and the phenomenon of globalization have brought—and still bring—diversity to the French nation. In fact, the French constitutional approach to these issues shows, as underscored by some authors, the highest levels of denial.[25]

To fully comprehend the normative reality of the Basque language in the French Constitution, two key articles of the Constitution must be analyzed: Article 2 and Article 75-1. Article 2 was revised after the constitutional amendment of 1992 crowned French as the language of the nation: "The language of the Republic shall be French." Later, the constitutional amendment of 2008 added Article 75-1, including regional languages in the national cultural heritage: "Regional languages are part of France's heritage." Both articles led to landmark Constitutional Council decisions.

Article 2 of the French Constitution and the Regional Languages

In 1992, a constitutional amendment was implemented in France, introducing for the first time in French constitutional history a reference to the language of the nation.[26] Indeed, until 1992 it was assumed but never written in the constitutional text that French was the language of the French nation. Therefore, introducing the mention of the French language in Article 2 was a significant symbolic gesture for the French language[27]—one that entailed major legal effects. This amendment, introduced to try to forestall the process of English becoming the everyday language of French citizens, operated with a "defensive logic."[28] At the same time, by crowning French as the nation's language, the amendment sought to soften the criticism of the sovereigntists who were irritated by the further European integration happening at the same time with the Treaty of Maastricht.[29]

Soon after, this constitutional provision was used in a series of key decisions. The first decision of the Constitutional Council referring to the amended Article 2 was the decision on the Autonomy of French Polynesia.[30] The Constitutional Council decided in this case that Article 2 on the use of the French language "only applies to public legal persons and to private legal persons in the exercise of a mission of public service, as well as to the users in their relations with the administrations and public services."[31] This decision established the mandatory use of French in the public sphere and in relationships with the administration. The constitutional judges decided here that teaching the Tahitian language and culture are allowed in French Polynesia, as long as teaching the Tahitian language is not mandatory—to be in accordance with the principle of equality.[32] This is related to the approach to equality discussed above, where, in the Constitutional Council's view, equality is the equivalent of homogeneity, with no inclusion of differences.

Following the decision of the Constitutional Council on French Polynesia, two other key cases revolved around Article 2: the ratification of the Language Charter (discussed below) and the London Agreement on patents. The latter addresses the translation of European patents. This agreement aims to reduce the cost of the translation of patents, and the Constitutional Council had to decide in 2006 on the constitutionality of Article 65 of the agreement regarding the partial translation of patents.[33] The Constitutional Council confirmed in this decision that Article 2 imposes the use of French in the domain of public law. Private law governs the legal relations between the patent holder and third parties, and so Article 2 of the Constitution did not apply in this situation. The Constitutional Council concluded, therefore, that the London Agreement did not violate Article 2 of the Constitution, since the imposition of French cannot be extended to legal relations under private law.

Not only did the Constitutional Council interpret Article 2 of the Constitution, so did the Council of State (*Conseil d'Etat*). In the famous case of the Diwan schools,[34] the Council of State stopped the inclusion of the immersive schooling system in the Breton language, using Article 2 of the Constitution.[35] In 2006, the Council of State annulled a provision of the internal rules of French Polynesia's territorial assembly,[36] referring to Article 2 of the Constitution. Article 15-1 of the internal rules considered the option for members of the assembly to speak either in French, in Tahitian, or in a Polynesian language.[37]

The Council of State also played a role in the ratification of the Language Charter by France.[38] Article 2 of the Constitution gave rise to issues regarding the use of the French language, and both the Council of State and the Constitutional Council defined the scope of protection of the French language by their interpretation. The landmark case regarding Article 2 and regional languages in France—and the Basque language by extension—is the decision of 1999, which will be discussed in the next section.

Article 2 of the Constitution and the Language Charter

When France signed the Language Charter in 1999, a constitutional element already consecrated the power of the French language in France, with the previously mentioned landmark constitutional case on French Polynesia. To assess whether the adoption of the Language Charter by France was lawful, research was conducted and, in 1999, three ministerial reports offered their conclusions on the compatibility of the Language Charter with the constitutional text. Following these reports, France signed the Language Charter on May 7, 1999. However, there had been a previous opinion released by the Council of State, arguing that the Language Charter was not compatible with the Constitution's newly added Article 2.[39] Thus, right-wing opposition members of Parliament (MPs) asked the Constitutional Council if an amendment to the Constitution was necessary to ratify the Language Charter.[40] Finally, in June 1999, the Constitutional Council announced the following:

> In granting special rights to "groups" of speakers of regional or minority languages within "territories" where such languages are used, [the Language Charter] infringes the Constitutional principles of the indivisibility of the Republic, equality before law and the unicity of the French people.[41]

In this decision, the *Sages* again underscored two main elements of the French constitutional tradition: On the one hand, all citizens are equal, and on the other hand, the nation is indivisible in terms not only of territory, but also in terms of population. This echoes the revolutionary approach to state unity and equality, in which no divisions are allowed inside the national community.[42] Yet, the Constitutional Council did not carefully read the text of the Language Charter, since, as is expressly stated in it, the treaty does not give any group rights to the linguistic minorities that it protects. Indeed, Article 5 of the Language Charter highlights that the territorial integrity and unity of the signatory states remain intact. Accordingly, the Constitutional Council's decision is highly questionable since the constitutional judges clearly did not understand the aim of the Language Charter.[43]

Speaking of this contestability, Trifunovska adds that "the [Language] Charter does not intend to create competition and antagonism between the official and regional or minority languages, but adopts an intercultural and multilingual approach."[44] In addition, Malo (2011) explains how the Constitutional Council "deliberately" places the doubt in the field of collective rights, when the question of compatibility of the Language Charter with the French Constitution actually has to do with the field of individual rights. The Constitutional Council seems to deny that the right to use a language is an individual right. Therefore, the *Sages* adopted a poorly reasoned decision regarding the Language Charter. In this sense, Woehrling underscored how, by subjectively claiming that a united country can only speak one language, the Constitutional Council wrongly "ethnicized" the concept of nation.[45] Thus, the decision of the Constitutional Council did not allow the beneficial impact that the Language Charter could have for regional or minority language in France.

At the very moment that French politicians were for the first time considering positive action on the taboo topic of minorities, the Constitutional Council decided to stop this action in the name of the French Republican traditional understanding of "equality." Various bodies have since then repeatedly spoken of the need to change the French approach to minorities.[46] The question of regional or minority languages is still being discussed in France.[47] Ratification of the Language Charter could have clarified the situation because "the absence of recognition equals a legal negation of the existence of minorities."[48] Throughout this research, we will encounter other examples of the attitude of the French courts toward regional language rights.

Article 75-1 and Other Regional Languages

In 2008, a constitutional amendment added a new article to the French Constitution, Article 75-1: "Regional languages are part of France's heritage."[49] This article can appear surprising in light of the constitutional heritage and tradition in France. In the previous discussion, we saw how the construction of the French nation and citizenship has a strong unitarian undertone, paired with an impossibility of adding any mention of minorities in the constitutional text. The introduction of Article 75-1 is a result of many years of social and political mobilization. Slowly becoming more open to minority issues and seeking to address a concern for a part of the French society, French politicians wanted to capture the reality of minority languages in the Constitution. Furthermore, "more than in any other country of Western Europe, the expansion of minority protection in France in the course of the last quarter of a century [...] has been entirely due to successful political mobilization, occasionally supported by minority nationalist violence as in the case of Corsica."[50] This would be an extremely positive step forward for linguistic minorities, where a French constitutional text would start the process of inclusion of French multiculturality. Not being able to ratify the Language Charter and not even signing the Framework Convention, some political forces started to shift the strategy to focus on the constitutional text.

Before moving forward to exploring what Article 75-1 entails and which rights it grants to the speakers of the regional languages, we should first explain the process of adopting this article in the amendment of 2008.

During the first reading, the National Assembly (*Assemblée Nationale*) proposed this formulation of Article 75-1: "The regional languages belong to its heritage" ("its" referring to the Republic).[51] The deputies who proposed this amendment aimed to add these words to the text of Article 1 of the Constitution after the mention of the decentralized organization of the Republic. This would be followed by Article 2, introduced in 1992. Reading both articles together, one would understand that the Republic contains regional languages that it has to protect, but with the nuance of French remaining the official language of the nation. Other deputies wanted to include the mention of regional languages in Article 2. The Senate, however, wanted to eliminate this mention of regional languages from the constitutional text altogether. During the second reading, the National Assembly decided to again include the protection of regional languages, by creating Article 75-1 in Title XII of the Constitution. This shows the division in France regarding the protection of regional languages, and where to include this protection. It is worth noting that Title XII of the Constitution refers to *territorial collectivities*,[52] whereas the original position of the protection of regional language in France was meant to be included in Title I, devoted to *sovereignty*.[53] Thus, regional languages are tolerated in the French Constitution as long as they are seen as an aspect of regionalism and not as a French sovereignty marker.[54] This links back to the French way of referring to historical linguistic minorities as "regional" languages, tying them to folklore and regional customs rather than leveling them up equally to other languages, notably French.

Commentators on this constitutional amendment already in 2008, Verpeaux among them,[55] showed their skepticism about including the protection of regional languages in the title on the territorial collectivities. In their view, the duty to protect regional languages should devolve not only upon regional authorities but also upon the state (for example, regarding education). Despite its limitations, this amendment raised the hopes of regional language speakers and some scholars;[56] both sides anticipated that the newly adopted Article 75-1 would open the door to litigation.

In 2011, the Constitutional Council delivered the decision *Madame Cécile L. et autres*,[57] which decided on the interpretation of Article 75-1. This case addressed the teaching of regional languages, in Article L.312-10 in the Code of Education. Madame Cécile L. and the other plaintiffs claimed that this article in the Code of Education breached Article 75-1 of the Constitution. In fact, they argued that Article L.312-10 did not guarantee the teaching of regional languages and regional cultures but only offered the possibility of teaching them. Additionally, they argued, this article seemed to impose a territorial limit on teaching regional languages. The Constitutional Council decided that Article 75-1 is not a right or a liberty guaranteed in the Constitution and, therefore, cannot be invoked by individuals to challenge it.[58] By doing so, the Constitutional Council confirmed the symbolic nature of Article 75-1: the Constitutional Council "stated that this constitutional provision did not form a *right* which could be invoked by individuals to challenge the constitutionality of the existing (and modest) legislative arrangements for the teaching of regional languages."[59] Thus, the symbolic nature of Article 75-1 is not accompanied by rights that regional language speakers could claim must be enforced in France.

Interestingly, Article L.312-10 of the Code of Education was amended in 2013 with the law on the orientation and programming for the refoundation of the school of the Republic.[60] Article 40 of the 2013 law rewrote Article L.312-10, included a reference to Article 75-1 of the Constitution, the "regional languages and cultures are part of France's heritage," and expanded their teaching to other regions by adding their teaching is favored "in the regions where they are spoken."[61] So, although Article 75-1 fell short in protecting regional languages and cultures because of the interpretation by the Constitutional Council, the legislature intervened later and tried to correct the issue that the plaintiffs raised in *Madame Cécile L. et autres*.[62]

When it comes to regional languages in France, the constituent power limited the use of the Basque language with the amendment of Article 2, and the constitutional judges highlighted the lack of linguistic rights for regional languages under Article 75-1. This leads us to analyze how the legislature has since intervened to regulate languages in France.

Key French Laws and the Basque Language

The amendment of Article 2 of the French Constitution in 1992 was followed by the Toubon Law, developing the linguistic content of the Constitution in the everyday life of the French citizen. Analyzing the 1994 Toubon Law is key to understanding the legal framework of the Basque language in France. In addition, more recent laws and bills having an impact on Euskara in France will be analyzed in this section.

The Toubon Law on the Use of the French Language

The Toubon Law of 1994[63] was adopted to implement the newly amended Article 2 of the Constitution and, at the same time, to update and expand the Bas-Lauriol Law.[64] Accordingly, Article 1 of the Toubon Law states that "the French language is a fundamental element of the personality and the patrimony of France. It is the language of education, work, exchanges, and public services."[65] The Toubon Law has, therefore, a militant objective to protect the French language. This is followed by an extension of the compulsory use of French to other areas such as manuals, warranty conditions of goods or services, invoices, advertisements, and more (Article 2). It imposes the use of French and extends to a series of key areas: trade, advertising, public display, scientific research, labor law, and education. Despite the general rule being the mandatory use of French in a variety of areas, the use of translations in other languages is accepted together with the French text, as long as the text in French is "as legible, audible or intelligible as the presentation in foreign languages" (Article 4).[66]

This overview of the Toubon Law shows its intrusive nature. The imposition of French seems to extend to all areas where language is used. Yet, this law was not accepted without a challenge in front of the Constitutional Council, and some members of Parliament challenged the constitutionality of this law.[67] The Constitutional Council decided on the unconstitutionality of certain elements of the law, notably for the lack of protection of the freedom of expression. First, the Constitutional Council decided that the Toubon Law cannot "impose the obligation to use a specific official terminology on public—or private—sector radio or television broadcasting companies, under the threat of penalties."[68] The imposition of using a certain terminology in media is, therefore, unconstitutional.[69] Also, the Constitutional Council decided that the Toubon Law "cannot [. . .] require private persons, other than in performance of a public service, to use words or expressions specified by regulation as official terminology under threat of penalties."[70] So, the *Sages* specified the legislature can only regulate the vocabulary to be used in the case of moral persons of public law and in the case of private individuals when performing a public service (Article 5 of the Toubon Law).

Regarding the regional languages in France, the Toubon Law seemed to be, a priori, pushing their use into a corner. However, it contained Article 21, which stated that the provisions of this law must be applied without creating any prejudice to the legal framework on the regional languages in France.[71] Article 21 also added that the Toubon Law is not opposed to the use of these regional languages. The Toubon Law adds in Article 11: "The language of instruction [. . .] is French, with exceptions justified by the *needs of teaching regional languages and cultures*."[72] Thus, Article 11 emphasizes that the language used in education is French, with some room, as an exception, for regional languages. As explained earlier, the Toubon Law was challenged in front of the Constitutional Council. It must be noted that Article 11 was not contested when the opposition deputies brought this law in front of the Constitutional Council. In addition, in its decision no. 94-345, the Constitutional Council did not examine this provision ex officio, giving to Article 11 a presumption of constitutionality.[73] Therefore, the Toubon Law led to the inclusion of this provision in Article L.121-3.2 of the Code of Education, giving room to maneuver in terms of teaching regional languages.

The New Territorial Organization of the Republic (NOTRe) Law and the Northern Basque Country

The law on the New Territorial Organization of the Republic (known as the NOTRe Law) of August 7, 2015,[74] is relevant to regional languages in France and their legislative protection. This law amended the General Code of the Territorial Collectivities (*Code general des collectivités territoriales*), and its main goal was to further President Hollande's project of decentralization.[75] In Chapter IV of the NOTRe Law, regulating the "shared competences in the areas of culture, sport, tourism, the promotion of the regional languages, the popular education, the grouping and the granting of aid and subsidies,"[76] Article 103 underscores "the responsibility in cultural matters is jointly exercised by the territorial collectivities and the state, while respecting the cultural rights set out in the Convention on the Protection and Promotion of the Diversity of Cultural Expressions of October 20, 2005."[77] This article is followed by Article 104, which introduces the following text in Article L.1111-4 of the General Code of the Territorial Collectivities: "Competences in matters of culture, sport, tourism, *promotion of regional languages* and popular education are shared between the municipalities, the departments, the regions and the communities with special status."[78]

Article 104 of NOTRe, therefore, expressly gives competence over the promotion of regional languages to municipalities, departments, regions, and communities with special status. This law marked a turning point for Basque speakers since it allowed for the creation of a first-ever administrative territory containing Iparralde, called the Agglomeration Community of the Basque Country (henceforth the Agglomeration Community), in 2017.[79]

Iparralde and the Agglomeration Community of the Basque Country

The Agglomeration Community is the largest agglomeration community of France both in landmass and in the number of municipalities it contains.[80] The creation of the Agglomeration Community was long awaited by the Basques from Iparralde. Before the French Revolution, the Basques from Iparralde had their administrative divisions with legal prerogatives attached:[81] the Estates of Lower Navarre (*Nafarroa Beherea* in Basque), the Estates of *Zuberoa* (Soule), and the representative Assembly of *Lapurdi* (Labourd). These were the equivalent of the *fueros* in the Southern Basque Country (*Hegoalde*).[82] Since these administrative divisions were abolished in the French Revolution of 1789, claims for an administrative division for Iparralde have always been in the minds of Northern Basques. This claim came back in force in the twentieth century, notably because of the sociopolitical changes felt around the world during the seventies and eighties. For instance, during the presidential campaign of François Mitterrand, proposition no. 54 included the creation of a "Département Pays Basque."[83] The creation of an administrative division for Iparralde did not happen, however, until January 1, 2017[84]—with the opportunity created by the NOTRe Law. Figure 2.1 shows the territory of the Agglomeration Community.

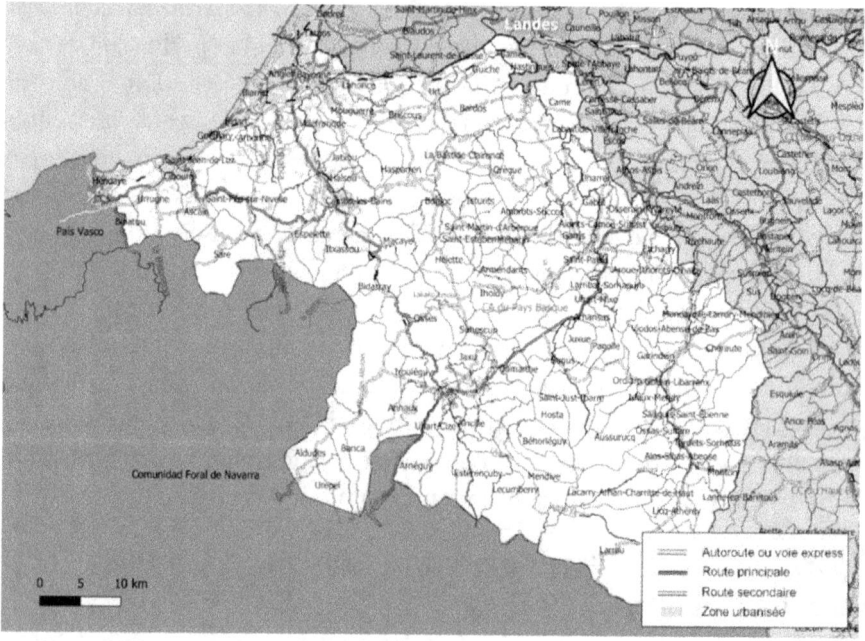

Figure 2.1. Map of the Agglomeration Community of the Basque Country.[85]

When looking into the competences of the Agglomeration Community, we notice that it fulfills the role of a local administration, albeit in a limited manner. Regarding minority language protection, the list of the competences of this institution contains linguistic and cultural policies. According to the official website of the Agglomeration Community,[86] these competences refer to the Basque and the Gascon languages, and the administration has already taken some initiatives regarding Euskara.

It is worth noting the efforts expended in Iparralde regarding the status and use of Euskara. Indeed, the mere existence of the Public Office of the Basque Language (POBL[87]) is a triumph in this matter.[88] The Agglomeration

Community works together with the POBL. Despite being a recently created entity, it also aims to improve the use of Euskara. The first policies adopted by the Agglomeration Community addressed linguistics, showing this institution's commitment toward the Basque language.[89] On the topic of Euskara, the Agglomeration Community has also created "improvement contracts,"[90] aimed at including and developing the presence of this language in the municipalities of Iparralde. The ultimate goal of these contracts is to provide a bilingual service to the citizens of Iparralde by their municipal governments. Thirteen municipalities have joined these "improvement contracts" so far.[91]

The Molac Law on the Heritage Protection and Promotion of Regional Languages

The latest legislation regarding the Basque language in France is the law on the heritage protection of the regional languages and their promotion, known as the Molac Law.[92]

The bill proposed by MP Molac sought to strengthen the protection of regional languages, notably in the areas of education and diacritic marks. Before the intervention of the Constitutional Council on this law,[93] it would have resulted in the inclusion of immersive schooling in regional languages in public schools (Article 4). This would have been a big step forward for regional languages. Together with this, the Molac Law aimed to financially support the schooling of children in regional languages when the option was not available in their municipality (Article 6). Finally, another key element of this law in favor of regional languages in France was the inclusion of the use of diacritic marks in civil status documents (*actes d'état civil*). This was a nod to the national discussion on the case of Fañch, a child whose name in Breton was not accepted in civil status documents because of its diacritic mark.[94] However, despite this law being adopted on April 8, 2021, it was challenged before the Constitutional Council, which, with decision no. 2021-818,[95] annulled (in May 2021) Articles 4 (previously mentioned) and 9.

Despite the Constitutional Council's decision diluting its full potential, the Molac Law has included the protection of regional languages in some areas of French law. Article 1 of the Molac Law managed to extend the heritage protection to regional languages, and Article 2 included regional languages as "national treasures." More importantly, Article 3 of the Molac Law amended Article 21 of the Toubon Law.[96] Article 21 now reads as follows: "The provisions of this law do not preclude the use of regional languages and public and private actions carried out in their favor."[97] This seems to extend the scope of protection of Article 21 of the Toubon Law a little bit further, to include public and private actions, when before Article 21 was limited to legislation and regulations. Articles 5, 6, and 7 of the Molac Law include the regional languages in education,[98] notably with the creation of Article L.312-11-2 in the Code of Education stating that regional languages are "taught during the normal school timetable, from kindergarten to high schools" with the goal of "offering education in regional languages to all students" (Article 7).[99] Finally, Article 8 of the Molac Law regarding official multilingual signs in French and regional languages was adopted.[100]

In contrast with the situation in France, the Basques in Spain have their language recognized as a co-official language in the BAC and Navarre, entailing more extensive linguistic rights. In the following section, we will analyze the Spanish legal framework and the Basque language.

Notes

1. Regarding France, the author will use the term "regional language" to be consistent with the French law. However, she does not believe this is the best term to use to refer to these languages because of its underlining value judgments, and the delimitation of these languages to "regional matters."
2. The unwritten norms with constitutional value being considered: Principes fondamentaux reconnus par les lois de la République, Principes à valeur constitutionnelle, Objectifs à valeur constitutionnelle.
3. The fundamental right of freedom of expression relating to minority languages will be discussed in part III.
4. Bertile gives a comprehensive account of the evolution of language rights in France, notably via the French Revolution, in Bertile, *Langues régionales ou minoritaires et constitution*, 2008.
5. Rosenfeld, "Constitutional Identity," 763.
6. Sieyès, *Qu'est-ce que le Tiers-Etat?*
7. Rouland, Pierré-Caps, and Poumarède, *Droit des minorités et des peuples autochtones*.

8 Rosenfeld and Sajó, *The Oxford handbook of comparative constitutional law*, 763.
9 Verpeaux, "L'unité et la diversité dans la République."
10 Decision of the Constitutional Council no. 91-290, of May 9, 1991: https://www.conseil-constitutionnel.fr/decision/1991/91290DC.htm (Accessed February 8, 2021).
11 Ibid.
12 Rouland, "La tradition juridique française et la diversité culturelle," 383.
13 Levade, "Discrimination positive et principe d'égalité en droit français," 55.
14 Levade, 60.
15 Debbasch, "La République indivisible, la langue française et la nation."
16 Debbasch, 58. Translated by the author. *"[les révolutionnaires ont] attaché plus d'importance à l'universalité des droits qu'à celle de la langue."*
17 The idea was to establish a law at a "national" scale, in opposition to different customary laws that were spread throughout the territory.
18 Debbasch, 59.
19 Adrey, "Language, Nation and State in French Linguistic Nationalism. History, Developments and Perspectives," 2009.
20 This decree was not applied in the end.
21 The Jacobin tradition is examined in Benoit-Rohmer, "Les langues officieuses de la France." See also chapter 4 "La France et les minorités" in Rouland, Pierré-Caps, and Poumarède, *Droit des minorités et des peuples autochtones*. In pages 338-344, the authors explore the issue from the linguistic perspective.
For a comprehensive analysis of the language policies in France, see Adrey, "Language, Nation and State in French Linguistic Nationalism: History, Developments and Perspectives," 2009.
22 Poggeschi, *Le nazioni linguistiche della Spagna autonómica*, 41.
23 Trifunovska, "The case of the Baltic states," 78. The scope of protection of the Language Charter would be applied to nine or ten of these languages, located in metropolitan France.
24 Gilbert and Keane, "Equality versus fraternity? Rethinking France and its minorities," 884.
25 Rouland, Pierré-Caps, and Poumarède, *Droit des minorités et des peuples autochtones*, 91.
26 Zabaleta Apaolaza, "Principios constitucionales sobre las lenguas en Francia," 96.

27 Adding to the symbolic meaning of writing down the French language as the language of the nation in the Constitution, the constitutional law no. 95-880, of August 4, 1995, with its Article 8, shifted the position of this declaration to place it first in Article 2. For the implementation of the new Article 2, the Toubon Law was created in 1994, setting the linguistic scene in France. The Toubon Law will be analyzed later in this chapter.
28 Poggeschi, *Le nazioni linguistiche della Spagna autonómica*, 31. Translated by the author: "una logica difensiva."
29 Benoit-Rohmer, "Les langues officieuses de la France," 9.
30 Decision of April 9, 1996, Autonomie de la Polynésie française. https://www.conseil-constitutionnel.fr/decision/1996/96373DC.htm (Accessed June 9, 2020).
31 Translated by the author: "usage du français aux personnes morales de droit public et aux personnes de droit privé dans l'exercice d'une mission de service public, ainsi qu'aux usagers dans leurs relations avec les administrations et services publics."
32 See part II for a discussion of the Basque language and education.
33 Decision no. 2006-541 of September 28, 2006, Accord sur l'application de l'article 65 de la convention sur la délivrance de brevets européens (accord de Londres). https://www.conseil-constitutionnel.fr/decision/2006/2006541DC.htm (Accessed June 9, 2020).
34 Diwan schools are associative schools conducting immersive schooling in the Breton language in France.
35 This decision will be developed further in part II, chapter 5.
36 Council of State, March 29, 2006. https://www.legifrance.gouv.fr/affichJuriAdmin.do?idTexte=CETATEXT000008262074 (Accessed June 9, 2020).
37 Article 15-1 of the internal rules of the territorial assembly of French Polynesia, as it appears in the decision of 2006. Emphasis added and translated by the author: "The Chairman directs the debates. He must be asked to speak. In plenary sessions, the speaker is seated. His or her speech must be in *French, Tahitian or one of the Polynesian languages* (...) ."
38 Analyzed in the next section of this chapter.
39 Council of State, opinion no. 359461, September 24, 1996, on the European Charter for regional or minority languages. Later, the Council of State also

stopped an attempt of ratification of the Language Charter with the opinion of July 3, 2015.
40 Benoit-Rohmer, "Les langues officieuses de la France."
41 Decision of the French Constitutional Council, June 15, 1999. http://www.conseil-constitutionnel.fr/conseil-constitutionnel/root/bank_mm/anglais/a99412dc.pdf (Accessed July 30, 2021).
42 Chicot, "L'autochtonie sur les territoires du Canada et de la France."
43 Guy Carcassonne explains how this decision was expressed without taking into consideration the already-mentioned elements of the Charter where it is evoked that the text does not grant group rights. In his opinion, the Constitutional Council had a "reaction of fear," and instead of performing an objective analysis, the constitutional judges allowed to give space to the "expression of hostile sentiments" of some judges; in Carcassonne, "Les interdits et la liberté d'expression," 61.
44 Trifunovska, "The case of the Baltic states," 77.
45 Woehrling, "Le droit constitutionnel français à l'épreuve des langues régionales," 81.
46 See Gilbert and Keane, "Equality versus fraternity? Rethinking France and its minorities," 884-886.
47 For instance, in 2015 there was a constitutional amendment project to ratify the Language Charter. However, on October 27, 2015, the Senate rejected this bill. Later, a bill on this topic was proposed by the MP Le Roux in 2017. After the bill was accepted by the National Assembly on January 31, 2017, the French Senate abandoned it. Since France will (apparently?) not ratify the Language Charter any time soon, in 2021 the Molac Law tried to develop the protection of regional languages in France but was limited by the Constitutional Council. This will be examined later in this chapter.
48 Translated by the author: "l'absence de reconnaissance *équivaut* à la négation juridique de l'existence des minorités." In Rouland, Pierré-Caps, and Poumarède, *Droit des minorités et des peuples autochtones*, 263.
49 "Les langues régionales appartiennent au patrimoine de la France."
50 De Witte, "Linguistic minorities in Western Europe: Expansion of rights without (much) litigation?" 40.
51 "Les langues régionales appartiennent à son patrimoine," ("à son" referring to the Republic).

52 Titre XII, Des collectivités territoriales.
53 Titre I, De la souveraineté.
54 This French approach contrasts with the Spanish approach, which pairs in Article 2 of its Constitution, the "right to autonomy," together with the "indissolubility" of the Spanish nation. The Spanish approach to autonomy and regional languages in the Constitution is explained in the following chapter.
55 Verpeaux, "La révision constitutionnelle à l'arrachée."
56 Malo, "Les langues régionales dans la Constitution française: à nouvelles donnes, nouvelle réponse?"
57 Decision no. 2011-130 QPC of May 20, 2011: https://www.conseil-constitutionnel.fr/decision/2011/2011130QPC.htm (Accessed August 27, 2021).
58 Considérant 3, translated by the author: "This article does not institute a right or freedom that the Constitution guarantees; that its infringement cannot therefore be invoked in support of a priority question of constitutionality on the basis of article 61-1 of the Constitution; that, consequently, the complaint is inoperative."
59 De Witte, "Linguistic minorities in Western Europe: Expansion of rights without (much) litigation?" 42.
60 Loi d'orientation et de programmation pour la refondation de l'école de la République (no. 2013-595, July 8, 2013).
61 Translated by the author: "As regional languages and cultures are part of France's heritage, priority is given to teaching them in the regions where they are spoken.
This teaching may be provided throughout schooling in accordance with procedures defined by agreement between the state and the local authorities where these languages are used.
The Conseil supérieur de l'éducation is consulted, in accordance with the powers conferred on it by Article L.231-1, on ways of promoting the study of regional languages and cultures in regions where these languages are used.
Optional teaching of regional language and culture is offered in one of two forms:
1. Teaching regional language and culture;
2. Bilingual teaching in French and regional languages.
Families are informed of the various options for learning regional languages and cultures."
62 The key element regarding regional languages in this amendment of 2013

was the introduction of bilingual teaching in regional languages in the French public schooling system. In 2021, the Molac Law tried to include immersive schooling in public schooling as well. This will be explored later in this chapter, as well as in part II.

63 Law no. 94-665, August 5, 1994, on the use of the French language. https://www.legifrance.gouv.fr/affichTexte.do?cidTexte=JORFTEXT000000349929&dateTexte=20200617 (Accessed June 17, 2020).
64 Law no. 75-1349, on the use of the French language, of December 31, 1975, is known as the Bas-Lauriol Law. This law made compulsory the use of French in public displays and commercial advertising and prohibited the use of any foreign term or expression in these areas.
65 Translated by the author. Article 1: "Langue de la République en vertu de la Constitution, la langue française est un élément fondamental de la personnalité et du patrimoine de la France. Elle est la langue de l'enseignement, du travail, des échanges et des services publics. [. . .] . "
66 Translated by the author : "[. . .] la présentation en français doit être aussi lisible, audible ou intelligible que la présentation en langues étrangères."
67 Decision no. 94-345. July 29, 1994. English version: https://www.conseil-constitutionnel.fr/en/decision/1994/94345DC.htm (Accessed June 17, 2020).
68 Ibid., paragraph 9.
69 The legal system surrounding media and its linguistic content will be analyzed in part III.
70 Ibid., paragraph 10.
71 The Molac Law recently revised Article 21, as will be explained below. Article 21: "Les dispositions de la présente loi s'appliquent sans préjudice de la législation et de la réglementation relatives aux langues régionales de France e' ne s'opposent pas à leur usage."
72 Translated, and emphasis added, by the author. Article 11: "la langue de l'enseignement (. . .) est le français, sauf exceptions justifiées par les *nécessités de l'enseignement des langues et cultures régionales.*"
73 Bertile, *Langues régionales ou minoritaires et constitution*, 94.
74 Law no. 2015-991. Loi portant nouvelle organisation territoriale de la République (NOTRe).

75 The process of decentralization of the Fifth Republic has been possible notably with the constitutional amendment of 2003 (constitutional law no. 2003-276 of March 28, 2003) on the decentralized organization of the Republic. https://www.legifrance.gouv.fr/affichTexte.do;jsessionid=1B2033987EA22A26B364D350BE05D197.tplgfr34s_2?cidTexte=JORFTEXT000000601882&dateTexte=20110211 (Accessed June 23, 2020).
This law amended Article 1 of the Constitution to include the organization of the Republic is decentralized ("*son organization est decentralisée*"). This law also developed the system of the territorial collectivities regulated in Title XII of the Constitution, which led later to the NOTRe Law.

76 Translated by the author. The original text reads: "Compétences partagées dans le domaine de la culture, du sport, du tourisme, de la promotion des langues régionales et de l'éducation populaire et regroupement de l'instruction et de l'octroi d'aides ou de subventions."

77 Translated by the author. The original text reads: "La responsabilité en matière culturelle est exercée conjointement par les collectivités territoriale' et l'Etat dans le respect des droits culturels énoncés par la convention sur la protection et la promotion de la diversité des expressions culturelles du 20 octobre 2005."

78 Translated, and emphasis added, by the author. The original text reads: "Les compétences en matière de culture, de sport, de tourisme, de promotion des langues régionale' et d'éducation populaire sont partagées entre les communes, les départements, les régions et les collectivités à statut particulier. [. . .]"

79 Communauté d'agglomération Pays Basque-Euskal Hirigune Elkargoa https ://www.communaute-paysbasque.fr/ (Accessed July 2, 2020).

80 Data extracted from the official website of the Agglomeration Community. This administrative division contains 308,323 inhabitants and 158 towns. Its territory extends to 110km in length and 70km in width. https://www.communaute-paysbasque.fr/eu/euskal-hirigune-elkargoa/lurraldea/translate-to-basque-en-chiffres (Accessed June 22, 2020).

81 Etats généraux de Basse-Navarre, Etats généraux de Soule, Biltzar du Labourd-Lapurtarren Biltzarra. Iparralde is formed by the territories of Lower Navarre, Soule, and Labourd.

82 Discussed later in chapter 3.

83 Proposal no. 54, translated by the author: "State decentralization will be a priority. Regional councils will be elected by universal suffrage, and the executive will be assured by the president and the bureau. Corsica will be given special status. A Department Pays Basque will be created. Prefects will no longer have authority over the administration of local authorities. The departmental executive will be entrusted to the president and bureau of the general council. Reform of local finances will be undertaken immediately. State supervision of local authority decisions will be abolished." See the 110 propositions in http://www.mitterrand.org/110-propositions-pour-la-France.html (Accessed June 22, 2020).
84 By the prefectural decree of July 13, 2016.
85 Wikimedia Commons, by Roland45 and contributors of OpenStreetMap. https://commons.wikimedia.org/w/index.php?curid=81797237 (Accessed June 22, 2020).
86 https://www.communaute-paysbasque.fr/ (Accessed June 23, 2020).
87 https://www.mintzaira.fr/eu/eep.html (Accessed February 19, 2020). Office Public de la Langue Basque—Euskararen Erakunde Publikoa. The POBL is a public interest group, formed by twelve people representing the four members of this institution. There are three representatives of the state, three representatives of the Nouvelle-Aquitaine region, three representatives of the Departmental Council of the Atlantic Pyrenees, and three representatives of the Agglomeration Community of the Basque Country.
88 More concrete practices of this institution will be examined in parts II and III.
89 Interview of Jean-René Etchegaray (2020), "Jean-René Etchegaray: 'La collectivité territoriale à statut particulier aurait plus d'efficience,'" by Goizeder Taberna, on *Mediabask*, February 21, 2020. https://www.mediabask.eus/eu/info_mbsk/20200221/jean-rene-etchegaray-la-collectivite-territoriale-a-statut-particulier-aurait-plus-d-efficience (Accessed February 24, 2020). With the adoption of these policies, the Agglomeration Community notably decided to increase the funding of the POBL.
90 Translated by the author "hobekuntza kontratuak" https://www.communaute-paysbasque.fr/eu/euskara-eta-gaskoia/euskara/bizitzeko/herriko-etxeetan (Accessed February 19, 2020).
91 As of July 2021.
92 https://www.legifrance.gouv.fr/loda/id/JORFTEXT000043524722/2021-07-28/ (Accessed July 28, 2021).

93 See part II, chapter 4.
94 This case created passionate debates in France, and further information can be found in French media. The parents of Fañch wanted to register the name of their child using the Breton name and its diacritic mark. However, the state refused to accept this name. A second case with the same name emerged later in November 2018 when the name Fañch was not accepted for a newborn. The reason behind the refusal in these cases is that the letter *ñ* does not belong to the list of the diacritic marks accepted by the circular of July 23, 2014. However, Article 57-2 of the Civil Code reads that the name of children is chosen by their father and mother. In the first case of the baby born in 2017, the High Court of Quimper did not grant the parents the right to name their respective children Fañch, but on November 19, 2018, the Court of Appeal of Rennes decided the use of the diacritic mark *ñ* did not go against the principles informing the drafting of public acts or Article 2 of the Constitution. This was later confirmed by the Cassation Court on October 17, 2019, which authorized both children to keep their (respective) names as Fañch. Yet, the same issue keeps repeating, with a new blocking of the name Fañch in February 2024 by the French administration.

For a comprehensive explanation, see Zabaleta Apaolaza, "Le ñ de la discorde: retour sur le contentieux Fañch et la transcription des noms et prénoms non français dans l'état-civil français—Eneritz Zabaleta."
95 https://www.conseil-constitutionnel.fr/decision/2021/2021818DC.htm (Accessed July 28, 2021). This decision is further analyzed in part II.
96 Analyzed previously.
97 Translated by the author: "Les dispositions de la présente loi ne font pas obstacle à l'usage des langues régionales et aux actions publiques et privée menées en leur faveur."
98 Article 6 is discussed in the previous paragraph.
99 Translated by the author: "Without prejudice to article L. 312-11-1, within the framework of agreements between the state and the regions, the Corsican collectivity, the European Collectivity of Alsace or the territorial collectivities governed by Article 73 of the Constitution, the regional language is a subject taught as part of the normal timetable in nursery and elementary schools, colleges and lycées in all or part of the territories concerned, with the aim of offering the teaching of the regional language to all pupils."

100 Article 8, translated by the author: "Public services may, in all or part of their territory, display translations of the French language into the regional language or languages in use on inscriptions and signs affixed to public buildings, public thoroughfares, waterways, transport infrastructures and the main institutional communication media, when they are installed or renewed."

3

Spanish Law and the Basque Language

The Spanish Constitution of 1978 represents a transition from an authoritarian regime to democracy. This text forged the current parliamentary monarchy of the Kingdom of Spain. However, the Spanish constitutional model is well known for another characteristic: The 1978 Constitution established the *Estado de las Autonomías* (State of Autonomies). This chapter is a two-part analysis: first, the Spanish Constitution as it relates to the Basque language, and second, the regional legal framework and the Basque language.

The Spanish Constitution and the Basque Language

The Constitution of 1978 created a decentralized system providing for recognition of minorities and minority languages. It was also set in the wake of a dictatorship that had prohibited any sort of cultural, ethnic, or linguistic differentiation in the Spanish territory.

Constitutional Heritage of Spain

The Spanish Constitution of December 29, 1978, marked the end of the authoritarian era in Spanish history. The death of General Francisco Franco in November 1975 allowed for the beginning of a democratic transition (referred to as "the transition"), and the Constitution of 1978 marked the reestablishment of a democracy in Spain. The major political parties negotiated this text, and it obtained approval by referendum.

To understand how the Constitution of 1978 comes into the picture of Spanish history,[1] we must at least mention the Second Republic (1931–1936). The Second Republic was proclaimed on April 14, 1931. Regarding the "territorial question" of Spain, the Constitution under the

Second Republic already established a system for granting devolution of political power to the regions willing to move toward self-government. In 1932, Catalonia was granted a Statute of Autonomy after referendum. This created tension, since the parties on the right were critical of the move.[2] This devolution of powers was also extended to the BAC and Galicia. In 1933, there was already a referendum in the BAC regarding this matter,[3] and in October 1936, the Statute of Autonomy of the Basque Country was enacted into law.[4] A referendum about Galicia was also organized, but the Civil War erupted before its approval.[5] We can see how the Second Republic already settled some of the features that would apply later, during the 1978 Constitution. However, between the Second Republic and 1978, Spain lived under the Francoist regime.

One of the factors that brought civil war to Spain and Franco to power was the belief among some sections of Spanish society that the unity of the country was broken because of the regional devolution of powers. This debate is often referred to as the "territorial question." Ferreres Comella emphasizes that Franco used these sentiments among the Spaniards "when he decided to dismantle the self-government that had been granted to Catalans and Basques," and "to persecute regional languages and cultures."[6] Fed by this, nationalist opposition in Catalonia and the Basque Country reinforced the opposition to Franco's regime. In the Basque Country, the struggle against the regime also attained a violent form with the birth of *Euskadi Ta Askatasuna* (ETA) in 1959.[7] The terrorist activities performed by this group truly challenged the Franco dictatorship, notably by killing the president of the government, Luis Carrero Blanco, in 1973.[8]

The adoption of the Law for Political Reform (by referendum on December 15, 1976) created the landscape for a regime change. This led to the elections of June 1977 that brought the drafting of the Constitution of 1978. The different parties negotiated this text to attain the widest consensus possible.[9] The Constitution was adopted with a clear majority of citizens. Rosenfeld believes the Spanish negotiated model was attained with a clear majority because citizens wanted to leave the fascist regime; they did not wish to have a second civil war; and they were willing to enter the European Union.[10] Yet, the turnout in the referendum was only 67.11 percent, notably because of politically motivated abstention. For instance, in the BAC, the Basque nationalist party PNV,[11] which was not satisfied with the degree of self-government attained under the new Constitution, encouraged abstention. Less than half (46 percent) voted in the referendum of the BAC. Thus, the referendum showed a vast acceptance of the 1978 constitutional text but still showed problems concerning the territorial question.

The Spanish Constitution and the State of Autonomies

The Spanish Constitution of 1978 set up a political system known as the State of Autonomies. The Kingdom of Spain is divided into seventeen autonomous communities and two autonomous cities (Ceuta and Melilla). One of the characteristic traits of the Spanish constitutional model is that "it sets a framework for a multi-ethnic polity."[12] In fact, the Spanish Constitution creates a system of devolution of powers to the autonomous communities but keeps the unity of the nation. This is clearly stated in Article 2 of the Constitution, where the "indissoluble unity of the Spanish Nation" is claimed.[13] Furthermore, Article 2 establishes the main principles of the State of Autonomies: It simultaneously affirms the unity of Spain and gives the right to autonomy.[14] The constitutional text also mentions "nationalities" and "regions" to distinguish between different levels of autonomous states. Arzoz goes further and defines the Spanish state as a "multinational quasi federal unitary state."[15] In this sense, it could be said the slogan of the 1978 Constitution is "unity and autonomy." This brings us back to the drafting of the Spanish Constitution, when a compromise was struck in trying to find "proper balance between national unity and according a meaningful measure of autonomy to ethnic communities, such as the Basques and the Catalans, who had been suppressed ruthlessly during the Franco regime."[16] Therefore, the Spanish state is not defined in the 1978 text as a federal state, or as a central state, but combines "the traditional ideology of the nation-state with limited recognition of territorial and cultural autonomy."[17] Part VIII of the Constitution regulates this territorial division of Spain, in which Article 137 states that Spain is territorially organized "into municipalities, provinces and Self-governing Communities that may be constituted." It adds, "All these bodies shall enjoy self-government for the management of their respective interests."

The two fundamental provisions recognizing collective identities in Spain are Article 2, with the right to autonomy of the nationalities and regions, and Article 3, containing the right to use various regional languages.[18] In addition, Articles 148 and 149 list the shared competencies between the regional administration and the central state. Article 148 lists the exclusive matters devolved to the autonomous communities, and Article 149 lists those matters exclusive to the central state.

Another peculiarity in the Spanish Constitution is the asymmetric model. That is to say, there is equality between the autonomous communities in the eyes of the Spanish Constitution, but asymmetry exists in some matters.[19] For instance, the BAC and Navarre have always showed some differences regarding their financing systems.[20] This asymmetry in financing is still a right for these two autonomous communities, and it is frequently discussed in politics and the media. This asymmetry, a major source of controversy between Catalonia and Madrid, was also one of the issues that sparked the Catalan crisis of 2017. The issue of the autonomous communities, and their asymmetry, is still not settled. The adoption of the new Catalan Statute of Autonomy in 2006[21] sparked another six autonomous communities to also change theirs, and resulted, after a long series of events, into the referendum on the independence of Catalonia in 2017.

Exploring the State of Autonomies and the asymmetric model in Spain indicates the complexity that the negotiated Constitution brought to the political organization of the Spanish territory. In fact, the asymmetric model generates tension between autonomous communities, adding to the existing tension between the central state and the regions. Yet, at the same time, it allows for the management of cultural and linguistic differences present in the different autonomous communities, such as the BAC and Navarre—where the Basque minority is accommodated.

In this section so far, we have described the overall regime of the Spanish Constitution and its particularities with the autonomous states. We can now move toward our main concern: the Spanish Constitution and its relationship with the Basque language.

Article 3 of the Spanish Constitution

The Constitution of 1978 established the State of Autonomies to accommodate different nationalities and minority cultures in a bigger Spanish framework.

Castilian is not the only language spoken, and Spanish culture is not the only one present in Spain. Some authors even suggest that in a European context, "Spain is probably the country with the highest number of minority-language speakers and the greatest degree of linguistic complexity."[22]

The Spanish Constitution of 1978 creates a framework of protection for regional or minority languages. This also includes the protection of Euskara. In the Preamble of the Constitution, the following is noted: "The Spanish Nation . . . proclaims its will to: . . . Protect all Spaniards and peoples of Spain in the exercise of human rights, of their cultures and traditions, and of their languages and institutions."[23]

Unlike the French Preamble or constitutional block, in the Spanish case there is a direct reference to regional or minority languages. In the corpus of the Constitution, Articles 3, 20.3, and 148.1.17 evoke language matters. However, the main protection of the Basque language in the Spanish Constitution resides in Article 3. This article gives an official status to other languages in Spain, in addition to Castilian:

1. Castilian is the official Spanish language of the state. All Spaniards have the duty to know it and the right to use it.
2. The other Spanish languages shall also be official in the respective autonomous communities in accordance with their statutes.
3. The wealth of the different language modalities of Spain is a cultural heritage, which shall be the object of special respect and protection.[24]

Through Article 3.2, the Spanish Constitution grants the recognition of official languages other than Castilian in the autonomous communities. As a matter of fact, formal bilingualism is recognized in certain territories. But what does it mean to have an official status for a language under the 1978 Constitution? To answer this question, we should turn to decision 82/1986 of the Spanish Constitutional Tribunal.[25] In this decision, the Constitutional Tribunal explains, to be official, a language should be recognized by public powers as a "normal means of communication within and between them" and also between private subjects "with full legal validity and effects."[26] This official recognition should not depend on the weight that the language carries in society. Following the linguistic system set by Article 3 and the autonomous communities, there are six bilingual regional territories in Spain: the BAC, the Balearic Islands, Catalonia, Galicia, Navarre, and Valencia.

Returning to the text written in the Constitution, Article 3.2 cannot be explained without mentioning Article 3.1. Before proclaiming the recognition of other languages than Castilian, the Constitution sets Spanish as the main language of Spain.[27] The text also reads: "All Spaniards have the duty to know it and the right to use it." As clearly explained by Agirreazkuenaga, this does not mean that the Constitution imposes the use of Castilian (even in the bilingual autonomous communities),[28] but it rather provides the choice of using either one of the two co-official languages.[29]

As mentioned earlier, the Spanish political system is a decentralized model that gives power to its autonomous communities, and these regional governments must decide on the protection of their languages. These Autonomy Statutes are, then, formally adopted by the Spanish Parliament (*Cortes generales*).[30] Therefore, by being limited to the autonomous communities, "the co-official status has territorial character" and "the linguistic model and the territorial model are intrinsically linked."[31] The autonomous communities that want to protect a regional language must adopt a Language Act, regulating the conditions and scope of protection of the language(s) concerned. Thus, the bilingual autonomous communities must regulate the use of the co-official languages. The majority of autonomous communities containing a regional or minority language have declared it "vernacular" in their territory, and "this symbolic recognition" can even have wide practical effects, "which go from justifying special promotion [. . .] to grounding a sort of priority in the actual language use of the autonomous authorities."[32] Since the regulation of languages is left in the hands of the autonomous communities by the Spanish constitutional order, there is no general regulation on languages at the national level despite the general principle of Article 3 of the Constitution. This has led to what has been referred to as the "territorial thinking" of language in Spain.[33]

A side effect of this territorialization is the non-protection of co-official languages outside of the autonomous community. For instance, if a citizen who speaks Catalan wants to enjoy their linguistic rights before institutions or authorities belonging to the central state, Spanish will be the only official language.[34] The same happens if a citizen who speaks Galician goes to another autonomous community—Extremadura, for instance—and wants to enjoy his or her linguistic rights. This citizen does not have his or her rights concerning Galician protected in Extremadura (in this example). The territorial protection of a minority language means that its protection is confined to the autonomous community's institutions and territory.

In addition to the protection by the Constitution, the Basque language is also protected by the international treaties adopted by Spain. Article 96.1 of the 1978 Constitution states the following: "Validly concluded international treaties, once officially published in Spain, *shall be part of the internal legal system.*" The international legal framework for the protection of the Basque language has already been discussed in chapter 1. Here again, the division of Spain into autonomous communities plays a fundamental role. Regarding the Language Charter, for instance, the protection of regional or minority languages provided by this text is only extended to the six autonomous communities that contain a co-official minority language.

Regional Laws and the Basque Language: The BAC and Navarre

When we study the legal status of Euskara, two autonomous communities should be considered: the BAC and Navarre. Both these autonomous communities recognize the co-officiality of Euskara with Spanish. Yet, when approaching these two regions, we must not forget the historical peculiarities of these two places. The territorial distinctiveness of the Basque Country has been present over centuries: "The lack of genuine exclusive political institutions common to the Basque territories has not prevented parallel developments that share certain features through time."[35] This translated into the development of provincial parliaments, the Juntas (or Assemblies), and the regulation of *fueros* (customary old laws). Regarding the historical territorial dimension, the Kingdom of Navarre maintained its statehood until 1620[36] and did not lose its self-government until 1789.[37] The other territories of Hegoalde[38] were subject to the Crown of Castile as a free association, sealed by a bilateral Covenant known as the *foral*[39] (statutory) system, maintaining their autonomy.[40] The BAC and Navarre still apply *fueros* later codified as covenants,[41] notably on personal status and inheritance. The regional parliaments update these. Even if they are often linked to the territories of Hegoalde, it must be emphasized that *fueros* existed on both sides of the Pyrenees. These laws started to extend gradually in the twelfth century and were in place until the end of nineteenth century.[42] The abolishing laws of 1836 and 1876, or even of 1841, were imposed in a context of war.[43] These rights were reinstated in 1878 for the BAC, reformulated and diminished in form, as had happened in Navarre too. They were abolished again by the dictatorial regime of Franco—except in Navarre and the province of Araba, as a reward for supporting the coup. Finally, these historical rights were brought back with the new democratic regime of 1978. Regarding the BAC, the historical rights are mentioned in the additional disposition of the Statute of Autonomy, and Navarre even mentions the *fueros* in the name of the Statute of Autonomy itself.[44]

The Law and the Basque Language in the BAC

The BAC is one of the two autonomous communities in Spain where the Basque language is co-official. This region is characterized by its proactive approach toward the protection and development of the Basque language. The linguistic policies put in place aim to achieve the full and real co-officiality of Euskara and Spanish. To achieve this, it is essential to establish a legal system that favors this approach. In the BAC, the legal framework for co-officiality comes from the Statute of Autonomy and the Law for the Normalization of the Basque Language of 1982 (the Normalization Law).

The Statute of Autonomy of the BAC and the Basque Language

Following what is expressed in the Spanish Constitution, the Statute of Autonomy of the BAC gives a co-official rank to the Basque language, together with Spanish.[45] Both languages have equal force in this territory. Among all the territories in which Basque is spoken, the BAC is the one in which Basque speakers enjoy the broadest fulfillment of their rights. Yet, it must be noted, Basque is still spoken by a minority of the population even in the BAC's territory.[46]

The Second Republic already granted linguistic rights to the BAC: The Statute of Autonomy of 1936, in Article 1.3, granted for the first time an official status to the Basque language, together with Castilian. However, this official rank to Euskara was only given in three of the four Basque territories in Spain: Araba, Bizkaia, and Gipuzkoa,[47] leaving Navarre outside the Autonomy Statute. Furthermore, Franco's troops quickly occupied Araba, making it difficult to implement the Statute of Autonomy, including its regulation on linguistic rights. This short period of recognition was followed by Franco's dictatorship, a key characteristic of which was the attempt to erase all cultural and political particularities, the Basque culture and language included. In fact, "the Fascist state laid down a linguistic policy to repress any demonstration of Basque or other minority languages in the State, prohibiting and punishing its use very violently."[48] Analyzing the fascist regime's prohibition and repression of the Basque language exceeds the scope of this research, but its impact was and still can be felt among Basque speakers and their linguistic rights.

The highest legal norm of the BAC is the Statute of Autonomy, known as the Statute of Gernika. It was approved by the organic law of December 18, 1979. Historical territories of Araba, Gipuzkoa, and Bizkaia form the BAC. The Statute of Autonomy leaves the door open for Navarre to join the autonomous community if it decides to do so. The sharing of competencies between the autonomous communities and the state is established in the Constitution in Articles 148 and 149. In the Statute of Gernika, the exclusive competencies of the BAC are listed in Title I.

The main reference to the status of the Basque language appears in Article 6 of the Statute of Autonomy.[49] This article recognizes a co-official rank to the Basque language, at the same level as Spanish.[50] This includes Euskara as a co-official language in administration and public services (Article 10.4 of the Statute of Autonomy). Additionally, the Normalization Law of 1982[51] and the Law of Local Institutions of the BAC of 2016[52] confirm the co-officiality of Basque and Spanish in public administration. Because this part of the book focuses on the legal framework of the Basque language, we will look closer at the Normalization Law of 1982.

Normalization Law 10/1982

Governing the basic normalization of the use of Euskara is Law 10/1982 of November 24, known as the Normalization Law. A normalization law in Spain is defined by the Constitutional Tribunal as:

> [A law that contains] provisions whose general objective is none other than to ensure the respect and to promote the use and the co-officiality of the language of the Autonomous Community and, to this end, positively correct a historical situation of inequality with respect to Spanish, allowing to achieve, progressively and within the requirements that the Constitution imposes, the widest knowledge and use of this language in its territory.[53]

The Normalization Law today "continues to be the keystone in the linguistic system [of the BAC],"[54] providing for concrete rights for the citizens of the BAC. The Normalization Law of 1982 proceeds to list them.

The Normalization Law of 1982 refers to Article 6 of the Statute of Autonomy in its Preamble, and it places itself as the development of this norm, reaffirming its commitment to the Basque language. In the Preliminary Heading, we can find the general principles governing the Normalization Law: the Basque language is the "lengua propia" (*own language*) of the BAC (Article 2); Basque and Spanish are co-official languages (Article 3); discrimination on grounds of language is prohibited (Article 4); and all citizens of the BAC have the right to know and use the official languages orally and in writing (Article 5). Article 5.2 lists the fundamental linguistic rights of the citizen:[55]

- a) Right to interact in Basque or Spanish orally and/or in writing with the Administration and any other Organism or Entity situated in the autonomous community.
- b) Right to receive an education in both official languages.
- c) Right to receive in Basque periodicals, radio, and television programs, and other media.
- d) Right to carry out professional, labor, political, and union activities in Basque.
- e) Right to express oneself in Basque in any meeting.

In addition, Article 5.3 emphasizes that "the public powers will guarantee the exercise of these rights, in the territorial scope of the autonomous community, so that they are effective and real."[56] The Normalization Law regulates the use of the Basque language in the areas of public administration (Chapter 1), education (Chapter 2), media (Chapter 3), as well as regulates social use and other institutional aspects (Chapter 4) and the use of Basque as the official written language (Chapter 5).

Both the Statute of Autonomy and the Normalization Law provide for a comprehensive framework for the protection and the development of the Basque language. This autonomous community has taken an activist role in the protection of Euskara, which deeply contrasts with the situation already discussed in France. The Basque government takes up the role of legislative protector of the Basque language. Yet, the BAC is not the only autonomous community in Spain that grants a co-official status to the Basque language together with Spanish. The next autonomous community we will analyze is the Foral Community of Navarre.

The Basque Language and the Law in Navarre

The legal system of the Basque language in Navarre mirrors the one in the BAC in that it is an autonomous community where Euskara is granted a co-official rank. However, the way in which the co-officiality is implemented is different and more complex since Navarre is divided into linguistic areas. This linguistic zoning is a headache for lawyers and citizens, who must juggle between different levels of language protection in a rather small territory.[57] The two key norms ruling the Basque language in Navarre are the Statute of Autonomy and the Law on the Basque Language.

Statute of Autonomy of Navarre and the Basque Language

Navarre also granted co-official status to the Basque language in the Statute of Autonomy,[58] but with a different regime than that of the BAC. To understand the legal framework of the Basque language in Navarre, let us consider the following assessment made by Xabier Arzoz:[59]

> Euskara is, nowadays, a minority language, but in not so remote times, when it was the language spoken by the majority of the inhabitants of Navarre. If today it is a minority language, it is because there has been a long historical process of linguistic substitution, with the complexity of all long historical processes.

The complex historical process of the loss of the Basque language in Navarre is important for understanding the legal regime that Navarre offers to Euskara.[60] Concerning the regulation of Euskara in Navarre, complexity is the watchword. Navarre is divided into three linguistic zones: the Basque-speaking area (in the north), the Mixed area (in the center), and the Spanish-speaking area (in the south).[61] This division gives an official status to the Basque language in the smallest area of the three, leaving the most populated part of the region in the Spanish-speaking (or non-Basque-speaking) area. Article 9.2 of the Statute of Autonomy grants co-official status to the Basque language only in the Basque-speaking area.[62] Concerning the Mixed and non-Basque-speaking areas, the Basque Language Act[63] regulates the protection of Euskara.[64] However, this act "intentionally leaves a huge discretion to the authorities" to define the content of the protection of the Basque language.[65] The linguistic territorial division of Navarre is shown in figure 3.1 below.

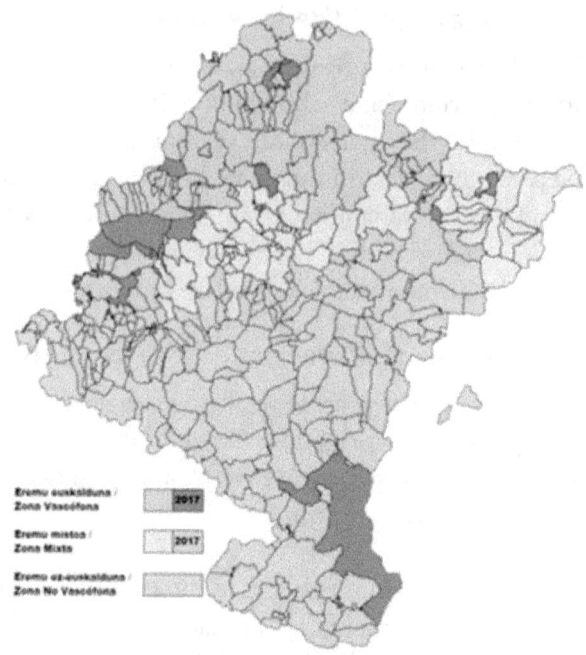

Figure 3.1. Map of the linguistic zoning of Navarre (updated with the latest revision of 2017).[66]

This linguistic territorial zoning is highly contested. In 2017, a social and political movement started asking the Navarrese government to abolish this linguistic division.[67] Regarding this linguistic zoning, and leaving the recent civil and political movements aside, Irujo and Urrutia rightly explain the two main issues of this territorial setting. In their words, on the one hand, linguistic zoning "jeopardizes the universal character of the diffusion and transmission of the language and culture" and on the other hand, it "discriminates against Basque speakers in the mixed zone and puts Basque outside the law in the south zone."[68] This approach definitively challenges the maintenance, protection, and development of a minority language that is classified as an endangered language by UNESCO.[69]

The adoption of the Statute of Autonomy has already been contested in Navarre. In an early draft of the statute, co-officiality had been granted to the Basque language in the entire territory.[70] Another criticism to the final text of the Statute of Autonomy was the vocabulary used to refer to the Basque language and linguistic rights.[71] Yet interestingly, the Statute of Autonomy did not explicitly decide on the geographical extension of each of the three linguistic divisions. The Statute of Autonomy left this decision for a future law. The lack of clear protection of the Basque language in Navarre was experienced by a large part of the Navarrese society as a "regrettable episode of ignorance" of the history and society of Navarre.[72] Other commentators[73] more moderately highlight the impracticality of the division of Navarre into linguistic zones.[74] Not only was this decision impractical and created headaches for politicians and lawyers, but also no explanation was given about this decision, or about which elements were considered to reach it. In addition, since Navarre is a territory populated by only a half a million inhabitants, where historically Basque was mostly spoken, experts believe that extending the co-official status of Basque to the entire territory would make more sense.[75]

Even if linguistic zoning was not the most advisable approach to be undertaken by the legislators concerning linguistic rights, the reality is that this regulation is still applied. This leaves a complex legal framework for Basque speakers in the Foral Community of Navarre, in another complex constitutional general regime of the State of Autonomies.

Law 18/1986 on the Basque Language

The Law 18/1986 on the Basque Language develops the principles on the Basque language contained in the Statute of Autonomy.[76] The objectives of this law appear in Article 1.2:[77]

a) To protect the right of citizens to know and use the Basque language and define the instruments to make it effective.
b) To protect the recovery and development of the Basque language in Navarre, indicating the measures to promote its use.
c) To guarantee the use and teaching of Basque in accordance with the principles of voluntariness, gradualness, and respect, in accordance with the sociolinguistic reality of Navarre.

Article 2 claims the Basque language to be one of the "*lenguas propias*" of Navarre (Article 2.1)[78] and states the co-officiality of Basque and Spanish in Navarre (depending on the linguistic areas). Following a similar structure to the law in the BAC, Article 3 prohibits discrimination on grounds of language and states that public institutions must respect this language law.[79] The final general norm, Article 4, grants citizens the right to address judges and tribunals in Basque.[80]

Concerning the linguistic zoning of Navarre, Article 5 sets out the three areas (Basque-speaking, Mixed, and non-Basque speaking) and states which municipalities belong to which area. Yet, some principles apply to all areas. For instance, Article 6 recognizes, regarding all citizens, "the right to use both Basque and Spanish in their relations with Public Administrations [. . .]."[81] Other principles include that the official *Journal of Navarre* will be published both in Basque and Spanish (Article 7), that the toponymy of Navarre will have official names in Spanish and Basque, depending on the linguistic area (Article 8), and that an official translation unit will be established by the government of Navarre (Article 9). The following chapters of the Law on the Basque Language pertain to language rights given to citizens depending on the linguistic area: Chapter II, the use of Euskara in the Basque-speaking area; Chapter III, the use of Basque in the Mixed area; and Chapter IV, the use of Basque in the non-Basque-speaking area. We will now discuss the key elements of these chapters.

For the Basque-speaking area, Articles 10 to 16 list the language rights of Basque speakers. All these rights address the relationship of citizens with the administration and public institutions. Thus, in this area, citizens have the right to use both languages equally in their relations with public institutions and the administration, and "[. . .] the appropriate measures shall be taken and the necessary means shall be adopted to progressively ensure the exercise of this right [. . .]."[82] All administrative acts are legally effective in both languages (Article 11), public institutions "will promote the progressive training in the use of Euskara of the personnel that provides services," and "each Administration shall specify the positions for which knowledge of Basque is mandatory" (Article 15).[83]

Article 11 adds that all administrative actions are valid and fully effective, regardless of the official language used, and "consequently, all acts involving bodies of the Public Administrations, as well as notifications and administrative communications must be written in both languages, unless all interested parties expressly choose the use of only one of them."[84] The authority writing the public document can decide in which language it shall be written, and in the case of having more than one authority, they can agree on the language in which it shall be written (Article 12). In addition, public notaries must issue in Spanish or Basque, as requested by the interested party, copies or testimonies, and translate them when necessary (Article 12). In any case, "they must issue in Spanish the copies that must take effect outside the Basque-speaking area" (Article 12).[85]

In the area of justice, the Navarrese citizen can use the official language of their choice (Article 14).[86] To implement fully these regulations regarding Basque and Spanish, Article 15 foresees that the public administration and companies should "promote the progressive training in the use of Euskara among the staff working in the Basque-speaking area," and therefore they "should specify the jobs for which knowledge of Basque is mandatory, and for the others it will be considered a qualified merit among others."[87] Finally, concerning the Basque-speaking area, the local entities shall use Spanish and Basque "in all its provisions, publications, urban road signs, and proper names of their places, respecting, in any case, the traditional ones" (Article 16).[88]

Regarding the Mixed area, citizens have the right to use both Spanish and Euskara when addressing the public administration of Navarre (Article 17).[89] To achieve the implementation of this right, the public administration can specify the job positions for which knowledge of Euskara is necessary (17.a) and value as a merit the knowledge of Euskara to access other positions (17.b).

Finally, Chapter IV, regarding the use of the Basque language in the non-Basque-speaking area, contains a single article: Article 18. This article also regulates the language used to address the administration and public institutions: "Citizens are recognized the right to speak in Basque to the Public Administrations of Navarre. [The administrations] may require the interested parties to translate into Spanish or use the translation services provided in article 9."[90] Article 18 regulates the Spanish-speaking (non-Basque-speaking) area, granting the right to address the administration both in Basque and Spanish. This does not mean, however, public administration from this linguistic area must provide their services in both languages. This results in all three linguistic areas of Navarre offering the right to address the administration in Basque.[91] This differs significantly from the policies concerning education or media, where the linguistic zoning interferes heavily with the rights of Basque speakers.

The language rights regarding the relationship of citizens with the administration is followed by principles concerning other areas: Title II is about education[92] and Title III elaborates on media.[93] These two areas (education and media), and their relationship with the law and context of the Basque language are analyzed in the following chapters of parts II and III.

Concluding Remarks of Part I

This section of the book, on the legal framework of the Basque language, provided an overview of the complexity of the laws regarding Euskara. International law sets a basic threshold for the protection of minorities and minority languages, but in the case of Euskara, it must face a key limit: the responsibility falling into the hands of the nation-state. For instance, France systematically claims reservations when rights concern minorities in its territory. The European legal framework is more interesting for the case of the Basque language, since this language can be protected under the Language Charter. Some other tools can be found at this level, such as the Framework Convention or the European Union law. Yet, the former is not signed by France and its protection in Spain is limited to the Roma community, and the latter shows limitations as well for the protection of Euskara. Hence, the main text protecting the Basque language (in Spain) is the European Charter for Regional or Minority Language (the Language Charter).

Regarding domestic law, the approach to minority language protection could not be more different between France and Spain. Analyzing the French legal framework about regional languages has shown the difficulties the Basque language faces for its protection. Despite recent attempts of the legislature to include the protection of minority languages, the rule remains the active protection of the French language, leaving the regional languages to the sidelines. The case of Euskara in Spain is different. The constitutional setting in Spain allows for a system of devolution of powers which favors the accommodation of different cultures and languages existing in the territory. Therefore, the autonomous communities of the BAC and Navarre used this opportunity to integrate the protection of the Basque language in their Statutes of Autonomy. The result differs and carries difficulties in Navarre, but the solution there is, nevertheless, better than in Iparralde, where there is the lack of proper linguistic positive action. In both cases (Navarre and the BAC), the norm givers incorporate the co-officiality of Spanish and Basque, which provides further protection to the Basque language. In Spain, linguistic minority protection is offered by Article 3 of the Constitution, the Language Charter, and elements of the international legal framework.

Now that we have the general (and broad) understanding of the law concerning the Basque language, we will home in on the reality of Basque speakers. Although we have focused our attention on the legal norms, we have not elaborated on the norm users. Norm users give meaning to legal norms, and discussing this other side of the law will enable the contextualized understanding of the legal framework and social embedding of the Basque language. To proceed, I will focus on two key areas of social life where language rights of linguistic minorities are essential: education (part II) and media (part III).[94]

Notes

1 Ferreres Comella gives an extensive account of this process in Ferreres Comella, *Constitution of Spain*.
2 In 1933, conservative parties held the power, bringing an extreme reaction from Catalonia that ended up with the suspension of the Catalan Statute of Autonomy. In 1936, however, the left won the elections and brought again the regional government in Catalonia.
3 https://www.euskadi.eus/informacion/resultados-segunda-republica-referendum-del-estatuto-de-autonomia-1933/web01-a2haukon/es/ (Accessed April 10, 2024).
4 The Basque Country here refers to the region of the BAC. For more information about the construction of the autonomous communities of Navarre and the BAC, see Martín María Razquin Lizarraga, "La organización territorial interna de los territorios forales."
5 The Statute of Autonomy was never approved in Galicia under the Second Republic.
6 Ferreres Comella, *Constitution of Spain*, 5.
7 ETA stopped its armed activity in 2011, and the complete disarmament happened in spring 2017. Other violent groups existed and acted, too, especially during the transition: Frente Revolucionario Antifascista y Patriota (a Marxist-Leninist organization), Fuerzas Armadas Guanches (Canarian nationalist group), Terra Lliure (Catalan nationalist group), and Loita Armada Revolucionaria (Galician nationalist group). On the other hand, during the seventies, an illegal death squad was created by the state—Grupos Antiterroristas de Liberación (GAL)—to do the dirty war against the political groups of the left and the ETA.
8 This president of the government was an admiral, and Franco had appointed him to guarantee the continuity of the regime in the future.
9 Ysàs, "La Transición española. Luces y sombras." The author explains consensus was the only viable option.

10 Rosenfeld and Sajó, *The Oxford Handbook of Comparative Constitutional Law*, 10. See also Ferreres Comella, *Constitution of Spain*.
11 Euzko Alderdi Jeltzalea-Partido Nacionalista Vasco (EAJ-PNV): the Basque Nationalist Party.
12 Rosenfeld and Sajó, *The Oxford Handbook of Comparative Constitutional Law*, 7.
13 Text extracted from the official English version of the Spanish Constitution available on the website of the Spanish Congress: https://www.boe.es/legislacion/documentos/ConstitucionINGLES.pdf (Accessed April 10, 2024).
14 Tudela Aranda, "Small Worlds in the Spanish Autonomic State," 139.
15 Arzoz, "New Developments in Spanish Federalism," 179.
16 Rosenfeld and Sajó, *The Oxford Handbook of Comparative Constitutional Law*, 12.
17 Arzoz, "New Developments in Spanish Federalism," 179.
18 Article 149 also refers to the territorial division, but the essential ones are Articles 2 and 3.
19 Interestingly, the French constitutional block has the equality between the *collectivités territoriales* as a Principle of Constitutional Value, being completely different from the Spanish approach.
20 Razquin Lizarraga, "La organización territorial interna de los territorios forales."
21 Sentencia Tribunal Constitucional, 31/2010: http://hj.tribunalconstitucional.es/HJ/es/Resolucion/Show/6670 (Accessed August 27, 2021). The controversy surrounding the "new" Autonomous Statute in Catalonia and its following ruling by the Constitutional Court was also one of the main elements opening the door for the Catalan crisis of 2017.
22 Pérez Medina, "The case of Spain," 105.
23 https://www.boe.es/legislacion/documentos/ConstitucionINGLES.pdf (Accessed: July 15, 2024).
24 https://www.boe.es/legislacion/documentos/ConstitucionINGLES.pdf (Accessed: July 15, 2024).
25 Decision 82/1986 of June 26. https://hj.tribunalconstitucional.es/es-ES/Resolucion/Show/645 (Accessed June 25, 2020).
26 Translated by the author. F.J.2: "[. . .] a language is official, regardless of its reality and weight as a social phenomenon, when it is recognized by the public authorities as a normal means of communication within and between them and in their relationship with private subjects, with full legal validity and effects. [. . .]"

27 Following this, the central state has taken the role of protecting the Spanish language.
28 Iñaki Agirreazkuenaga, "Euskararen Araubide Juridikoa Autonomia Erkidegoan, Nafarroan eta Ipar Euskal Herrian," 19.
29 It must be highlighted here, however, that the decision 84/1986 of the Constitutional Court explained that Article 1.2 of the Normalization Law of the use of Galician (3/1983) that wanted to implement the duty of all Galicians to know the Galician language was contrary to Article 3.1 of the Constitution. Article 1.2, as originally written, said all Galicians must know the Galician language. This was interpreted by the Constitutional Tribunal as being an imposition of knowing the language, going against Article 3.1 of the Constitution that reads, "Castilian is the official Spanish language of the State. All Spaniards have the duty to know it and the right to use it." Here, the Constitutional Tribunal clearly indicated the difference between the official language of the State, and the co-official languages of Spain (Article 3.2 of the Constitution). https://www.boe.es/buscar/pdf/1983/DOG-g-1983-90056-consolidado.pdf (Accessed: July 15, 2024).
30 Article 146 of the Constitution: "The draft Statute of Autonomy shall be drawn up by an assembly consisting of members of the Provincial Council or inter-island body of the provinces concerned, and the respective Members of Congress and Senators elected in them, and shall be sent to the Cortes Generales for its drafting as an Act."
31 Arzoz, "The implementation of the European Charter for Regional or Minority Languages in Spain," 83.
32 Arzoz, ibid., 84-86.
33 Yet, it must be noted that Part II of the Language Charter applies to the entire territory of Spain.
34 The following examples are purely illustrative examples created by the author.
35 Bengoetxea, "The Formal and the Ideal Euskal Herria: Plural Identities and Laws," 340.
36 It is true the larger part of the Kingdom of Navarre fell to the Castilian-Aragonese union in 1515, but the rest persisted until the French Revolution.
37 Bullain, "Identidad vasca en tránsito," 113.
38 As a reminder, the BAC contains three provinces: Gipuzkoa, Bizkaia, and Araba.

Together with Navarre, they form the Southern Basque Country (*Hegoalde*).
39 The term "foral" is still used now. It englobes de statutory and customary laws that are still in place.
40 Bengoetxea, "The Formal and the Ideal Euskal Herria: Plural Identities and Laws," 340.
41 Ayerbe, "Las fuentes del Derecho territorial vasco y navarro."
42 Ibid. Ayerbe gives an excellent account of the chronology and variety of the *fueros*.
43 Bullain, "Identidad vasca en tránsito," 113. See also, Bullain, "Esparterismo berria eta eskubide historikoak."
44 Organic Law 3/1979, December 18, 1979, the Statute of Autonomy of the BAC. Additional disposition, translated by the author: "Acceptance of the system of autonomy established in this Statute does not imply the renunciation by the Basque People of the rights to which they may have been entitled as such by virtue of their history, which may be updated in accordance with the provisions of the legal system." Navarre named its Statute of Autonomy the "Law of reintegration and improvement of the foral regime of Navarre" (Organic Law 13/1982, August 10, 1982).
45 Organic Law 3/1979, December 18, 1979, the Statute of Autonomy of the BAC. https://www.boe.es/buscar/pdf/1979/BOE-A-1979-30177-consolidado.pdf (Accessed June 19, 2020). Spanish version.
46 Urrutia Libarona, "Estatuto jurídico del euskera en el País Vasco," 417.
47 These three territories join to form the Autonomous Community of the BAC.
48 Urrutia and Irujo, "The Basque Language in the Basque Autonomous Community (BAC)," 167.
49 Autonomy Statute of 1979, Article 6, translation from Urrutia and Irujo (ibid.): Euskara, own language of the Basque People will have, like Spanish, official status in the Basque Country, and all its inhabitants will have the right to know and use both languages. The common institutions of the autonomous community, taking into account the sociolinguistic diversity in the Basque Country, will guarantee the use of both languages, regulating their official status, and they will arbitrate and regulate the measures and resources required to assure its knowledge. Nobody can be discriminated against for reasons of language. The Royal Academy of the Basque language—Euskaltzaindia is the official consultation institution referring to Basque. As Basque belongs to the heritage of other Basque territories and

communities, in addition to the links and correspondence which the academic and cultural institutions maintain, the Basque Country Autonomous Community can request that the Spanish government hold and present, when appropriate before the General Courts for authorization, treaties or agreements which permit cultural relations to be set up with States where these territories or communities are located in order to safeguard and promote the Basque language.

50 See also the decision of the Constitutional Court of Spain, 337/1994, of December 23, where the judges explained that languages that share official status also means a *co-living* of those languages. https://www.boe.es/buscar/doc.php?id=BOE-T-1995-1790 (Accessed April 15, 2024).

51 Law 10/1982, of November 24, basic for the normalization of the use of the Basque language (básica de normalización del uso del euskera) https://www.boe.es/buscar/act.php?id=BOE-A-2012-5539 (Accessed June 19, 2020). The constitutionality of this law was analyzed in the decision of the Spanish Constitutional Tribunal 82/1986 of June 26.

52 Ley de Instituciones Locales de Euskadi. https://www.boe.es/diario_boe/txt.php?id=BOE-A-2016-4171 (Accessed July 30, 2021).

53 Decision 337/1994, of December 23. Translated, and emphasis added, by the author. http://hj.tribunalconstitucional.es/es-ES/Resolucion/Show/2854 (Accessed June 25, 2020).

54 Urrutia and Irujo, "The Basque Language in the Basque Autonomous Community (BAC)," 167.

55 Translated by the author.

56 Translated by the author.

57 The territory of Navarre consists of 10,391 km^2 and has 647,554 inhabitants (in 2019).

58 Law 13/1982, of August 10, Organic Law of Reintegration and Improvement of the Foral Regime of Navarre (Ley Orgánica de Reintegración y Amejoramiento del régimen Foral de Navarra): http://www.lexnavarra.navarra.es/detalle.asp?r=87 (Accessed September 25, 2019).

59 Pérez Fernández et al., *Estudios sobre el estatuto jurídico de las lenguas en España*, 387.

60 Monreal Zia offers a comprehensive explanation of the Basque language in Navarre throughout history, in Monreal Zia, "Origen de la Ley del Vascuence de Navarra."

61 The name given to these linguistic areas is contested and controversial. In the non-Basque-speaking area, Basque is spoken, even if the number of Basque speakers is very limited. The author will use this translation, despite sharing the criticism that the name is not correct, since it suggests no Basque is spoken in southern Navarre. The name given to this area suggest Basques do not exist in this area, which does not help their precarious situation.
62 Article 9.2: "Basque will also have the character of official language in the Basque-speaking areas of Navarre. A foral law will determine these zones, will regulate the official use of Basque and, within the framework of the general legislation of the State, will order the teaching of this language."
63 Law 18/1986 of December 15, Ley Foral del Vascuence.
64 Irujo and Urrutia translate this law in Irujo and Urrutia, "Basque in the Foral Community of Navarre(CFN)," 201-203.
65 Arzoz, "The implementation of the European Charter for Regional or Minority Languages in Spain," 95.
66 In mid-gray, the "Basque-speaking" area; in light-gray, the "Mixed" area; and in dark-gray, the "non-Basque-speaking" area. Map from Wikimedia Commons, by Barasoaindarra., CC BY-SA 3.0, https://commons.wikimedia.org/w/index.php?curid=3132223 (Accessed June 24, 2020).
67 The political parties Bildu, Aralar-Nabai, I-E, and Geroa Bai voted in favor of this motion, but the vote against from UPN, PSN, and PPN stopped this process on December 11, 2017.
68 Irujo y Urrutia, "Basque in the Foral Community of Navarre(CFN)."
69 Moseley, *Atlas of the World's Languages in Danger*.
70 Irujo y Urrutia, "Basque in the Foral Community of Navarre(CFN)," 199.
71 Even if these changes might seem small and unimportant, we can currently clearly see how changing a few words makes a major impact: *Euskera* (Basque language) became *vascuence* (Basque language in some archaic writings; also the formulation used under Franco) and *impulsar* (improve, boost) became *proteger* (protect). However, the main change remains the limitation of the official status of the Basque language to one part of the territory.
72 Monreal Zia, "Origen de la Ley del Vascuence de Navarra." 519.
 Translated by the author: "a painful episode of ignorance on the part of the legislature about the linguistic history of the country itself or perhaps of self-

consciousness and self-hatred of cultural heritage."
73 Kasares, "Hikuntz eskubideak Euskal Herrian: zer eskubidez ari garen eta zertan diren." 81.
74 Changes in 2017 helped balance out this division into linguistic zones, where some areas switched from being "Mixed areas" to "Basque-speaking areas" or from "Non-Basque speaking areas" to "Mixed areas." This was a result of a political shift in Navarre from 2010 to 2017. This shift was a response to the regressive language policy of the previous conservative governments in Navarre (starting in 2000). See Arzoz, "Legal Mobilisation at the Subnational Level: The Case of Language Rights in the Spanish Autonomous Community of Navarre."
75 Agirreazkuenaga, "Euskararen Araubide Juridikoa Autonomia Erkidegoan, Nafarroan eta Ipar Euskal Herrian." 30. The issue of linguistic zoning for the granting of linguistic rights to Basque speakers in Navarre is often raised by the monitoring mechanisms of the Language Charter.
76 Foral Law 18/1986, of December 15, on Euskera. http://www.lexnavarra.navarra.es/detalle.asp?r=1822 (Accessed September 25, 2019).
77 Article 1.2 of the Law on the Basque Language 18/1986. Translated by the author: "Son objetivos esenciales de la misma:
a) Amparar el derecho de los ciudadanos a conocer y usar el vascuence y definir los instrumentos para hacerlo efectivo.
b) Proteger la recuperación y el desarrollo del vascuence en Navarra, señalando las medidas para el fomento de su uso.
c) Garantizar el uso y la enseñanza del vascuence con arreglo a principios de voluntariedad, gradualidad y respeto, de acuerdo con la realidad sociolingüística de Navarra. [. . .] "
78 Article 2 of the Foral Law 18/1986, translated by the author:
"1. Castilian and Basque are Navarre's own languages and, consequently, all citizens have the right to know and use them.
2. Castilian is the official language of Navarre. Euskera is also so under the terms set forth in Article 9 of the Organic Law of Reintegration and Improvement of the Foral Regime of Navarre, and in those of this Foral Law."
79 Article 3, translated by the author:
"1. The public authorities shall adopt such measures as may be necessary to prevent discrimination of citizens on the basis of language.

2. The public authorities shall respect the linguistic norm in all actions deriving from the provisions of this Foral Law and the provisions that develop it.

3. The official consultative Institution, for the purposes of establishing linguistic rules, shall be the Royal Academy of the Basque Language, from which the public authorities shall request as many reports or opinions as they deem necessary to comply with the provisions of the preceding paragraph."

80   Article 4, translated by the author: "Citizens may apply to the Judges and Courts, in accordance with the legislation in force, to be protected by the linguistic rights established in this Foral Law."

81   Article 6, translated by the author: "All citizens are recognized the right to use both Basque and Spanish in their relations with the Public Administrations, under the terms established in the following chapters."

82   Translation of Article 10 by the author: "All citizens have the right to use both Basque and Spanish in their relations with the Public Administrations and to be attended to in the official language of their choice. To this end, the appropriate measures shall be adopted and the necessary means shall be provided to progressively ensure the exercise of this right. In files or proceedings in which more than one person is involved, the public authorities shall use the language established by mutual agreement between the parties involved."

83   Article 15, translated by the author:

1. The Public Administrations and the Companies of public character will promote the progressive training in the use of Euskara of the personnel that provides services in the Basque-speaking area.

2. Within the scope of their respective competences, each Administration shall specify the positions for which knowledge of Basque is mandatory and for the others it shall be considered as a qualified merit among others." Article 16, translated by the author: "The Local Entities of the Basque-speaking area shall use Spanish and Basque in all their provisions, publications, urban road signs and proper names of their places, respecting, in any case, the traditional ones."

84   Translated by the author: Article 11: "All administrative actions shall be valid and shall have full legal effect regardless of the official language used. Consequently, all acts in which bodies of the Public Administrations intervene, as well as administrative notifications and communications, must be written in both languages, unless all interested parties expressly choose to use only one."

85 Translated by the author: Article 12: "Public documents must be drawn up in the official language chosen by the grantor or, if there is more than one grantor, in the language agreed upon by them.
The public notaries must issue in Spanish or Basque, as requested by the interested party, the copies or testimonies and translate when necessary matrices and documents under their responsibility.
In any case, they shall issue in Castilian the copies that are to have effect outside the Basque-speaking area."
86 Article 14, translated by the author: "In their relations with the Administration of Justice, all citizens may use the official language of their choice, in accordance with the provisions of the legislation in force."
87 Article 15, translated by the author.
88 Article 16, translated by the author.
89 Article 17, translated by the author:
"All citizens have the right to use both Basque and Castilian to address the Public Administrations of Navarre."
To guarantee the exercise of this right, the said administrations may:
a) Specify in the public offer of employment of each year, the positions to access to which the knowledge of Basque is mandatory.
b) Value as a merit the knowledge of Euskera in the calls for access to the other posts."
90 Article 18 translated by the author.
91 Concerning the right to be answered in Basque in public administration, staff must be trained in this language. The Foral Decree 55/2009 of June 15 lists the requirements concerning the knowledge of Basque depending on the linguistic area: http://www.lexnavarra.navarra.es/detalle.asp?r=29849 (Accessed October 4, 2019).
92 The 1986 Law on the Basque Language makes distinctions in education depending on linguistic zoning. See part II, chapter 4.
93 See part III, chapter 6 OR 7.
94 These areas of social life are inspired by the Language Charter, which lists seven key areas where language rights should be protected for regional or minority languages: education (Article 8), judicial authorities (Article 9), administrative authorities and public services (Article 10), media (Article 11), cultural activities and facili-

ties (Article 12), economic and social life (Article 13), and transfrontier exchanges (Article 14). Because of time and space limitations, the author chose to focus on these two examples. First, education was chosen since it is a pivotal element in language transmission and recovery. Second, the example of media was chosen because it is fundamental in joining both the public sphere and language transmission as well as offers a platform for these minority languages to be heard.

Part II

Education and the Basque Language

Because the Basque language is an endangered minority language, different strategies have been implemented for its revitalization. One of the main strategies has been education. Education focuses on perpetuating the intergenerational transmission of language, fostering the visibility of it, enhancing its value, and creating new speakers. This is a rather difficult task, because "by targeting educational systems, minority language activists often challenge assimilatory logic and nationalist legacies that have defined state-level language planning and policy making in the modern era."[1]

In the BAC, traditionally, education has been primarily in Spanish, except for religious education that was bilingual, and initially predominant, in Basque. This pattern has remained stable over the years: Basque has been perceived as the informal language, and Spanish has been the language of power and formality. However, the demand for inclusion of the Basque language in education, and education in Basque as a teaching language, progressively increased. Civil society even created clandestine Basque schools during the Franco era to respond to this demand. This led to the current situation, in which the presence of Basque in education is significant.

During the nineteenth century, the number of Basque speakers in Navarre was already decreasing, and the awareness of a need to protect this language was gaining force. The Basque elite realized that the decline in Euskara-speaker numbers was a result of the unification of education in Spain by the Moyano Law of 1857. In response to this decline, in 1877 Navarrese intellectuals and philologists founded the Navarrese Society of Basque (*Nafarroako Euskara Elkargoa*). These figures denounced the high rate of school failure among Basque-speaking children who were "a monolingual group immersed in a classroom [with a] language foreign to them."[2] This evolved, and discussion about the need for education in Basque, or bilingual education (Spanish and Basque), gained force during the Spanish Second Republic (1931–1936). The events of 1936 curtailed Basque-language schooling, and the Civil War and the repressive regime that followed did Basque schooling few favors. Finally, the teaching of Basque as a subject in the public school system was introduced in 1973 and evolved toward the system we know today.

In Iparralde, the evolution of Basque in education was different. The construction of the French nation was marked by an opposition to regional languages since the early days of the 1789 revolution. This led to new linguistic policies in education and administrative measures to erase local languages. The heyday of the diffusion of the French language in education occurred during the Third Republic (1870–1939). This diffusion was favored by the well-known Ferry laws of the 1880s. One of the goals of these educational laws was the linguistic unification of the country. Following this trend, Article 14 of the application decree of the 1881 Education Law read that "only French may be used in schools." Finally, by the time of the First World War, France was already mainly French-speaking, and the modernization and industrialization after the Second World War accelerated the process.

The first step toward the revitalization of a regional or minority language is to focus on the transmission of the language via education. Thus, it is key to start teaching children from a very young age. As we have previously seen, this was achieved in the Basque case, to a greater or lesser extent, depending on the territory. Yet, limiting the teaching *of* and *in* Euskara to only early stages of schooling also limits the language. It needs to reach higher levels of education. Why would anybody want to learn in Euskara if they would need to switch to French or Spanish when entering higher education? The inclusion of Euskara in universities is crucial, not only to showcase the "utility" of the language, but also to include this language inside the academic sphere. Including Euskara in universities introduces Basque speakers to the top spheres of highly trained and qualified citizens and professionals, and it makes Euskara part of academic discussions. Accordingly, Basque society has focused on including Euskara as part of the study selection in universities. This is noteworthy, because such an offering in higher education is a significant achievement for regional or minority languages.

From this introduction, one can see the heterogeneity of the legal frameworks regarding Euskara in education. Thus, when discussing education in Basque, we face a kaleidoscope: Depending on which territory we are stepping in, the shape of the offer varies. Yet, like in the case of a kaleidoscope, even if the shapes vary, the same colors apply. In this chapter and the next, we will scrutinize the legal framework of education and the Basque language, as well as the role of the public and legal actors on this matter to understand the social embedding of the law on the Basque language in education.

Notes

1 Heidemann, "In the Name of Language: School-Based Language Revitalization, Strategic Solidarities, and State Power in the French Basque Country," 55.
2 López-Goñi, "Basque Schools in Navarre: The Early Stages, 1931-1936," 570.

4

Legal Framework of the Basque Language in Education

Examining the legal system is crucial to understand the intersection of education and the Basque language. The BAC, Navarre, and Iparralde do not share the same legal frameworks in terms of Euskara and education. In fact, the legal culture toward regional or minority languages in Spain and France varies considerably, and the area of education is no exception. In the following analysis, we will explore the legal framework of Basque in education in Spain and the relevant autonomous communities, followed by the legal framework of Basque in education in France.

Education and the Basque Language in Spain

Spain is bound by the Language Charter, in which education in regional or minority languages is protected by Article 8.[1] This chapter covers all stages of education, from preschool to university and higher education. It also covers adult and continuing education; the teaching of the history and the culture that is reflected in the regional or minority language; requests that signatory states provide teacher training; and the establishment of a supervisory body or bodies. Honoring Article 8 of the Language Charter,[2] it is assumed education in regional or minority languages is offered throughout all stages of education in Spain.[3]

Regarding the domestic legal framework on the matter, we will explore the framework that applies to the entire Spanish territory concerning regional or minority languages and education. Thereafter, we will discuss the legal regulation of languages in education in the BAC and Navarre.

The Framework

To understand the framework of the Basque language and education in Spain, it is essential to know how the Constitution protects the right to education, and more importantly, how the central state and the autonomous communities share competences in the field. Article 27 of the Constitution protects and regulates the right to education and the freedom of education (paragraphs 3 and 6),[4] yet it does not address said education's linguistic dimension. The following analysis will focus on the linguistic aspect of the regulation of education in Spain.

General Rules and Competence Matters: Education and the Basque Language in Spain

Article 148.1.17 of the Constitution[5] establishes that the autonomous communities can promote "culture and research and, where applicable, the *teaching of the self-governing community's language.*"[6] Even so, this article does not mention expressly how this teaching must be performed: which educational models must be implemented in Spain, or how many hours must be devoted to teaching Spanish or any other official language, for instance.

Establishing a model for teaching the co-official languages of the autonomous communities in Spain raises several questions. For Milian i Massana, when talking about language and education, two main questions must be addressed.[7] First, there must be rules based on which language(s) must be learned mandatorily and, therefore, must be included in the curriculum. Second, there is the question of which language(s) can or must be used as the medium for teaching other subjects. Regarding the first aspect, a main question is the number of hours that must be devoted to teaching different languages. Since the constitutional text is unclear about regulation of language and education, two views could be taken. On the one hand, one could argue that the right to education contains the right for the pupil to be taught in their mother tongue, or to pick the teaching language among the official languages. In this case, the public powers would not be entitled to determine the language of instruction. On the other hand, one could argue the right to education has no linguistic content and therefore public authorities have the right to decide the language of instruction. We will examine the second view.

The central state and the autonomous communities (Articles 148 and 149 of the Constitution) share the competences over education.[8] Looking at the competences listed, exclusive competences of the central state on education are mentioned in Article 149.1:[9] "Regulation of the conditions relative to the obtaining, issuing and standardization of academic degrees and professional qualifications and basic rules for the development of Article 27 of the Constitution, in order to guarantee the fulfillment of the obligations of the public authorities in this matter." This article is an enhancement of Article 27 of the Constitution. Yet, this only means the central state must regulate the standardization of academic degrees and professional qualifications on the one hand, and that it must develop Article 27 on the other. Article 149 remains, therefore, vague in terms of what it specifically means to develop Article 27 or what kind of competences the central State holds in terms of education.

Regarding the competences of the autonomous communities and education, Article 148 does not shed much light on the matter. In fact, Article 148 only contains one mention of education. Article 148.1 refers to the teaching of co-official languages in Spain in the following way: "[The Autonomous Communities may assume competence over] the promotion of culture, of research and, when applicable, the teaching of the language of the Autonomous Community." Thus, despite not referring to education directly, Article 148 does mention the teaching of the "language of the Autonomous Community." This implies that there is sharing of powers regarding education, at least in linguistic matters.

Yet, in a multilingual state such as Spain, regulating education in co-official languages has had a long trajectory filled with constitutional disputes. As noted by the Constitutional Court in decision STC 337/1994, "Unlike the Constitution of 1931, whose Article 50 incorporated a regulation of the official languages in relation to education, the fundamental norm in force today does not include a similar precept."[10] This lack of regulation by the Constitution has led to various cases concerning language and education before the Spanish Constitutional Tribunal.

The Spanish Constitutional Tribunal and Education in Co-official Languages

By interpreting the Constitution, the Constitutional Tribunal has shed light on the limits of language rights in education. These limits are extracted from pairing Articles 3 and 27 of the Constitution. The official character of a language in the Spanish Constitution carries the duty of the public authorities to include in obligatory fashion the study of this language in education for all students.[11] In addition, when Article 27.2 of the Constitution mentions "the full development of human personality," it also implies a linguistic content to the right to education (one's own language being a part of the human personality). This is even more relevant when a minority language is at issue.

Yet, in a country where multiculturalism and multilingualism create tensions, the Spanish Constitutional Tribunal had to decide. In the early stages of the Statutes of Autonomy, the Constitutional Tribunal decided on the teaching of co-official languages. In decision 87/1983, the Constitutional Tribunal claimed that co-officiality of languages "implies that both languages must be taught with the intensity that allows to achieve this objective."[12] Decision 88/1983, about the minimum hourly requirements of teaching of the Castilian language, followed.[13] The government of the BAC brought this case before the Constitutional Tribunal claiming that Royal Decree 3087/1982 on the setting of minimum teachings for the higher cycle of basic general education breached the sharing of competences between the central state and the autonomous communities.[14] Among other things, a key element raised by the BAC was that it considered the protection of the Basque language a constitutional obligation not only of the autonomous communities (via Articles 149.1.17 of the Constitution and Article 6.2 of the Statute of Autonomy) but also of the central state (via Article 3 of the Constitution). Despite not agreeing with the BAC on the other points, the Constitutional Tribunal did acknowledge that ensuring the knowledge of co-official languages falls under the responsibility of both the central state as well as the autonomous communities. The tribunal recognized Article 3 of the Constitution requires the state and the autonomous communities to ensure the knowledge of both co-official languages (Spanish and Basque in this case).[15] Therefore, the responsibility is shared and is not exclusive to the autonomous communities.

Later, in decision 337/1994 of December 23, the Constitutional Tribunal decided that Article 27 does not guarantee the right to receive one's entire education in one of the two official languages. In addition, the tribunal declared there is no right to freely choose the "teaching language" (*lengua vehicular*), i.e., the language in which students are taught.[16] However, in this case, regarding the Catalan language, the Constitutional Tribunal highlighted also that, in the context of linguistic normalization in Catalonia, it is legitimate that Catalan is in the center of the educational model, "as far as this does not exclude Castilian as a teaching language."[17] This underscores the purpose of the education regulations, in the linguistic normalization of Catalan, on which the Catalan government is trying to correct the historical inequalities or imbalances that exist regarding the two official languages. In the same decision 337/1994, the Constitutional Tribunal corrected the vagueness of Article 27 by stating that in the autonomous communities where various official languages coexist, inhabitants have the right to receive education in one language that they understand. Later, in its decision of 31/2010, the Constitutional Tribunal added the nuance that the teaching in Castilian must be present in the whole educational curriculum, and not only in basic studies.

The Constitutional Tribunal also clarified the competences regarding education and regional or minority languages in Spain via the same decisions. If we go back to the previously mentioned decisions 87/1983 and 337/1994, we can see the tribunal started clarifying the domain of competences of language(s) and education. First, in the *Fundamento Jurídico* (Legal Basis; F.J.) 5 of decision 87/1983, the Constitutional Tribunal decided that Article 3 of the Constitution implies the responsibility of the central state and the autonomous communities to ensure knowledge both of Castilian and co-official languages. Later, in the F.J.9 of decision 337/1994, the tribunal underscored that both the central state and the autonomous communities are entitled to determine the use of both co-official languages as the teaching language in education. This early jurisprudence of the Constitutional Tribunal set a shared competence between the central state and autonomous communities. Yet, in parallel, the tribunal also split the competences regarding language and education in Spain. In decision 87/1983, the tribunal declared that the central state holds the competence over arranging minimum education requirements, in order to establish a common education throughout Spain. Therefore, the central state is entitled to lay down the minimum requirements of teaching of Castilian since it is the only common official language throughout the territory. Regarding the competence over deciding on the teaching in the rest of the co-official languages, in the F.J.5 of decision 87/1983, the Constitutional Tribunal decided that it was an exclusive competence of the respective autonomous communities. The Constitutional Tribunal confirmed this dual approach in decision 337/1994.

Finally, the latest constitutional decision on education and language is from February 20, 2018.[18] This decision of the Constitutional Tribunal 14/2018 addressed the Organic Law for the Improvement of Educational Quality (of 2013).[19] Regarding the books' standpoint on minority and regional languages and education, this Organic Law included a financial obligation to the autonomous communities: When education solely in Spanish was not provided in the public system, the state could impose on the autonomous communities the assumption of the cost of schooling these children in the private schools doing so. When the High Inspection for Education was called to decide on this, it decided this financial obligation was "reasonable" and "appropriate." However, the Constitutional Tribunal decided in February 2018 that the Organic Law exceeded its scope and that no financial burden could be imposed on the autonomous communities with such vague criteria. Furthermore, the Constitutional Tribunal decided it was unconstitutional for the central state to decide on plurilingual education, via regulation, without consulting the autonomous communities having co-official languages.

We have seen that education matters are divided between the central state and the autonomous communities in Spain. In the following part, we will examine the legal frameworks of the BAC and Navarre regarding education and Euskara.

Autonomous Communities and Education: The BAC and Navarre

Based on the constitutional text, the autonomous communities have competence over the area of education and co-official languages. We will separately consider the autonomous communities of the BAC and Navarre.

Legal Framework of Education in the Basque Language in the BAC

As mentioned in the introductory remarks before this chapter, the Basque language is in continuous contact with Spanish and French. In the BAC, Castilian and Euskara are co-official. To overcome the decline of Basque speakers and the stigmatization of this language throughout the centuries, education has always been key to its revitalization.

As explained by Lontxo Oihartzabal during his interview,[20] the Basque education system had to be reinvented during the transition. Since Franco installed a single education system, with teaching in one language, and with the monopoly of the church, all the new regional governments in Spain had to start from scratch. In the case of the BAC, and in Navarre, the first issue the drafters of the new schooling system encountered was a lack of teachers who were able to speak in Basque.

According to Oihartzabal, less than 10 percent of teachers were Basque speakers. Indeed, the Francoist educational system was effective in lowering the number of Basque speakers, and lowering the quality of their knowledge of Euskara, since among the ones who could speak Basque, very few felt confident enough to be teaching in that language. In this setting, the drafters of the schooling system—Oihartzabal among them—faced two challenges: they had to create a bilingual schooling system, when for decades no teaching of Basque had been available, and they had to do this with very few Basque speakers among teachers and parents.[21] This is how the tripartite system was born: Model A, Model B, and Model D.[22] This system puts an emphasis on the freedom of choice of parents. Before exploring these models further, we should focus on the legal framework regulating the place of Basque in education in the BAC. It must be emphasized that the BAC offers the same "freedom of language of education" in all stages of education.[23]

The two main legal instruments on education in the BAC are the Normalization Law 10/1982[24] and the Law on the Basque Public School (Law 1/1993 of February 19[25]). These two laws implement Article 6 of the Statute of Autonomy,[26] establishing Castilian and Basque as the two official languages of the territory. Also, the Statute of Autonomy adds, in Article 16, that the BAC has competence on education "in all its extension, levels and degrees, modalities and specialties, without prejudice to Article 27 of the Constitution and the Organic Laws developing it."[27] Based on these laws, the public school system in this autonomous community is divided into three categories.[28]

Model A offers a curriculum taught in Spanish with Basque as a subject (weak model of bilingualism). Model B offers a curriculum equally taught in both Spanish and Basque (partial immersion). Model D offers a curriculum taught in Basque with Spanish as a subject (total immersion). There is freedom of choice for the parents among these three models, according to Article 15 of the Normalization Law, as well as Article 5.e of the 1/1993 Law.[29] In fact, as pointed out by Oihartzabal during his interview, the drafters of the school system wanted to create a "democratic environment" where parents could choose which linguistic model they wanted for their children. Urrutia Libarona says that this freedom of choice has led to the growth of one model (Model D), and the decline of another (Model A).[30] Social demand for Model D has indeed increased throughout the years, and the demand for Model A has declined.[31]

Urrutia Libarona also considers that the decline of the demand for a curriculum mainly taught in Spanish is linked to a "social awareness" that the Model D provides "the most balanced levels of knowledge of the official languages." This has been confirmed to be true over the years.[32] During his interview, Oihartzabal explained the reasons behind splitting the public education into three models (in contrast with the Catalan model).[33] When designing the models, the drafters wanted to install a system almost fully in Model D, with an option of Model B, since the objective was to create individuals who were both proficient in Basque and Castilian. Oihartzabal expressed how the drafters were uncomfortable with creating Model A, being aware that it would not reach the goal of creating fully bilingual individuals, both in Castilian and Basque. They did, nonetheless, rightly calculate that this model would decline over time; Model A is decreasing immensely.[34] Yet, despite their discomfort, and facing the reality of the bleak number of speakers in the BAC after the Francoist dictatorship, the drafters were forced to include other options. Hence, an immersive-only school system would have been strictly impossible to implement. The policymakers opted, then, to leave the decision of the linguistic menu in the hands of the parents.

It is widely known and stressed by authors that this tripartite model has still not achieved its goal.[35] By the time they finish their years of mandatory education, not all pupils have attained fluency in Basque, especially those enrolled in Model A. In addition, it is also often said that attaining a fluent level of Basque does not merely rest on the shoulders of the education system. Teacher 1, from a public primary school in Gipuzkoa, emphasized the difficulties public schooling in Model D faces with children whose out-of-school lifeworld is quasi-exclusively in Castilian. For these children, even if enrolled in Model D, the only place where they use Euskara is school, making their evolution toward full bilingualism very difficult. The Basque government is aware of this issue and, over the past few years, has focused on promoting the social use of the Basque language.[36] Thus, even if the school system has a major role to play to reach the goal of creating fully bilingual citizens in the BAC, it must be accompanied by other elements (e.g., sociolinguistic environment, attitude toward the Basque language, linguistic attitudes and practices of family and friends, presence in the media, etc.).

The BAC offers the most protective approach toward the Basque language and education among all the Basque territories. The decision was taken to offer freedom of choice and different degrees of bilingualism in school. This system has proved to be efficient, as shown by sociolinguistic reports,[37] but it still needs further improvement to achieve the goal of creating fully bilingual citizens in the BAC, both in Basque and Castilian.

Legal Framework of Education in Basque in Navarre

Today's situation of official languages and education in Navarre takes different shapes. The main legal texts regulating education and Euskara in Navarre are the Law on the Basque Language[38] and its implementation by Foral Decree 159/1988 of May 19,[39] regulating the integration and the use of Euskara in non-university studies.

Within the 1986 Law on the Basque Language, education—together with media—holds a substantial place. Indeed, whereas the first preliminary heading of the Law on the Basque Language invokes a variety of areas (e.g., public administration and justice), the entirety of Title I is dedicated to education. In the regulation of education, this law provides a variety of elements (introducing Basque in the curriculum, training of teachers) but does so in a general way, leaving a large discretionary power to the Navarrese government. Therefore, to find more specific legal rules, we must look for Foral Decrees:[40] Foral Decree 159/1988, on non-university education; Foral Decree 160/1988, which regulates jobs for which qualifications in Basque are required and sets quotas for these jobs and the knowledge of Basque language;[41] and Foral Decree 161/1988, on public school centers for teaching Basque to adults.[42]

The most important decree on the matter is the above-mentioned Foral Decree 159/1988, establishing a system of schooling models. These models correspond to the three systems established in the BAC, with differences regarding the territorial distribution of Navarre. The territorial division into linguistic areas by the Law on the Basque Language in Navarre has direct implications for the regulation of languages in education.[43] Foral Decree[44] 159/1986 for non-university studies creates a series of different linguistic schooling systems: Models A, B, D, and G.[45] In the Basque-speaking area, the three models containing Euskara must be offered since Basque is co-official (A, B, and D). Regarding the Mixed area, learning Basque is voluntary and, thus, parents have the choice of enrolling their children in a curriculum exclusively taught in Spanish (G), in addition to the three other models (A, B, and D), depending on the demand of teaching in Basque by parents. Finally, in the Spanish-speaking area, the two options available are the curriculum in Spanish (Model G) or Model A (if there is enough demand).

This linguistic zoning, paired with the educational models, creates inequalities among Basque speakers in Navarre. "The most direct consequence of the language models is that parents in the non-bascophone zone cannot choose education through the medium of Basque."[46] Yet, this is not the only consequence of limiting the offering of education in Basque to some linguistic zones. As mentioned in chapter 3, zoning hinders the universality of the transmission of the language and, even if zoning guarantees co-officiality of Basque in the North of Navarre, it "discriminates against Basque speakers in the mixed zone and puts Basque outside the law in the south zone."[47]

To deal with this situation, another element of education in Basque has emerged: the Ikastola schools.[48] Indeed, Ikastola schools offer immersive education in Basque, notably in the "Spanish-speaking area." Nonetheless, the teaching in Basque in these areas, and by extension, the presence of Ikastola schools, is controversial in Navarre.[49]

To sum up, Navarre offers a complex legal system, paired with multiple choices of schooling. This system, rather than offering a variety of choices, creates difficulties for proper access to education in Basque. However, Ikastola schools provide Model D education where public schooling usually does not allow for it. The example of Navarre shows the different layers for the regulation of education in Euskara. When researching education in Euskara in Navarre, three elements should be kept in mind: first, the linguistic area in which one is located; second, the choice of parents between the models available; and third, the resources provided by the administration in terms of education for the development of the Basque language—the latter being constantly criticized by the Basque-speaker community in Navarre.

This analysis has addressed non-university education in Spain, focusing on the case of the BAC and Navarre with respect to the Basque language. Another crucial stage in the inclusion of regional or minority languages in education concerns higher education.

Higher Education and the Basque Language in Spain[50]

When discussing the current legal framework of universities in Spain,[51] the main law regulating this matter is the Organic Law of the University System.[52] Once again, the devolution of powers in Spain comes into play. The higher education system follows the main rules on education we have already discussed: The central state sets the general rules, and the autonomous communities set the specific rules for their territory. Following this, for the case of regional or minority languages, in the autonomous communities where a co-official language is present, the teaching *in* and *of* this language can be extended to higher education. Thus, for exploring the Basque language in universities, we need to investigate the regulations in the BAC and Navarre.

The regulation of universities in the BAC is addressed in Law 3/2004 on the Basque university system, known as the Basque University Law.[53] Following the system of devolution of powers, the BAC has the competence over education and research (Article 16 of the Statute of Autonomy).[54] This devolution of power must follow the minimum requirements set by the Spanish Organic Law of Universities 6/2001 that sets the general rules on university degrees, such as the organization of public and private universities, the structure of university degrees, exam requirements, etc. The Basque University Law lays down its principles and objectives in Article 3. In this first article of Title I, Article 3 defines the Basque university system as being an integral part of the Basque educational system (Article 3.1) and asks the Basque university system (containing both the private and public universities) to contribute to the economic, scientific, and cultural development of the Basque society, and to its cohesion and well-being (Article 3.2). Article 3.3 highlights that the universities must promote democratic values and social justice, and respect human rights, and Article 3.4 calls for the respect of fundamental rights and freedoms of thought, creation, and development of the individual.

On the Basque language, Article 3.3 continues by saying "[universities] shall also encourage the defense, study and promotion of the Basque cultural heritage in general, and of the Basque language in particular."[55] Another key element about the Basque language in the 2004 Basque University Law appears in Article 6, regarding the objectives of the Basque university system. Article 6.1.e reads: "The Basque university system has as fundamental objectives [. . .] the progressive incorporation of the Basque language into all areas of knowledge, thus contributing to the *normalization of its use.*"[56] Article 7 sets the guiding principles, and, among them, two interesting elements appear. On the one hand, Article 7.f claims that one of the guiding principles of the Basque universities is the "responsibility of the public authorities to guarantee and ensure the *effective fulfillment of the right to receive university teaching in Basque*";[57] and on the other hand, Article 7.i adds a cross-border collaboration with the other areas where Basque is spoken: "Promotion and development of collaboration and coordination agreements with the universities of Navarre and the Northern Basque Country."[58] This links back to Article 2,[59] which called for the promotion of "relations and collaborations" with other university institutions in other territories that also share the Basque language or that have a project of "promoting the use of the Basque language." Furthermore, the end of Article 2 reads: "Priority relationships will be established with the rest of the universities located in the Basque Country."[60] Finally, the fundamental article of the Basque University Law about the Basque language is Article 11, which regulates the use of languages in the universities.[61] Article 11.1 consecrates both Castilian and Euskara as the official languages of the Basque university system, and Article 11.3 requires universities to adopt necessary measures to guarantee the "right to study in Basque and the right to live in that language."[62] This means that the co-officiality of Euskara does not stop at the classroom and must permeate university life.

In Navarre, the same Organic Law of Universities 6/2001 sets the general legal regime, and the Foral Law 8/1987 on the Creation of the Public University of Navarre sets the regulation of the autonomous community.[63] Navarre has the power to regulate university education (Article 47 of the Statute of Autonomy[64]). Yet, no mention of the Basque language is made in this law, which only contains the general elements regarding the creation of the Public University of Navarre (UPNA).[65] To access more information about the Public University of Navarre, we should consult its Statutes, approved by Foral Decree 110/2003.[66]

The Statutes of the UPNA contain some elements on the Basque language. Chapter V regulates the Basque language in the university (Article 118 to Article 125). According to Chapter V, all members of the UPNA have the right to know and use both Castilian and Euskara (Article 118.1). This translates into the right to address the Navarrese government institutions and university administration in either of these languages (Article 119.1.a); to express oneself in either of these languages in university meetings (Article 119.1.b); and to receive and offer teaching, and carry out projects, exams, or tests in Basque, in those subjects that are offered in this language (Article 119.1.c).[67] Article 120 establishes the language planning of the Basque language in academic activities, in accordance with the demand and social needs. Finally, regarding language planning, Article 123 of Foral Decree 110/2003 orders the UPNA to establish relations with public and private institutions that work in the realm of the Basque language.

Education and the Basque Language in France

The Preamble of the 1946 French Constitution protects the right to education, and in the French constitutional block, the principle of freedom of education belongs to the Fundamental Principles recognized by the laws of the Republic,[68] as the Constitutional Council held in decision no. 77-87.[69] The right to education and freedom of education are also included in Articles L.111-1[70] and L.151-1[71] of the Code of Education, respectively.

When discussing education in France, we should keep in mind the *acquis* (the acquired fact) that French citizens have in their minds when talking about education. In fact, when talking about public education in France, three notions are taken for granted: the education is free and guaranteed by the state, public education is secular, and education requires teachers and students to be philosophically and politically neutral.[72] Yet, there is no direct link made between language and education. Under the Fifth Republic, there is an assumption that the language of the "School of the Republic" is French,[73] fed by a long historical process.

With this in mind, we will examine the legal framework of education in Euskara in France, followed by the regulatory acts on the matter, as well as Euskara's place in higher education in France.

The Framework

As comprehensively analyzed by some authors,[74] it took some time for the French language to arrive to schools. From revolutionary times until the Third Republic, French was imposed slowly as the single language of national education. Interestingly, during the Fourth Republic, the regional languages of France started to enter education with the Deixonne Law of 1951.[75] This law set the foundation of the regional language education system we know today in France. This law was the first legal text offering (restricted) recognition of minority languages in education. The novelty of this law was to authorize the teaching of regional languages in all stages of education (from primary school to university).

It pertained to all the regional languages of France, even if, in its Article 10, the law mentions four of them to be taught starting the following academic year: Breton, Basque, Catalan, and Occitan.

The Deixonne Law introduced the teaching of regional languages as an optional subject only (Article 3.2.), setting out an approach to minority languages in French education which has been preserved until today.[76] This law was extremely vague, with "provisions [. . .] defined in ways that make their fullest implementation unlikely,"[77] and the decrees for its implementation were not released until the late sixties. In addition, the body of educators was not trained to teach these languages. Nonetheless, the Deixonne Law set the precedent establishing the regime still mainly prevailing today. The novelty of introducing regional languages in French schools was undeniably a big step forward in terms of protecting and recognizing these languages. However, the idea behind this law appears in its Article 2,[78] in which the lawmaker explains the use of the regional languages must be made as an accessory, to facilitate the study and learning of the French language.[79] Therefore, the Deixonne Law does not recognize regional languages in their own right, but as a medium for the better learning of the French language. This law serves French first, not granting full importance to the regional languages in education.

The second main law dealing with regional languages and education in France is the Haby Law on education, from July 11, 1975.[80] Despite underscoring the primacy of French, this law implemented in its Article 12 the possibility of teaching regional cultures and languages throughout all stages of schooling,[81] and it included training measures for teachers. However, once again, the education of regional languages was made optional. This meant that the teaching of regional languages was subject to the willingness of parents to send their children to these classes and the willingness of teachers to teach them. More importantly, this law includes, in Article 18, a possibility for exceptions for the purpose of the "realization of an educational experiment"[82]—an element that will be useful for education in Euskara and starting immersive classes in public primary schools (see next section of this chapter). A later (1989) law—the Jospin Law[83]—reiterates the option of teaching regional languages in its first article.[84]

The last general law regarding education and regional languages in France is the Toubon Law of 1994.[85] As already mentioned in part I, Article 21 of the

Toubon Law declared that the provisions contained in this law must be applied without creating any prejudice to the legal framework on regional languages in France, and that this law does not oppose the use of regional languages. Also, Article 11 emphasized that the language of education is French, with some room, exceptionally, for regional languages. Finally, a legislative regulation on education and regional languages in 2013[86] introduced bilingual schooling both in French and in regional languages (Article 40[87]).[88]

Despite offering some possibilities for the studying of regional languages, the general approach to regional languages in French public education remains clear: Learning regional or minority languages must be optional only, and their use is conditioned by their inferior status to the French language. More importantly, these principles are still the ones present in the Code of Education.

The above principles were entrenched in constitutional law by the decision of the Constitutional Council of 1991 regarding the status of the territory of Corsica.[89] In this decision, the *Sages* discussed the topic of education and regional languages. In the *considérants* (paragraphs of the decision) 35 and 37, the judges underscored that teaching a regional language complies with the principle of equality only when this teaching has an optional character and is not mandatory.

Following up on this decision, the Constitutional Council decided on the immersive schools in Breton called "Diwan." Before diving into the decisions, we should keep in mind that the right of freedom of education allows for the creation of private schools both in France and Spain. Usually, these schools can receive public funding if they fulfill certain conditions (follow the curriculum set by the National Education, prepare students for the same official exams, etc.) by signing a contract with the state. In this case, in France, Diwan schools have offered immersive schooling in the Breton language since the seventies, but they remain private schools, despite having some agreements with the state.[90] Yet, the immersive private schools in regional languages in France strive for their inclusion in the public schooling system alongside the other schooling options.

The Constitutional Council decided on the inclusion of Diwan schools in the public system on May 28, 2001, and added decision no. 2001-456 of December 27, 200, regarding the budget law of 2002 (*Loi des finances* of 2002). In this decision, the Constitutional Council used the newly introduced Article 2 of the Constitution and applied it to education. This was a first, since before 2001, the decisions regarding languages and education were examined under the principle of equality. In 2001, however, the Constitutional Council affirmed in *considérant* 49 that according to Article 2 of the Constitution, there cannot be an imposition of a language other than French in public schools. By doing so, the Constitutional Council erroneously understood the inclusion of an immersive option of schooling alongside other options implied the imposition of a different language than French. The Constitutional Council, with this decision, seemed to indicate that because immersive schooling would offer another option for students, it would somehow impose the learning of regional languages on those who do not want to study them. Therefore, by safely placing the discussion in terms of Article 2 of the Constitution, the constitutional judges did not tackle the issue of integrating Diwan schools into the public education system and relied on a previous decision on the matter adopted by the Council of State.[91]

Along the same lines, the decision on the organic law about the autonomy status of French Polynesia also mentions education and regional languages.[92] In the *considérants* 69 and 70, the Constitutional Council decided that teaching a regional language during regular hours cannot be mandatory—for the pupils, nor for the teachers. As noted by Bertile, the key element to notice with this decision of the Constitutional Council is that, regarding teaching *of* a regional language, the Council uses the discourse of equality, but in 2001, regarding teaching *in* a regional language, the Council uses the discourse of Article 2.[93]

Another case on the matter of regional languages and education concerns Article 75-1. The case *Mme Cécile L et autres* (Mrs. Cécile L and others) of 2011[94] brought another layer to the jurisprudence of the Constitutional Council in matters of regional languages and education. As explained in part I, in 2008, the constitutional amendment introduced Article 75-1, including regional languages for the first time in a French constitutional text. The contested Article L.312-10 read: "Teaching of regional languages and cultures *can be provided* throughout schooling. The High Education Council is consulted, in accordance with the powers conferred on it by Article L.231-1, on the means to promote the study of regional languages and cultures *in the regions where these languages are used*."[95] Article L.312-10 did not guarantee the teaching of regional languages and regional cultures, and it also seemed to impose a territorial limit on the teaching of regional languages. The applicants claimed these provisions did not guarantee an effective protection of teaching of regional languages, and, therefore, breached Article 75-1 of the Constitution. The Constitutional Council refused to examine the constitutionality of the law on the grounds that Article 75-1 was not a directly enforceable provision.[96] The constitutional judges declared that "this constitutional provision did not form a *right* which could be invoked by individuals to challenge the constitutionality of the existing (and modest) legislative arrangements for the teaching of regional languages."[97] Yet this case could have been a good opportunity for the Constitutional Council to introduce a fresh perspective on education and regional or minority languages in France, since a new and more protective provision was introduced in the Constitution for regional languages.

Over the years, it seems that the option of teaching regional languages in France has become engraved in stone. However, no text is crystal clear on providing a definition on this optional character. Bertile rightly questions who the beneficiary of this optional character is.[98] In fact, education concerns a wide range of actors: from administrators to teachers, and from parents to children. Her analysis shows that texts contradict themselves, and that the optional character can equally be applied to students, teachers, and administration. Looking at the jurisprudence confirms this approach and strongly underscores there is no right to education in a regional language; both by the Council of State[99] and the Constitutional Council.[100] Also, as shown in the Diwan case, immersive schooling, despite being an option alongside other schooling modalities (private and religious schools), is seen as an imposition of regional languages.

Finally, recent events threatened the rules set in stone regarding immersive schooling in regional languages in French public schools. The French National Assembly adopted the Molac law on April 8, 2021,[101] with 247 votes in favor and 76 against, and 19 abstentions. This marked a historic win for the regional languages in France. Yet, the constitutionality of the law was challenged at the Constitutional Council, resulting in the decision no. 2021-818, that limited the scope of this law.[102]

We will examine this decision, which analyzed the constitutionality of Articles 4, 6, and 9 of the Molac law. Interestingly, the deputies contested Article 6,[103] but the Constitutional Council also examined the constitutionality of Articles 4 and 9 ex officio. In this decision, the Constitutional Council sanctioned articles of the Molac law, notably Articles 4 and 6, regarding immersive schooling.[104]

Article 6 of the Molac law was created to make teaching of regional languages more accessible by financially helping children who needed to go to another municipality's private primary school to receive education in a regional language.[105] To do so, it modified Article L.442-5-1 of the Code of Education. The Constitutional Council argues that Article 6 does not result in imposing a language other than French, nor would it grant the right to use a language other than French with the administration. It also notes the inclusion of this financial help does not breach Article 2, and thus, considers that Article 6 is in accordance with the Constitution (para. 13).[106]

More importantly, Article 4 of the Molac law amended Article L.321-10 of the Code of Education, regarding the teaching of regional languages, adding a third point that includes immersive education.[107] The Constitutional Council poorly argued the unconstitutionality of Article 4, saying this article of the Molac law breached Article 2 of the Constitution by including immersive schooling.[108] In fact, the Constitutional Council argued that since immersive schooling is not limited to the teaching of a regional language, but rather uses this language as the "main language of instruction and as a language of communication within the school,"[109] Article 4 breached the Constitution. The Constitutional Council seems to indicate that Article 4 did include immersive schooling as an *option* alongside other forms of schooling, and it mentions immersive schooling should be performed without hindering "the objective of a good knowledge of French."[110] The position of the Court was reiterated in the comment published following the 2021 decision.[111] Once again, the Constitutional Council seems to follow the "anxiety logic"[112] of automatically pairing immersive schooling with imposition of a language other than French, hence discriminating against regional languages.

When we consider education in Basque and international law, the position of France follows the same direction. In fact, France does not seem to want to help the development of the teaching of regional languages. On this topic, the Convention on the Rights of the Child should be mentioned. In this Convention, Article 28 declares the right of the child to education, and Article 29 refers to the direction that the education of children should take.[113] Interestingly, Article 29.1.a mentions "the development of the child's personality," and Article 29.1.c protects "the development of respect for the child's parents, his or her own cultural identity, language and values, for the national values of the country in which the child is living, the country from which he or she may originate, and for civilizations different from his or her own." Finally, Article 30 of the Convention reads: "In those States in which ethnic, religious or linguistic minorities or persons of indigenous origin exist, a child belonging to such a minority or who is indigenous shall not be denied the right, in community with other members of his or her group, to enjoy his or her own culture, to profess and practice his or her own religion, or to use his or her own language." As already noted in part I, Article 30 has a reservation by France, claiming that this article would be contrary to Article 2 of the Constitution. In the international law area as well, France seems to hinder the further development of schooling in regional or minority languages.

This analysis has shown that the teaching of the Basque language in France must follow pre-established rules: The education in Euskara must be optional, and its use in teaching is allowed as a complement to the use of the French language. This section demonstrates that the legal framework regarding education and regional languages in France has not improved much over the years. In fact, the latest decision of 2021 shows an impasse that the Constitutional Council is not willing to overcome just yet. The law corpus is essential to examine when one wants to understand the legal framework surrounding education and the Basque language in France.[114] However, laws are not alone in the realm of regulating education, and regulatory acts have plenty to say on this matter.

The Regulatory Acts and Education in Basque

In terms of the legal framework surrounding education and regional languages in France, not only is it essential to consider the laws, but also the regulatory acts implementing these laws. Following the trend set by the Deixonne Law, the *circulaire*[115] of February 17, 1969, laid down the option of teaching regional languages.[116] Later, for the first time, the decree of July 10, 1970,[117] installed the optional test of these languages in the *Baccalauréat* (high school diploma, baccalaureate) exam. In 1982, the well-known *Circulaire* Savary intervened to set up the teaching of regional languages from nursery school to higher education.[118] This *circulaire* marked a positive turning point for regional languages in France. It established more precise elements regarding schedule and content for the teaching of regional languages. The *Circulaire* Savary provided a language-teaching plan lasting three years for Breton, Corsican, Occitan, and Basque. It specified that the state had to take central responsibility to promote regional languages in public schooling with express measures such as exams, training programs, and the production of teaching material. These measures remained optional but were a big step forward for regional languages, and thus, for Euskara.

Later, the *circulaire* of December 30, 1983,[119] on the guidance text on the teaching of cultures and regional languages, set the principle of bilingual education between French and regional languages. This *circulaire* was enabled by the previously mentioned Haby Law and is essential for the landscape of education and regional languages in France today. In fact, even if until 1983 education in France authorized the teaching *of* regional languages, this *circulaire* enabled the teaching *in* regional languages. Using the method of a *circulaire* helped to stretch the rigid law. This led to the academic inspection of the Ministry of National Education to propose an experiment wherein the public school of Sara would use a bilingual model, in Basque and French, in 1983.[120] This model used a parity of hours between the two languages.[121] Indeed, the *circulaire* of 1983 specifies the terms of this experimentation. On June 23, 1994, this *circulaire* was completed by an order of the Ministry of National Education,[122] authorizing students of bilingual classes to take the *Brevet des collèges*[123] history-geography exam in the regional language. Even though the principle of bilingualism in French public education is the object of constant criticism, the right to it was reaffirmed by the *circulaire* Darcos-Bayrou of April 7, 1995.[124]

Two orders by Jack Lang, minister of national education, boosted this tendency to reaffirm a space for bilingual education. First, the order of July 31, 2001, provided, on the one hand, for the creation of public primary, middle, and high schools where the education was bilingual using the immersive method.[125] On the other hand, this order provided for public primary, middle, and high schools where "regional language sections" were to be set using the bilingual method of hourly parity.[126] However, these highly progressive attempts to further bilingualism in French education were brought in front of the Council of State by teacher's trade unions. The Council of State suspended the order of July 31, 2001, in an injunction on October 30, 2001, *SNES et autres*. Facing this suspension, the Ministry of Education had two reactions. First, it modified the order of July 31, 2001, by the order of February 25, 2002.[127] Being faced with the reality of Article 2 of the Constitution by the Council of State, the ministry changed the previous order by removing any reference to an education in immersive fashion and the creation of these schools. The only schools kept in the order were the ones offering sections of "regional languages" providing hourly parity between French and regional languages. In a second round, the ministry came back to the first idea by introducing, in the order of April 19, 2002, an immersive model in regional languages in public schools. This second order was inevitably brought again in front of the Council of State, which, unsurprisingly, suspended it in an injunction on July 15, 2002.[128] This back-and-forth fight between the Ministry of Education and the Council of State on the Diwan schools ended with two decisions of the Council of State on November 29, 2002, annulling the contested orders.[129]

As a result of the legal framework of education and regional languages in France, from the linguistic point of view, there are three main educational models: a model of exclusive use of French as the teaching language (monolingual model), the use of French as the teaching language with the introduction of regional languages in non-compulsory fashion (regional language option), and a bilingual model with equal hourly allocation to French and the regional language (bilingual model).[130] Compared with the educational offering in Hegoalde, the offering in Iparralde would correspond to Model G (exclusively in French), Model A (a regional language class option within an otherwise exclusive offering in French), and Model B (bilingual). Yet, Ikastola schools are providing immersive education (Model D) in Iparralde as well.[131] These schools fall under the realm of private schools, with a contract with the state. Founded based on associations fostering and providing immersive education in regional languages, they are known as associative schools.[132] This name also helps them to be differentiated from other private schools (usually religious). These immersive schools will be examined in the following chapter, but it must be noted that since 1969, they have been pioneers in offering the teaching *of* Euskara and *in* Euskara. As previously mentioned, the right of freedom of education enables these schools to exist in France.

The legal framework regarding education and the Basque language in France seems to be far narrower than the one across the Pyrenees. Still, regional languages have managed to hold a place in public schooling in France. In fact, the protection and revitalization of Euskara has always been driven by civil society and pushed by social movements.[133] Thus, despite the limitations of the legal framework of education and regional languages, France offers (not without difficulties) education in Basque. Further contextualization of this point will be provided in the next chapter.

Higher Education and the Basque Language in France

The regulation of Basque in higher education in Iparralde is extremely scarce compared to the BAC and Navarre. Considering the legal framework of regional languages in France, this comes as no surprise. The latest norm regarding university teaching in France[134] is the Law of July 22, 2013, on higher education and research.[135] This law updated the legal framework of higher education in France, notably the objectives of the public service of higher education. According to Article L.123-3 of the Code of Education (modified by Article 7 of the Law of 2013, previously mentioned), the goals of higher education in France are: initial and continuous training (L.123-3-1); scientific and technological research (L.123-3-2); guidance, social promotion, and professional integration (L.123-3-3); the dissemination of humanist culture (L.123-3-4); participation in the construction of the European Higher Education and Research Area (L.123-3-5); and international cooperation (L.123-3-6).[136] Despite regional languages not being included, the general principles of education, in Article L.312-10 of the Code of Education reads that "teaching of regional languages and cultures can be provided throughout schooling,"[137] suggesting that the teaching of regional languages in higher education is not prohibited. How this translates into accessing higher education in Basque will be examined in the next chapter.

The analysis of the legal framework ecosystem of the Basque language and education reveals the profound correlation between law and society. Furthermore, the analysis also suggests a deep interrelation between the Basque speakers (norm users) and the legal framework. Indeed, law, and especially for the regulation of education in Euskara, must be scrutinized under the prism of social context. The Basque language and regulation of education are interconnected, and one cannot understand law without understanding the environment in which it is applied. Therefore, understanding the different approaches and their consequences for one and the same language needs the support of contextualization.

Notes

1 See full text of Article 8 in Appendix 1.
2 https://boe.es/buscar/doc.php?id=BOE-A-2001-17500 (Accessed August 7, 2020). Concerning Article 8, Spain is bound by paragraph 1, a.i; b.i; c.i; d.i; e.iii; f.i; g; h; and i; and paragraph 2.

3   Further analysis of the monitoring reports of the Committee of Experts shows that many autonomous communities in Spain do not fulfill the level of obligations entered by Spain in the field of education. For instance, Galicia, Valencia, and the Balearic Islands do not offer full immersive education in their regional languages, but only bilingual education models. This is not what the Language Charter imposes under the obligations ratified by Spain. As we will see later, even the BAC shows some deficiencies regarding professional and vocational education.
4   Appendix 1.
5   For articles 148 and 149 of the Spanish Constitution, see appendix 1.
6   Emphasis added by the author. Note the official English translation of the Constitution uses the term "self-governing communities" to refer to the autonomous communities.
7   Milian i Massana, Más sobre derechos lingüísticos, 117.
8   The system of devolution of powers in Spain has been previously explained in part I, chapter 3.
9   Aragón Reyes, "Las competencias del Estado y las Comunidades Autónomas sobre Educación," 193.
10 Translated by the author. STC 337/1994, of December 23, 1994, F.J.6 http://hj.tribunalconstitucional.es/HJ/es/Resolucion/Show/2854 (Accessed July 5, 2018).
11 Milian i Massana, *Más sobre derechos lingüísticos*, 195.
12 Translated by the author, STC 87/1983, of October 27, 1983, F.J.5 http://hj.tribunalconstitucional.es/HJ/es/Resolucion/Show/215 (Accessed July 5, 2018).
13 STC 88/1983. http://hj.tribunalconstitucional.es/HJ/es/Resolucion/Show/216 (Accessed July 5, 2018).
14 Royal Decree 3087/1987, of November 12, 1987, on the establishment of minimum teaching requirements for the higher cycle of General Basic Education (Translated by the author. Originally: Decreto Real 3087/1987, de 12 de noviembre, sobre fijación de enseñanzas mínimas para el ciclo superior de Educación General Básica).
15 Ibid. F.J.4, translated and emphasis added by the author: "todos los habitantes de Euskadi tienen el derecho a conocer y usar ambas lenguas (Article 6.1 del Estatuto). Ello supone, naturalmente, que ambas lenguas han de ser enseñadas en los centros escolares de la Comunidad con la intensidad que permita alca-

nzar ese objetivo. *Y es de observar en este mismo sentido que tal deber no deriva sólo del Estatuto, sino de la misma Constitución.*"

16 Translating "*lengua vehicular*" is a hard task. This term refers to the language used for teaching—the language through which the teacher communicates. Therefore, in this book we will refer to it as the "teaching language."

17 Translated by the author. See the decision: https://www.boe.es/buscar/doc.php?id=BOE-T-1995-1790 (Accessed April 15, 2024).

18 As of July 2020.

19 Translated by the author. Ley Orgánica para la Mejora de la Calidad Educativa (LOMCE).

20 See appendix 2 for Oihartzabal's bio.

21 In 1979, out of every three adults living in the BAC, one was born outside the BAC, and a second one had a mother or a father that was born outside the BAC. Spanish immigration to the BAC had been very important in the fifties, sixties, and seventies. In those conditions, it was very difficult to implement an aggressive or radical policy of language recovery. Long-term language planning was instead favored. See Mezo, *El palo y la zanahoria*.

22 For university studies, two other options are available: The students can study either in Euskara or in Castilian. See discussion on higher education below.

23 Arzoz, *Bilingual Higher Education in the Legal Context. Group Rights, State Policies and Globalisation*, Volume 2:138.

24 This law was analyzed in depth in part I, chapter 3. This law installed the right to use either Basque or Castilian as the teaching language and was followed by the 138/1983 Bilingualism Decree of July 11 that created the three models. https://www.euskadi.eus/y22-bopv/es/bopv2/datos/1983/07/8301433a.pdf (Accessed July 6, 2018).

25 Law 1/1993, of February 19, on the Basque Public School. http://noticias.juridicas.com/base_datos/CCAA/pv-l1-1993.t1.html#t1 (Accessed July 6, 2018). Before this law, the Basque education system was tripartite: public, private, and Ikastola schools. Among other things, this 1993 law clarified the status of Ikastola schools. This is analyzed further below.

26 The Statute of Autonomy of the BAC was explained in part I, chapter 3.

27 Translated by the author. Full Article 16 of the Statute of Autonomy: "In application of the provisions of the first additional provision of the Constitution,

the Autonomous Community of the Basque Country is responsible for education in all its extension, levels and grades, modalities and specialties, without prejudice to Article 27 of the Constitution and Organic Laws that develop it, of the powers attributed to the State by Article 149.1.30º of the same and of the high inspection necessary for its compliance and guarantee."

28 Established by Decree 138/1983, of July 11. https://www.legegunea.euskadi.eus/x59-preview/eu/contenidos/decreto/bopv198301433/eu_def/index.shtml (Accessed March 17, 2021).

29 Law 1/1993, of February 19, on the Basque Public School. http://noticias.juridicas.com/base_datos/CCAA/pv-l1-1993.t1.html#t1 (Accessed July 6, 2018). Before this 1993 law, the Basque educational system since 1982 was divided between three categories: public, private and Ikastola schools. This law and its context are analyzed in the next chapter.
The Statute of Autonomy of the BAC was explained in chapter 3.

30 Urrutia Libarona, "Estatuto jurídico del euskera en el País Vasco," 440.

31 Model A was predominant in 1983, whereas in 2017 it contained less than 10 percent of all mandatory education-aged students. See chapter 5.

32 Flors-Mas y Manterola, "Els models lingüístics de l'educació obligatòria a la Comunitat Autònoma Basca i a Catalunya."

33 In the autonomous community of Catalonia, as planned by Law 1/1998, of January 7, 1998, on Linguistic Policies, Catalan is used as the teaching language in education. The approach taken by the Catalan linguistic model implies more presence of Catalan than Castilian throughout the schooling years, without the division into models such as in the BAC or Navarre. Thus, public education works mainly with a total immersive model. Yet, these two approaches aim to attain the same goal: that students are bilingual by the end of their school years.

34 Oihartzabal even confessed during his interview that he had the impression that the Model A is dying faster than what they had predicted.

35 Urrutia Libarona, "Hizkuntza eskubideak eta euskara hezkuntza sisteman," 183.

36 For instance, with the dynamic of Euskaraldia—an initiative in all three Basque administrative territories with the aim of creating social conditions for speaking Basque. See https://euskaraldia.eus/es/ (Accessed April 29, 2021).

37 According to the VI. Sociolinguistic Survey (from 2016, published in 2017), among the inhabitants older than sixteen in the BAC, 33.9 percent are Basque

speakers, 19.1 percent understand (but don't speak) Basque, and 47 percent are monolingual. The number of Basque speakers has grown steadily over the years, notably because of education. In fact, the lower we go in age groups, the higher number of Basque speakers there are. This will be further explored in the next chapter. https://www.euskadi.eus/contenidos/informacion/ikerketa_soziolinguistikoak/eu_def/adjuntos/VI_INK_SOZLG_EAE_Aurkezpen_publikoa_20161014.pdf (Accessed August 7, 2020).
38 Education is regulated in Title II of this Foral Law 18/1986. This law was analyzed in part I, chapter 3.
39 http://www.lexnavarra.navarra.es/detalle.asp?r=28807 (Accessed August 7, 2020).
40 Foral Decrees are decrees adopted by the government of Navarre.
41 http://www.lexnavarra.navarra.es/detalle.asp?r=28806 (Accessed August 7, 2020).
42 Foral Decree 161/1988, of May 19, 1988, approving the regulations on the operation and organization of the Basque language teaching centers for adults of the Government of Navarre and on the granting of aid to private entities promoting the teaching of Basque language for adults (private Euskaltegis and Gaueskolas). (Translated by the author, originally: Decreto Foral 161/1988, de 19 de mayo, por el que se aprueban los reglamentos de funcionamiento y organización de los centros de enseñanza del Euskara para adultos del Gobierno de Navarra y de concesión de ayudas a entidades privadas promotoras de la enseñanza del Euskara para adultos (Euskaltegis privados y Gaueskolas)). http://www.lexnavarra.navarra.es/detalle.asp?r=28805 (Accessed August 7, 2020).
43 The linguistic zoning of Navarre is explained in part I, chapter 3.
44 Foral Laws or Decrees are laws adopted by the regional Parliament of Navarre.
45 Model A refers to schooling in Spanish, with Basque as a subject. Model B refers to bilingual teaching, in which both Spanish and Basque are used. Model D refers to teaching in Basque, with Spanish as a subject. Finally, Model G refers to schooling exclusively in Spanish, without Basque as a subject. It must be noted a few options are available in Model G or Model A, in which children can learn other languages such as English or French, but to stay focused on the example of Euskara, we will only discuss the variations in models as they apply to the Basque language specifically.
46 Oroz Bretón y Sotés Ruiz, "Bilingual Education in Navarre: Achievements and Challenges," 29.

47 Irujo y Urrutia, "Basque in the Foral Community of Navarre(CFN)," 204-5.
48 Ikastola schools are analyzed in greater depth in the next chapter.
49 Aldasoro Lecea, "La evolución de la enseñanza en euskera en Navarra: una perspectiva pedagógica.". The argument put forward by those who oppose the presence of Ikastola schools in this area of Navarre is that because Basque is not co-official in this area, the immersive teaching in the Basque language goes against the law, even if it is performed under Ikastola schools that are private. This argument does not make sense to the author who believes, even if this geographical area is legally hostile to the teaching of the Basque language, it cannot be banned in the private sphere.
50 Analyzing higher education and related law is extremely interesting because it brings together a series of fundamental rights such as freedom of education and the independence of universities and professors. However, these very rich topics exceed the scope of our analysis on education and the Basque language. Therefore, the author will give a general introduction of this topic of higher education and the Basque language, without exploring further the richness of the regulation of higher education and what it entails.
51 The author will focus on public universities in this book.
52 Ley Orgánica 2/2023, de 22 de marzo, del Sistema Universitario https://www.boe.es/buscar/act.php?id=BOE-A-2023-7500 (Accessed April 24, 2025).
53 Basque University Law: Law 3/2004, of February 25, on the Basque University System (Translated by the author: Ley vasca de universidades: Ley 3/2004, de 25 de febrero, del Sistema Universitario Vasco) https://www.ehu.eus/documents/1277275/1277448/ley_vasca_universidades.pdf/abeb76ef-9e8b-4622-8569-bfd8077652e3?t=1370521277000 (Accessed July 23, 2020).
54 Article 16, translated by the author: "In application of the provisions of the First Additional Provision of the Constitution, the Autonomous Community of the Basque Country is responsible for education in all its extension, levels and grades, modalities and specialties, without prejudice to Article 27 of the Constitution and Organic Laws that develop it, of the powers attributed to the State by Article 149 1.30ª of the same and of the high inspection necessary for its compliance and guarantee."
55 Translated and emphasis added by the author. Article 3.3, translated by the author: "Likewise, universities should promote education in democratic values

and social justice and in respect for human rights. They shall stimulate and support initiatives complementary to ordinary education that entail the transmission of values corresponding to human dignity and solidarity among all peoples and cultures. They shall also encourage the defense, study and promotion of the Basque cultural heritage in general, and of the Basque language in particular."

56 Translated and emphasis added by the author.
57 Translated and emphasis added by the author. Article 7.f, translated by the author: "The responsibility of the public authorities to guarantee and ensure the effective fulfillment of the right to receive university teaching in Basque, promoting for this purpose the regulatory developments and positive action measures deemed necessary, within the general university policy."
58 Translated by the author. Article 7.i: "The promotion and development of collaboration and coordination agreements with the universities of Navarre and the Northern Basque Country to the extent that they so wish, and in particular with regard to the right to free movement of students, so that standardized mechanisms will be established for their admission to the Basque university system."
59 Translated by the author. Article 2: "The university system is formed by all the universities based in the territory of the Autonomous Community of the Basque Country, and in it will be integrated those that in the future will be created or recognized by the Basque Parliament. Likewise, within the system, relations and collaboration with other university institutions located in other territories that share the cultural body of the Basque language or project for the future will be promoted with the aim of promoting the use of the Basque language, through the coordination of teaching, research, cultural activities and mobility among the students and teaching staff of the aforementioned university institutions, in order to promote the use of the Basque language, and all of this within the scope of the European nations. Priority relations will be established with the rest of the universities located in the Basque Country."
60 Ibid.
61 Other articles of this law concerning the Basque language regulate the language requirements for the staff, the documents, and publications. The same thing happens concerning the Foral Law on the Creation of the Public University of Navarre (discussed below). The author is not going to address this side of the Basque language in higher education in this book.

62 Translated by the author. Article 11.3: "The universities shall adopt the necessary measures in accordance with what is established in this respect in their own regulations and specific plans, guaranteeing in its entirety the right to study in Basque and to live in that language."
63 (Translated by the author) Foral Law 8/1987, of April 21, 1987, on the Creation of the Public University of Navarre http://www.lexnavarra.navarra.es/detalle.asp?r=2923 (Accessed July 23, 2020).
64 Article 47, translated by the author: "The regulation and administration of education in all its extension, levels and grades, modalities and specialties is the full competence of Navarre, without prejudice to the provisions of the constitutional precepts on this matter, of the Organic Laws that develop them and of the competences of the State with regard to the regulation of the conditions for obtaining, issuing and homologation of academic and professional degrees and of the high inspection of the State for their compliance and guarantee."
65 The Public University of Navarre (public university)—*Universidad Pública de Navarra*—should not be confused with the University of Navarre (private university)—*Universidad de Navarra*.
66 Foral Decree 110/2003, of May 12, 2003. https://www.unavarra.es/digitalAssets/103/103198_100000estatutos-ntegrados.pdf (Accessed July 23, 2020).
67 Some entire study programs are available in Basque. For the academic year 2021–2022, the undergraduate degrees in education are available entirely in Euskara, while some courses are available in Basque in other degree programs. See http://www.unavarra.es/euskara/ensenianza-en-euskera/oferta-academica?languageId=100000 (Accessed February 17, 2021).
68 Principes fondamentaux reconnus par les lois de la République.
69 Decision no. 77-87. http://www.conseil-constitutionnel.fr/conseil-constitutionnel/francais/les-decisions/acces-par-date/decisions-depuis-1959/1977/77-87-dc/decision-n-77-87-dc-du-23-novembre-1977.7529.html (Accessed August 31, 2018).
70 Article L.111-1 of the Code of Education https://www.legifrance.gouv.fr/codes/section_lc/LEGITEXT000006071191/LEGISCTA000006151327/#LEGISCTA000006151327 (Accessed March 12, 2021).
71 Article L.151-1 of the Code of Education https://www.legifrance.gouv.fr/codes/section_lc/LEGITEXT000006071191/LEGISCTA000006151331/#LEGISCTA000006151331 (Accessed March 12, 2021).

72 Nicolau y Lupu, "The Child's right to education and culture in French legislation," 257.
73 This was later added to the legal corpus with the Toubon Law of 1994. The Toubon Law is analyzed in part I, chapter 2.
74 Bertile, *Langues régionales ou minoritaires et constitution: France, Espagne et Italie*, 59. Additionally, Adrey dedicates a full chapter to the study of the historical evolution in France. See Adrey, *Discourse and struggle in minority language policy formation*, 107-41.
75 Law no. 51-46 of January 11, 1951.
76 As we will see, the optional character of the teaching of regional languages poses an issue for the implementation of immersive schooling in France. The author does criticize this optional character. She believes offering an immersive schooling system in public schools does not mean the imposition of learning regional languages to those students; rather, it offers a broader linguistic choice of education. This is discussed below, as well as in the next chapter.
77 Adrey, "Language, Nation and State in French Linguistic Nationalism: History, Developments and Perspectives," 2009, 133.
78 Translated and emphasis added by the author: "Pedagogical instructions will be sent to rectors with a view to authorizing teachers to use local languages in primary and nursery schools *whenever they can benefit from them for their teaching, particularly for the study of the French language.*"
79 Bertile, *Langues régionales ou minoritaires et constitution*, 2008, 92-93.
80 Law no. 75-620, July 11, 1975. https://www.legifrance.gouv.fr/jorf/id/JORFTEXT000000334174 (Last accessed: May 2024)
81 Article 12, translated by the author: "Regional languages and cultures may be taught throughout the school curriculum. "
82 Translated by the author.
83 Translated by the author: Orientation Law on Education, no. 89-486, July 10, 1989 (originally: Loi d'orientation sur l'éducation). https://www.legifrance.gouv.fr/jorf/id/JORFTEXT000000509314 (last accessed: Mai 2024).
84 Emphasis added and translated by the author. Article 1: "Schools, collèges, lycées and higher education establishments [...] provide training whose content and

methods are adapted to the economic, technological, social and cultural developments of the country and its european and international environment. *This training may include the teaching of regional languages and cultures at all levels.*"
85 The Toubon Law is examined in part I, chapter 2.
86 Law no. 2013-595 of July 8, 2013 on the orientation and programming for the refoundation of the school of the Republic (translated by the author. Originally: Loi n° 2013-595 du 8 juillet 2013 d'orientation et de programmation pour la refondation de l'école de la République). https://www.legifrance.gouv.fr/affichTexte.do?cidTexte=JORFTEXT000027677984&categorieLien=id (Accessed August 5, 2020).
87 Article 40 of the Law no. 2013-595 of July 8, 2013. See appendix 1. For the criticism of the bilingual model, see below.
88 Article 21 was modified by the Molac law, examined below. The sanction of the Molac law by the Constitutional Council (decision n° 2021-818, May 21, 2021) concerning immersive schooling is examined below.
89 Constitutional Council, decision no. 91-290, May 9, 1991.
90 The same applies for Ikastola schools practicing immersive schooling in Basque, analyzed in the next chapter.
91 See the next chapter.
92 Constitutional Council, decision no. 2004-490, February 12, 2004.
93 Bertile, Langues régionales ou minoritaires et constitution, 2008, 84.
94 Decision no. 2011-130 QPC, May 20, 2011.
95 Translated and emphasis added by the author. "Le Conseil supérieur de l'éducation est consulté, conformément aux attributions qui lui sont conférées par l'article L. 231-1, sur les moyens de favoriser l'étude des langues et cultures régionales *dans les régions où ces langues sont en usage.*"
96 For the examination of Article 75-1 and the French Constitution, see part I, chapter 2.
97 De Witte, "Linguistic minorities in Western Europe: expansion of rights without (much) litigation ?" 42.
98 Bertile, *Langues régionales ou minoritaires et constitution*, 2008, 116.
99 The decision of the Council of State, April 15, 1996, *Association des parents d'élèves pour l'enseignement du Breton* (Parents' Association for Teaching Breton, translated by the author), underscores the optional nature (for teachers) of

teaching regional languages, and that there is no obligation for the administration to provide the teaching of such languages. The decision of the Council of State, on June 1, 1979, *Association Défense et promotion des langues de France* (Association for Defending and Promoting the Languages of France, translated by the author), denies implicitly the existence of a right to access teaching in regional languages.

100 The decision of the Constitutional Council no. 96-373, on the autonomy statute of French Polynesia, underscores the optional character of learning regional languages for the students, and the decision no. 2001-454 on the law relating to Corsica underscores the optional character both for students and teachers.

101 See part I, chapter 2.

102 Translated by the author: Decision n° 2021-818 of May 21, 2021, on the Law relating to the heritage protection of regional languages and their promotion. https://www.conseil-constitutionnel.fr/decision/2021/2021818DC.htm (Accessed July 13, 2021).

103 See https://www.conseil-constitutionnel.fr/sites/default/files/as/root/bank_mm/decisions/2021818dc/2021818dc_saisinedep.pdf (Accessed July 13, 2021).

104 For this research, our discussion will focus on the sanction of Articles 4 and 6 and will not elaborate on Article 9 concerning the diacritic marks.

105 This applied to private primary schools under contract with the State.

106 Paragraph 13, translated by the author : "First, the contested provisions do not have the effect of imposing the use of a language other than French on a legal person governed by public law or a person governed by private law in the exercise of a public service mission. Nor do they have the effect of enabling private individuals to avail themselves of a right to use a language other than French in their relations with administrations and public services, or of compelling them to do so. On the other hand, the mere fact of providing, under the conditions set out in the contested provisions, for a municipality to contribute to financing the schooling of a pupil residing on its territory and wishing to attend a primary school under an association contract located on the territory of another municipality, on the grounds that it provides regional language teaching within the meaning of 2° of article L. 312-10, does not infringe the first paragraph of article 2 of the Constitution."

107 "Immersive teaching in the regional language, without prejudice to the objective of a good knowledge of the French language."

108 Paragraph 20, translated by the author: "Consequently, by providing that the teaching of a regional language may take the form of immersive teaching, article 4 of the law in question infringes article 2 of the Constitution. It is therefore contrary to the Constitution."
109 In paragraph 19, translated by the author: "The preparatory work for the law in question shows that the immersive teaching of a regional language is a method that does not simply teach this language, but uses it as the main language of instruction and as a language of communication within the school."
110 Translated by the author. Article 4 of the Molac Law.
111 Comments by the Constitutional Council on the decision: https://www.conseil-constitutionnel.fr/sites/default/files/as/root/bank_mm/decisions/2021818dc/2021818dc_ccc.pdf (Accessed July 14, 2021).
112 Schmalz, "Beyond an Anxiety Logic: A Critical Examination of Language Rights Cases before the European Court of Human Rights."
113 See appendex 1.
114 University studies will be explored later in this chapter.
115 A *circulaire* is used in the French public administration to explain or develop a rule. The ministry usually writes it; several ministries can also collaborate. The *circulaires* can be either binding or nonbinding. The nonbinding ones interpret a law or regulation to have a homogeneous implementation in the country. They can be seen as recommendations coming from the ministry or ministries. The binding ones, on the other hand, are considered new legal rules. In fact, these *circulaires* can be contested in court. This helps the administrative judge control the legality of the *circulaires*.
116 Circulaire nº. IV-69-90, of February 17, 1969.
117 Decree nº. 70-650, of July 10, 1970.
118 Circulaire no. 82-261, The teaching of regional cultures and languages in the national education system, of July 1, 1982 (translated by the author).
119 Circulaire no. 83-547, of Decembre, 1983, Guidance text on the teaching of regional cultures and languages. Translated by the author.
120 The town of Sara (Sare, in French) is in Iparralde.
121 This experiment was based in the authorization of conducting educational experiments created by the Haby Law of 1975. See Zabaleta Apaolaza, "Inmersión lingüística y Constitución: una perspectiva francesa," 99.

122 Order relating to the modalities for awarding the national patent diploma to candidates in third-grade classes in bilingual French-regional language sections, of June 23, 1994. Translated by the author

123 An official diploma given to students at the end of *3ème*, at the end of the college. In the US, this is the equivalent of the ninth grade, or freshman year of high school. In France, the ninth grade is considered to be the last year of middle school.

124 Circulaire no. 95-086, of April 27, 1995, on the teaching of regional languages and cultures.

125 Article 3 of this order defines the immersive method as being characterized by the use of the regional language as the main language of teaching, as well as the language of communication in the school.

126 According to Article 3 of the order, the principle of hourly parity constitutes teaching half of the time in the French language and the other half in the regional language. We will discuss in the next chapter how this requirement is usually not fulfilled.

127 Translated by the author: Order amending the order of July 31, 2001, relating to the establishment of bilingual education in regional languages either in "regional languages" schools, middle schools and high schools, or in "regional languages" sections in schools, colleges and high schools, March 6, 2002.

128 Council of State, UNSA Education, and others, July 15, 2002. Translated by the author.

129 Council of State, SNES, and others, and Council of State, UNSA, and others. Translated by the author.

130 Yet, as we will see in the next chapter, the bilingual model is not actually granting half of the curriculum to be taught in Euskara. In fact, the "bilingual" model in Iparralde contains only classes of history and geography in Basque, and Basque language classes. This is a common criticism of the bilingual model in Iparralde, notably by teachers of this model who see their hands tied when trying to form fully bilingual children (see interviews of teachers in the following chapter).

131 In 2019, the French Ministry of National Education, the Public Office of the Basque Language, and Seaska signed a Convention for 2019-2022, continuing their collaboration. Seaska ("cradle" in English) is the name of the federation of Ikastola schools, immersive schools in the Basque language in the Northern

Basque Country. https://www.mintzaira.fr/fileadmin/documents/Aktualitateak/Prentsaurrekoak/2019/Seaska_20190716/SEASKA_2019_2022_hitarmena_izenpeturik.pdf (Accessed August 17, 2020).
132 These schools are currently grouped under "Eskolim," a federation of immersive schools in regional languages since 2009.
133 Harguindeguy y Itçaina, "Towards a Consistent Language Policy for the French Basque Country? Actors, Processes and Outcomes."
134 As of December 2020.
135 Law No. 2013-660 of July 22, 2013, relating to higher education and research, translated by the author. https://www.legifrance.gouv.fr/affichTexte.do?cidTexte=JORFTEXT000027735009&categorieLien=id (Accessed July 23, 2020).
136 Article L.123-3, Code of Education. See appendix 1.
137 Translated by the author.

5

Context of the Basque Language and Education

The analysis of the legal framework regulating education in Euskara already gives clues about the importance of the context. From the necessity of teachers fluent in Basque to the creation of Ikastola schools, we can see the need to study the real-life dynamic of the legal norms regulating education in Euskara. Analyzing the key actors of education in Basque will provide this insight.

These actors will be divided between public and private, and no attempt will be made to be comprehensive in listing all the actors. Yet, these public and private actors are essential to help us better understand the regulation of education and the Basque language. They have shaped—and still do—the educational offerings in Basque, and they strongly influence and are strongly influenced by the law. In the following analysis of the relationship between law and its context, we will explore courts, public institutions, public funding sources, and universities, as well as the role of associative schools, parents, and teachers.

Public Actors

Public schooling serves a large number of students in the three administrative regions of the Basque Country, and therefore, public actors have a great deal to say regarding education in Basque. First, we will examine courts in France with respect to immersive schooling in regional languages. Second, we will examine the public funding and education in the Basque language. And third, we will look at the factors at play at the intersection of higher education and the Basque language.

The Role of Courts in Regulating Immersive Teaching in France

Examining courts under the lens of context might seem surprising.

Indeed, the analysis of courts usually belongs to the legal framework. However, while courts in general function as interpreters of the law ("norm givers" in MacCormick's terms), regarding immersive teaching in France, the take of French courts on multilingual teaching could be described as legal countermobilization. While in Spain courts have settled disputes about linguistic issues in education,[1] the French courts have decided to relegate immersive schooling outside the public school of the Republic, clashing with policy makers, that is, the primary norm givers. The distinctiveness of the role of the French courts in regional language immersive teaching justifies its discussion in this section.

Public actors hold a major role in education. In France, public education is one of the pillars of the Republic in the nation-state imaginary. We have previously explored the evolution and the place of regional languages in education in France, and we have noticed how the presence of regional languages in education in France is marked by its optional character. Over the years, regional languages have been introduced in French public education as optional subjects. Therefore, regional languages can be studied with different formulas, ranging from a couple of hours per week to bilingual options, where students learn a couple of elements of their curriculum in the given language instead of in French.[2] The French approach to regional languages in education seems characterized by a lack of courage or even immobilism. Still, some attempts were made to try to include immersive education in Breton in the French public schools.

We have already mentioned in chapter 4 that various associative schools exist in France, providing immersive schooling in regional languages. Regarding the Basque language, Ikastola schools (joined under the Seaska association) offer immersive education. For the Catalan language, Bressola schools perform this function; for the Occitan language, Calandreta schools; for the Alsatian language, ABCM Zweisprächigkeit schools; and for the Breton language, Diwan schools.[3] These schools have articulated their willingness to join the public schooling system.[4] Some attempts toward the inclusion of these schools in the public system were made under the presidency of François Mitterrand, but the project was abandoned in 1984.[5] The associative schools since then have remained in the private educational and legal systems. We will focus our attention on the Diwan schools since they attempted integrating immersive schooling into French public schools.

In their fight to join the system of public education, Diwan schools walked farthest along the road of recognition. Created in 1977, Diwan schools can be defined as the equivalent to Ikastola schools for the Breton language. In 1985, Article 28 of the budget law (*loi des finances rectificatrice de 1985*) included the integration of Diwan school teachers into the public schooling system, starting the path of the "publicization" of immersive schools. Nonetheless, the Constitutional Council decided[6] in its *considérant* 7[7] that the procedure used to integrate the teaching staff of Diwan schools via this 1985 budget law did not comply with the Constitution.

This first step, therefore, was not big enough for the introduction of immersive schooling into the public system. In fact, the fate of immersive schools remained untouched for almost ten years. It was not until 1994 that associative schools in France were aligned, with a contract, to private schools. This means, as explained by Article L.442-5 of the Code of Education, that these schools are under the control of the state, which imposes teaching rules and programs. This legal status entitles these schools to state funding for the remuneration of teachers and for the operating expenses of the functioning of classes at the same level as the public school classes. Therefore, 1994 marked a step forward for immersive schools since their recognition as private schools allowed much-needed funding, enabling their survival. A few years later, Diwan schools started to move things faster.

Jack Lang, minister of education, and Andrew Lincoln, the president of Diwan schools, signed a protocol of agreement[8] on May 28, 2001, to shift Diwan schools from private to public status. Various parents and union brought the Ministry of Education's decision to the Council of State. In this decision,[9] the Council of State had to answer the claims brought mainly by the SNES (the National Union of Second-Degree Teachers), asking for the suspension of the process of integration of Diwan schools within the public education system. Accepting the claims of emergency (Diwan schools were going to be introduced into the public system from January 2002 onward), the Council of State decided to suspend the integration of immersive schooling into public education. The decision of the Council of State was followed by that of the Constitutional Council.

In a decision on the law for the 2002 budget,[10] the Constitutional Council decided the fate of the immersive schooling model in France. In this decision, the Constitutional Council examined Article 134 of the budget law for that year. This article dealt with nominating and granting tenure to teachers of primary and secondary Diwan school education, if—and only if—these schools were integrated into the public schooling system. The *Sages* decided (*considérant* 52)[11] that Article 134 did not constitute a decision on the integration of these schools into the public system and delegated this decision, under the control of their judge, to the competent administrative authorities. The Constitutional Council concluded, with this reservation of interpretation, the conformity of Article 134 to the Constitution. Interestingly, Bertile[12] notes that the Constitutional Council, in its *considérant* 49,[13] uses Article 2 in matters of education for the first time, instead of using the principle of equality as before.

The Constitutional Council not committing entirely but rather whispering its position on the constitutionality of immersive schooling, the Council of State decided on the conformity of the matter. Indeed, the minister of education wrote two *circulaire*s in 2002: one regarding the inclusion of "regional language schools" (primary and secondary) and "regional language high schools," and another regarding recruiting and training workers for these schools. This led to a second injunction, in which the Council of State decided on the annulment of these two *circulaires*.[14] Finally, the Council of State released a decision on November 29, 2002.[15] In this administrative litigation, the Council of State confirmed the previous orders. In *considérant* 5,[16] the Council of State argued that immersive schooling goes beyond the requirements of learning a regional language and beyond the possibilities of derogation of using the French language, as authorized in the Code of Education. Therefore, by deciding on the limits of use of regional languages, the Council of State did not allow immersive schooling to enter the public education system.

The Diwan school case(s) raises two main thoughts. First, we find the Constitutional Council deciding in 2001 on a matter that does not relate to education, but nevertheless still affecting immersive schooling. Certainly, it is interesting to note that the Constitutional Council wrongly assumes the introduction of immersive schooling will create an imposition of regional languages in education (*considérant* 49).[17] The creation of immersive schools or classes was never considered a substitute to other multilingual, bilingual, or unilingual education offerings, but rather as an addition. Sadly, the Constitutional Council made a restrictive interpretation of inclusion of immersive schooling system. We have seen how in 2021 this position remains unchanged.[18]

Second, it seems rather odd that the Council of State decided on the requirements of learning regional languages and their limits. By deciding that immersive schooling "goes beyond the requirements of learning a regional language," the Council of State ignores the reality of regional languages in France, where, even with a bilingual offering, the number of speakers is diminishing quickly.[19] A quick look at language-planning literature or language-revival policies in other countries with minority languages shows the importance of granting weight to regional or minority languages' presence in education. In addition, the Council of State does not expressly justify why the immersive schooling "goes beyond the requirements of learning a regional language." The Council of State seems to veto the immersive schooling per se, and, shielded under performing a legality check, performs a suitability check of the inclusion of immersive education in French public schools.[20] Hence, the Council of State's decision seems rather ill-informed and lacking in legitimacy.

The example of Diwan schools shows a systematic exercise of the High French Courts holding on to unilingualism against a further inclusion of regional languages in the public education system. Yet, the Diwan schools' cases happened because of a positive shift in the attitude of the Ministry of Education toward regional languages that collided with the conservative and traditional mindset of French courts. Therefore, the Diwan cases are bittersweet for regional languages, since they display a continuity in the practice of French courts, with a glimpse of positive action from policy makers. For the case of the Basque language, the example of Diwan schools showed that there was room for inclusion of Ikastola schools in the public system—progress that the approach of the French courts stopped. The Constitutional Council's 2021 decision reiterated this.[21]

Another way in which public actors influence the presence and spread of Euskara in education is via public funding. In the case of Euskara, public funding regarding Basque language and education is worth noting when exploring its context.

Public Funding and Education in Basque

One key element of public actors in education is public funding. Education has a cost, and any linguistic policy or educational policy needs financial support. In the case of linguistic minorities, the political point of view is divided between perceiving funding education in these languages as a cost or as an investment. To support the revival of a minority language or its transmission, funding policies should be seen as investments. Regarding Euskara, funding can appear in terms of financing programs for students and teachers or financing Basque schools.

The previously mentioned Normalization Law 10/1982[22] sought to attain perfectly bilingual children at the end of mandatory education (Article 17) and thus, the regional administration had to take appropriate measures. That law was followed by Decree 138/1983 on the regulation of the use of official languages in non-university education in the Basque Autonomous Community (the BAC).[23] The order that developed this decree on August 1, 1983, explained in its Article 12 that the Education and Culture Department "shall adopt the necessary measures"[24] inside and outside the classroom to foster the use of Basque in school. Following these rules, and to fulfill their objective, the education institutions of the BAC created NOLEGA[25] (Development of the Law of Normalization/*Normalizazio Legearen Garapena*) to introduce more Euskara in education and its administration. Therefore, when looking at public funding and education, we notice that the early laws of the BAC planned to create resources to promote Basque in schools. For the 2017–2018 academic year, NOLEGA released a public call for funding of 150,000 euros.[26] In the case of the BAC, different programs provide funding toward education in Euskara. Apart from the annual budget line going toward education, there are other programs: IRALE and ULIBARRI.[27]

IRALE[28] (*Irakasleak Alfabetatu eta Euskalduntzea,* Making teachers literate in Basque) is devoted to teaching Basque or improving the level of Basque of teachers of non-university education in the BAC (from both private and public education). For 1976–1977, in a survey conducted by Siadeco,[29] only 5 percent of teachers in public education considered themselves Basque speakers in the BAC. Yet, inhabitants of the BAC were asking for teachers who were able to teach both in Castilian and Basque. Accordingly, teachers needed to be trained to be able to teach in Basque, and the IRALE program started with this objective in mind. The Basque government's education department began IRALE during the 1981–1982 academic year. There are now five centers (two in Bilbao, one in Donostia-San Sebastián, one in Vitoria-Gasteiz, and one in Eibar). IRALE also collaborates with other external schools, known as "Euskaltegi,"[30] which are schools for teaching Euskara to adults. Additionally, IRALE offers didactic and methodological training for the teaching of the Basque language and sociocultural training for the Basque curriculum.

With IRALE, teachers are excused from their duties for a period (half a year, or a full year) to learn or improve their Basque language skills, and the training is provided for free while full-salary is retained. This training is open to any teacher or education professional in the BAC. For teachers who choose to learn or improve their Basque language skills, their temporary replacements' salaries are also covered fully by the Basque government for the public schools and at least 80 percent for the private schools. The maximum length authorized for the training is three years (when freed and with a replacement). It must be said that now almost all the newly appointed teachers are Basque speakers and almost all the schools in the BAC have mostly Basque-speaking teachers. Because of this trend, in which the need for IRALE is less and less needed, this program now offers new services. Those services include assessing the level and quality of Euskara in teaching materials, measuring linguistic levels, and counseling regarding the Basque language.

The Basque government also offers ULIBARRI, a program for the normalization of language in schools. For the 2017–2018, ULIBARRI received funding of 50,000 euros. The idea of this program answers to the logic established by the 10/1982 Normalization Law of 1982.[31] According to its last update,[32] about four hundred schools take part. The schools that enter ULIBARRI make efforts to strengthen the use and the quality of Basque, and they are protected by the Department of Education. Such schools are given priority when assessing initiatives for the expansion and consolidation of Euskara. Since the schools that join the program must have as one of their goals the strengthening of Euskara, they are asked to have their own program of linguistic normalization. In fact, when joining ULIBARRI, schools create a program to foster the use of Euskara in all areas (use by students, by parents, by staff, by teachers, and more), and these programs are revised every four years.

Regarding Navarre, the government offers funding for non-university teachers to attend courses. They can attend classes in public or private centers, but these courses cannot be taken during teaching hours.[33] The teachers who are eligible for this funding are from public schools or private schools (under contract). The Navarrese government finances 50 percent of the registration fee if teachers attend 80 percent of the course. Seventy-five percent of the funding is allotted to public school teachers and 25 percent to the private school teachers. For the 2019–2020 academic year, the government of Navarre provided a maximum of 8,000 euros for the teaching or improvement of Basque among its teachers.

Focusing on public actors and education in Euskara, one cannot forget tangible actions taken by public institutions and administration, which usually translate into funding. From institutional activism to transregional cooperation, we will explore the public funding and education in Basque.

Cooperation, Funding, and Education in Euskara

Because Euskara is in a border area, collaboration and cooperation have always been present between the Basque people. Regarding the Basque language, and in a European context, transfrontier cooperation is increasing steadily. In the case of education and public funding, we will elaborate on an activist collaboration first and on a newly established institutional collaboration second.

Political Activism Beyond Law: The Case of Xalbador School

A regional government financing the work of a secondary school in another country may sound astonishing. Yet, the province of Gipuzkoa (one of the three provinces of the BAC) decided to finance the Ikastola Xalbador (in Kanbo/Cambo-les-Bains in Iparralde), which was experiencing major financial difficulties.

Xalbador was founded in 1983, the first secondary school of Seaska, and became the first immersive secondary school in Iparralde. As mentioned earlier, not including immersive schools into the French public system increases the costs of maintaining Ikastolas in France, and Xalbador was facing major difficulties. It needed many upgrades to infrastructure and had to find financial support. The regional elections in 2011 marked a turning point with the victory of the Bildu coalition for the Gipuzkoa region, and Martin Garitano became the general deputy (*Diputado general*).[34] Bildu, a Basque nationalist coalition and demonstrating a high commitment to the Basque language and culture, decided to proceed with a quite astonishing grant for the Xalbador school.

In fact, in 2013, the Deputation of Gipuzkoa decided to allocate a direct grant of 200,000 euros for the renovation and expansion of Xalbador. The Council of Deputies of Gipuzkoa approved this agreement on April 23, 2013. This agreement on directly funding the renovations at Xalbador school was extended to cover 600,000 euros worth of work from 2013 to 2015. However, the state attorney filed an appeal against the collaboration agreement between Xalbador and the Deputation of Gipuzkoa on May 15, 2013, arguing the territorial overreach and lack of competence of the Deputation. The Deputation of Gipuzkoa, therefore, did not continue the funding from 2013 onward, waiting for the decision of the court.

The Superior Tribunal of Justice of the Basque Country decided on the matter on January 22, 2015.[35] The agreement of April 23, 2013, had consisted in reducing the general budget of Gipuzkoa by 200,000 euros in favor of the Association of Ikastola schools (*Ikastolen Elkartea*). This resulted in granting a subsidy of 200,000 euros to Xalbador and an authorization of 600,000 euros in total for the works at Xalbador between 2013 and 2015. The Superior Tribunal of Justice underscored the territoriality of the competences of the Deputation of Gipuzkoa, based on the constitutional regime (Articles 137 and 141-1) and the autonomic regime (Articles 1, 2, 31, and 36).[36] Also, the tribunal emphasized how no single connection could be found between the grant conceded to Xalbador (in France) and the competences of the Deputation of Gipuzkoa (including the purpose of the grant, its effects, and the connection with the Foral territory).

Interestingly, the defendants mentioned the Language Charter to justify the agreement and the grant, as a tool to promote the Basque language beyond the territory of Spain.[37] On this matter, the tribunal considered the Language Charter as an instrument that can be used beyond the borders of a state, but does not legitimize the Deputation of Gipuzkoa to create agreements producing effects, with charges in its budget, outside its territorial scope. Therefore, the tribunal concluded there was no justification for the actions of the Deputation of Gipuzkoa and that the grant authorized by this institution did not serve the general interests that the deputation should represent and support.

This case shows how activism went too far, beyond the limits established by law. Indeed, the Superior Tribunal rightly underscored the framework that the Deputation of Gipuzkoa must work within when deciding on the regional budget. Even if the idea behind the action—helping a school in need, with which there is a linguistic and cultural connection—might appear to be a noble act, the reality is that taxes from the Gipuzkoa inhabitants are not meant to be spent in another country.

Finally, another reading of this case might be the interconnection between the three territories in the Basque Country. Albeit clumsily and without legal authority to do so, the Deputation of Gipuzkoa tried to establish some sort of financial solidarity. This might be food for thought for future relationships between the Basque government and the POBL (Public Office of the Basque Language), which have already established a collaboration.

Continuing with the idea of financial solidarity, we will now discuss regional collaboration and education in Euskara.

Regional Collaboration and Education in Basque

Since its creation in Iparralde in 2004, the POBL has advanced the development of the Basque language and education in Iparralde.

The collaboration between the Basque government (government of the BAC) and the POBL[38] started in 2007, with a renewal of the agreement every five years, to foster and develop linguistic policies in Iparralde.[39] This office renewed an agreement with the government of the BAC on April 28, 2018. This agreement signed on April 28, 2018, showed important improvements, also in terms of education. On April 25, 2017, it was decided the funding of 2018 was going to be 1,930,000 euros (the POBL contributing 1,530,000 and the Basque government contributing 400,000). On April 30, 2018, the decision regarding the budget for 2018 was published.[40] Among those 1,930,000 euros, 1,550,000 went to the promoters linked with the POBL[41] and 380,000 euros went toward other private agents in Iparralde through a call for projects. Regarding the promoters linked with the POBL, for 2018, primary and secondary education in Basque received 496,000 euros in total from this funding: Seaska received 405,000 euros; Ikas-bi, 40,000; Biga bai, 23,000; and Euskal Haziak, 28,000 euros. In addition, teaching Basque to adults received 500,000 euros via AEK.[42] Therefore, almost one million euros was directed toward education and Euskara from the budget of 2018, and that's only counting the promoters who have an agreement with the POBL via the collaboration between this institution and the Basque government.

Other agents also received funding from this 2018 budget line. As a matter of fact, 380,000 euros was kept for a public call for funding. Among the projects that were accepted for funding, two were linked to teaching Basque to adults (students of Angelu/Anglet who offer training; and the *Jakinola* project, to create online modules to learn Basque). Two kindergartens also received funding because they conduct activities in Basque (Bayonne's kindergarten, Luma, for the project of psychomotricity and music therapy; and Biarritz's kindergarten, Ohakoa, for three workshops—"sound and music," "reading and stories," and "singing and dancing").

Interestingly, looking at the budget decisions for 2018, one can see the key focus is education.[43] The majority of promoters who have an agreement with the POBL and the Basque government are concerned with education and teaching Basque to adults. Also, in the secondary budget line, four projects linked to education received funding. The biggest commitments and economic efforts are directed to education in Iparralde. Together with the Basque government, the POBL sees in education the key to the recovery of the Basque language in Iparralde. Also, it is worth noting that the promotors who received the biggest share of funding are AEK, for the teaching of Basque to adults in Iparralde, followed up by Seaska, for the Ikastola schools in Iparralde.

For 2023 (the latest call as of 2024),[44] the overall budget was the same (1,930,000 euros). Regarding education and Basque, the sums remain similar: 405,000 euros for Seaska, 40,000 euros for Ikas-Bi, 23,000 euros for Biga-Bai, 28,000 euros for Euskal Haziak. For teaching Basque to adults, AEK received 520,000 euros. The 2024 data confirms, once again, the commitment of both institutions to education in Basque in Iparralde.

Higher Education and the Basque Language in Context

In Spain, the higher education system needed to be rethought with the new democratic era. Public universities were established both in the BAC and Navarre: the Universidad del País Vasco-Euskal Herriko Unibertsitatea (the University of the Basque Country) and the Universidad Pública de Navarra (the Public University of Navarre).

The public universities of the BAC, Navarre, and Iparralde[45] comply in one way or another with Article 8.1.e of the Language Charter. In the BAC, we will examine the University of the Basque Country (UPV-EHU). Since its creation in 1980,[46] it provides for 70 percent of the research realized in the BAC. The University of the Basque Country consists of thirty-one schools grouped on three campuses (one in each historical territory).[47] Among the three administrative areas, this public university concentrates the biggest offering of higher education in Euskara, and the highest number of students and professors who study or work in this language. For the 2017–2018 academic year, the UPV-EHU enrolled 44,076 students,[48] and almost half of those students decided to study in Basque.[49] This number has increased over time, as shown by figure 5.1:

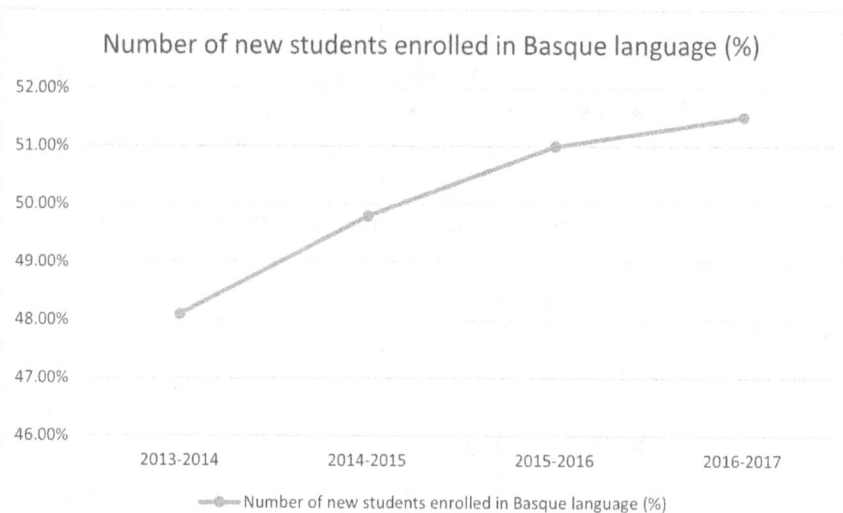

Figure 5.1. Number of new students enrolled in Basque language (%) at the University of the Basque Country (UPV/EHU) between 2013 and 2017[50]

Figure 5.1 shows that just over 48 percent of students at the UPV-EHU decided to study in Basque for the 2013–2014 academic year. This number has been increasing over the years; for the 2016–2017 academic year, among the newly arrived undergraduates, 51.5 percent decided to study in Basque. If we consider news in the press, we can see how this number is slowly increasing, attaining 43.4 percent for 2023–2024.[51] The offering of studying *in* Euskara in higher education seems to be working in the BAC. As a matter of fact, when consulting the linguistic model of origin from students who take the university entrance exam, for the year 2019, most students were coming from Model D.[52] This might explain the increase in students choosing to conduct their university studies in Euskara: They are used to using the Basque language in a learning environment, and thus, want to continue using it in higher education.

For the region of Navarre, the Public University of Navarre (UPNA) was created in 1987 by the Parliament of Navarre, and in 1989 this Navarrese university started teaching to 500 students.[53] UPNA consists of three campuses, and for the 2022–2023 academic year had 10,000 students.[54] Interestingly, regarding the Basque language, for the 2020–2021 school year, the UPNA announced an increase in its offer in Euskara.[55] In fact, in 2020–2021 the UPNA offered a degree in history and heritage, and another in nursing, in Euskara. Yet, the publication of the 2020 UPNA personnel in the *Official Gazette of Navarre*, shows that out of 563 university employees, only thirty-three have a bilingual profile.[56] This shows that accessing higher education or UPNA administration in Basque is rather limited. Trying to improve the accessibility of higher education in Basque in Navarre, the UPNA presented in 2021 the Master Plan for Basque Language Teaching 2021–2024 (*Plan Director de las Enseñanzas en Euskera 2021–2024*).[57] The plan recognizes the percentage of students who speak Basque is slowly increasing, and therefore, the UPNA should implement more teaching in Basque. Therefore, the plan's objective is to steadily increase the availability of credits taught in Basque in UPNA.

For Iparralde and higher education in Basque, the situation is different. As we have discussed in part I, chapter 2, the legal framework of France is not very progressive toward the Basque language, and as we have analyzed chapter 4, public education in regional languages in France also has more obstacles than in Hegoalde. Therefore, there is only one undergraduate degree in only one university where one can learn in Basque.[58] The university we are going to compare to the UPV-EHU and UPNA is, thus, the University of Pau and the Adour Region (UPPA)[59] that offers an undergraduate degree in Basque studies.[60] Using information provided by UPPA's website, for the academic year 2017–2018, twenty-one students participated in the first year of an undergraduate degree in Basque studies. The goal of the Basque studies program of the UPPA (as listed on its website) is to help Basque-speaking students strengthen their knowledge of the Basque language as well as broaden and deepen their knowledge of the Basque culture. After getting this undergraduate degree, the students can study for three different masters, two being in another university:

> Option 1 is the master's in Basque studies[61] (*Master Etudes Basques*) at the University Bordeaux Montaigne.[62] Despite this master's program belonging to the University of Bordeaux Montaigne, it is taught in Bayonne and is linked to the IKER research center[63] (research center on the Basque language and Basque texts) at the UPPA campus. This master's program aims to prepare students who want to continue research in this subject or become teachers of primary education in the Seaska immersive schools.

Option 2 is the master's in teaching, education and training professions[64] (*Master mention Métiers de l'Enseignement, de l'Éducation et de la formation*) at the University Bordeaux Montaigne for students who want to teach in secondary education in public or private schools.

Option 3 is the master's (Master Mention Métiers de l'enseignement, de l'éducation et de la formation-Second degré (MEEF) Lettre et Langues). This master's program aims to prepare students to become teachers of primary education both for public schools and Seaska schools.

After obtaining a master's in Iparralde, students have the option of working toward a PhD in Basque studies at the IKER research center, which belongs to the University Bordeaux Montaigne.

Finally, when discussing higher education in Euskara in Iparralde, the program "Eskola futura" must be mentioned. This program is not limited to Iparralde or Euskara but is rather a cross-border collaboration between different administrations and universities. The Euroregion NAEN led this project, and the EU[65] cofinanced it via interreg POCTEFA[66] funds (2014–2020 program[67]). This project sets a new scheme to help students access education and exams required to teach in French/Basque and French/Occitan bilingual schools to fill the need of teachers who can teach in those languages in France. This shows local administrations and the universities are collaborating within the legal limits to improve education in Euskara via the training of teachers.

Implementing Basque studies from the undergraduate program through to the PhD is a major step forward for the teaching of Euskara in higher education in Iparralde. However, it is mostly limited to the teaching *of* Euskara rather than *in* Euskara.

The example of the higher education offer in Euskara in Iparralde shows two contrasting views: On the one hand, this example shows the strict linguistic limits set by the French system when it comes to education. On the other hand, it shows the tenacity of Basque speakers and the sensibility of universities and local administrations to include their language in all stages of education and be successful, making the most of what is allowed under the limits set by the law.

However, it is still not possible for a student in Iparralde to study anything other than Basque studies in Euskara.[68] The student would need to cross the border. Indeed, the reality of the offering in Basque in higher education results in the migration of students. Students in Iparralde or Navarre who want to study in Basque usually move to the BAC to do so. It would be interesting to have public data analyzing the number of students coming from Iparralde or Navarre to go study in Basque in the BAC. Despite looking, the author could not find any public record. More research could be performed on this matter.

It is essential to explore the role of public actors in education. In fact, since education is one of the duties of a state, public institutions have a lot to say about it. Regarding education in Euskara, we have seen the different degrees of responsibility taken between the governments of the BAC and Navarre, each with a very different approach to funding to create more teachers proficient in Basque or to introduce further Basque language use in schools. In addition, we also note that, sometimes, it is not a regional government nor the ministry of education that acts to develop the Basque language in education. For instance, in the case of Iparralde, a public institution helped by a cross-border agreement is taking on this role of promotor of Basque in education. The other side of the coin is shown by the constant difficulties posed by courts when trying to expand the teaching of regional languages in French public schools.

We have seen how public actors can influence the reality of education in Euskara: Courts, institutions, and administration are essential. Yet, education does not fall only in the hands of public actors. Indeed, private actors have also a lot to say on the subject.

Private Actors

As is often the case, the education offered in the Basque Country is not merely in the hands of public institutions. Private schools also play a role.[69] Research on private actors is often limited to private schools, but it is crucial to study private individuals as well. Parents and the choice they make when enrolling their children into school say a lot when analyzing the relationship between law and its context. Finally, a proper contextualization of education and Euskara would not be complete without the input of teachers.

Ikastola Schools

Ikastola schools are key actors in the Basque schooling ecosystem. One cannot understand the richness and interconnection of education and the Basque language on both sides of the Pyrenees without understanding the place that Ikastolas hold in Basque schooling.

The Ikastola schools preceded the current legislation on the Basque language in education. These schools were the first to implement an immersive model of teaching in Basque. Their model currently falls under the "Model D" in the BAC and Navarre. As explained by Masa,[70] Ikastolas started as a popular initiative, as a reaction to the only two education alternatives that were present at that time: public and private. In fact, these two options did not meet the needs of a group of Basque people, who considered Euskara as a key element of their identity. Before the Spanish Civil War, one could count about thirty Ikastola schools in the regions of Bizkaia and Gipuzkoa. After 1947, Ikastola schools started to reemerge clandestinely, and in the 1960s, the spread of these schools became stronger and harder to control. In Iparralde, the movement of Ikastola schools happened in a parallel manner. On this side of the border the Basques did not suffer from the same authoritarian regime as in Hegoalde, but they were still dealing with acculturation that took place over decades which led to the discontent of some parents. These parents decided, in 1966, to create the first class entirely taught in Basque in the city of Baiona (Bayonne). In 1969, the first Ikastola schools opened their doors.[71]

The Ikastola schools in Iparralde have been united under the Seaska association since the beginning (May 24, 1969).[72] Seaska is one part of a broader association called Ikastolen Elkartea, which encompasses all the regional groupings of Ikastola schools. This association was created to group the alliance of Ikastolas from Gipuzkoa, Bizkaia, Araba, Navarre, and Seaska. This association works in a transborder fashion, elaborated further in a previous article.[73] Yet, while the Ikastola schools are cooperatives in Hegoalde, they are "associative schools" in Iparralde.

One might wonder where Ikastola schools belong in the Basque schooling ecosystem. Born as a social movement, these schools managed to enter the legal arena in different forms. In the BAC, after hiding in the dark, Ikastolas entered the official arena of education with the adoption of the Statute of Autonomy and Euskara being authorized in school. Indeed, with the Royal Decree 1049/1979 of April 20, 1979, Ikastola schools could legally be recognized as schools.[74] Later, the Basque Parliament adopted Law 15/1983, creating the legal status of Ikastolas.[75] This law created "Euskal Ikastolen Erakundea" (the Basque Institute of Ikastolas), a public law entity with its own and independent legal personality, linked to the department of education and culture of the BAC. The objective of this institute was to promote and offer education in the Basque language at all non-university levels.

Article 1 of Law 15/1983 read: "The 'Basque Institute of Ikastolas' is created as a Public Law Entity, with its own legal personality and independent from the Administration of the Autonomous Community [. . .]. The creation of this Autonomous Organ will be considered as *a transitory step toward the consolidation of the Basque Public School* [. . .]." The expression emphasized in Article 1 was brought before the Constitutional Tribunal by the central state (STC 137/1986, November 6, 1986[76]). It was argued that Ikastolas could not be a part of the public schooling system: Since Ikastolas were offering education in Basque, they were too specific to the BAC to be extended to the rest of Spain, and therefore, could not be considered as public education. The Constitutional Tribunal in 1986 interpreted the concept of "Basque Public Education" more neutrally. In this decision (F.J.1), the Constitutional Tribunal clarified that when talking about "Basque Public Education," one is talking about "a group of schools sustained with public funds, in which, without prejudice to the teaching of Castilian, the language that is used is Basque."[77] Therefore, introducing Ikastolas in "Basque Public Education" was judged to be constitutional. In addition, using decision 82/1986 (of June 26, 1986), the Constitutional Tribunal validated the possibility of teaching in Euskara, since it has constitutional validity via Article 3.2 and also validity by the Statute of Autonomy's Article 6.1 (F.J.1).

This decision by the Constitutional Tribunal, however, did not shed light on the legal nature of Ikastolas in the BAC: Were they public or private? Law 15/1983 seemed to place them into the public education sphere, but the court's interpretation seemed to place them into the private education category. The Basque Parliament tried to resolve this issue with Law 10/1988 (June 29, 1988) on the integration of Ikastolas in public education.[78] This law set Ikastola schools, in its statement of reasons, as a third alternative in the school realm. In fact, the law mentioned public schools, private schools, and Ikastola schools separately.[79] Yet, this law also established the basis for the then-upcoming integration of Ikastolas into either the public or the private education sphere.

The law from 1988 was followed by Law 1/1993 of February 19, 1993, on Basque public education.[80] This law set a three-month period for Ikastolas to decide if they wanted to join the public sphere or the private sphere. This phenomenon was erroneously identified by Bertile, when she explained that Ikastolas are divided into two regimes: those belonging to the public system and those belonging to the private sphere.[81] In reality, some Ikastolas decided to join the public system, and therefore became *Eskolas*, and others decided to remain a private entity and remained *Ikastolas*. This means that Ikastolas only belong to the private sphere now (after 1993), and those who entered the public system do not belong to the Ikastola family anymore. Thus, Ikastola schools provide "Model D" in private education in the BAC and Navarre. Even if Bertile's reading lacked precision regarding the Eskolas, one could still see that Ikastola schools have two legal regimes, not in the public/private dichotomy but rather in the Hegoalde/Iparralde dichotomy. In fact, as explained above, Ikastolas in Iparralde are associative schools, whereas in Hegoalde they are mainly cooperatives.

Yet, the interest of the analysis does not rest in the dichotomy between the two legal regimes of Ikastolas. The focus, in this case, must be shifted toward the law of 1993. In fact, if we look at the "law in books," we only understand that the Basque Parliament wanted to avoid a tripartite division of education. If we look at the context, however, we realize much more was at stake than reducing the educational system to the public/private model.

The political climate surrounding the law of 1993 was extremely tense. The Basque Parliament was in the hands of PNV-EAJ[82] in 1993 (after the elections of 1990) with twenty-two seats, followed by PSE-EE[83] with sixteen seats, and Herri Batasuna (HB)[84] with thirteen seats.[85] During the early nineties that followed the dark eighties in the Basque Country, HB was a very strong opposition. One can recall the active role that the ETA and state police violence had in the politics in the BAC in the eighties as well as the economic difficulties of the region. Even if the atmosphere was cooling down from that of the eighties, Law 1/1993 was adopted in a contentious climate. Violence was still present in politics and the everyday life of Basques. There were twenty-five ETA victims in 1990, forty-six in 1991, twenty-six in 1992, and fourteen in 1993. Some of the targets were politicians, mainly from PP and PSE-PSOE. In 1984, ETA killed Enrique Casas Vila (PSE-PSOE) and in 1995, ETA killed Gregorio Ordóñez Fenollar (PP). During the same period, HB, being a very active left nationalist party, suffered from the repression of the GAL.[86] Javier Pérez de Arenaza y Segorbe (HB) and Santiago Brouard (HB) were killed in 1984, followed by the murder attempt of Alfonso Salazar Uriarte in 1989 (which instead killed the postman who carried the letter bomb). The issue of Basque schools was immediately politicized and escalated. As explained by the example of Teacher 1,[87] the division among those who wanted to join the public system and those who wanted to keep the identity of Ikastola schools created tensions in towns and cities, furthering the already existing tensions in Basque society.

In this tense political climate, where a law was introduced to clarify and simplify the education offering in the BAC, one could ask where the issue of Law 1/1993 was. The issue was money. Indeed, by not entering the public schooling system, Ikastolas would not receive all the financial help they had been receiving from the Basque government. It is important to note that even if the majority was held by the PNV-EAJ, the matters on education were in the hands of PSE-PSOE—a non-nationalist party. This side of the debate claimed that the option of entering the public education system must be offered to Ikastolas. In fact, Ikastolas "created" the current immersive education system in Basque and, therefore, should be offered the recognition of their public service by entering the public school realm. On the other side of the debate, opponents claimed Ikastolas should keep the funding while remaining private, since they were an initiative of citizens when studying in Basque was not available. The position on either joining the public education system or remaining in private education became a political position.

In the end, Ikastolas were mainly pragmatic and made decisions according to their financial needs. Teacher 1 remembers how, in the case of the Ikastola of their small town of Gipuzkoa, the decision was clear when looking at the finances: The Ikastola could not sustain itself without the funding that was being received from the Basque government. They decided that offering education in Basque to the children of the town was more important than keeping the Ikastola status. This brought plenty of challenges, since the public school and the Ikastola decided to merge. This meant a lot of work from both sides trying to join both philosophies and methodologies. In the case of Teacher 1's town, the merging schools decided to work with a mediator from the beginning. Because the shared goal was to offer free education in Euskara to the children of the town, they eventually managed to join forces and create a public school. In other cases, Ikastolas prioritized their independence—notably the independence of their educational methods—and decided to remain in the private sphere.

Finally, in Navarre,[88] there are fifteen Ikastola schools today.[89] When analyzing the Ikastola schools in Navarre, one must take into account the linguistic zoning of the territory.[90] Five of these schools are in the Basque-speaking area (Altsasu, Bera,

Elizondo, Etxarri-Aranatz, and Lesaka), four are in the non-Basque-speaking area (Lodosa, Tutera, Viana, and Irunberri), and six are in the Mixed area (Atarrabia, Iruñea, Lizarra, Zizur Txikia, and Tafalla and Zangoza—which, since June 2017, moved from the non-Basque speaking area to the Mixed area). Therefore, as of 2018, two-thirds of Ikastolas are outside the Basque-speaking area. This shows, first, the commitment of parents and of Basque speakers in the Mixed and non-Basque-speaking areas toward the Basque language. Second, it shows that Ikastolas in Navarre are still following the same purpose that made them start: filling the gap in education, where full education in Euskara is not available. Third, in the Basque-speaking area, Ikastola schools have the same role as in the BAC: to provide a private alternative to the public system.

As we analyze the context surrounding Ikastola schools, we notice that they were, and still are, constantly communicating with the law. The dialogue starts from the inception of Ikastolas, when they influenced the law by showing and creating a demand for the presence of Basque in education. They began as a bottom-up operation: They were started by the norm users. Oihartzabal (see Appendix 2) underscored how the drafters of the schooling models based their approach to the three educational models (A, B and D) on the work that Ikastolas had already done. The function of law as a regulator is shown when they shaped the Basque public school (Eskola). In that process, there was also a dialogue between law and Ikastolas, and between political parties and citizens. Finally, law also affects Ikastolas. In the case of Ikastolas in Iparralde and in Navarre, the lack of access to immersive education in Basque woke up the civil society, leading to the creation of Ikastolas. In Iparralde, the associative schools of Ikastolas are filling the gap of private and public education in which immersive schooling in Basque is not available. In Navarre, Ikastolas are mainly present outside the Basque-speaking areas, where access to the Model D is not available for parents and their children. Ikastolas, being a dynamic phenomenon, constantly in interaction and dialogue with law and civil society, are an excellent example of the conversation between law and context. They showcase a bottom-up dynamic about immersive schooling in Euskara. They are also a key private actor to consider when painting the Basque education landscape.

Yet Ikastola schools are not the only private actors with a say about education. One should not forget that parents, i.e., the norm users, created and still manage Ikastolas. Along the same lines, by choosing to which school they will send their children, parents strongly affect the educational reality for the Basque language.

Parents' Choice and Education in Basque

When looking at the context of the legal framework of education and the Basque language, it is clear that parents play a key role. These private actors are the recipients of the legal rules since they decide which educational option to choose for their children. They are norm users. The parents' choice in matters of education and language determines policies and changes in the future. They are also the ones using the possibilities (or restrictions) produced by law, and their use of law is what gives meaning to the black letter law. This analysis will be developed in three steps, taking one administrative territory at a time.

Data from the BAC

To understand the legal framework of Euskara and education in the BAC in its context, we should analyze the data available on school enrollment. Both the data on public and private schools must be taken into consideration here, since Ikastola schools belong to the private category, and Models B and A tend to be more present in private schools than in public schools. Regarding the BAC, for the 2021–2022 academic year,[91] 52 percent of primary education students attended a public school, and 50 percent of secondary education did so too. Therefore, as can be seen from figure 5.2, during the first stages of education, the decision to educate children in public or private school is almost equal.

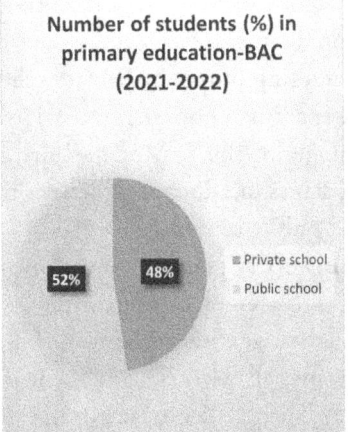
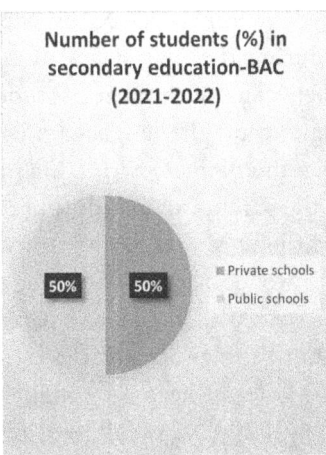

Figure 5.2. Choice of education in the BAC, private versus public, for primary and secondary school children in the 2021–2022 school year (%).

Regarding the number of students enrolled in infant and primary education by language in the BAC, figure 5.3[92] explains the evolution from 1983 to 2020.

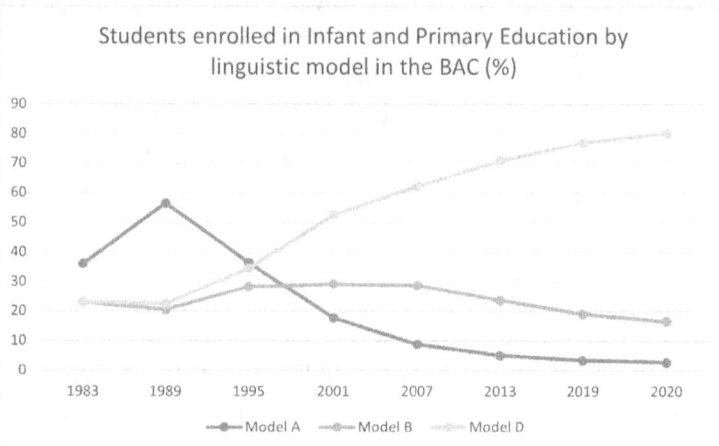

Figure 5.3. Percentage of students enrolled in infant and primary education by linguistic model in the BAC (1983–2020)

During these first stages of education, as can be seen in figure 5.3, for 2020–2021, more than 80 percent of children attend Model D for primary education, followed by Model B, scoring 16.5 percent. This shows how, during the first stages of education in the BAC, even if the difference between the number of students attending public or private schools is not significant, the language model that parents choose shows a large gap between the models, with a high percentage for the D Model. Thus, in the BAC, the parents' choice during the first stages of education inclines mainly toward the D Model, both in private and public schools.

If we look at the data about non-university general education (figure 5.4),[93] we see the apparent pattern of early stages of education is replicated until students reach the last year of their general education. This data shows Model D keeps the highest score overall with 68.1 percent of students in 2020–2021, followed by Model B with 16.6 percent and ending with Model A with 14.7 percent.

Context of the Basque Language and Education

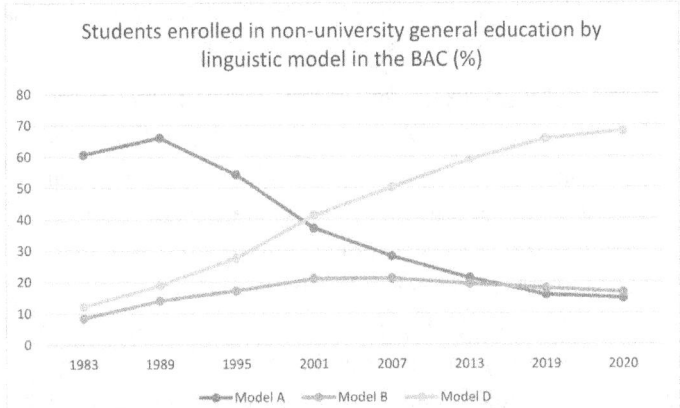

Figure 5.4. Percentage of students enrolled in non-university general education by linguistic model in the BAC (1983–2020)

Regarding further stages of education, the division between public and private schools of students seems to remain almost equal in 2022–2023: for bachillerato (Baccalaureate),[94] public schools attract 47 percent of students; and for the different vocational training cycles, public schools hold 57 percent of students (see figure 5.5[95]).

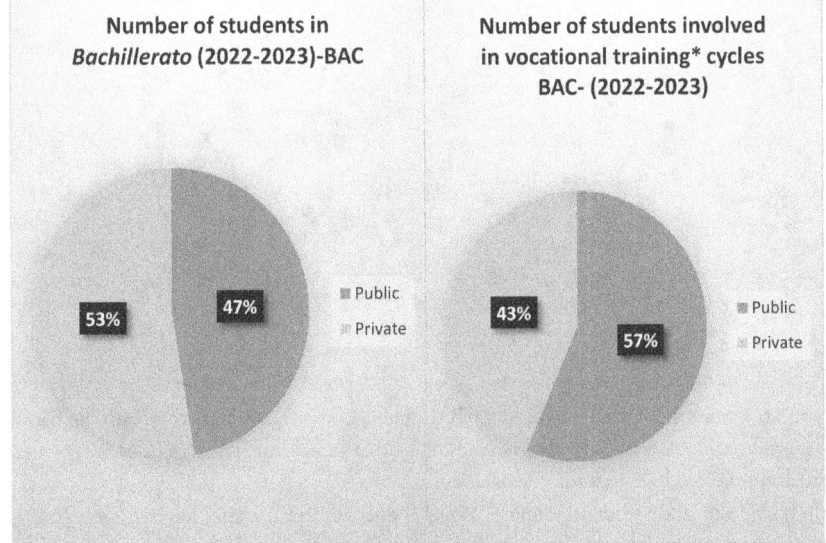

Figure 5.5. Choice of education in the BAC, private versus public, for bachillerato versus vocational training cycles in 2022–2023 (%).

*The data for vocational training cycles includes intermediate and higher vocational training, learning of tasks and specialization courses of vocational training.

During the academic year 2022–2023, for bachillerato, 67 percent of students followed Model D, 7 percent followed Model B, and 26 percent followed Model A (figure 5.5). Despite the margins being closer than in primary education, the tendency of students to gravitate toward Model D, therefore, also happens at this stage. For vocational training,[96] on the other hand, most students are in Model A. In fact, regarding vocational training, Model A attracts 52 percent of students, Model B gets 21 percent, and Model D has 27 percent (figure 5.6).[97] Considering that the offering and demand of linguistic models are linked, this might indicate that the offering of vocational training is mainly in Model A, and therefore, students attend mainly Model A. This could also indicate that most students of vocational training want to study in Model A, and thus, the offering of Model A is higher.

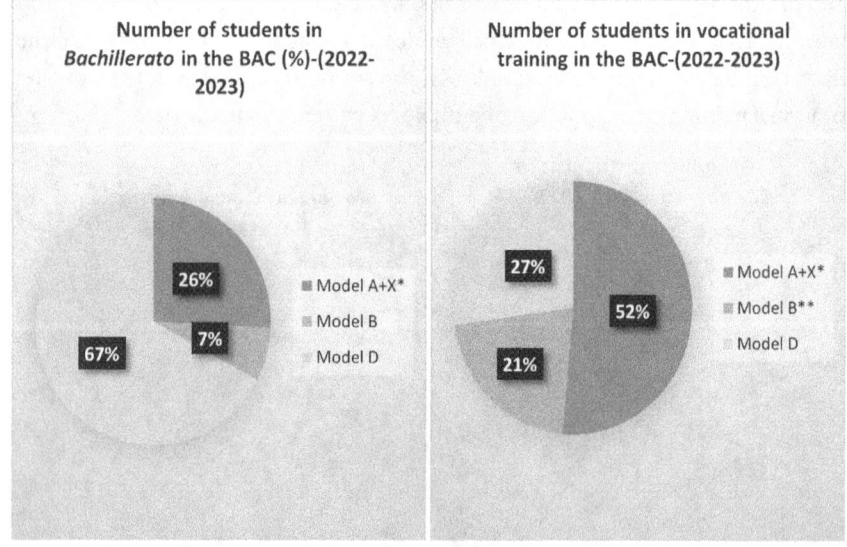

Figure 5.6. Choice of linguistic model in the BAC, public and private schools combined, for bachillerato and vocational training students in the 2022–2023 school year (%)
*The data provided by Eustat joins Model A and X.
** In bachillerato and vocational training, Model B does not legally exist. However, some groups of students are taught some subjects in the Basque language, assimilating this category, known as reinforced Model A, into the linguistic model (Model B).

Searching in the list of vocational training cycles in the BAC for the 2020–2021 academic year,[98] in a word search by models, Model A scored 780 programs, while Model D scored only 159 (Model B scored 77 results). This preliminary search shows the gap between A and D models in vocational training in the BAC. Searching for the reasons behind the difference between vocational training and general secondary education or higher education seems to direct us toward the socioeconomic background of the students, or their Basque language proficiency. This correlation calls for further study, falling outside the scope of this book. However, during the interviews with teachers (examined below), the issues between academic success and language, and socioeconomic background, already arose.

Finally, data for the 2022–2023 academic year mimics the above-mentioned tendencies (figure 5.6). Adding up all non-university stages of education, 68 percent of students attend Model D, followed by Model B with 17 percent, and Model A at 15 percent. This is shown in figure 5.7 below.[99]

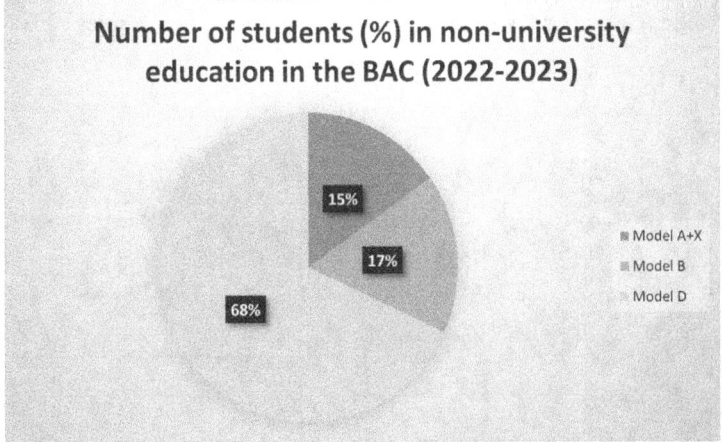

Figure 5.7. Choice of educational model in the BAC for all non-university students in the 2022–2023 school year (%).

Among these students, 53 percent are enrolled in public school, while 47 percent are enrolled in private school (figure 5.8).[100] Figure 5.8 examines the linguistic model chosen by the parents for their children both in private and public schools. The 2023–2024 data shows the overall preference for Model D

(82 percent in public schools and 54 percent in private schools), with Model B scoring higher in private schools (30 percent).

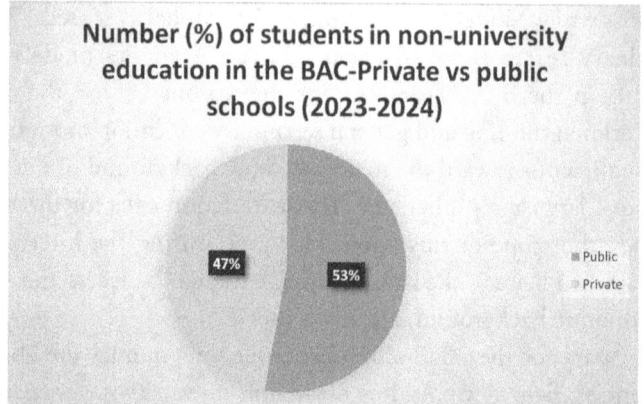

Figure 5.8. Choice of public versus private schools in non-university education in the BAC for the 2023–2024 school year (%).

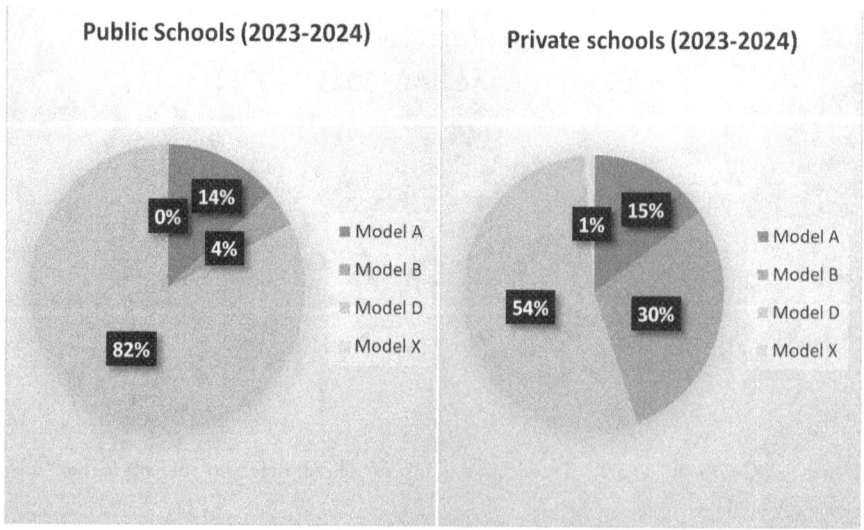

Figure 5.9. Educational model chosen in the BAC for all non-university students, in public versus private school, for the 2023–2024 school year (%).

When asked about the reasons why parents send their children to her school that only offers Model D, Teacher 1 explained there are a variety of factors. First,

Context of the Basque Language and Education   151

her school is the only school offering Model D in her town, attracting the parents who want their children to be schooled in immersive fashion in Euskara. Another element helping parents to choose is the physical proximity of the school and/or the parents' linguistic background (being Basque speakers or not). However, Teacher 1 emphasized that the parents' financial situation is increasingly a key factor. She noticed that the socioeconomic background of the parents is changing. She is seeing an increasing demand for public schooling, not only because of the belief in free public education or the linguistic schooling system, but also because families cannot afford other options.

When asked about why she chose to send her two daughters to an Ikastola school in Oñati, a Basque-speaking town of Gipuzkoa,[101] Susana Arrese[102] explained that she was motivated to do so by practicality. She also had an emotional attachment to Txantxiku Ikastola, where she had studied. During her research, the author encountered various parents who brought up their emotional attachment to the school or Ikastola. Overall, parents seem both pragmatic and sometimes emotional when deciding where to enroll their children.

Data from Navarre

The latest data available regarding school choice in Navarre shows a vast spread between different linguistic models across the years (from kindergarten to the end of high school). Table 5.1 shows this spread:[103]

2022–2023 Academic Year								
General non-university education								
Students by linguistic model								
	MODEL G		MODEL A		MODEL B		MODEL D	
	Public	Private	Public	Private	Public	Private	Public	Private
Early primary education (2nd cycle)	4,673	4,246	2,635	808		28	3,759	1,099
Primary education	13,490	9,665	5,834	2,063		90	8,639	2,499

Secondary Education	11,703	8,570	1,361	882	7		5,434	1,656
Bachillerato*	3,555	3,131	199	123			1,912	352
Training cycles*	9,037	2,750					934	
Basic Vocational Training Cycles	658						42	

* Includes face-to-face, evening, and distance learning.

Table 5.1. Choice of educational model in Navarre for non-university students (in all three linguistic areas combined) for the 2022–2023 school year (number of students).

This table illustrates that for the 2022–2023 academic year, Model B is at the bottom of the list of the choice of parents in Navarre across all ages. This, however, is probably because of the limited availability of this model. Both in public and private schools, Model G contains the highest number of students. In both kinds of schools, Model G is followed by Model D, and Model A comes in third. To analyze the issue of linguistic model choices by parents, we need to zoom in to see more concrete data.

Using data from table 5.1, we can see that, for 2022–2023, the percentage of students attending a public school for primary education is 66 percent.

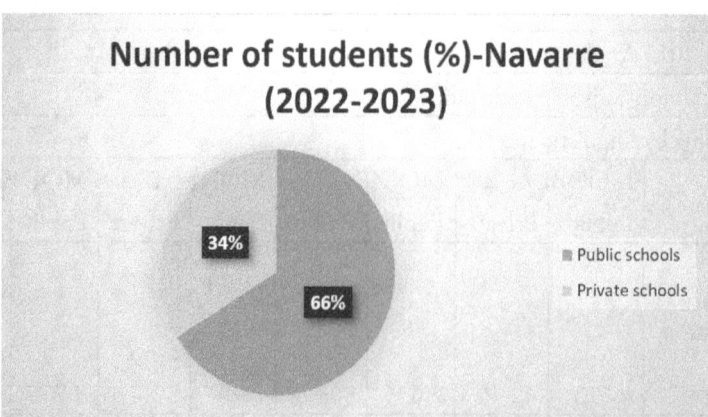

Figure 5.10. Choice of education in Navarre, private versus public, for early primary school children in the 2022–2023 school year (%).

If we look at the choice of linguistic model in Navarre, for primary education (figure 5.10), both public and private schools joined, 55 percent of students attend school in Model G, 26 percent in Model D, and 19 percent in Model A. Model B scores close to 0 percent. In the choice of the parents regarding the linguistic model of their children for primary school, we can already notice the big division that exists in Navarre about language.

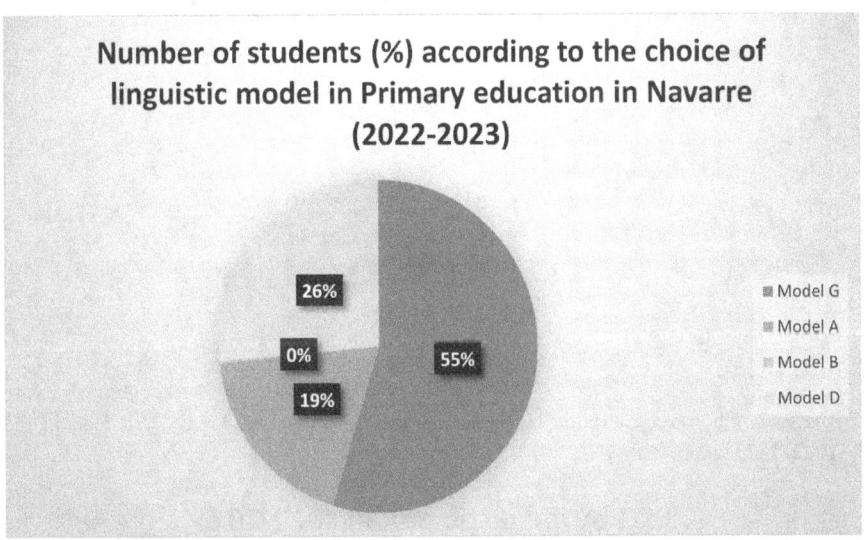

Figure 5.11 Choice of educational model in Navarre for primary school children in the 2022–2023 school year (%).

Regarding the primary stages of education in Navarre, as the previous figures show, we can notice the presence of the social cleavage concerning language in the choice of the parents of the linguistic model of their children. For further information on the schooling system in Navarre, we must analyze the mandatory secondary education (ESO). During these secondary schooling years, data shows the preference of public schools persists, with 62 percent of students attending public schooling facilities in Navarre for the 2022–2023 academic year (figure 5.12). Yet, regarding linguistic models, Model G enjoys an increase, scoring 68 percent of students (figure 5.12). Model D still holds second place with a steady 24 percent. Model A decreases to 8 percent, and Model B comes in last with a score close to 0 percent.

As we can see, the pattern repeats itself with more intensity the further on the trajectory of the education system we go in Navarre, with a wide preference for public schooling over private schooling and wide preference for Model G, followed by Model D.

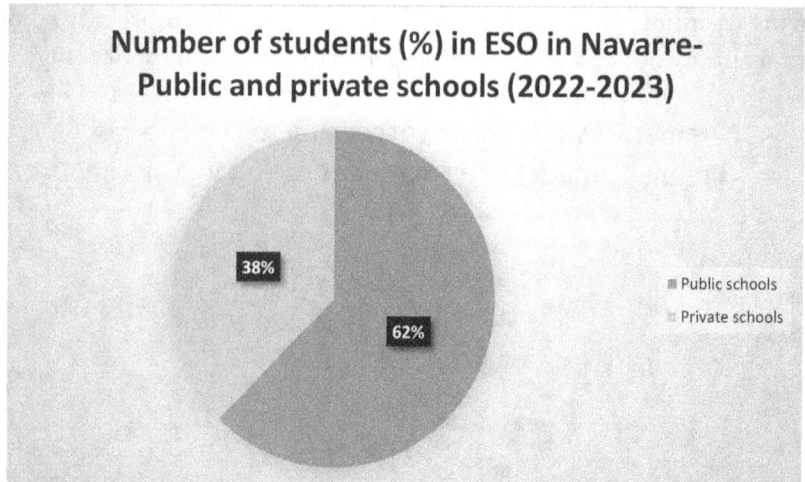

Figure 5.12. Choice of education in Navarre, private versus public, for ESO students in the 2022–2023 school year (%).

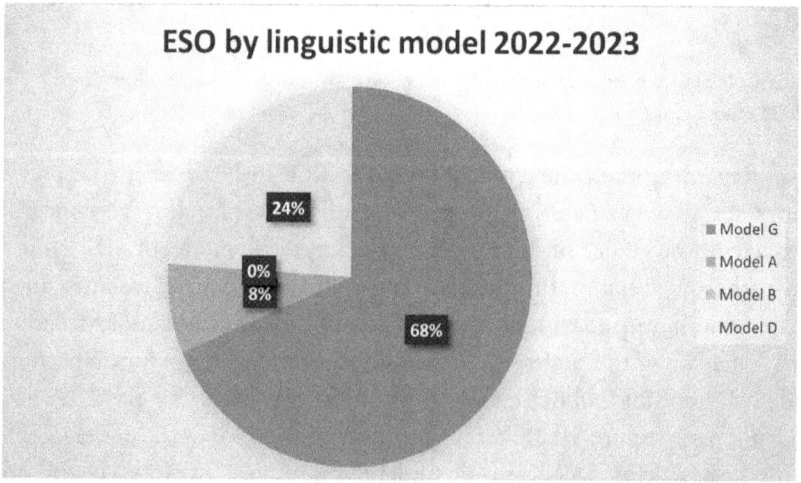

Figure 5.13. Choice of educational model in Navarre for ESO students in the 2022–2023 school year (%).

When we arrive at the last stages of "general" education in Navarre (during the two last years of high school—bachillerato), the choice for public schooling increases once again to 61 percent of students for the 2022–2023 school year (figure 5.14).

The tendency noted in the earlier stages of education is also confirmed in the data (figure 5.15) regarding linguistic models of bachillerato in 2022–2023. In fact, Model G increases to 72 percent of students, followed by Model D with 24 percent, and Model A with 4 percent.[104]

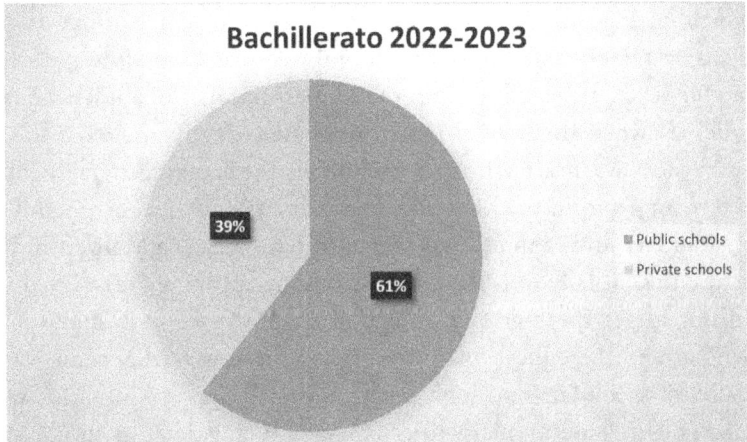

Figure 5.14. Choice of education in Navarre, private versus public, for ESO students in the 2022–2023 school year (%).

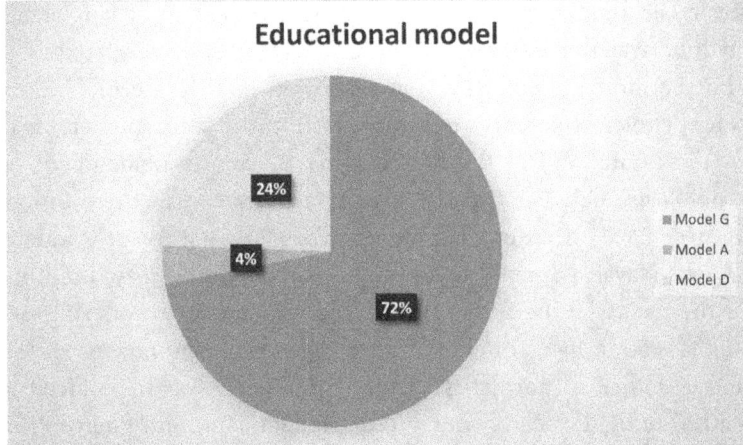

Figure 5.15. Choice of educational model in Navarre for bachillerato in the 2022–2023 school year (%).

One first observation could be that, unlike in the BAC, the linguistic model preferences seem much more heterogenous in Navarre. Indeed, the first model chosen is the one with teaching entirely in Spanish, but second place is held by the model in which the curriculum is taught entirely in Basque. Model A (teaching in Spanish, plus a Basque-language class) holds third place, while the model that offers the curriculum being taught evenly in both languages does not capture the attention of Navarrese parents. Yet, it is worth noting that the choice of parents in Navarre regarding linguistic models is extremely conditioned by linguistic areas. Therefore, it is highly predictable (even expected) to find the highest number of students enrolled in Model G, when this model is the most offered (this model is the most offered in the Navarrese territory as a whole, in the biggest geographical parts of the territory, and in the highest-populated cities). Also, there tends to be fewer secondary and schools, and they also tend to be centralized in bigger towns or cities, usually in Mixed or non-Basque-speaking areas. Finally, one should not forget the high percentage of students of the Basque-speaking area who attend the educational offerings in the BAC rather than Navarre, especially for secondary and higher education.[105] Thus, taking into account that since 2017 some municipalities changed linguistic areas in Navarre to integrate into the Mixed area (and one to integrate into the Basque-speaking area), it would be interesting to see whether the upcoming data shows an increase in enrollment in the models that include the Basque language, since those will be available in more territories in Navarre.

Furthermore, recent issues have showed in the case of Navarre the enrollment choice of parents does not tell the entire story. In fact, regarding Iruñea (the capital and in the Mixed area),[106] parents' demand for Model D has not been met. For the 2020–2021 academic year, the municipality of Iruñea decided to reduce the number of slots granted to Model D in schools. The Navarra Suma[107] coalition leads the municipality (holding thirteen of the twenty-seven seats) and decided to reduce the offering of early stages of education in Basque for children aged eighteen months and under, claiming a "return to normality." Indeed, Model D was introduced in the 2016–2017 academic year,[108] notably in the Donibane and Fuerte Príncipe-Printzearen Harresi schools, which now have shifted again toward offering models in Spanish with English, and no Model D. This decision created tensions among the political opposition (notably EH Bildu and Geroa Bai) but also from the parents who want to educate their children in Euskara and now see their chances of doing so extremely reduced. As a matter of fact, with the regression of these two schools into a Spanish model, only two public schools—Txantrea and Arrotxapea—would offer Model D in Iruñea, both in the northern part of the city. Both schools being on one side of the city hinders the choice of parents since, as explained by the teachers interviewed in this research, proximity to the school is an extremely important factor influencing the choice of parents, notably when children are very young. Also, the lower the number of schools offering Model D, the lower the number of spots available for children.

When analyzing the landscape of education in Euskara in Navarre, we discover that linguistic division—and by extension the schooling division—creates complications in everyday life. Certainly, the division of the educational offering based on the linguistic areas has a social impact, perpetuating the linguistic inequalities in the different areas of Navarre. For instance, in the Mixed area, there is a large increase in the number of Basque speakers, notably because of the schooling models available. Yet, the impact is limited, as the Basque speakers find themselves frustrated in everyday life by facing limitations in accessing media, administration, and higher education in Euskara. Another example concerns the Basque-speaking area, where 10 percent of the population of Navarre lives, and find themselves in "linguistic isolation."[109] Additionally, other everyday life activities are inconvenient for Basque speakers: Most medical facilities are in Pamplona (Mixed area), making it more difficult for Basque speakers to obtain medical advice or services in Basque.

Data from Iparralde

There is no data from the French Ministry of Education regarding education in Iparralde, since education is administered mostly centrally, unlike in Spain. In the databases accessible on the websites of the French National Education Ministry, the Academy of Bordeaux, and the Department of Pyrenees-Atlantiques, no information is made available about Basque in schools, or even regional languages in general. The information available (on regional languages and number of students) appears in the national data on secondary education and learning of languages.[110] This data analyzes the number of students in secondary education in relation to the second language they are studying (data for the year 2016). In table 5.2, we notice that 0.7 percent of secondary level students study a regional language in France. This percentage considers all levels of secondary schooling and all models offered to learn regional languages (from a couple of hours per week, to immersive systems in private schools). Table 5.2 also shows the predominance of public schooling over private schooling in secondary education. Even if table 5.2 gives us an indication of the ratio (0.7%) of students studying regional languages compared to other (and bigger) languages, this data joins all regional languages taught in France together and, therefore, cannot give us specific data regarding the Basque language.

	Total of students learning languages	Total of students studying regional languages
Total	5,579,354	38,509
Percentage	100 percent	0.7 percent
Public schools	4,398,836	31,558
Private schools	1,180,518	6,951

Table 5.2. Number of students studying regional languages in secondary education in France in 2016-2017.

Consulting data on regional languages, the Department of Evaluation, Forecasting, and Performance published an information note[111] in November 2021 on "The teaching of languages in secondary education in 2020." In this information note, data shows that for the 2020–2021 academic year, 1 percent of students studying secondary education in France (public and private schools included) study a regional language. Yet, here as well, all regional languages taught in France are grouped together.

Luckily, the POBL's website provides some answers. In fact, one can find information provided in the database to help parents to find schools where Basque is taught. For the 2018–2019 academic year, eighty-five primary schools offered the teaching of the Basque language in bilingual fashion (bilingual here meaning an hourly parity between teaching in French and Basque) and thirteen schools offered Basque in immersive fashion (only in kindergarten).[112] For private schools, the database separates religious schools and Seaska schools.[113] There are thirty-two private primary schools offering bilingual classes and sixteen private immersive schools (also only in kindergarten). Finally, for primary schooling, twenty-six Ikastola schools in Iparralde offer immersive education in Basque. The inclusion of some experimentation with immersive schooling in early stages of public education in Iparralde[114] is possible because of the protocol signed in 2011 between the Academy of Bordeaux, the National Education Ministry, and the POBL.[115]

As for secondary education,[116] there are fourteen public secondary schools offering bilingual education and thirteen private, Catholic, secondary schools. For immersive secondary education, there are three Seaska secondary schools. Table 5.3 illustrates this data.[117]

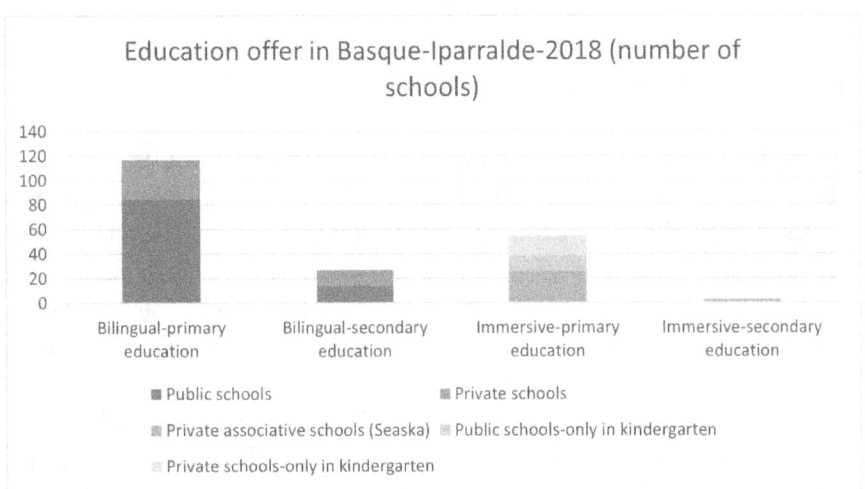

Table 5.3. Number of bilingual and immersive education offerings in Euskara in Iparralde, for primary and secondary education during the 2018–19 school year.

Another way we can understand the relationship between parents' choices and the situation of the Basque language is to use the data provided by the

VII. Sociolinguistic Survey (from 2021). According to the report dedicated to Iparralde,[118] 20.1 percent of people there are Basque speakers, and 9.4 percent are receptive speakers. Those who do not understand or speak Basque remain the majority at 70.5 percent (figure 5.16).

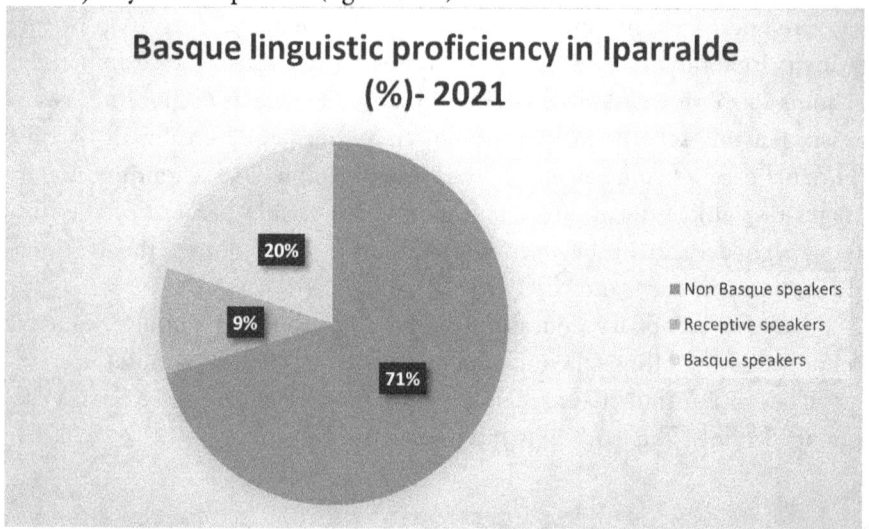

Figure 5.16. Level of Basque linguistic proficiency in Iparralde (%), 2021.

Even if the number of Basque speakers is decreasing in Iparralde, this last survey shows that, over time, the number of young speakers is increasing. In table 5.4, we notice a slow increase of Basque speakers in the younger generations (25–34 and 16–24 age groups). In fact, if we look at the data over time (from 2001 to the last one to date in 2021), we notice the decrease of the older Basque speakers but the increase among the youngest generations (table 5.4).

This is linked to the increasing sensitivity of inhabitants of Iparralde to the Basque language, to the growing educational offering in Euskara and, to the increasing willingness of parents of enrolling their children in immersive or bilingual schooling systems in the future (figure 5.17).

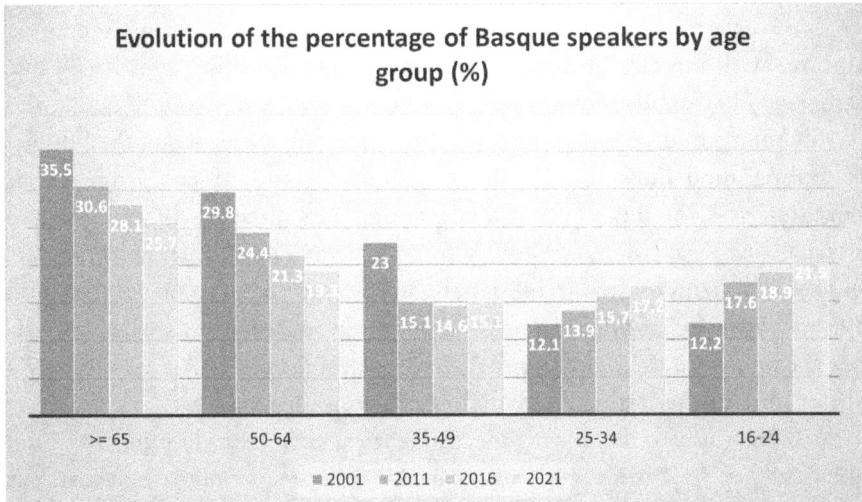

Table 5.4. Evolution of the number of speakers by age groups in Iparralde (%), 2001–2021.

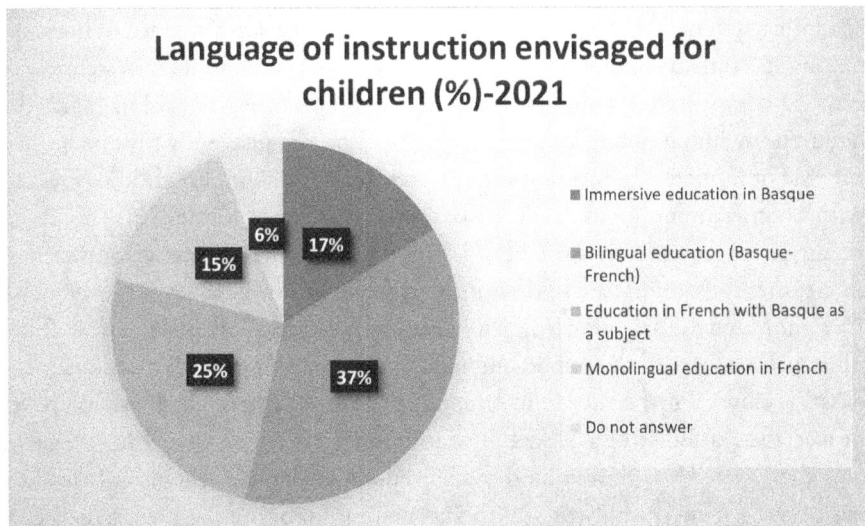

Figure 5.17. Language of instruction envisaged for children (%), according to the VII Sociolinguistic Survey (2021)

Over time, parents in Iparralde seem to keep choosing schooling options with Euskara in them. Regarding public schooling and the Basque language in Iparralde, Eztitxu Harignordoquy[119] explained that parents who enroll their children in bilingual public teaching instead of other public schooling modalities usually show enthusiasm toward the language. A common case she has seen is when grandparents do speak Basque but did not pass it to the parents, resulting in a lost generation. Therefore, the parents enroll their children in bilingual schooling for them to be able to speak Basque with the grandparents. Another common situation is when parents see the benefit of their children being schooled bilingually and connected to the culture of the territory in which they live.

When asked about why she thought parents keep deciding to enroll their children in Ikastola schools in Iparralde, Edurne Manterola[120] believes the appeal of Ikastolas is not merely the immersive schooling system, but also the monitoring of children and the role given to parents in the Ikastola system. In addition, Xan Aire[121] believes Seaska has managed to put in place an immersive schooling system but needs to improve the tools to develop the usage of Euskara among its students. The immersive schooling system in Iparralde is essential to him, to compensate for the sparseness of Euskara in everyday life of Iparralde children—without falling into the replacement of a language. By this, he means the role of immersive education is not to replace a monolingual child in French with another monolingual child in Basque. This fear of immersive schooling, he argues, is completely mistaken. Manterola adds the success of Seaska lies in creating fully bilingual children in Iparralde, both in Basque and in French. Harignordoquy did acknowledge in her interview it was difficult to create fully bilingual students in the public bilingual system because of its limitations (discussed below). Furthermore, in Aire's view, Ikastola schools in Iparralde have proven the feasibility of a Model D or immersive schooling model in Iparralde and its success. He believes that the achievement of Ikastola schools in Iparralde has been their successful work on the normalization of the Basque language, at least in the domain of education. Yet, looking ahead, Aire believes the upcoming

Context of the Basque Language and Education

challenge of Ikastola schools in Iparralde is to improve the linguistic quality, notably in the informal areas of life.

This context provided by the interviewees confirms that parents who have an attachment to the Basque language would send their children to bilingual or immersive schooling option, which seems obvious. However, those who believe in the immersive system or those who prefer the monitoring of children offered by Seaska would send their children to an Ikastola.

Yet, despite the positive evolution of education in Euskara in Iparralde, the sociolinguistic survey shows a very low use of Basque, hindering the efforts of educators. In fact, students and speakers barely speak Basque in their daily life. Among those who can speak Basque, only 1 percent use it actively more than French, 6 percent use it as often as French, 11 percent use it less often than French, and 3.4 percent use Euskara very little in their everyday lives. More importantly, if we look at the evolution over time (figure 5.19), the use of Basque is declining.

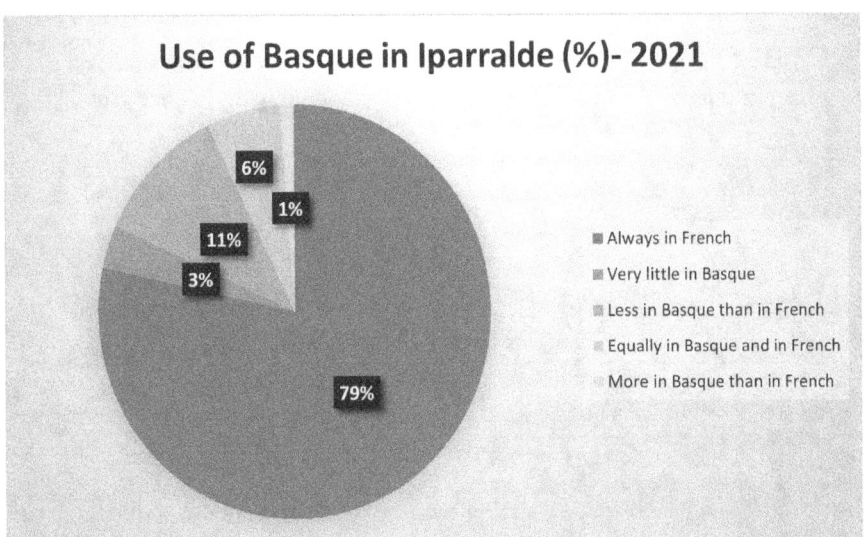

Figure 5.18. Use of Basque in Iparralde in 2021 (%).

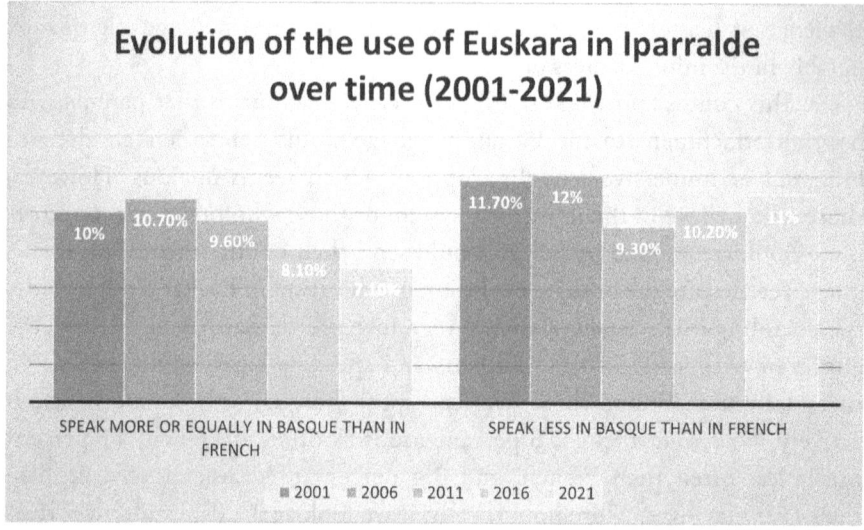

Figure 5.19. Evolution of the use of Euskara in Iparralde over time, from 2001 to 2021 (%).

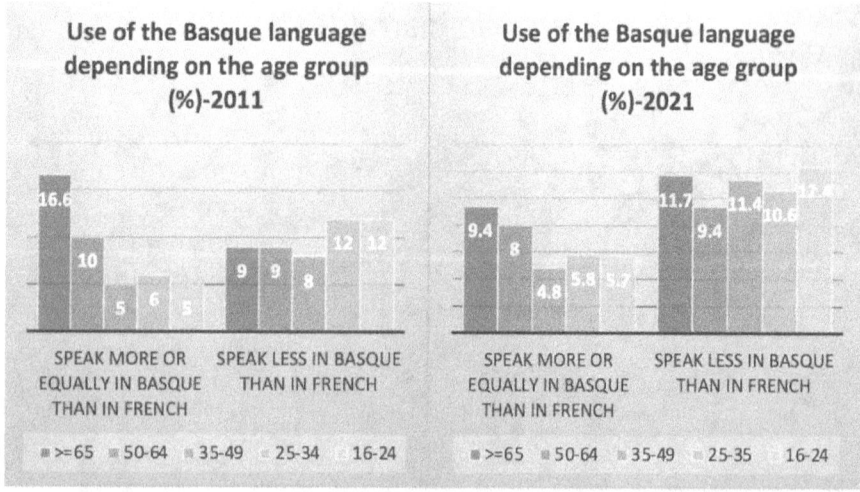

Figure 5.20. Evolution of Euskara use in Iparralde by age groups, comparing 2011 and 2021 (%).

As the data presented in table 5.4 shows, there has been a slight increase in the creation of Basque speakers in the 16–34 year age range, suggesting the success of the educational offering. However, this slow increase, paired with the lack of opportunities to use Basque in the streets (especially among new Basque speakers) contributes to the overall decrease of the use of Euskara (figures 5.18, 5.19, and 5.20). In addition, as pointed out by the VII Sociolinguistic survey, for Iparralde, as of 2021, only 15.1 percent of folks in the 35–49 year age range are Basque speakers (table 5.4). This number has also decreased in older generations. Moreover, despite a slight increase, only 21.5 percent of 16–24 year olds are Basque speakers, which is not enough to ensure the survival of Euskara. This indicates the need for a stronger implementation of education in Basque and shows the limits of the bilingual education model available in France. In fact, the conclusions of the mentioned report show how, even if the number of speakers is growing among the younger generations, their ability to speak Basque is decreasing. Thus, young people truly need more exposure to the Basque language.[122]

Finally, to fully grasp a contextualized view of education in Basque, we must examine the other actors, the teachers, and their everyday interactions with educational policies linked to the Basque language.

Teachers and Education in Basque

The role of teachers for the transmission of the Basque language is essential. Their views and their realities offer a perfect contextualization of the reality of Euskara and education.

Teacher 1, in the town of Hondarribia in Gipuzkoa, has been teaching for more than thirty-five years. She started teaching in the private Catholic schools and soon moved to teaching in an Ikastola. This Ikastola later joined with the town's public school and became public in 1994. She has worked there since, experiencing the (linguistic) evolution of the town's children over the years. In Hondarribia, Model D is only available in the public school, so Teacher 1 teaches exclusively in Euskara. The Basque language is also exclusively the language Teacher 1 uses with her coworkers. She notices how the social reality and linguistic reality of this once-fishing town has drastically evolved. In fact, more and more Spanish-monolingual parents live in Hondarribia[123] and send their children to the public school, where Model D is taught.

Also, recently, Teacher 1 noticed that the number of bilingual (Spanish-Basque) families seem to be increasing. This is important to note, since teaching in Euskara to (Spanish) monolingual children is very different than teaching in

Euskara to children coming from Basque-speaking families, or bilingual families. The latter category can help children with their homework much more easily than the first category, for instance. This example seems trivial, but Teacher 1 notices the added difficulties that the children who hear no Euskara at home have, in comparison with the other children. Indeed, when she started teaching, the language of home was mainly Euskara, whereas now it is predominantly Spanish. This is not only the case in homes where parents do not know Euskara, but also the case in homes where, despite the parents knowing the language, do not use it. This means, after the summer holidays, children who do not hear Euskara at home arrive with difficulties to regain the pre-summer level of Basque they had. The situation was even more alarming in 2020 with the lockdown because the COVID-19 pandemic, where these children barely hear or speak Basque for months at a time.

These difficulties, however, are not insurmountable. Those who continue their schooling in Model D and are (usually) greatly supported during their schooling years do achieve a decent level of bilingualism, according to Teacher 1. The issue remains, as we have already discussed, the social use of Euskara. Teacher 1 notices that the children who use the Basque language socially tend to lean toward a greater bilingualism or proficiency in Euskara, whereas those who only use it in a school setting tend to find it difficult to use later.

A teacher in Navarre, Amaia Silvo has taught both in a non-Basque-speaking area and in the Mixed area. Furthering the interest of comparison, the non-Basque-speaking area where she taught was a small town in rural Navarre, whereas she teaches now in the capital, Iruñea, the biggest city of Navarre. Silvo is originally from a Basque-speaking town in Gipuzkoa, and she ended up teaching for one year in the non-Basque-speaking area of the Rivera of Navarre, where it is estimated more than half the population is of Moroccan origin. In fact, this immigrant population usually comes to Navarre to work in the agricultural sector. In the non-Basque-speaking area, there is the option to learn Basque as an optional class, if there is enough demand.

Thus, Silvo was teaching the optional class to children who were at the same time learning Spanish and/or English (the Spanish-English bilingual model was available in that school too). She mentions that the option of studying Basque was available because the director of the school, an Andalusian woman, believed learning Basque (even if a little bit) was useful for these children. Yet, Silvo noticed that at the beginning of their schooling, parents enrolled the children in the class to learn Basque. But as they grew up, the children lost interest in learning that language, as did the parents, resulting in a decrease in enrollment. Also, because Basque was optional, it competed with a class called "workshop," where students used their time to work on topics discussed in class, or with the class on religion. Finally, Silvo explained to the author that these children were very young and struggling to learn Spanish first; they were sometimes paired with English and viewed learning Basque at the same time as a burden. Also, in the town in which these children were living, no social life could be made in Basque and barely anything could be accessed in Basque. On the flip side, by the end of the academic year, some of the children were able to have a basic conversation in Euskara.

The next year, for the 2019–2020 academic year, Silvo was teaching in Iruñea, in the Arrotxapea school, with Model D. She noticed that the parents there had made the choice of sending their children to Model D, and therefore, their support of the Basque language was more pronounced compared to the situation she had previously experienced in the Navarrese Rivera area. In Iruñea, she teaches using Euskara as the teaching language. She noted that in her 2019–2020 class of nineteen children, ten had Basque-speaker families; eight had parents who really wanted their children to learn Basque; and one student who was enrolled in this school because of other factors, mainly the proximity of the school. She noticed the speaking level of Basque of her students was good but that the students had trouble writing in Basque. Finally, she stated that despite being Basque speakers, children at her school tend to socialize in Spanish.

Interestingly, Silvo noted some socioeconomic differences in Navarre between the Model D students and the Model A or G students in the same school. She believes some parents make the choice of enrolling their children in Model D because of this socioeconomic difference, knowing they will have classmates with higher socioeconomic status. She mentioned that this is true in the San Francisco school, where Model D, PAI,[124] or G are available. In this school, where her partner teaches, Spanish-speaking models contain children of parents who have a low socioeconomic status, whereas Model D draws those children whose parents have a higher socioeconomic status. It is a pattern that perpetuates itself. For her, it was shocking to see, in a school where the linguistic model offering was vast, and available to any child, that the children's profiles were so different between the models, and that the choice of linguistic models was so tied to the socioeconomic background.

A teacher of the Basque language in secondary schools of Miarritze (Biarritz) and Angelu (Anglet), Harignordoquy works in the French public bilingual system. As a teacher of the bilingual program in public schools of Iparralde, she also teaches history and geography in Basque. She previously taught in the high school of Donibane-Garazi (St-Jean-Pied-de-Port). Teaching in Iparralde's inland (Donibane-Garazi) or coastal area (Miarritze) is different, even in the French public system. With the inland being more Basque-speaking than the coast, she noticed the relationship with Euskara was different between the two areas. In Donibane-Garazi, her students were mainly from Basque-speaking homes, while her students in Miarritze or Angelu are mainly from French-speaking homes.[125] Thus, despite being, in theory, enrolled in the same program, Harignordoquy's students varied greatly from one school to another in their level of attaining fluency in Euskara.

Harignordoquy mentioned that she tries to use Euskara as a teaching language as often as she can, but that this stratregy depends on the level of the student. In her experience, the relationship with the language also differs among the students. She noticed that those who were brought up in Euskara have an appreciation of the language, and therefore, enjoy having classes in Basque. Regarding the students who do not have Euskara as a mother tongue, some really enjoyed learning it and considered themselves lucky to be given the opportunity to learn this language. Others were forced by parents to learn the language or even have parents who are not at all interested in the language (despite sending their children to a bilingual model of schooling).

Interestingly, in all schools in which Harignordoquy has taught, most students use French to socialize, limiting the use of Basque to the classroom. Harignordoquy highlighted, like the previous two teachers, the importance of the social use of the language to improve students' Euskara skills in the classroom and beyond. Yet, this was not the only issue in Iparralde she pointed out. In fact, she emphasized that the so-called "bilingual" model does not grant equal hours to both languages in the curriculum. Only six hours are devoted to teaching the Basque language and history and geography in Euskara. Moreover, she explained that there is no official curriculum in Basque the teacher must follow, making the monitoring of the children and their level of Euskara more difficult. This results in not having fully bilingual children at the end of their schooling, despite that being the goal. Also, often, children decide to drop studying in Euskara when they enter high school. Furthermore, the most recent reform of the *Baccalauréat*, the Blanquer Act of 2019,[126] has diminished the presence (and status) of regional languages incredibly, putting the study of Euskara (or other regional languages) in direct competition with other classes.[127] Incidentally, this reform gave more credits to studying Latin than regional languages.

Concluding Remarks of Part II

Education is an extremely difficult matter to regulate, let alone the teaching of minority languages in the classroom. Not only do different political views intervene in what education should be, or how it should be regulated, but also in views on multiculturalism and multilingualism. Regarding our case—that of the Basque language—two different points of view have been taken. One concerns the introduction of the Basque language in education, with a slight variation in Navarre, following the main suggestions brought by the literature on language planning for the recovery of minority languages. If we look at the stages of reversing language shift by Fishman,[128] access to public schools in Basque, from kindergarten to higher education, fulfills all the requirements. The BAC would be placed in the higher part of the stages, "passed- to transcend diglossia." Navarre, in theory would be in the same place as the BAC, but the lack of access and difficulties of access to higher education in Basque in Navarre must be noted. In Iparralde, there is a different point of view on minority language education. We note that France is lower ranked in Fishman's stages of reversing language shift than the other two Basque administrative territories. France's linguistic policy—notably in education—seems to place the country in the lower stages of reversing language shift. This means that France is still trying to attain diglossia. Also, France's attitude and policies over the years have varied little, resulting in a stagnation of the stages of language shifts. In fact, to move on to improving the situation, regulations and policies (paired with the attitude of high courts) need to go further.

Despite offering different norms on Euskara and education, law in action shows that three main schooling systems are available throughout the entire Basque Country with the help provided by Ikastola schools: Model A, Model B, and Model D. The linguistic degrees of particular programs within a model vary somewhat, but they can be safely categorized in these models.

In fact, the Spanish domestic law, with the work undertaken by the BAC and Navarre, goes beyond the minimum standard of protection of Euskara in education. This is especially the case in the BAC, a region that has been proactive in transforming the norm of co-official languages into reality, particularly in the domain of education. Despite not yet fulfilling the desired full bilingualism in all children, the BAC seems to be on the right path. Navarre demonstrates the difficulties that linguistic territorial division brings into the reality of education and the Basque language. However, Ikastola schools help fill the gap of immersive schooling where such an offering is not otherwise available. Finally, France is a curious case. The legal framework is generally hostile toward the recognition of the officiality of regional languages, but it nevertheless includes them in education. The issue remains the optional character of studying regional languages, placing them at a lower rank. Also, the "anxiety logic" about immersive schooling by the French courts has stopped this model from entering public schools. In the French case as well, associative schools help to provide immersive schooling in regional languages in France.

The example of education and the Basque language shows the importance of norm users when analyzing the law—the "institutional normative order."[129] Parents, teachers, policy makers, university students, and civil movements have shaped and continue to shape the everyday education in Basque in all three administrations of the Basque Country.

This part II has examined the Basque language and the area of education. Another area of social life worthy of our attention regarding Euskara is media (part III).

Notes

1 Spanish courts, however, have also shown a similar "anxiety logic" as seen in the French courts—particularly in the last decades regarding the Catalan-medium immersive schooling in Catalonia. This shows the Spanish courts are not always benevolent toward immersive education either.
2 This must not be mistaken with other options, where curriculum is taught in other languages, but not in regional or minority languages (for instance, in Spanish, English, or German).
3 These schools have been grouped under the association "Eskolim" since 2009.

4   For instance, the statutes of Seaska and Diwan mention expressly this goal.
5   Zabaleta Apaolaza, "Inmersión lingüística y Constitución: una perspectiva francesa," 100.
6   Decision 85-203 of December 28, 1985. https://www.conseil-constitutionnel.fr/decision/1985/85203DC.htm (Accessed February 17, 2021).
7   Translated by the author: "Considering that Article 28 of the Amending Finance Act for 1985 provides that staff teaching in the bilingual classes of the 'Diwan' association are to be integrated into the body of primary school teachers under conditions to be specified by decree in the Conseil d'Etat; that the Amending Finance Act for 1985 does not provide for the creation of new posts or the opening of new appropriations to implement this provision; that such a provision, which is not of a financial nature within the meaning of Article 1 of the Order of January 2, 1959, is not one of those that can be included in a Finance Act; that, consequently, it was adopted according to a procedure that does not comply with the Constitution."
8   http://discours.vie-publique.fr/notices/013000555.html (Accessed August 27, 2018).
9   Council of the State, October 30, 2001, National Union of Second Degree Teachers (SNES) and others. Translated by the author.
10 Decision 2001-456 of December 27, 2001, about the finance law of 2002. Translated by the author. https://www.conseil-constitutionnel.fr/decision/2001/2001456DC.htm (Accessed August 10, 2018).
11 Translated by the author. "Considering that Article 134 is not intended to and cannot have the effect of deciding on the principle of integrating such establishments into the public education system; that it will be up to the competent administrative authorities, under the control of the judge, to decide, in compliance with Article 2 of the Constitution and the legislative provisions in force, on a request for integration; that, subject to this reservation, Article 134 is not contrary to the Constitution."
12 Bertile, *Langues régionales ou minoritaires et constitution*, 2008, 83.
13 Translated by the author: "Considering that, while the State and local authorities may provide assistance to associations for the protection of regional languages, it follows from the aforementioned terms of Article 2 of the Constitution that the use

of a language other than French may not be imposed on pupils in public education establishments, either in the life of the establishment or in the teaching of subjects other than those of the language in question."

14 Council of State, July 15, 2002, UNSA and others. Translated by the author.
15 https://www.legifrance.gouv.fr/affichJuriAdmin.do?idTexte=CETATEX-T000008146764&dateTexte (Accessed August 20, 2018).
16 Translated and emphasis added by the author: "Considering that, according to the 'immersion' method introduced by the Minister of Education's decree of April 19, 2002 and circulaire no. 2002-103 of April 30, 2002, which supplements it, the regional language is used either exclusively in nursery schools, or as the main language of instruction and communication in primary and secondary schools and establishments; that the methods thus defined for learning the regional language, according to which the activities in the various fields provided for in the curricula are practiced in the regional language, limit teaching in French, in primary education, to learning the French language and mathematical concepts, and in secondary education to two subjects per level; *that such prescriptions go beyond the necessities of learning a regional language and thus exceed the possibilities for derogation from the obligation to use French as the language of instruction* authorized by the provisions of Articles L. 121-3 and L. 312-11 of the Education Code; thus, the provisions of the decree of April 19, 2002 and circulaire no. 2002-103 of April 30, 2002 ignore these legislative provisions; consequently, the plaintiff unions and groups are entitled to request their annulment."
17 *Considérant* 49, translated by the author: "The aforementioned terms of Article 2 of the Constitution mean that the use of a language other than French may not be imposed on pupils in public education establishments, either in the life of the establishment or in the teaching of subjects other than those of the language in question."
18 See the previous chapter.
19 Moseley, *Atlas of the World's Languages in Danger*.
20 Zabaleta Apaolaza, "Inmersión lingüística y Constitución: una perspectiva francesa," 102.
21 See the previous chapter.
22 See Part I, Chapter 3.
23 Translated by the author. Decree 138/1983, of July 11, 1983, regulating the use of the official language in non-university education in the Basque Country.

http://www.euskadi.eus/bopv2/datos/1983/07/8301433a.pdf (Accessed August 24, 2021).

24 Translated by the author: "The Department of Education and Culture shall adopt the necessary measures to guarantee the use of Basque in the school environment, making it a habitual means of expression both inside and outside the classroom."

25 http://www.nolega.euskadi.eus/es (Accessed August 31, 2018).

26 http://www.euskadi.eus/gobierno-vasco/-/ayuda_subvencion/2017/nolega/ (Accessed August 31, 2018).

27 Another funding program exists for funding teaching materials in Basque, called EIMA. https://www.euskadi.eus/eima-presentacion/web01-a3eima/es/ (Accessed May 24, 2024).

28 http://www.irale.hezkuntza.net/web/guest (Accessed August 21, 2018).

29 See the history behind IRALE in https://irale.hezkuntza.net/es/presentacion-e-historia (Accessed July 15, 2024). Siadeco is the Society of Applied Research for Community Development (http://www.siadeco.eus/en/identidad/ last accessed on July 15, 2024).

30 Euskaltegi schools are public schools that teach Euskara to adults. Their equivalent in the private sector are *Alfabetatze Euskalduntze Koordinakundea* (AEK) schools, mentioned in the introduction in relation to the *Korrika* fundraising event. AEK is present in all three territories of the Basque Country, while Euskaltegi schools are only present in the BAC and Navarre.

31 The ULIBARRI program was created by the Decree 84/2019, of June 11.

32 http://www.ulibarri.euskadi.eus/eu (Accessed August 21, 2018).

33 See the latest call for the 2019–2020 academic year: https://bon.navarra.es/es/anuncio/-/texto/2020/159/4 (Accessed August 14, 2020). The data mentioned in this paragraph corresponds to this academic year.

34 The "General Deputy" is the head of the Deputation (provincial deputation). In this case, Martin Garitano was the head of the Deputation of Gipuzkoa. "Deputation" is the literal translation of *Diputación* (in Spanish) or *Diputazioa* (in Basque). It refers to the provincial government.

35 Decision 419/2015 of January 22, 2015 http://www.poderjudicial.es/search/contenidos.action?action=contentpdf&databasematch=AN&reference=7341306&links=&optimize=20150401&publicinterface=true (Accessed August 22, 2018).

36 Fourth paragraph on the Law Fundamentals (Fundamentos de Derecho, translated by the author) of the decision.
37 The author could not find any mention to which specific article(s) of the Language Charter they were referring.
38 Even though Navarre also signed a collaboration with these two institutions on June 15, 2018, we are going to use the data available that concerns only the BAC and POBL. The agreement: https://www.irekia.euskadi.eus/uploads/attachments/11903/Eranskina_EUS_2018_EEP-EJ-NAF_Logoduna.pdf?1529061166 (Accessed August 26, 2018).
39 This agreement was completed in 2024 between the BAC Basque government and the POBL: https://www.mintzaira.fr/fileadmin/documents/Appel_a_projets/2024/Partenariat_OPLB-Gvt_CAE_Annexe_2024.pdf (Accessed: July 17, 2024). The latest renewal (as of 2024) of this agreement between the Administrations of BAC and Navarre, with the POBL is from 2022, for the period between 2021 and 2025: https://www.mintzaira.fr/fileadmin/documents/Aktualitateak/Prentsa-agiria/PO_Hiruko_Ituna_Annexe_2022_fr.pdf (Accessed: July 17, 2024).
40 https://www.irekia.euskadi.eus/uploads/attachments/12068/AkordioaEEP.pdf?1531503353 (Accessed August 27, 2018).
41 These promoters from Iparralde have signed agreements of collaboration with the POBL: Seaska (association of Ikastola schools of Iparralde), Ikas-bi (association of parents of public bilingual schooling in Basque), Biga bai (another association of parents of public bilingual schooling in Basque), Euskal Haziak (association of parents and teachers of Catholic, private bilingual schooling in Basque), AEK (private schools teaching Basque to adults), Euskal Irratiak (association of five radio stations in the Basque language in Iparralde), Uda-Leku (leisure and summer camp centers conducted in Euskara), and Bertsularien Lagunak (association for the promotion and teaching of Bertsolaritza in Iparralde).
42 The remaining funds were directed toward other activities not linked with education.
43 This tendency has been maintained over the years. For instance, see the funding for 2020 below.
44 Cooperation funds for 2023: https://www.mintzaira.fr/fileadmin/documents/D2023_Note_de_presse_F_20230705.pdf (Accessed: July 17, 2024).

45　In this book the author will only focus on the public university offerings, since the three administrative regions have public universities offering higher education in Basque—which is not always the case with private universities. In addition, in Iparralde, only one undergraduate program is available in the Basque language and it is in the public university. Therefore, for comparison matters, it also makes sense for the author to focus only on the public universities. It must be said, however, that in the BAC, private universities also provide programs in the Basque language.

46　Inspired in the Basque University of 1936, the University of the Basque Country as such was created in 1980. It joined higher education institutions created earlier, such as some schools of Sarriko (Economics and Business, Medicine, and Science), the Nautical School, the University School of Business Studies of Bilbao, and engineering technical schools.

47　See Eusko Ikaskuntza's Auñamendi Encyclopedia. http://aunamendi.eusko-ikaskuntza.eus/es/universidad-del-pais-vasco/ar-153761/ (Accessed July 16, 2020).

48　https://www.ehu.eus/es/web/gardentasun-ataria/datu-orokorrak (Accessed July 16, 2020).

49　For the 2013–2014 academic year, the number of students studying in Euskara was 48.11 percent, and this number increases over the years.

50　Figure created and translated by the author using data from the evaluation report of the II Master Plan for the Basque language, 22. This evaluation report was published in April 2018. https://labehu.eus/wp-content/uploads/2018/05/Euskararen_II_Plan_Gidariaren_Ebaluazio_txostena_gazt.pdf (Accessed July 17, 2024).

51　https://www.ehu.eus/es/-/comienza-el-curso-2023-2024-en-la-upv-ehu (Accessed July 17, 2024).

52　According to the data from Eustat, in the year 2019, 11,361 students passed the university entrance exam, and 7,826 of those were coming from Model D. Data from https://www.eustat.eus/banku/id_2320/indexLista.html (Accessed August 6, 2020).

53　http://www.unavarra.es/conocerlauniversidad/historia/historia-y-cronologia (Accessed July 16, 2020).

54　http://www.unavarra.es/conocerlauniversidad/datos-basicos (Accessed July 16, 2020).

55 http://www.unavarra.es/sites/actualidad/contents/noticias/2020/06/20-06-12/la-upna-amplia-en-varios-grados.html (Accessed August 14, 2020).
56 Published on March 2, 2021, Resolution 143/2021: https://bon.navarra.es/es/anuncio/-/texto/2021/48/10 (Accessed July 16, 2021).
57 https://www.unavarra.es/digitalAssets/209/209438_1000002021-24_Plan_Director_EUSKERA_UPNA.pdf (Accessed July 17, 2024).
58 The undergraduate degree in Basque studies offered at UPPA can be followed by a master's program at the University of Bordeaux Montaigne. For those who want to further their studies, a PhD can be performed in Basque studies at both universities, associated with the IKER research center.
59 Université de Pau et des Pays de l'Adour (UPPA). https://www.univ-pau.fr/fr/index.html (Accessed July 19, 2024).
60 https://formation.univ-pau.fr/fr/catalogue/arts-lettres-langues-ALL/licence-12/licence-langues-litteratures-et-civilisations-etrangeres-et-regionales-32_1/l1-l2-l3-parcours-etudes-basques-IGXEMPVL.html (Accessed July 16, 2020). In a similar fashion, under the undergraduate program "Licence langues, littératures, civilisations étrangères et régionales," the study of other regional languages is available—such as Breton, Catalan, Corsican, Creole, Occitan, or Tahitian—in French universities.
61 https://formations.u-bordeaux-montaigne.fr/fr/catalogue-des-formations/master-XB/master-etudes-basques-master-euskal-ikasketak-KQQN7MMA.html (Accessed July 19, 2024).
62 https://www.u-bordeaux-montaigne.fr/fr/index.html (Accessed July 19, 2024). It must be noted this university is outside the three territories we are analyzing in this book, but nevertheless offers two courses (MA) in Basque language, explained in this part.
63 https://www.u-bordeaux-montaigne.fr/fr/recherche/equipes_de_recherche/iker.html (Accessed July 19, 2024).
64 https://formations.u-bordeaux-montaigne.fr/fr/catalogue-des-formations/concours-de-l-enseignement-meef-2d-degre-capes-XB242/master-meef-lettres-KQRR6GHE.html (Accessed July 19, 2024).
65 https://www.euroregion-naen.eu/en/ (Accessed July 19, 2024).
66 https://www.poctefa.eu/fr/ (Accessed July 19, 2024).
67 https://2014-2020.poctefa.eu/fr/ (Accessed July 19, 2024).

68 In 2023 the collaboration between the UPV-EHU, the UPPA, and the University Bordeaux Montaigne, together with the POBL, created a university degree of Journalism in Basque (Kazetaritza euskaraz-Journalisme en langue basque) for 2023–2025. This project also shows the willingness of universities and local institutions to foster higher education in Euskara. https://www.mintzaira.fr/fileadmin/documents/Aktualitateak/Prentsaurrekoak/2023/2023_04_27/Presidentaren_hitzartzea__-_Conf._de_presse_OPLB_2023.04.27.pdf (Accessed July 19, 2024).
69 In this research, we will not discuss private religious schools.
70 Masa, "Ikastolas as a Social Innovation Phenomenon: a case study," 178.
71 To know more about the history of Seaska and the Ikastolas of Iparralde, see Garat y Aire, *Seaska 40 urte euskararen alde*.
72 Seaska in Basque means "cradle."
73 Palacin Mariscal, "Ikastolen Elkartea, example of effective transfrontier cooperation under the European Language Charter."
74 Royal Decree 1049/1979, of April 20, 1979, on the integration of the Basque language in education in the BAC. https://www.boe.es/diario_boe/txt.php?id=BOE-A-1979-12160 (Accessed July 12, 2018).
75 Translated by the author: Law 15/1983, of July 27, 1983, creating the "Euskal Ikastolen Erakundea-Basque Institute of Ikastolas" and approving the Legal Statute of Ikastolas. https://www.legegunea.euskadi.eus/x59-preview/es/contenidos/ley/bopv198301525/es_def/index.shtml (Accessed August 6, 2020).
76 http://hj.tribunalconstitucional.es/en/Resolucion/Show/700 (Accessed August 6, 2020).
77 Translated by the author. F.J.1.
78 http://noticias.juridicas.com/base_datos/CCAA/pv-l10-1988.t1.html#t1 (Accessed July 17, 2018).
79 Text emphasized and translated by the author. "Starting from the existence of the public network, the private network and the ikastola network, the reorganization of the Basque non-university education system aims to consolidate a single Basque Public School."
80 https://www.euskadi.eus/y22-bopv/es/bopv2/datos/1993/02/9300650a.shtml?BOPV_HIDE_CALENDAR (Accessed July 17, 2018).
81 Bertile, Langues régionales ou minoritaires et constitution, 2008, 310.

82 Partido Nacionalista Vasco-Euzko Alderdi Jeltzalea (PNV-EAJ), is the Basque Nationalist Party. It is a Basque nationalist and regionalist political party. This party currently operates in the BAC, Navarre, and Iparralde. Politically it is often described as being Christian-democratic, social-democratic, and conservative-liberal.

83 Partido Socialista de Euskadi-Euskadiko Ezkerra (PSE-EE) is the Socialist Party of the Basque Country. It acts as the regional affiliate of the Spanish Socialist Worker's Party (PSOE). Politically, it is a social-democratic party.

84 Herri Batasuna, "Popular Unity" in English, was a far-left Basque nationalist coalition. Politically, it was a Basque nationalist and separatist left-wing socialist coalition party. This coalition was founded in 1978 to call for a "no" in the referendum validating the 1978 Spanish Constitution. This party was later made illegal by the Supreme Court in 2003 (confirmed in 2009) for its link to ETA. In fact, the case made it to the European Court of Human Rights (case of *Herri Batasuna v. Spain*), where, in 2009, the decision by the Spanish Supreme Court was confirmed.

85 Eusko Alkartasuna-EA ("Basque Solidarity," a Basque nationalist democratic and non-denominational party) had nine seats, Partido Popular-PP ("The People's Party," a conservation and Christian-democratic political party in Spain) had six seats, Euskadiko Ezkerra-EE ("The Basque Country Left," a Basque socialist coalition) had six, and Unidad Alavesa ("Alavese Unity," a political party from the province of Alava, that defended this province needed to create its own separated Foral community, similar to Navarre) had three.

86 Grupo Antiterrorista de Liberación (GAL) was an illegal death squad active in the 1980s. This paramilitary group was found to be financed by the Spanish Ministry of the Interior, performing state terrorism, usually targeting ETA members.

87 See appendix 2.

88 López-Goñi, "Basque Schools in Navarre: The Early Stages, 1931–1936," gives an accurate historical account on the evolution of Ikastola schools in Navarre.

89 http://www.nafarroakoikastolak.net/Ikastolak.asp (Accessed July 17, 2018).

90 Explained in part I, chapter 3.

91 Figure 5.2 is created and translated by the author using the following data from Eustat: https://www.eustat.eus/elementos/ele0000100/alumnado-de-ensenan-

zas-de-regimen-general-en-la-ca-de-euskadi-por-territorio-historico-titularidad-del-centro-y-nivel-de-ensenanza/tbl0000108_c.html for primary education and http://www.euskadi.eus/contenidos/informacion/graficosmatr1314/es_def/adjuntos/graficos_17-18/EAE_sarea_OBLI.pdf for secondary education (Accessed July 18, 2018).

92 Figure 5.3 is created and adapted by the author using the following data from Eustat: https://en.eustat.eus/indic/indicadoresgraficosvista.aspx?idgraf=16357&opt=0&tema=300 (Accessed July 20, 2024). Note that the original data refers to "linguistic models" as "language models." It also uses "in Spanish" for Model A, "Bilingual" for Model B, and "in Basque" for Model D. The author has adapted this vocabulary to be more consistent with the rest of the book.

93 Figure created and adapted by the author using data from Eustat: https://es.eustat.eus/indic/indicadoresgraficosvista.aspx?idgraf=16356&opt=0&tema=300 (Accessed July 20, 2024). Note that the original data refers to "linguistic models" as "language models." It also uses "in Spanish" for Model A, "Bilingual" for Model B, and "in Basque" for Model D. The author has adapted this vocabulary to be more consistent with the rest of the book. Non-university general education is understood in Spain as containing all general education from kindergarten to the end of secondary education (private and public combined). For more information, see https://eurydice.eacea.ec.europa.eu/national-education-systems/spain/organisation-education-system-and-its-structure (accessed July 20, 2024).

94 Last two years of high school (which are not mandatory to complete). Some students choose (public or private) trade school or vocational training instead of continuing in the traditional high school setting.

95 Figure created and adapted by the author using data from Eustat: https://en.eustat.eus/elementos/ele0000000/students-enrolled-in-the-basque-country-by-ownership-of-the-centre-and-level-of-education-according-to-historical-territory-and-sex-202223/tbl0000081_i.html (accessed July 20, 2024).

96 Includes Intermediate and Higher Vocational Training, Learning of tasks and Specialization Courses of Vocational Training.

97 Figure 5.5 created and adapted by the author using data from Eustat: https://en.eustat.eus/elementos/ele0000100/students-enrolled-in-non-university-general-education-in-the-basque-country-by-territorial-area-of-school-ac-

cording-to-education-level-and-language-model-202223/tbl0000106_i.html (Accessed July 22, 2024).
98 https://ivac-eei.eus/es/ (Accessed July 22, 2024).
99 Figure 5.6 was created and adapted by the author using the following data from Eustat: https://www.eustat.eus/elementos/ele0000100/alumnado-matriculado-en-ensenanzas-de-regimen-general-no-universitarias-en-la-ca-de-euskadi-por-ambitos-territoriales-del-centro-segun-nivel-de-ensenanza-y-modelo-linguistico-202223/tbl0000106_c.html (Accessed July 22, 2024).
100 Figures 5.7 and 5.8 are created and adapted by the author using the following data from Eustat: https://www.eustat.eus/elementos/ele0002400/alumnado-matriculado-en-ensenanzas-de-regimen-general-no-universitarias-en-la-ca-de-euskadi-por-territorio-historico-y-nivel-de-ensenanza-segun-titularidad-del-centro-y-modelo-linguistico-avance-de-datos-202324/tbl0002427_c.html (Accessed July 22, 2024).
101 Oñati is an "arnasgune," a place where the percentage of Basque speakers is very high, and where Basque is commonly heard and used.
102 Susana Arrese (see appendix 2) is a parent of two daughters who went to Txantxiku Ikastola in Oñati (one of the first Ikastolas created).
103 Table 5.1 has been created by the author using the data available at the official website of the Department of Education for the government of Navarre: https://www.educacion.navarra.es/web/dpto/estadisticas/estadistica-de-datos-basicos (Accessed August 5, 2020).
104 There is no offering for Model B in the 2022–2023 academic year for bachillerato in Navarre.
105 Higher education has been examined earlier (in the previous chapter).
106 Iruñea in Basque, Pamplona in Spanish.
107 Coalition of the following political parties: Unión Pueblo Navarro, Ciudadanos, and Partido Popular de Navarra—all usually opposed to the strengthening or protecting of Euskara in Navarre.
108 This reform increased the number of slots in Basque from 164 to 408 children, while reducing the slots in Spanish and Spanish-English by 255.
109 Term used by Oroz Bretón y Sotés Ruiz, "Bilingual Education in Navarre: Achievements and Challenges."
110 As of August 2018. http://cache.media.education.gouv.fr/file/2017/82/6/depp-rers-2017-eleves-second-

degre-maj-dec-2017_861826.pdf (Accessed August 27, 2018). The following table 5.2 has been created, adapted, and translated by the author using this data.
111 Information Note n° 21.26. https://www.education.gouv.fr/l-enseignement-des-langues-vivantes-dans-le-second-degre-en-2020-326035 (Accessed July 22, 2024).
112 http://www.mintzaira.fr/fr/services-en-langue-basque/ecoles.html (Accessed August 8, 2018) We must note that teaching immersive classes or bilingual classes are not exclusive from each other; therefore, some schools appear in both categories.
113 Seaska is the federation of Ikastola schools in Iparralde. The difference between general private schools and associative schools in France was explained in chapter 4.
114 For more details on this experimentation, see Zabaleta Apaolaza, "Inmersión lingüística y Constitución: una perspectiva francesa," 102.
115 http://web64.ac-bordeaux.fr/fileadmin/fichiers/circos/anglet/Documents/BILINGUISME/Protocole_experimentation_pedagogique.pdf (Accessed March 17, 2021).
116 http://www.mintzaira.fr/fr/services-en-langue-basque/colleges-lycees.html (Accessed August 8, 2018)
117 Table 5.3 has been created by the author to give a clear vision of the schooling offered in Euskara in Iparralde, using the data of the POBL website for the 2018–2019 academic year.
118 http://www.mintzaira.fr/fileadmin/documents/Enquete_sociolinguistique/Sintesia_2016_euskaraz.pdf (Accessed August 8, 2018). All of the tables and figures that follow in this chapter are extracted from this report. https://www.mintzaira.fr/fileadmin/documents/Aktualitateak/Prentsaurrekoak/2023/2023_03_30/Synthese_des_resultats-fr.pdf (Accessed July 22, 2024). All the following figures and tables are created and translated by the author using this data.
119 Eztitxu Harignordoquy is a teacher of bilingual classes in Basque in public secondary schools of Iparralde. See appendix 2.
120 At the time of the interview (2019), she was the principal of the Piarres Larzabal secondary school and has been teaching in Seaska since 1986. See appendix 2.
121 Xan Aire is the coordinator of the linguistic project of Seaska. See appendix 2.
122 Dynamics such as Euskaraldia (https://euskaraldia.eus/) or Mintzalasai

(https://mintzalasai.eus/) try to start developing the use of Euskara in everyday life.

123 While most non-Basque speakers are Spanish-speaking (either being originally from the Basque Country or Spain, or emigrating from a Spanish-speaking country abroad), it must be noted the increasing immigration is not merely Spanish-speaking, even in the town of Hondarribia. Lately, the immigrating families arrive also from Central and Eastern Europe, or countries from Africa (for example, the town of Hondarribia has a significant population arriving from Senegal). Also, often these families are not monolingual: they might bring a series of languages from home (Polish and Ukrainian for instance) *and* speak Spanish, thus are not technically monolingual. For the sake of clarity, we are going to join all the families of non-Basque-language speakers under the label of "Spanish-speaking," despite not all of them being Spanish-speaking *monolingual* families.

124 Programa de Aprendizaje de Inglés (PAI) is a program where some classes are taught in English. PAI can go hand in hand with the three models. This means students can enjoy Model A-PAI, Model B-PAI, or Model D-PAI. It does not hinder the study of Euskara.

125 Here, too, some students are not coming from strictly French-speaking families. In fact, Harignordoquy mentioned she has some students coming from the UK and Brazil. The norm being that non-Basque-speaking children coming from strictly French-speaking families, the author will refer to them as "French-speaking."

126 Law n°2019-791 of July 26, 2019 for a school of trust (translated by the author, originally *Loi n°2019-791 du 26 juillet 2019 pour une école de la confiance*) https://www.legifrance.gouv.fr/jorf/id/JORFTEXT000038829065/ (Accessed July 15, 2021).

127 The data provided about the effects of this reform by the Public Office of the Breton Language is enlightening. See the report "High school reform and territorial language teaching in France. The challenges of Act 2019-791 of 26 July 2019 'pour un école de la confiance,' the so-called 'Blanquer Act,' " published by the Network to Promote Linguistic Diversity (NPLD): https://www.npld.eu/our-publications/ (Accessed July 15, 2021).

128 Fishman, *Can Threatened Languages Be Saved?*, 466.

129 MacCormick, "Institutional Normative Order: A Conception of Law."

Part III

The Basque Language and Media

Media plays a key role in the development and maintenance of minority languages. When researching media—and correlatively freedom of expression—we generally hear little about minority languages and their rights. In relation to media or freedom of expression in the main European societies, attention is immediately shifted to the majority language(s) of a country. As a matter of fact, media in major languages are key actors in building a common European social imaginary and, even more importantly, in the creation of a state-level identity.[1] When talking about minority language speakers and media, this chapter will reflect not only on the legal and social dimension of media in Basque, but also on the connection between freedom of expression and (minority) language rights. Both the negative and the positive aspects of the right to freedom of expression and minority language rights will be discussed, as well as what characterizes these two aspects. When they are linked to language rights, we will define the negative freedom of expression as the non-prohibition of using the language of one's choice. Supporting this idea, the Supreme Court of Canada stated the following:

> Language is so intimately related to the form and content of expression that there cannot be true freedom of expression by means of language if one is prohibited from using the language of one's choice. Language is not merely a means or medium of expression; it colors the content and meaning of expression.[2]

Not only did the Canadian Supreme Court decide already in 1988 on the built-in relationship between language and freedom of expression, but also in 1993, the Human Rights Committee delivered a decision on the matter. Indeed, in *Ballantyne, Davidson, and McIntyre v. Canada*, the committee granted a wide approach to freedom of expression, adding to it commercial expression.[3] On the positive aspect of freedom of expression and language rights, we will argue that it is defined as the right to receive information in one's language.[4] These rights might seem superficial or stretched for those who are not a minority language speaker or who can access media in their native language easily. Yet, "like many rights which are asserted (such as the right to work), it only seems important to those who do not possess it."[5] It is true, in the case of any language, that the number of readers and writers will be lower than the number of speakers, but this issue is extremely accentuated in the case of minority languages.[6] Also, the activity of building both a European and a state identity by the major language media "may exert hard pressure concealing another expression of Europe, formed by minority language communities that claim their place on the construction of an inclusive European social imaginary and, besides, on the empowerment of citizens and their own community reality."[7] Therefore, protecting and implementing these rights are of critical importance for minority language speakers. This is the reason behind this chapter exploring media and the Basque language.

Euskara is highly linked to orality, as for centuries it relied on the oral passing of knowledge, culture, and language. With the institutionalization of the regions of the BAC and Navarre, one could think this led to the production of media in Basque. However, the media produced in the Basque language is not as recent as one might imagine. The first newspaper published in the Basque language that we know of was in 1834—a biweekly newspaper in Donostia-San Sebastián during the Carlist War.[8] The second time the Basque language appeared in a newspaper publication was in Iparralde. Joseph Augustin Chaho[9] published two issues of *Uscal Herrico Gaseta* in 1848, when presenting himself to the legislative elections. He was looking for Basque-speaking voters.[10] At the end of the nineteenth century, the electoral struggle between the "xuriak" (*the whites*, conservatives) and "gorriak" (*the reds*, republicans) created two very important weeklies in the history of Basque journalism: There was *Le Réveil Basque* (active between 1884 and 1892), published in Pau. Opposing this publication and political position was *Eskualduna*, a newspaper receiving support from the Catholic right, close to the bishopric of Bayonne. This was the longest-running weekly publication in Euskara to date (from 1884 to 1944). It was shut down for its support of the German Nazi invaders during the Second World War and later was replaced by *Herria*. The beginnings of the publications in Basque were linked, therefore, to politics.

Trying to get some distance from the political world, movements for developing true journalism in Euskara started at the end of the nineteenth century and the beginning of the twentieth century, led by Resurrección María de Azkue.[11] Before the Civil War in Spain, the most important newspaper written in Basque was *Argia* (1921–1936) from Donostia-San Sebastián. Sadly, the Civil War and, later, the dictatorship of Franco marked a cessation in the development of journalism in Basque. Yet, one can get a sense of how journalism and the Basque language could have developed with two small examples. On the one hand, the first Basque daily journal was written in Basque. This newspaper—*Eguna*—was published from the beginning of January 1937 until mid-June 1937. On the other hand, the official daily of the Basque Country (*Euzkadi'ko Agintzaritzaren Egunerokoa*, Euzkadi's Daily Newspaper) was publishing in Basque the legal and administrative provisions of the Basque government under the presidency of Jose Antonio Aguirre (the first *lehendakari*, from 1936 to 1960).[12] This means that the tendency seemed to be going toward media written in Euskara.

When democracy was reestablished in Spain, several other types of media in Euskara were born, but two main media outlets marked a new beginning: *Euskal Irrati Telebista* (EITB), the Basque public radio and public television, and *Euskaldunon Egunkaria* (Egunkaria), the daily newspaper written in Basque.[13] EITB was the first public media outlet created exclusively in Basque to promote "Basque culture and language," and it was later divided into two channels (two television channels and two radio stations), one in Castilian and the other in Basque.[14] The media bestowal of recognition and power to a language is especially important in the case of a minority language.[15] This was well understood by the Basque administrative bodies, notably in the beginning of the normalization process of the Basque language in the BAC. As a matter of fact, when the Basque Parliament was established in 1980, the creation of public media in

Basque was immediately invoked. Agirreazkuenaga explains that it was decided to immediately launch a public radio in Euskara because a pool of professionals was already available thanks to the *Radio Popular* station, which had a Basque-speaking audience that would follow them.[16] However, at the same time, the viability of a public television station exclusively in Basque was questioned.

The BAC currently still has public and private media outlets entirely in Basque. In Iparralde and Navarre, access to media in Euskara is slightly more complicated, but possible. Both the negative and positive aspects of freedom of expression and language rights are covered to a greater or lesser extent throughout the three Basque administrations. What is the impact of the legal framework in this matter? What solutions have Basque speakers and institutions found to create and develop access to media in Basque? To answer these questions, we will elaborate on the legal framework surrounding media and the Basque language and its context.

Notes

1. Zabaleta et al., "European minority language media and journalism: Framing their marginal reality," 276-277.
2. *Ford v. Québec*, 1988, para. 40 https://decisions.scc-csc.ca/scc-csc/scc-csc/en/item/384/index.do (Accessed 26 July 2024).
3. *Ballantyne, Davidson, McIntyre v. Canada*, 1993 https://www.legal-tools.org/doc/90u36m/ (Accessed 26 July 2024).
4. Both the positive and negative aspects of freedom of expression and (minority) language rights are further analyzed in the following chapters.
5. Cormack, "Problems of Minority Language Broadcasting: Gaelic in Scotland," 102.
6. Cormack, "Minority Language Media in Western Europe," 44.
7. Zabaleta et al., "European minority language media and journalism: Framing their marginal reality," 277.
8. Díaz Noci, "La langue basque dans les médias de la Communauté Autonome Basque," 109-110.
9. Influential Basque writer, journalist, politician, and linguist from Iparralde.
10. Díaz Noci, "La langue basque dans les médias de la Communauté Autonome Basque," 110.
11. Díaz Noci, 112. Resurrección María de Azkue was a priest, writer, musician, and academic. He was the first head of *Euskaltzaindia*, the Royal Academy of

the Basque Language. He was very influential and made major contributions to the study of the Basque language.
12 Díaz Noci, 113. Jose Antonio Aguirre was a Basque nationalist politician and the first president (*lehendakari*) of the Provisional Government of the Basque Country. Despite being the first lehendakari, because of the Civil War, he shortly left on exile to France, where he presided over the Basque government in exile until 1940. When France was invaded by Germany, he escaped by moving through different countries to end up in New York—where he also presided over the Basque government in exile.
13 Both EITB and the private newspaper *Euskaldunon Egunkaria* will be explored in the next two chapters.
14 Díaz Noci, "La langue basque dans les médias de la Communauté Autonome Basque," 114.
15 Earlier, this empowering role of media was also understood by Basque speakers. This is brilliantly analyzed in Agirreazkuenaga, "The role of the media in empowering minority identities: Basque-language radio during the Franco dictatorship (1960s–1976) and their influence as identity catalysts."
16 Agirreazkuenaga., ibid., 505.

6

Legal Framework of Media and the Basque Language

Minority languages are usually underrepresented in the media, notably in the case of Spain and France.[1] The role of law in regulating language use of the media is particularly prominent regarding public service media: Since they belong to the public sector, the general regulation of official languages tends to include them. However, the language used by private media can also be affected by legal norms that restrict or promote the use of languages. Thus, the legal framework surrounding media and Euskara concerns mainly public media but, to a lesser extent, manages to permeate private media.

The following analysis of the Basque language and media addresses this landscape. Analyzing the legal corpus of the media in Euskara, notably the domestic legal corpus, is key to understanding how a minority language media exists, develops, and survives. We will explore the legal framework regarding this matter in Spain, in France, and at the European level.

Spain, Media, and the Basque Language

Media in Spain is regulated by a general framework at the national level but also through the autonomous communities. Therefore, to understand media and Euskara in Spain, we will discuss the legal framework of Spain, followed by that of the autonomous communities of the BAC and Navarre.

To grasp the legal framework of Spain, we must examine both the regulation of media and language as well as the distribution of competences on media between the central state and the autonomous communities.

The General Rules on Media and Languages

Article 20 of the Constitution, together with Article 149 regarding the sharing of competences, regulate the media. Article 20 is dedicated to the freedom of expression, and Article 20.3 sets the regulation and organization of public media by the law and under parliamentary control.[2] This article also underscores the access to these media of the significant social and political groups, respecting the pluralism of society and diverse languages of Spain. Therefore, Article 20.3 already mentions the language plurality of Spain and its necessary presence in public media.

Article 4.3 updated by the General Audiovisual Communication Law 13/2022.[3] states that the operators of audiovisual services "will promote the knowledge and dissemination of the official languages in the State and their cultural expressions."[4] Yet, this responsibility falls in the hand of publicly owned operators, since they "will contribute to the promotion of the cultural industry, especially that of audiovisual creations linked to the different languages and cultures existing in the State."[5] In addition, General Audiovisual Law 7/2010 includes Article 5, which affirms the right to cultural and linguistic diversity in Spain: "Everyone has the right to an audiovisual communication that includes open programming that reflects the cultural and linguistic diversity of the citizenry"[6] (Article 5.1) and sets the rules to do so. The second paragraph of Article 5 goes further and grants the autonomous communities with co-official languages the power to approve additional rules for promoting media in those languages.[7] Some authors have argued,[8] therefore, that the national media institutions, such as *Radio y Televisión Española* (Spanish Radio and Television, RTVE[9]), should showcase the linguistic and cultural diversity of Spain and not merely focus on offering monolingual programs in Spanish,[10] which is currently the case.

Thus, as we have just seen, rules regarding media relate back to freedom of expression or to its linguistic content. Yet, another general aspect of media that we must consider in Spain is its financing, notably the financing of public media. In a country where most media outlets are in the hands of private companies, the funding of public media outlets is very important. This funding is not in the hands of the central state. Focusing on the example of press, one should note, since the nineties, Spain is the only country in the EU where the regions—autonomous communities—are exclusively responsible for direct press subsidies.[11]

After the democratic transition, there were three types of direct press subsidies in Spain and other types of indirect subsidies. The granting of subsidies was criticized for the lack of transparency during the first democratic government (1977–1982).[12] The following government (social democrats-PSOE) in 1982 retained only the three direct subsidies previously in place: for the consumption of newsprint produced in Spain, for circulation, and for technological restructuring. Keeping these direct subsidies especially benefited the big newspapers, since no mechanism was put into place to favor or help smaller media outlets. This, however, did not last long. The General State Budget Act 37/1988 abolished direct subsidies. This was also encouraged by Spain's desire to access the European Economic Community (EEC). As a matter of fact, in 1988, the European authorities underscored that, for Spain to access the EEC, this country would be required to abolish subsidies for nationally produced newsprint because it would infringe on competition rules.[13] Yet, Act 37/1988 went far beyond what was expected from the EEC, abolishing any type of subsidy by the central government. As a result, since 1990, only the reduced-rate of the Value Added Tax (VAT)[14] has remained as an indirect subsidy for Spanish newspapers.

The example of direct press subsidies already shows the important role that the autonomous communities play in the media landscape in Spain. This is further emphasized in the case of co-official minority languages. Indeed, the 7/2010 Audiovisual Law articulates in the second paragraph of Article 5.1 that the autonomous communities with a co-official language "have the right to approve additional rules for the audiovisual communication services within their sphere of competences to promote audiovisual production [in that language]."[15] Once again following the trend of the 1978 Constitution and the devolution of powers, the media in Euskara mainly falls under the umbrella of regional competences.

The Distribution of Competences on Media

Interestingly, if we look at Articles 148 and 149 of the Spanish Constitution, in which competences are distributed between the central state and the autonomous communities, the competences over media seem to belong to the central state (Article 149), as Article 148 does not mention media. Yet, Statutes of Autonomy list among their competences "creating and maintaining their own television, radio, and press"[16] for instance. Therefore, at first glance, the distribution of powers for the media seems rather confusing in Spain. Luckily, the Spanish Constitutional Tribunal clarified that powers over the media are shared between the central state and the autonomous communities. Decision 78/2017 gives us useful insight into the doctrine elaborated by the tribunal over the years on this matter.[17]

Regarding the division of powers over media regulation in Spain, the Constitutional Tribunal has established a double criterion that needs to be applied with caution,[18] based on Articles 149.1.21 and 149.1.27 of the Constitution. Article 149.1.21 affirms that the central state holds exclusive competence over the "general system of communications," while Article 149.1.27 declares that the central state holds exclusive competence over "basic rules relating to the organization of the press, radio and television and, in general, all the means of social communication, without prejudice to the powers vested in the Autonomous Communities related to their development and implementation." Considering that the former article is more expansive than the latter, the Constitutional Tribunal considers the rule for dividing the powers in the area of media must be interpreted restrictively to avoid "unjustifiable exclusion from the autonomic competences."[19] In other words, Article 149.1.27 of the Constitution allows for the articulation of a regime of shared competences between the state and the autonomous communities,[20] according to which "it corresponds to the State to dictate the basic regulations, with the Autonomous Community assuming powers of legislative development that in any case must respect those basic regulations, a regulatory power also of development, and, finally, the executive function corresponding to the matter."[21] This way, the exclusive power of the central state is to regulate the general regime.[22]

The Constitutional Tribunal believes it is "constitutionally legitimate for the State to regulate from a unitary conception all forms of telecommunication,"[23] given the intrinsic unity of the phenomenon. The Constitutional Tribunal also decided that Article 149.1.21 of the Constitution grants exclusive competence to the state regarding the "general communications regime," which includes all the regulatory powers and even the attribution of the powers of execution to configure a unitary system for media in Spain.[24] The general regulation by the state includes the planning and control of the radioelectric spectrum: the determination of broadcasting channels, assignment of frequencies, allocation of multiple channels for each demarcation, and technical characteristics of local digital television stations.[25] The Constitutional Tribunal in 2016 reiterated this:

"[The central State exclusively deals with] the assignment of frequencies and powers for each of the uses, in compliance with the international discipline of the subject, as well as the anticipation of other problems."[26] In a nutshell, the Constitutional Tribunal has decided that the central state has the power of regulating the operating conditions of media in a unitary fashion.[27]

Following the criterion established by the Constitutional Tribunal, the power of the autonomous communities must intervene only to *develop* the general regulations provided by the central state. Furthermore, linking back to the distribution of powers, the Constitutional Tribunal decided those technical aspects clearly related to the regulation of media "remain within the exclusive State competence" granted by Article 149.1.21;[28] whereas the direct relationship between the media and the fundamental rights of communicating and receiving information, and freedom of expression (Article 20 of the Constitution) is in the hands of the autonomous communities. This means that the technical aspects of media and their regulation remain a central state matter, and the autonomous communities intervene in the fundamental rights aspect of the media, notably in the right to inform and receive information in a co-official language.

Finally, another key element for the Constitutional Tribunal on this matter is the risk of Article 149.1.21 "emptying the content of the autonomous jurisdiction."[29] Yet, the tribunal affirms that Articles 149.1.21 and 149.1.27 "necessarily limit and counterbalance each other, preventing the mutual emptying of their respective contents."[30] Both powers on regulating media (from the central state and the autonomous communities) limit each other and thus cannot be separated.[31]

In Spain, the promotion of a language using media policies gets prioritized when it concerns co-official languages. The previously examined Audiovisual Law 7/2010 and the updated 13/2022 Law include the linguistic particularities of the autonomous communities. Therefore, in addition to the sharing of competences clarified by the Constitutional Tribunal, Law 7/2010 enables the autonomous communities to regulate on language matters their local media and co-official languages. Regarding the Basque language, the active role taken by the government in the BAC (and some attempts by Navarre) show the concern of regional governments to showcase Euskara in media. In fact, the BAC and Navarre have a key role in media in Basque. Because of the system of devolution of powers existing in Spain, these two autonomous communities have shaped the landscape of the media in Euskara. Thus, having discussed the legal framework of media and the Basque language in Spain, we now focus on the autonomous communities where Basque is recognized: the BAC and Navarre.

Autonomous Communities and Media in Basque: The BAC and Navarre

Law 46/1983 of December 26 already set up a regional channel of national television in the Basque Country, Galicia, and Valencia (later Madrid and Andalusia).[32] Yet, the distribution of powers enabled the creation of regional media. For the case of media in Basque, we will examine the legal framework on the matter for the BAC and Navarre.

Legal Framework of Media in Basque: the BAC

As we have seen, the Constitution does not clearly express the sharing between the autonomous communities and the central state for the subject of media, but this often appears in the Statutes of Autonomy. In the BAC, the Statute of Autonomy mentions the relationship that media and the Basque language have in its territory.

Article 19.1 states that the BAC will create laws on the development of basic norms on media, respecting Article 20 of the Constitution. The BAC claims in its Statute of Autonomy, therefore, its competences over media in its territory, but underscores cooperation with the central state in relation to the national media (Article 19.2). Finally, in Article 19.3, the Statute of Autonomy affirms that the BAC can "regulate, create, and maintain its own television, radio, and press, and in general, all the social communication media for the achievement of its goals."[33]

If we look at Normalization Law 10/1982,[34] we notice that the entire third chapter is exclusively devoted to the use of Basque in the media. Article 22 of the Normalization Law recognizes the "right of all citizens to be informed by the mass media equally in Basque and in Castilian."[35] Article 22 also entails an active role on the part of the Basque government to "increase the presence of the Basque language in media" for a "progressive equalization of the use of both official languages."[36] Article 23 of the Normalization Law's third chapter addresses regional public media and instructs the Basque government to "promote the preferential use of Basque in the media of the Autonomous Community, in order to guarantee the equalization of both languages established in [Article 22]. The next element addresses the regional programs of the national public media and thus, Article 24 mentions that the Basque government "will promote linguistic normalization in RTVE broadcasting centers in order to ensure an adequate presence of Basque [. . .]." This relates back to the division of powers regarding media we have already discussed, with the Spanish Constitutional Tribunal establishing that the central state decides on the general rules of media and the autonomous communities decide on the development of these general regulations.

Finally, Article 25 of the Normalization Law completes Article 22 by listing the areas in which the Basque government must enhance the diffusion and use of the Basque language, and the possibilities of its effective use.[37] These areas are:
- Broadcasting (radio)
- Press and publications
- Cinematography
- Theatre and shows
- Media for image and sound reproduction

Interestingly, television is not approached as an extension of the *Televisión Española* but rather as another public television setting, a service of its own. This started with an agreement signed on October 3, 1980, between the Councillor of Culture of the Basque government, Ramón Labayen, and the managing director of RTVE, Fernando Arias-Salgado. This agreement included a slot in Basque to be broadcast in the *Telenorte* regional news.[38] This meant main headlines were read in Basque, translated from Spanish. A similar policy was applied in radio. Regarding radio, however, especially between 1984 and 1991, two spaces found their place in Basque, with *Radio 4*, where the journalist Argi Dorronsoro founded, in Euskara, a magazine and a space for music (*radiofórmula*).[39] Cobreros already highlighted, in 1989, that the RTVE did not fulfill the role of media for a bilingual society.[40] This is the role undertaken by the Basque media (following Article 19.3 of the Statute of Autonomy), while respecting Article 20 of the Constitution. Consequently, EITB entered the arena.[41]

In 1982, the Basque government listed among its objectives the creation of a Basque-language radio and television. That same year, with the law 5/1982, *Euskal Irrati Telebista* (Basque Radio-Television, EITB) was created,[42] followed by Decree 157/1982 that created *Euskal Telebista* (Basque television). The idea was to create a television channel entirely in Basque with the main objectives being the protection and diffusion of Basque culture and the Basque language.[43]

When analyzing media and the Basque language in the BAC, we must mention Decree 231/2011 of November 8 that regulates both private and public media in the BAC. This decree, about the audiovisual communication in the BAC, contains specific elements on the Basque language. Article 7.2.c states that the rules for the attribution of broadcasting licenses must expressly state the number of licenses reserved for broadcasting in Basque.[44] In addition, Article 9 affirms that there must necessarily be a license reserved for television broadcasting entirely in Basque in each service zone if the number of licenses to be awarded is greater than three (Article 9.1).[45] For radio broadcasting, at least one-third of the licenses must be reserved for broadcasting exclusively in Basque when the population of the service zone is more than 100,000, and if the number of licenses to be awarded is greater than three (Article 9.2). Also, in the competition for the adjudication of licenses for radio broadcasting, at least one license must be reserved when the population of the service zone is less than 100,000, and if the number of licenses to be awarded is greater than or equal to two (Article 9.3). Interestingly, Article 9.5 allows for discarding the previous rules (Articles 9.1 to 9.4) when no offering is presented for broadcasting entirely in Basque. The same applies when the offerings presented to broadcast entirely in Basque do not meet the needs of the service, according to the thresholds established in rules of the tender. The decree also mentions the commitment of the Basque government with the promotion of the Basque language in media, in Article 10 devoted to evaluation criteria.[46] Article 10 lists the evaluation criteria and, among them, we find the "commitment to broadcast programming in Basque" (Article 10.1.f).[47]

Finally, and more importantly, the Audiovisual Communication Decree of 2011 defines media's function of public service in its Article 21.[48] Regarding the Basque language, in the first part of the article, the decree underscores the role of public media in protecting "the cultural and linguistic uniqueness of the Basque Country" (Article 21.1).[49] And it adds (in Article 21.2) the following: "Providers of audiovisual public communication service will ensure in their media a presence of the Basque language equivalent, at least to the rate of Basque speakers in the service area, according to the data made public in the latest sociolinguistic map published by the Basque Government."[50] This shows the commitment of the BAC toward media in Euskara despite being in a complex media environment. As Kelly-Holmes puts it: "The media system in the (Spanish) Basque Country is a complex one both structurally and linguistically [. . .]. Thus the Basque language is competing for its place on media run by the Spanish state, the Basque autonomous Government and private media systems against the dominant Castilian language."[51]

This analysis has shown that the BAC has placed media in Euskara among its priorities regarding the normalization of the Basque language. We will now examine how the power of the autonomous communities over the regulation of media and their co-official languages is translated in Navarre.

Legal Framework of Media in Basque: Navarre

In Navarre, the media in Basque appears in the Statute of Autonomy. The Statute of Autonomy mentions in its Article 55 that Navarre must develop the legal corpus about the regime of television and radio broadcasting (Article 55.1),[52] as well as developing the laws and executing the basic norms of the central state concerning the press and media in general (Article 55.2). Also, Article 55.3 underscores that Navarre "can regulate, create, and maintain its own press, radio, and television, and media in general, for the fulfilment of its purposes."[53] Thus, Article 55 means that Navarre has authority over legislation on regional radio and television broadcasting, and media in general. Yet, despite the authority that the Statute of Autonomy gives to Navarre in terms of developing a legal corpus on local media or media in Basque, not much has been developed on the matter. Furthermore, Navarre has not created its own public television or radio broadcaster, making it impossible to comply with the linguistic positive obligations in the media field arising from the Basque Language Act of 1986.

The Foral Law 18/1986 on the Basque Language,[54] in its Article 27, affirms that the Navarrese public administration should promote the presence of the Basque language in public and private media.[55] As a matter of fact, mirroring the Normalization Law of the BAC, the law of 1986 dedicates its Title III to media. To comply with this obligation, *Euskarabidea* holds the role of promoting the presence of the Basque language in public and private media in Navarre, as well as creating support plans and agreements (regulated under the Foral Decree 130/2015 of August 28, by which the Statutes of Euskarabidea are approved).[56]

On January 25, 2017, the government of Navarre approved the first Strategic Plan of the Basque Language (2016–2019).[57] Among other things, this first plan includes the "social use" of Basque, where funding is foreseen for the Basque language in media. The latest call for funding[58] was published in the Foral Order

16E/2021 for the "use of Basque in written press, radio, and online media, as well as for the implementation of Information and Communication Technologies (ICT) and digitization processes in the media for 2021."[59] This order establishes the basis for the allocation of the following funds: 895,912 euros for promoting the presence of Basque in media, and 25,000 euros for the development of apps for the promotion of the Basque language in the digital environment. Order 16E/2021 also contemplates the possibility of increasing the budget for these grants by up to 24,088 euros in the case of budget availability. The results were published in May 2021.[60] These grants are managed by Euskarabidea, an institution which plays a key role regarding the Basque language in Navarre. Among the list of the functions of Euskarabidea, we find the following assignments that relate to Euskara in media:

- Increase the presence of the Basque language in the social media of Navarre.
- Propose, manage, and control the calls and agreements to promote Basque in the public and private media.
- Promote the emergence of Navarre's information and communication technologies in Navarre.[61]

Euskarabidea is a powerful tool for the promotion of media in Basque for Navarre, even if it still has not managed to provide the support that the media in Euskara finds in the BAC.

Finally, private media in Navarre is regulated via the Foral Decree 5/2012 on the audiovisual communication services of Navarre.[62] The Basque language is also included in this regulation, with Article 12.e stating that, for the assessment conditions for the granting of broadcasting licenses, broadcasting in Basque will be considered.

The BAC has strong legal assets to establish and develop media in the Basque language, and Navarre seems to fall short even if there is potential with the existent legal corpus. With these two examples, we can already start noticing different layers for the regulation of media in Euskara. This discussion leads us to the other side of the border, to examine the landscape of media in Euskara in France.

France, Media, and the Basque Language

In France, the press or media is mainly regulated via general laws, and no specific law can be found on regional languages and media. But freedom of the press is protected under Article 11 of the 1789 Declaration of the Rights of Man and of the Citizen. Additionally, the law of July 29, 1881, on the freedom of the press, defines the freedoms and responsibilities linked to the French press. This law was modified to include matters linked to the discrimination and fight against racism, such as the Pleven Law of July 1, 1972. The Pleven Law also included the prohibition of insult or defamation toward individuals or groups in relation to their origin, or to their belonging—or not belonging—to an ethnic group, a nation, a race, or a religion. The Gayssot Law of July 13, 1990, added the prohibition of negation of crimes against humanity performed by the Nazi regime. There are, of course, more legal norms regarding media in France, notably those regulating the independence of the press[63] or fake news.[64]

This shows that the regulation of media in France seems to be very concerned about pluralism. In fact, the Constitutional Council decided on October 11, 1984,[65] that the pluralism of daily newspapers of political and general information is "in itself an objective of constitutional value." This decision was followed by laws or decisions about pluralism and the independence of the press,[66] and updating the legal corpus to apply to the internet.[67]

This preliminary overview of the regulation of media in France tells us that an emphasis is put on protecting against discrimination or defamation, but linguistic minorities are not directly mentioned. Yet, even if the main concern of the legal corpus in France toward the press has been under the lens of freedom of expression, manipulation of news, negationism, racism, or even pluralism, there are, still, laws that mention the regional languages and media in France.

The Legal Framework: France

The NOTRe Law on the new territorial organization of the Republic[68] is relevant when talking about media and regional languages in France. Chapter IV of this law concerns shared competences[69] "in the field of culture, sport, tourism, *promotion of regional languages*, popular education and regrouping of instruction, and the granting of grants or subsidies."[70] In this law, Article 103 starts by emphasizing that "the responsibility in cultural matters is jointly exercised by the territorial collectivities and the State, while respecting the cultural rights set out in the Convention on the Protection and Promotion of the Diversity of Cultural Expressions of October 20, 2005."[71] It is followed by Article 104, which inserts the following in the General Code of the territorial collectivities:[72]

"The competences in culture, sport, tourism, promotion of regional languages, and popular education are shared between municipalities, departments, regions, and special status communities."[73] Therefore, regions and local authorities have a say in regulating and/or promoting regional languages.

However, the key law regarding media and the Basque language in France is Law 2009-258 on audiovisual communication,[74] updating Law 86-1067 of 1986 on freedom of communication. This law also regulates private media. Article 3-1 of the law of audiovisual communication explains that the Audiovisual High Council (*Conseil supérieur de l'audiovisuel*) "guarantees the exercise of the freedom of communication" as well as "contributes to the actions in favor of the social cohesion and the fight against discrimination in the domain of audiovisual communications."[75] More importantly, this council must ensure "the defense and the illustration of the French language and the French culture," while fighting against "discriminations in the domain of audiovisual communication" and ensuring the programming "mirrors the diversity of the French society."[76]

Regarding the use of languages, Article 20-1 sets the rules for media in France: "*The use of French is mandatory* in all programs and advertising messages of audiovisual communication organization and services, whatever their mode of dissemination or distribution, with the exception of cinematographic and audiovisual works in their original version."[77] Thus, the general rule about media in France, unsurprisingly, is the mandatory use of French in public media outlets. Yet, there are some limits to this general rule.

Article 28 includes the regional languages together with the French language in the programming of music in the radio broadcastings (2 bis),[78] while including the need to ensure the "respect of the French language" (4 bis).[79] Albeit small, this contribution still grants some presence to the regional languages in radio broadcasting. Regarding the radio and television broadcasting not using the frequencies assigned by the Audiovisual High Council, Article 33 explains that a decree by the Council of State fixes the provisions to "ensure the respect for the French language and the influence of the French-speaking world [the *francophonie*] as well as those relating to the broadcasting, on radio services, of musical works of French expression or interpreted in a regional language in use in France" (Article 33-5).[80]

Regarding the public sector of audiovisual communication, Article 43-11[81] explains that these companies must "implement actions in favor of social cohesion, cultural diversity, and the fight against discrimination, and offer a program reflecting the diversity of French society." In addition, they also should "promote the French language and, where applicable, regional languages and highlight the diversity of France's cultural and linguistic heritage." Hence, the promotion of regional languages is included in the public sector of public media in France. This extends to the *France Télévisions* public company since, according to Article 44, it should "design and broadcast regional programs that contribute to the knowledge and influence of these territories and, where applicable, to the expression of regional languages."[82] The landscape concerning media and languages in France follows a similar logic to the one we have seen previously regarding education (part II): the general rule is the mandatory use of French in public media, with some inclusion of regional languages.

After looking at the legal framework of media and the Basque language in France, it is worth focusing on the regional and local framework. In fact, after exploring the diverse general regulations, one could ask how this translates into the reality of Basque speakers in Iparralde.

Iparralde and Media in Basque

Having analyzed the legal framework of France[83] and the landscape of education in Basque in Iparralde, it should be no surprise that mass media in Iparralde is mainly broadcast in French. Like in many cases regarding the Basque language or Basque culture, media in Euskara also remains mainly in the hands of private actors. The next chapter will elaborate more on the public and private actors in this matter. This section will focus on the regulation of broadcasting in Basque in public media in Iparralde.

There is, in fact, a limited inclusion of regional languages within the public media system. Regarding television, *France Télévisions* contains the France 3 national channel, devoted to providing programming that "contributes to the knowledge and influence of the territories and, where appropriate, to the *expression of regional languages*" (Article 3.2 of Decree 2009-796).[84] This channel offers national, regional, and local news and is thought to be a channel portraying the local culture(s) and language(s). More importantly, Article 40 of the 2009 Decree states that "France Télévisions ensures that, among the services it publishes, those which offer regional and local programs contribute to the expression of the main regional languages spoken in metropolitan France and overseas."[85] This means that, in practice, via the France 3 channel, some presence of regional languages in French public television is guaranteed.

Yet, data from 2022 shown on a web page[86] of the France 3 public television channel shows that, in 2022, only 10:46 hours were broadcast in Basque, second-to-last place among regional languages broadcast on French public television (figure 6.1).[87]

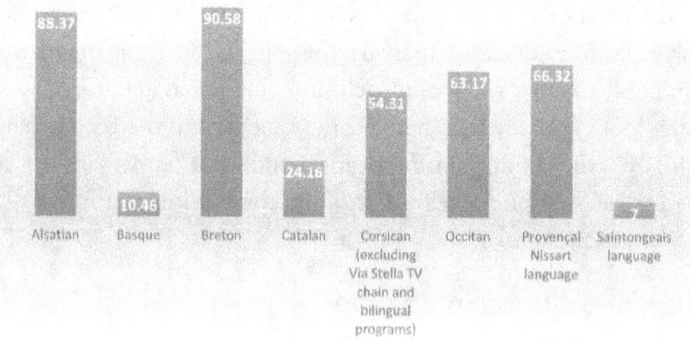

Figure 6.1. Hours broadcasted in regional language on France 3 TV channel (2022).

If we keep looking at the programming offered by France 3 (available on its website[88]), we notice the scarcity of programs airing in Euskara: We can only find *Txirrita*, a twenty-six-minute-long cultural magazine program broadcast once every two Sundays at 10:10 a.m.

Despite being included in public television broadcasting, the Basque language seems to have a rather limited presence, notably when compared, as previously mentioned, to the efforts made in the BAC to provide co-official television, with ETB1 fully broadcasting in Basque. In Iparralde, the efforts made by the French government for the inclusion of Euskara in public television relegates the language to a biweekly cultural magazine.

In a study commissioned by the POBL, published in October 2019[89] on the "attendance and consumption of media in Iparralde and media and streaming in Basque language,"[90] the results showed[91] that 41 percent of Basque speakers and receptive speakers would like to see an improvement in a local television station having content in Basque. Among those, 64 percent of those consuming France 3 would like to see more content in Basque.

Regarding public media in Iparralde, Euskara is also included in radio broadcasting. If we take a look at Radio France's mission and job specifications (Radio France mission statements),[92] Article 6 of this text reads that Radio France should "ensure that local stations contribute to the expression of regional languages."[93] Basque content in French public radio can be found in the France Bleu Pays Basque station.[94] Yet, the study of 2019 by the POBL shows 50 percent of Basque speakers and receptive speakers who listen to France Bleu Pays Basque would like to have more content in Basque on this radio station.[95]

To assess the prospects of the future of media in Basque language, it is worth noting, despite the low number of Basque speakers in Iparralde, compared to the BAC, for example, 42 percent of the population over thirteen years that were interviewed regularly or occasionally consume at least one media outlet with content entirely in Basque.[96] It is even encouraging that the study shows that non-Basque speakers regularly or occasionally consume at least one media outlet in the Basque language: 12 percent Euskal Irratiak (radio) and 14 percent EITB.[97]

Now that we have discussed the legal framework of media in Euskara in Spain and in France, as well as specifically in the BAC, Navarre, and Iparralde, we should look at the European legal framework on media and the Basque language.

The European Legal Framework, Media, and the Basque Language

To explore the European legal framework of the Basque language and media, we will analyze the European Union framework in relation to media in minority languages, the Language Charter and media in Basque, and the European Convention on Human Rights and media in Basque through the prism of freedom of expression.

The European Union and Media in Basque

One could imagine that the European Union laws' effect is limited in regard to media. Yet, the European Union does help promote Euskara in culture. Moreover, Article 167 of the TFEU stresses the importance of cultural diversity.[98] Article 167(4) reads: "The Union shall take cultural aspects into account in its action under other provisions of the Treaties, in particular in order to respect and to promote the diversity of its cultures." This means that even when regulating media, the diversity of cultures should be promoted. One might ask if all cultures or their languages are included in this definition.

Some elements of European Union law show the importance of minority languages. For instance, decision no. 1934/2000/EC of the European Parliament and of the Council of July 17, 2000, on the European Year of Languages 2001 affirms, in its fourth paragraph of the Preamble: "All the European languages, in their spoken and written forms, are equal in value and dignity from the cultural point of view and form an integral part of European cultures and civilization."[99] The equal value and importance of languages is also highlighted in Article 2, when explaining the objectives of the European Year of Languages (Article 2.a).[100] Yet, at the same time, this decision acknowledges that "the languages question is one of the core and unresolved matters, for there is a deep divide between majority and minority languages across the most fundamental areas of language development such as education, status, media and publishing, competence and use."[101]

Interestingly, the latest directive regarding media also mentions languages. Directive 2010/13/EU of the European Parliament and of the Council of 10 March 2010, known as the Audiovisual Media Services Directive,[102] highlights the importance of media pluralism. It also mentions the importance of a regulatory framework for the pursuit of broadcasting activities to "ensure optimal conditions of competitiveness and legal certainty for Europe's information technologies and its media industries and services, as well as *respect for cultural and linguistic diversity.*"[103] Moreover, paragraph 78 authorizes putting into place active policies in favor of a specific language.[104] Yet, these paragraphs belong to the Preamble and not to the directive's actual text. Therefore, these do not constitute binding norms and can only serve for the interpretation of operational provisions of the directive itself. If we look at the text of the directive, there are no rules on linguistic content. Despite including some elements that could be of value for linguistic minorities in the Preamble, the Audiovisual Media Services Directive is rather meaningless in its enforceable rules for them.

Even if, a priori, not much is said in the EU legal corpus on media and minority languages, we can detect hints in some documents that indicate the importance of languages and cultural diversity. Another important aspect to consider when exploring the European legal framework of media and Euskara is the Language Charter.

The European Charter for Regional or Minority Languages

Article 11 of the Language Charter regulates media. The article must be read together with the charter's Article 7[105] because it defines the objectives and principles that the text should pursue. Despite having no enforcement mechanism, the Language Charter has a monitoring system to assess how effectively it is implemented in each of the signatory states. These assessments are highly valuable to qualify media and the regional or minority language concerned. Therefore, we will briefly analyze the reports regarding Spain to discuss the health of Basque in media in the territories of the BAC and Navarre.

The topic of media in Basque both in Navarre and the BAC has been brought up by the Language Charter's reports over time. Early on, during the first report in 2005, the Committee of Experts encouraged the creation and maintenance of a private radio station and television broadcasting in Basque in both territories.[106] Furthermore, in this first round, the Committee of Ministers recommended adopting "a structured approach, with a view to strengthening the use of Basque in the private electronic media in the Basque Country and in broadcasting in general in Navarre."[107] The Committee of Experts in 2019 once again raised the issues of accessing television and radio in Basque in Navarre,[108] despite the improvements made in the case of EITB.[109]

After the first report, successive reports consistently emphasized the precariousness of Euskara's presence in media in Navarre. In the second evaluation report of the Committee of Experts in 2008,[110] for the Basque language in Navarre, the main issues emphasized dealt with the lack of presence of Euskara in the media. This was followed by the evaluation report of 2012,[111] in which the Committee of Experts recommended improving the cooperation between the BAC and Navarre to access media in Euskara in Navarre.[112] The same recommendations were presented in the committee's 2016 evaluation report.[113]

The Language Charter's evaluation system provides helpful information on the health of Euskara in Spain, notably in the case of media. The need to improve the situation of media in Euskara in Navarre seems to be a recurrent theme, as well as the need to increase the cooperation between the two Basque autonomous communities. But is the Language Charter efficient in improving the health of media in Basque in the BAC and Navarre? It's true the Committee of Experts keeps track of the issues the Basque language faces in both territories[114] and that recommendations are being made. Yet, the Language Charter does not make a major difference in regard to the use of Euskara in media. Experts interviewed for this chapter also agree on this matter: The Language Charter helps to give another layer of legal protection and provides a much-needed record of the evolution, but sadly it does not strongly influence the everyday use or inclusion of the Basque language in media.[115]

The European Convention on Human Rights and Media in Basque: Freedom of Expression

When looking into the European Convention on Human Rights in relation to media and its linguistic dimension, one understands that the fundamental right of freedom of expression ties both things together. In other words, freedom of expression is materialized by language.[116] Indeed, language and freedom of expression are inextricably linked, and therefore, protection of freedom of expression should hold some language content, especially in the case of minority languages. Indeed, as mentioned in the introduction to part III, in the case *Ballantyne, Davidson, and McIntyre v. Canada*, the Human Rights Committee found that freedom of expression includes "the freedom to express oneself in a language of one's choice."[117] Thus, it is interesting to analyze if the European Court of Human Rights interprets the European Convention on Human Rights (the Convention) as including the linguistic dimension into its right to freedom of expression.[118]

Looking into the text of the Convention, we notice that this treaty does not contain many linguistic rights. In fact, the linguistic rights we discover in the text are the ones regarding fair trial (Article 5.2) and the rights of the detained (Article 6.3.a). As noted by Henrard,[119] Article 9 (freedom to manifest a belief) has not been understood by the Strasbourg Court as giving any language rights. Nevertheless, recent case law brings a new era on linguistic rights under Article 10, despite not yet bringing positive duties for the state parties.[120]

Freedom of Expression and Minority Languages, under the European Convention on Human Rights

Together with its privileged position in liberal democratic constitutions, freedom of expression also holds a privileged position in the landscape of fundamental rights. This position was underscored by the jurisprudence of the European Court of Human Rights (the Court) for the first time in *Handyside v. United Kingdom*, where the Court highlights: "Freedom of expression constitutes one of the essential foundations of such a society, on the basic conditions for its progress and for the development of every man."[121] Later, in *Arslan v. Turkey*, the Court adds that "freedom of expression constitutes one of the essential foundations of a democratic society and one of the basic conditions for its progress and for each individual's self-fulfillment."[122] Considering these two cases together, we can find how the Court links freedom of expression not only to the basic needs for a liberal democratic society, but also to the importance for each individual as entitled to human rights.

Despite the Court deciding on the limits to freedom of expression, the case law on this topic argued before the Court shows how freedom of expression is interpreted in a comprehensive way.[123] However, freedom of expression is not an absolute right and encounters some limits. As a matter of fact, the Court considers in the Convention's Article 10.2 the option of limiting this right. When analyzing a case regarding Article 10—as expressed in *Handyside*—the Court decides that the limitation of freedom of expression is legitimate if it is "prescribed by law," has a "legitimate aim," and is "necessary in a democratic society," which should be grounded on the existence of a "pressing social need."

One cannot help but observe that because language is the tool of communication, freedom of expression and language are interconnected. Indeed, language is the means we use to express ourselves and define our identity. Furthermore, "freedom of expression is, in at least two respects, of special relevance for minorities. It allows them to express their own identity as well as to advocate a change of current Government policies of particular relevance to their lives and identity."[124] Following this reasoning, we can safely claim that freedom of expression has a major relevance for the rights of linguistic minorities. In fact, language in this case is both the tool and the identity marker. For linguistic minorities, using a minority language is crucial not only for "self-expression" but also for "self-fulfillment."[125] Schmalz adds that "language forms an essential medium of culture and identity, it is crucial for knowledge and narratives, literature and rituals."[126] Following this thread, we could ask ourselves what the interpretation of the Strasbourg Court has been regarding freedom of expression and linguistic minorities. Hence, if we move from the analysis of the text of the Convention toward the interpretation of the Court, we find that language-related rights appear beyond the above-mentioned Articles 5.2 and 6.3.a.

Freedom of Expression and Minority Languages in the Case Law of the European Court of Human Rights

When discussing freedom of expression and minority languages, one should investigate the case law of the Strasbourg Court and how it does or does not protect the use of these languages. Also, it must be emphasized that no article of the Convention (ECHR) protects language rights, although it has dealt with them on different occasions.[127]

Before diving into Article 10, this analysis must consider relevant case law regarding languages and minority languages under other articles of the Convention. A case that should be discussed—despite not being directly linked to Article 10 of the Convention—is the Belgian linguistics case.[128] This language-related case had to do with Articles 8 and 14 of the Convention, and Article 2 of the Protocol 1. In this case, the Court claimed that sending children to a French language school was the parents' choice and not imposed by the Belgian law. More importantly, the Court also claimed that Article 2 of Protocol 1 does not grant a right to education in one's own language. Therefore, the first approach of the Court to linguistic minorities was rather restrictive about any protection of language rights. The Court also took this restrictive approach in 2001 in *Cyprus v. Turkey*.[129]

Another case relating to language under Article 8 is *Mentzen v. Latvia*.[130] This case concerned the spelling of a surname in accordance with the spelling rules of the Latvian language. The applicant claimed that the transcription of her surname violated her right to respect her private and family life (Article 8). The Court claimed, however, that the Latvian authorities did not overstep the margin of appreciation, a legal principle that gives countries room to interpret and apply human rights in their own way.[131] Once again, language rights had to confront the wall of a restrictive interpretation from the Court.

Yet, we can read a new narrative regarding linguistic rights in the jurisprudence of the Strasbourg Court. Indeed, the same year as *Cyprus v. Turkey*, the Court faced another case: *Association Ekin v. France*.[132] This case concerned an alleged violation of Articles 10 and 6 by France.[133] The case involved the *Ekin* association, which released a book in French, Spanish, Basque, and English under the title of *Euskadi at War* in 1987. This book was banned by the French minister of the interior using Section 14 of the Law of 1881, which granted him the right to impose an absolute ban in France for the circulation, distribution, or sale of any documents written in a foreign language, or any document from foreign origin, even if written in French. Thus, the publication was banned because of its "foreign origin" and because it was seen as a threat to the public order because of the topic it portrayed.

It must be noted that case law established the concept of "foreign origin" and the conditions for the application of this rule. The nationality and place of residence of the authors, the fact that the publication was a translation, the country in which it was published or printed, the fact that foreign assistance was provided, and/or the presence of foreign documentation and inspiration were all factors indicating a foreign origin to the jurisprudence of the Council of State.[134] The status of foreign publication was decided considering all these indicators taken together. In this case, the publication was banned because it was considered that four of five chapters were written by Spanish authors and the documentation used for the publication was mainly from Spanish origin. The Strasbourg Court decided that there was no definition of the concept of "foreign origin" and also no indication on the grounds allowing these publications to be banned, producing "results that are at best surprising and in some cases verge on the arbitrary, depending on the language of publication or the place of origin."[135] Therefore, the Court concluded that the ban "did not meet a pressing social need and was not proportionate to the legitimate aim pursued."[136]

This case, regarding a Basque association publishing a book on the Basque terrorism issue in Basque, already allows us to start thinking about Article 10 and minority languages. The use of language wasn't directly relevant in this case but probably played a role in the decision to censor the book. Interestingly, thinking about this case from the language perspective, one can imagine if the publication had only been in Spanish, the French authorities probably would not have bothered to prohibit it. This could be seen as an example of what Schmalz calls an "anxiety logic,"[137] where a book on the issue of Basque terrorism, published in Basque (among other languages) is immediately placed in the context of threats to political unity. In any case, through this case, we can see that freedom of expression under Article 10 started to evolve slightly in the Court's language toward a right containing some sort of protection of the use of a language.

The discussion of the linguistic side of freedom of expression entered the arena again following the decision of *Egitim ve Bilim Emekçileri Sendikasi v. Turkey*,[138] and even further with *Sükran Aydin v. Turkey*.[139] These two decisions bring the protection of use of language under the scope of freedom of expression in the private sphere settings.

The 2013 case of *Sükran Aydin* is extremely important for the linguistic content of freedom of expression. This case had to do with five candidates who used Kurdish during their campaigns. These individuals were living in regions with large Kurdish populations, and a law at that time prohibited the use of any language other than Turkish in campaigning. In this case, we must not lose sight of the Court underscoring that the Convention does not guarantee the right to use a language and does not guarantee per se the right to use a particular language in communications with public authorities for electoral purposes. In addition, the Court expressed that Article 10 does not cover matters such as the choice of working language in a parliamentary assembly.[140] Moving from this point, the Court acknowledges that the case concerns the imposition of "a linguistic restriction" on persons in relations "with other private individuals."[141] Thus, the Court considers that the imposition of the use of Turkish, even during speeches in an election period, goes against Article 10:

The Court reiterates that Article 10 encompasses the freedom to receive and impart information and ideas *in any language* that allows persons to participate in the public exchange of all varieties of cultural, political and social information and ideas . . . in such contexts, *language as a medium of expression undoubtedly deserves protection under Article 10*.[142]

The Court, in *Sükran Aydin*, already adds a linguistic connotation to Article 10, since it considers that language is a tool of expression that needs to be protected. Paragraph 52 relates, therefore, to the democratic dimension of freedom of expression, in which language is seen as an essential tool for a democratic liberal society. At the same time, the Court also includes the "identitarian" dimension of the language in this case, since in paragraph 55, the Court recognizes that the language used by the applicants was Kurdish—their mother tongue—and was also the mother tongue of the people receiving the information. Following this, the Court declares: "The right to impart one's political views and ideas and the right of others to receive them would be meaningless if the possibility of using a language that could properly convey those views and ideas were diminished owing to the threat of criminal sanctions."[143]

The case of *Sükran Aydin* calls for an additional explanation. Following Guset's analysis, two readings of the case can be performed.[144] On the one hand, reading paragraph 51 and paragraph 52 together, one can find a narrow understanding of the state's margin of appreciation, since the Court underscores that Turkey was the only state among twenty-two to pair the use of minority languages in electoral speeches with fines and imprisonment punishments. On the other hand, the Court highlights that "the Convention does not guarantee per se the right to use a particular language in communications with public authorities or the right to receive information in a language of one's choice."[145] Here, the Court emphasizes that freedom of expression does not include a right to use the language of one's choice in communication with public authorities. Still, the decision *Sükran Aydin* is of fundamental importance in bringing an understanding of the right of freedom of expression—by the Strasbourg Court—as containing a linguistic dimension, even if limited to the private life and social life sphere.

Albeit slowly, the Strasbourg Court seems to be willing to develop a broader understanding of freedom of expression that would also include the linguistic dimension of this right. Nevertheless, the *Sükran Aydin* case marks the meeting point between the Human Rights Committee and the European Court of Human Rights of the intrinsic link between freedom of expression and language.

It is worth noting, as Schmalz pointed out,[146] the partly dissenting opinion on the case by Judge Keller, in which it is argued the importance of language use as a "core human rights issue" would have required examining Article 14 of the ECHR (prohibition of discrimination).[147] This links back to the various dimensions that language rights encounter: They are linked to freedom of expression, the right to education (see part II), and prohibition of discrimination, to name a few. In addition, when dealing with linguistic minority rights, other elements come into play. In the *Sükran Aydın* case, attention was paid to the use of Kurdish. In fact, the Court considered that Kurdish was the mother tongue of the applicants as well as the people to whom the discourses were addressed. Some of them did not even understand Turkish. Schmalz rightly extracts two arguments from this: On the one hand, the significance of the mother tongue "as the language in which persons would be best able to express themselves," and on the other, the question of understanding the use of Kurdish was justified because some recipients did not understand Turkish.[148] This shows, according to Schmalz, the Court's reasoning of languages "goes beyond the mere question of understanding and conveyance of information."[149] In this case, the Court does understand the implications of language for this minority community: "While a speech is a momentary act, language is also reflective of more durable features for a person such as her affiliation with a group and her familiarity with a certain culture. This is particularly the case, when the language at stake is the person's mother tongue."[150] Thus, for a minority language, freedom of expression gets another important layer added. The use of the mother tongue, while linked to freedom of expression, in the case of minorities should be carefully considered when talking about limiting this right.

Linguistic minorities know more restriction than freedom. This chapter addressed the issue of the relationship between language rights and freedom of expression. Focusing on Article 10 of the ECHR regarding freedom of expression and its relationship with minority languages helped us to see that even if the international environment already settled on the intrinsic link between language and freedom of expression, the Strasbourg Court has had some difficulties formalizing this linkage. However, the recent evolution of the jurisprudence of the Court seems to introduce the protection of language rights through Article 10—under certain circumstances. Even if this is the case, we cannot forget that the apparent new protection setting provided by the

Court is not enough for the protection of regional or minority languages. Yet, although the European Court of Human Rights is still not granting any language rights per se, the above discussed cases seem to open—if not a door—at least a window, for the further elaboration on freedom of expression and use of regional or minority languages.

Notes

1 Rigoni, Navarro, y Saitta, "Les médias des minorités culturelles et linguistiques en Espagne, en France et en Italie," 56.
2 Spanish Constitution, Article 20.3: "The law shall regulate the organization and parliamentary control of the mass communication means under the control of the State or any public agency and shall guarantee access to such means by the significant social and political groups, respecting the pluralism of society and of the various languages of Spain." For the English version of the Spanish Constitution, see https://www.senado.es/web/conocersenado/normas/constitucion/detalleconstitucioncompleta/index.html?lang=en#a13 (Accessed July 24, 2024).
3 This law was updated by the General Law 13/2022 of Audiovisual Communication of July 7th. Originally, Ley 13/2022, de 7 de julio, General de Comunicación Audiovisual. https://www.boe.es/buscar/act.php?id=BOE-A-2022-11311 (Accessed May 2025)
4 Article 4.3 of the Law 7/2010, translated by the author.
5 Ibid.
6 Translated by the author.
7 See the discussion regarding this division of competences below.
8 See Cobreros Mendazona y Pizzorusso, *El régimen jurídico de la oficialidad del euskara*.
9 The RTVE is regulated under the Law 17/2006. https://www.boe.es/buscar/act.php?id=BOE-A-2006-9958 (Accessed July 26, 2024).
10 The Law 17/2006 (ibid.) includes Article 3.2.e. that affirms RTVE should "promote the territorial cohesion, the plurality, and the linguistic and cultural diversity of Spain" (translated by the author).
11 Fernández Alonso y Blasco Gil, "Press subsidy policies in Spain in the context of financial crisis (2008-2012): An analysis of the Catalan case,". 172.
12 Fernández Alonso y Blasco Gil.

13 Fernández Alonso y Blasco Gil., 173.
14 The VAT (in Spanish IVA, *Impuesto sobre el Valor Añadido*) is an indirect tax on consumption derived from the purchase of goods or professional services.
15 Translated by the author.
16 Article 19 of the Statute of Autonomy of the BAC. Translated by the author. The Statutes of Autonomy and the media in Basque are examined later in this chapter.
17 Decision 78/2017, of June 22. http://hj.tribunalconstitucional.es/es-ES/Resolucion/Show/25385 (Accessed May 28, 2021).
18 See decisions 168/1993, on the Law 31/1987 of Organization of the Telecommunications (translated by the author, FJ4), 244/1993, relating to the conflict on the competences over the procedure for obtaining administrative authorizations for the installation and operation of radio-electric installations for the reception of television programs transmitted by satellite (FJ2), 5/2012, relating to the conflict of competences over the use of radio frequencies without administrative authorization (FJ5), and 235/2012, relating to the conflict of competences over the administration of Justice, airports, telecommunications and television (FJ6).
19 Decision 78/2017, FJ4, translated by the author.
20 Decisions 108/1993 FJ3, 168/1993 FJ8, 127/1994 FJ8, and 5/2012 FJ6.
21 Decision 78/2017, FJ4, translated by the author: "Article 149.1.27 [of the Spanish Constitution] allows the articulation of a system of shared competences between the State and the Autonomous Community, according to which the State is responsible for issuing basic regulations, with the Autonomous Community assuming legislative development competences, which in any case must respect those basic regulations, a regulatory power also for development, and finally, the executive function corresponding to the matter.
22 See decisions 8/2012 FJ16, 168/1993 FJ4, and 31/2010 FJ85.
23 Decision 168/1993, FJ4. Translated by the author.
24 Decision 31/2010 FJ85.
25 Decision STC 235/2012, FJ7.b.
26 Translated by the author. Decision 8/2016 FJ3.
27 See decisions 8/2012 FJ4 and FJ11; 235/2012; 72/2014 FJ3 and FJ6; 168/1993 FJ4; 8/2016 FJ3; and 180/2000 FJ12.
28 Translated by the author, decision 78/2017 FJ4: "The point of connection

that allows selecting the application of one or the other title is, on the one hand, the direct relationship of radio broadcasting, as a means of social communication, with the fundamental freedoms and rights contained in Article 20 [of the Spanish Constitution] and referring in some way to the right to communicate and receive information and to freedom of expression, a circumstance that makes both radio and television a phenomenon, in essence, not different from the press; in these cases Article 149.1.27 [of the Constitution] plays as a rule of distribution of competences. On the other hand, technical aspects clearly related to the regulation of the support or instrument used by radio and television—radioelectric, hertzian or electromagnetic waves—fall within the exclusive state competence under Article 149.1.21 [of the Constitution] to organize the public radioelectric domain; a domain that it is not useless now to recall, is susceptible of different uses for other types of communications that are also carried out by means of radioelectric waves and different from broadcasting; reason for which it is necessary a unitary organization of the problem through the assignment of frequencies and powers for each one of the uses, in compliance with the international discipline of the subject, as well as the foresight of other problems such as, e.g., the avoidance of interference with the radio and television broadcasting, as well as the avoidance of interference with the radio and television broadcasting, e.g., the avoidance of interference." See also Decisions 168/1993 FJ4, 244/1993 FJ2, 5/2012 FJ5, and 235/2012 FJ6.

29   Decision 168/1993 FJ4.
30   Translated by the author, decision 78/2017 FJ4: "[...] it is clear that both titles "necessarily limit and counterbalance each other, preventing the mutual emptying of their respective contents and, in this sense, they cannot be totally separated; although it is obvious that they should not overlap [...] when it comes to providing coverage for a given legal regulation. And this, precisely, in order to avoid the emptying of the regime of competence sharing provided for in Article 149.1.27 [of the Constitution], to the benefit of the State and to the detriment of the autonomous competences in radio and television matters."
31   See decisions 168/1993 FJ4 and 244/1993 FJ12.
32   https://www.boe.es/buscar/doc.php?id=BOE-A-1984-250 (Accessed November

11, 2020)
33   Translated by the author.
34   See the analysis of the Normalization Law in part I, chapter 3.
35   Translated by the author. Article 22: "The right of all citizens to be informed by the mass media equally in Basque and in Castilian is recognized. To this effect, the Government shall adopt the measures leading to increase the presence of the Basque language in the mass media, tending toward the progressive equalization of the use of both official languages."
36   Translated by the author.
37   See appendix 1.
38   Díaz Noci, "Los medios de comunicación y la normalización del euskera: balance de dieciséis años". 446.
39   Díaz Noci., ibid., 446-447.
40   Cobreros Mendazona y Pizzorusso, *El régimen jurídico de la oficialidad del euskara*.
41   The Basque Public Television Network EITB (previously named ETB) will be examined below.
42   Law 5/1982, of May 20, 1982, on the creation of the Public Entity "Basque Radio Television" (translated by the author. Originally: Ley 5/1982, de 20 de Mayo, de creación del Ente Público "Radio Televisión Vasca") https://www.euskadi.eus/bopv2/datos/1982/06/8200684a.pdf (Accessed October 14, 2020).
43   Díaz Noci, "Los medios de comunicación y la normalización del euskera: balance de dieciséis años,". 447.
44   Article 7, translated and emphasis added by the author: "Rules of the tender:
1. It is incumbent upon the Governing Council to approve the bases of the contest.
2. The bidding conditions shall contain, as a minimum, the following elements:
a) Licenses to be granted, the service area and technical characteristics;
b) Conditions for the provision of the service, with an expression of those that are considered essential;
c) If applicable, the number of licenses reserved for full broadcasting in Basque;
d) Documentation accrediting the requirements and legal capacity;
e) Evaluation criteria and their weighting, as well as the minimum thresholds that, if applicable, are established;
f) Guarantees that, if applicable, must be deposited; and

g) Composition of the Evaluation Committee"
45 See appendix 1.
46 Article 10. *Translated and emphasis added by the author: "Evaluation criteria:*
1. For the awarding of licenses, the following criteria shall be assessed, with the weighting attributed to them in the bidding conditions:
a) Programming proposal
b) Economic and structural proposals
c) Technological proposal
d) Contribution to the plurality of the supply of audiovisual communication service providers.
e) Promotion of employment
f) Commitment to broadcast programming in Basque
2. In the case provided for in Article 28.3 of Law 7/2010, of March 31, 2010, General Law on Audiovisual Communication, the terms and conditions of the call shall include the experience of the bidders, their solvency and the means they have for the operation of the license, as criteria to be taken into account in the award."
47 Translated by the author.
48 Translated and emphasis added by the author. Article 21: "Function of the audiovisual public service and its control:
1. It is the responsibility of the providers of the public audiovisual communication service to promote the protection of the cultural and linguistic uniqueness of the Basque Country, to foster tolerance and encourage peaceful coexistence, to promote the equality of men and women and to contribute to the eradication of sexist violence, as well as to pay special attention to the dissemination of knowledge, arts and sciences.
2. The providers of the public audiovisual communication service shall ensure in their media a presence of Basque at least equivalent to the number of Basque speakers in the service area, in accordance with the data made public in the latest sociolinguistic map published by the Basque Government.
3. The governing bodies of the local entities shall be responsible for identifying the public service contents, as well as for controlling the management and compliance with the public service function."
49 Translated by the author. "Basque Country" here refers to the BAC.
50 Ibid.
51 Kelly-Holmes, Moriarty, y Pietikäinen, "Convergence and divergence in

Basque, Irish and Sámi media language policing," 229.

52   Article 55 of the Statute of Autonomy of Navarre, translated by the author:
"1. Navarre is responsible for the legislative development and implementation of the radio and television broadcasting system under the terms and in the cases established in the Law regulating the Legal Statute of Radio and Television.
2. It is also responsible for the legislative development and implementation of the basic rules of the State relating to the press regime and, in general, of all means of social communication.
3. In accordance with the provisions of the preceding paragraphs, Navarre may regulate, create and maintain its own press, radio and television and, in general, all means of social communication for the fulfillment of its purposes."

53   Translated by the author.

54   See part I, chapter 3.

55   Article 27, translated by the author:
"The Public Administrations shall promote the progressive presence of Basque in the public and private media.
To this end, the Government of Navarre will elaborate plans of economic and material support so that the media use Basque in a habitual and progressive way.
2. In television and radio stations, and in the other media managed by the Foral Community, the Government of Navarre shall ensure the adequate presence of the Basque language."

56   The Navarrese institution Euskarabidea studies and advises the development of the regulation on the use of the Basque language in Navarre. Its function appears in the Foral Decree 303/2019 of November 6.

57   El plan estratégico del Euskera (2016–2019). This 2016-2019 Strategic Plan has been updated by the 2020-2027 Strategic Plan: https://gobiernoabierto.navarra.es/sites/default/files/pee_borrador_inicial.pdf (Accessed May 31st, 2025).

58   To date (June 2021).

59   https://bon.navarra.es/es/anuncio/-/texto/2021/52/14 (Accessed June 3, 2021).

60   https://www.navarra.es/documents/48192/6870827/Resoluci%C3%B3n_19E-2021_CSV.pdf/a38d4025-6fc3-de80-4d6f-4e23c-be94c53?t=1620290295651 (Accessed June 3, 2021).

61 Translated by the author. See the full list in http://www.euskarabidea.es/euskara/eginkizunak (Accessed June 3, 2021).
62 http://www.lexnavarra.navarra.es/detalle.asp?r=25576 (Accessed June 21, 2021).
63 See the order of August 26, 1944, that prohibits the concentration of press units.
64 See two propositions of organic laws issued by the National Assembly and adopted on July 3, 2018.
65 Decision no. 84-181, October 11, 1984.
66 See anti-Hersant Law n° 84-937 of October 23, 1984, and the Law n°86-897 on the reforming the legal status of the press of August 1, 1986.
67 Regarding the internet, the Council of State was asked if there was a need for a specific regulation of the internet and digital networks. In December 1998, after a study was conducted, the judges decided that the legislation on media is applicable to the internet.
68 See part I, chapter 2.
69 The shared competences in France do not compare directly to the devolution of powers toward the autonomous communities in Spain. The shared competences in France are administrative and not legislative in nature. This means that French legislation is ranked higher than what the French regions might decide.
70 Translated and emphasized by the author.
71 Translated by the author.
72 Code général des Collectivités Territoriales.
73 Translated by the author.
74 https://www.legifrance.gouv.fr/loda/id/JORFTEXT000020352071/ (Accessed June 11, 2021).
75 Translated by the author.
76 See ibid.
77 Translated and emphasis added by the author.
78 Article 28, 2°bis, translated by the author: "The substantial proportion of musical works of French expression or interpreted in a regional language used in France, which must reach a minimum of 40 percent of songs of French expression, at least half of which must come from new talents or new productions, broadcast during significant listening hours by each of the radio services authorized by the Superior Council of audiovisual, for the portion of its programs composed of variety music."

79 Translated by the author. Article 28, 4°bis: "Provisions to ensure respect for the French language and the influence of the French-speaking world [the *Francophonie*]."
80 Article 33, 5° translated by the author.
81 Article 43-11 translated by the author.
82 Article 44 translated by the author.
83 See part I, chapter 2, notably on the constitutional situation of Euskara in France.
84 Article 3 of the Decree no. 2009-796, June 3, 2009. Translated by and emphasis added by the author: https://www.legifrance.gouv.fr/loda/id/JORFTEXT000020788471/ (Accessed June 15, 2021).
85 Translated by the author.
86 https://www.francetvpro.fr/contenu-de-presse/59676441 (Accessed July 26, 2024).
87 Figure 6.1 created and translated by the author using the data from the map provided by France 3: https://view.genially.com/65158f7b0aa29a00111b4672 (Accessed July 26, 2024).
88 https://www.francetvpro.fr/contenu-de-presse/60406169?parent=59676441 (Accessed July 26, 2024).
89 Despite this study being published in October 2019, it was published in the website of the POBL in January 2020. https://www.mintzaira.fr/fileadmin/documents/Aktualitateak/OPLB_RAPPORT_FREQUENTATION_MEDIAS2019.pdf (Accessed July 26, 2024). For the summary of this study see https://www.mintzaira.fr/fileadmin/documents/Aktualitateak/OPLB_Frequentation_medias_-_Note_de_synthese_-_09.01.2020.pdf (Accessed July 26, 2024).
90 Translated by the author. Originally *"Etude sur la fréquentation et la consommation des médias au Pays Basque et des médias et émissions en langue basque."*
91 See page 3 of the summary of the study. https://www.mintzaira.fr/fileadmin/documents/Aktualitateak/OPLB_Frequentation_medias_-_Note_de_synthese_-_09.01.2020.pdf (Accessed July 26, 2024).
92 Translated by the author, originally: *cahier des missions et des charges de Radio France* https://www.csa.fr/Reguler/Espace-juridique/Les-textes-de-references/Decrets-et-arretes/Decrets-portant-cahiers-des-charges-des-services-publics-de-communication-audiovisuelle/Decret-portant-approbation-du-cahier-des-missions-et-des-charges-de-Radio-France (Accessed June 15, 2021).
93 Translated by the author: "The company contributes to the promotion and illustration of the French language in compliance with the recommendations

of the National Commission of Communication and of Freedoms. It ensures the quality of the language used in its programs. It ensures that local stations contribute to the expression of regional languages."

94 https://www.francebleu.fr/pays-basque (Accessed 26 July 2024).
95 See page 4 of the summary of the Study. Ibid.
96 See page 7 of the Summary of the study. Ibid.
97 See page 7 of the Summary of the study. Ibid.
98 Article 167 of the TFEU:
"1. The Union shall contribute to the flowering of the cultures of the Member States, while respecting their national and regional diversity and at the same time bringing the common cultural heritage to the fore.
2. Action by the Union shall be aimed at encouraging cooperation between Member States and, if necessary, supporting and supplementing their action in the following areas:
• improvement of the knowledge and dissemination of the culture and history of the European peoples,
• conservation and safeguarding of cultural heritage of European significance,
• non-commercial cultural exchanges,
• artistic and literary creation, including in the audiovisual sector.
3. The Union and the Member States shall foster cooperation with third countries and the competent international organisations in the sphere of culture, in particular the Council of Europe.
4. The Union shall take cultural aspects into account in its action under other provisions of the Treaties, in particular in order to respect and to promote the diversity of its cultures.
5. In order to contribute to the achievement of the objectives referred to in this Article:
• the European Parliament and the Council acting in accordance with the ordinary legislative procedure and after consulting the Committee of the Regions, shall adopt incentive measures, excluding any harmonisation of the laws and regulations of the Member States,
• the Council, on a proposal from the Commission, shall adopt recommendations."
99 Decision no. 1934/2000/EC of the European Parliament and of the Council of July 17, 2000 on the European Year of Languages 2001.

https://publications.europa.eu/en/publication-detail/-/publication/f9d1b376-a25f-4678-a99f-c4e947a4c9fc/language-en (Accessed April 25, 2019).
100 Article 2.a: "The objectives of the European Year of Languages shall be: (a) to raise awareness of the richness of linguistic and cultural diversity within the European Union and the value in terms of civilisation and culture embodied therein, acknowledging the principle that all languages must be recognised to have equal cultural value and dignity."
101 Zabaleta et al., "European minority language media and journalism: Framing their marginal reality," 278.
102 This directive was revised in 2018. https://eur-lex.europa.eu/legal-content/EN/ALL/?uri=CELEX%3A32010L0013 (Accessed August 20, 2020).
103 Paragraph 4 of the Audiovisual Media Services Directive, emphasized by the author.
104 "In order to allow for an active policy in favour of a specific language, Member States remain free to lay down more detailed or stricter rules in particular on the basis of language criteria, as long as those rules are in conformity with Union law, and in particular are not applicable to the retransmission of broadcasts originating in other Member States."
105 See Dunbar, "Article 7. Objectives and principles."
106 Basque television broadcasting will be analyzed briefly below and more in depth later, in chapter 7. https://rm.coe.int/CoERMPublicCommonSearchServices/DisplayDCTMContent?documentId=09000016806dba65 (Accessed May 14, 2021). Page 69.
107 See ibid., page 167, point 4.
108 See Committee of Expert's evaluations and recommendations, para. 34. https://search.coe.int/cm/Pages/result_details.aspx?ObjectId=090000168096fa01#_Toc6923307 (Accessed June 21, 2021)
109 The broadcasting of EITB in Navarre is explained below.
110 https://rm.coe.int/CoERMPublicCommonSearchServices/DisplayDCTMContent?documentId=09000016806dba68 (Accessed April 26, 2019).
111 Ibid.
112 Ibid., page 141, para. K.
113 https://rm.coe.int/CoERMPublicCommonSearchServices/

DisplayDCTMContent?documentId=09000016806f0658 (Accessed April 26, 2019).

114 Baztarrika Galparsoro, "A Look at the European Charter for Regional or Minority Languages from the Point of View of the Basque Language and the Basque Country."

115 See interview details in the following chapter.

116 Guset, "Le volet linguistique de la liberté d'expression selon la Cour européenne des droits de l'homme : le long chemin d'une consécration encore inachevée,". 813.

117 Human Rights Committee (1993). *Ballantyne, Davidson, and McIntyre v. Canada*, para 11.4.

118 Freedom of expression is contemplated in Article 10 of the ECHR.

119 Henrard, "A patchwork of "successful" and "missed" synergies in the jurisprudence of the ECHR," 341.

120 Discussed below.

121 *Handyside v. United Kingdom*, December 7, 1976, para. 49.

122 *Arslan v. Turkey*, July 8, 1999, para. 44.

123 For more information: https://www.echr.coe.int/Documents/Guide_Art_10_ENG.pdf (Accessed June 17, 2021).

124 Henrard, "A patchwork of "successful" and "missed" synergies in the jurisprudence of the ECHR," 352.

125 We can also add that, apart from "self-expression" and "self-fulfillment," in the case of linguistic minorities, the use and transmission of the language additionally has the role of self-preservation.

126 Schmalz, "Beyond an Anxiety Logic: A Critical Examination of Language Rights Cases before the European Court of Human Rights," 103.

127 See part I, chapter 1, on the legal framework. The European Court of Human Rights has dealt with language rights mainly in matters of private and family life (Article 8), freedom of expression (Article 10), and the right to education (Article 2, additional Protocol 1).

128 Case relating to certain aspects of the laws on the use of languages in education in *Belgium v. Belgium*, July 23, 1968. See part I, chapter 1. https://hudoc.echr.coe.int/fre#{%22itemid%22:[%22001-57525%22]} (Accessed July 26, 2024).

129 *Cyprus v. Turkey*, May 10, 2001. https://hudoc.echr.coe.int/Eng#{%22itemid%22:[%22001-59454%22]} (Accessed July 26, 2024).

130 Also known as *Mencena v. Latvia*, December 7, 2004. https://hudoc.echr.coe.int/eng#{%22itemid%22:[%22001-70407%22]} (Accessed July 26, 2024).
131 Ibid., 31.
132 *Association Ekin v. France*, July 17, 2001. https://hudoc.echr.coe.int/eng#{%22itemid%22:[%22001-59603%22]} (Accessed July 26, 2024).
133 We are going to leave aside the alleged violation of Article 6.
134 Association Ekin v. France, para. 27. Ibid.
135 Ibid., para. 60.
136 Ibid., para. 63.
137 Schmalz, "Beyond an Anxiety Logic: A Critical Examination of Language Rights Cases before the European Court of Human Rights."
138 *Egitim ve Bilim Emekçileri Sendikasi v. Turkey*, December 25, 2012. https://hudoc.echr.coe.int/eng#{%22itemid%22:[%22001-113410%22]} (Accessed July 26, 2024).
139 *Sükran Aydin v. Turkey*, May 27, 2013. https://hudoc.echr.coe.int/eng#{%22itemid%22:[%22001-116031%22]} (Accessed July 26, 2024).
140 Ibid., para. 50. The Court illustrates this reasoning with the following cases: *Mentzen v. Latvia, Kozlovs v. Latvia, Fryske Nasjonale Partij and Others v. the Netherlands, Association "Andecha Astur" v. Spain*, and *Brik-Levy v. France*.
141 Ibid., para. 52.
142 Ibid., end of para. 52. Text emphasized by the author.
143 Ibid., para. 55.
144 Guset, "Le volet linguistique de la liberté d'expression selon la Cour européenne des droits de l'homme: le long chemin d'une consécration encore inachevée," 824-825.
145 Sükran Aydin v. Turkey, para. 50.
146 Schmalz, "Beyond an Anxiety Logic: A Critical Examination of Language Rights Cases before the European Court of Human Rights," 109.
147 Quoted from *Sükran Aydin v. Turkey*, at Partly Dissenting Opinion of Judge Keller, para. 3.
148 Schmalz, "Beyond an Anxiety Logic: A Critical Examination of Language Rights Cases before the European Court of Human Rights," 109-10.
149 Schmalz, 110.
150 Schmalz, 115.

7

Context of Media and the Basque Language

When exploring media in the Basque language, one cannot merely look at the legal framework. Law alone does not cover the entire story of media in Euskara. Media is dynamic, and so is Basque society. Understanding the context is key to gaining a clear picture of the situation of Basque speakers and the legal regulation of their media. Nonetheless, the context is full of variables, and there are many points of view we could take to perform this analysis. Before moving forward, we will prioritize media platforms fully in the Basque language, leaving bilingual or monolingual (Spanish or French) media platforms in the background.[1] Also, in this chapter, we will consider the key actors with respect to the media and the Basque language, following the structure of the previous part II on education. These actors are chosen for their relevance in shaping (or having shaped) the media landscape in Basque and the reality of Basque speakers. They are influenced by law, and they influence back—together with the speakers—the law. In terms of structure, this chapter will proceed to a division of actors into two categories: public actors and private actors.

Public Actors

Public actors are key actors putting law into practice. Public radio and television stations have held an extremely important role in the recovering of Euskara in the BAC, as well as in Navarre—not without controversy. In the case of radio stations in Basque in Navarre, both the administration and the courts have been crucial in shaping the reality of Basque speakers and their access to these stations. We will elaborate on the example of the *Euskalerria Irratia* case, showcasing the difficulties the Basque language endures in Navarre. Also, no accurate portrait of the role of public actors in relation to media in Euskara can be provided without mentioning public funding. In a difficult setting for minority languages, public support is essential in creating, developing, and maintaining media. Transborder cooperation is also key in this area for media in Euskara. Finally, unique horizons are being explored with new technologies and media in Basque, notably by the *2deo* audiovisual laboratory.

EITB: Basque Public Television and Radio Broadcasting

Euskal Irrati Telebista (EITB) is the Basque public television and radio in the BAC, and it broadcasts in all three administrative territories of the Basque Country. EITB was created as a tool for the normalization of the Basque language. Indeed, EITB has the role of spreading both "formal" Euskara and "colloquial" Euskara.[2] EITB was created by Law 5/1982 of May 20. The public company (*sociedad anónima pública*) EITB Media[3] now encompasses the media entities developed by EITB:

1) *Eusko Irratia* (Basque Radio), dedicated to the production of radio programs and broadcasting them. This radio contains different networks, known as EITB Irratia (EITB radio): Euskadi Irratia (in the Basque language, created in 1982); Radio Euskadi (in Castilian, created in 1983); EITB Musika (specializing in music; bilingual and created in 2001); Gaztea (devoted to music in the Basque language, with a young audience in mind, created in 1990); Radio Vitoria (mainly in Castilian, created in 1934 and broadcast in the region of Araba); and EITB Euskal Kantak (created in 2019, devoted to music in Basque).

2) *Euskal Telebista* (Basque Television), producing and broadcasting television. Interestingly, these channels are broadcast in the BAC, Navarre, *and* Iparralde. The channels are: ETB1 (created in 1982, entirely in the Basque language); ETB2 (created in 1986, entirely in Castilian); ETB3 (for children and youngsters, in the Basque language, created in 2008); ETB4 (entertainment, in Castilian and Basque, created in 2014); and EITB Basque (international distribution for cable and the internet, in Basque and in Spanish, previously called ETB Sat, created in 1996).

3) *EITBNET*, created in 2004, is dedicated to content dissemination online. It mainly focuses on the maintenance of its apps and website (www.eitb.eus).

Law 5/1982, which created EITB, specifies that the general director is elected by the Basque government. After the amendment to the law of 1982, in 1998, the Parliament elects the general director. This change in the elective process, however, has not resulted in a change in the political affiliation of the elected general directors. Since 1982, all the general directors have belonged to the Basque Nationalist Party (EAJ-PNV), with one exception (Alberto Surio, PSE-EE, the Basque Socialist Party, between 2009 and 2013).

EITB Under Reform

Over the last few years, the Basque Parliament has tried to reform EITB. It has received proposals about the reshaping of EITB from various experts. We discussed some points of the proposals made by Kike Amonarriz[4] during his interview.[5] Amonarriz was asked to adapt the offer of EITB to the new sociolinguistic reality of the BAC as well as to the changes prompted by new technologies and their use. In the report he presented before the Basque Parliament,[6] he recalls that the 5/1982 law for the creation of EITB lists the roles of EITB in relation to the normalization of the Basque language:

1- To preserve the linguistic equilibrium of radio and TV broadcasting in the BAC.
2- To offer to the Basque-speaking community an entire program in Basque.
3- To promote the linguistic normalization of Basque, collaborating with and reinforcing the work developed in the educational system and in Basque culture, in general.
4- To take into consideration the cultural and linguistic plurality of Basque society.

Before talking about reshaping EITB, or making any changes, some points must be underscored. EITB has been an excellent tool for the normalization of the Basque language and has clearly been instrumental to the advancement of Basque speakers over the years. One key aspect of EITB, which Amonarriz also emphasized during his interview, is "socializing the Standard Basque language (Batua)" and making the Basque language a regular language (heard and used every day for different topics) rather than an exceptional one. Another thing he emphasized in the report and the interview is that EITB has created common cultural and social references.[7] Furthermore, EITB has provided the infrastructure for creating and producing in Euskara—essentially creating an industry for television in Basque. Also, it has enabled the use of Euskara as a working language. Last, in the words of Amonarriz, "it [EITB] has opened the world to the Basque language and the Basque language to the world."[8]

In the report he delivered to the Parliament, Amonarriz explained that these objectives must be revisited, confronting them with contemporary reality. Amonarriz is aware of the crossroads at which Basque policy makers in media currently find themselves. On the one hand, a generation that mainly studied in Model D[9] is entering the job market and starting families. And on the other hand, their use of the Basque language, despite their knowledge, is decreasing, even in the "arnasguneak."[10] This means that the children of these "Basque millennials" will live a linguistic generation gap, in which their parents speak a language but do not use it, and therefore, these children may not see the need to learn it. Considering that English has entered the Basque household and is more used than Basque worldwide, why would these children find the need to speak their mother tongue, or even to learn it? This is precisely where media policies must shift the popular mindset, Amonarriz explains. This is the time in history when media can change this future scenario.

By changing the programming offerings and, thus, the consumption of media in Basque, media can change (to a certain degree) the use of the Basque language and can help close the future linguistic generation gap scenario. Amonarriz emphasized that education alone cannot regenerate Euskara. Education and media must go hand in hand toward this goal. They have been working together in the past, and they still do today; they need to keep working together in the future. More than ever, in Amonarriz's view, the linguistic future depends on entertainment, media, and the work environment. Also, when it comes to EITB, he explains that most of the employees of EITB (also in ETB2 and Radio Euskadi) know Basque or understand it, and future employees will receive full linguistic training in the language.

Amonarriz emphasizes three points for the "redefinition of EITB." First, he underscores the evolution and growth of the radio and TV offerings since the creation of EITB has increased the gap between the offerings in Basque and in Castilian. This makes EITB—despite its limits—the only entity that could decrease this gap. Another thing to consider is the economic crisis that has significantly limited EITB's budget.[11] Amonarriz suggests rethinking the linguistic redistribution of this budget. Finally, Amonarriz argues, if the linguistic-functional distribution persists between ETB1 and ETB2, the subaltern situation of Basque will become chronic in the future; therefore, he calls for the rewriting of the law regulating[12] EITB as well as for the reshaping of EITB itself, especially when it comes to the linguistic-functional distribution.

When asked about how many different media outlets help to promote Euskara, in the "Basque Sociometer 67"[13] made by the Sociological Survey Office of the Basque Government (zero being the lowest and ten being the highest score), the best rated were ETB1, the BAC Euskadi Irratia, and Gaztea (8.4, 8.0, and 7.9 points, respectively). On the other side, Radio Euskadi received 6.2 points and EITB2 the low score of 5.2. Thus, citizens are aware that media in Basque performs the role of normalization and promotion of the Basque language. For Amonarriz, the score obtained by ETB2 especially shows the urgent need for a redefinition of this channel.

Amonarriz believes that having Basque as the language of reference in EITB in the shortest amount of time possible is key for the renewal of EITB, given these new societal parameters. The strategy to adopt in the future, in his opinion, is the following:

1- Prioritize the media in Basque, so that those stations/channels and programs become the spine of EITB. This would also imply pushing forward the channel ETB1 (contrary to having it as a secondary channel).
2- Overcome the linguistic division between the channels.
3- Maintain the media outlets in Basque (ETB1, ETB3, Euskadi Irratia, and Gaztea) as areas where the Basque language can thrive, known as "arnasguneak." This means Basque would be prioritized but does not mean Spanish would be excluded. If the situation requires it, Castilian would be dubbed or subtitled in Basque.
4- Make ETB2 and Radio Euskadi bilingual, giving more weight to interventions or content in Basque.
5- Impart in all programs a favorable discourse on linguistic coexistence, multilingualism, and revitalization of Euskara, both to Basque speakers and to the population that does not know the language.

To do so, Amonarriz offers some suggestions. He notes that there is a substantial inequality between the offerings in Basque and those in Spanish. There is also a need to integrate more fiction into the Basque offering, such as movies or TV series. For the children, there is a need to renovate and promote the programming of ETB3:

Children need new points of reference for their linguistic practices, and we need to foster their consumption of culture in Euskara. Finally, he suggests that ETB1 needs to keep offering sectoral contents (such as *Teknopolis*[14]), since these programs have an impact on their sector and/or can be used as a support for education.

From the perspective of the Basque language, it is a priority to produce the largest quantity possible of audiovisual products and put them in the hands of the speakers. Amonarriz highlights how entertainment television programs play a crucial role in the development of a language. Indeed, via those programs, Euskara is promoted, its use is reinforced, linguistic references are socialized, cultural contents make themselves known, and the recreational function of the language is reinforced. It is widely agreed that EITB is—and will remain—the main producer, engine, and agent of audiovisual content in Basque. In the imagined future reconfiguration of EITB, this public media entity would need to continue to produce in Basque certain types of programs or audiovisual content—or, when considered appropriate, to dub or subtitle them.

In the report, Amonarriz also highlights the need to reinforce the relationship between various institutions and EITB for an effective change in Basque media. These include: different internal agents of EITB, coordinated work with the Department of Language Policy in relation with the Department of Education, and collaboration with the University of Basque Country and other universities; relations with the other administrations of the Basque Country,[15] as well as with other media outlets in Basque; new spaces of collaboration and complementarity with other media in Basque, especially with local radio and television stations; and collaboration with cultural agents. These collaborative spaces would work to, among other things, lower the costs of production; enhance the impact of media; strengthen the linguistic community; widen the net of professionals; and integrate new voices, faces, and ways of talking during the regular broadcasts. Amonarriz mentions how Sarasua[16] claims the future of Basque television should include a wider spectrum of radio and television stations in Basque. He calls for a more "multipolar" offering, even if he recognizes the central value of EITB, especially in terms of objectives to achieve in the medium or short term.

Additionally, this expert in media in Basque includes two interesting points in his report. Amonarriz underscores the importance of incorporating French (and to a lesser extent, Occitan) in Basque media. Following this line of thought, he introduces the idea of a cofinancing by the administration of Iparralde (*Communauté d'Agglomération Pays Basque*). In addition, he claims it would be advisable to introduce the most used languages of the immigrant population in the programs on EITB to answer to a reality that is increasingly more plurilingual and multicultural. This would help us know and understand each other better and would guarantee the use and transmission of other languages, as well as bring these new citizens closer to the Basque language and Basque culture. Another minority that Amonarriz to which wants to draw attention is the community of people with hearing and vision impairments, who are often forgotten in the discourse of minority languages, language rights, and/or communication and media. Offering subtitles or audio description in Euskara would be useful for them but also for those who are learning or want to improve their knowledge of Basque.

Finally, Amonarriz calls for the inclusion of other radio and television media outlets that operate from the BAC in the process of normalization and recovery of Euskara. He claims that these media outlets, in exchange for public funding or public money via advertisements, should be asked to integrate Basque into their programming, which is not always the case.

As mentioned above, EITB broadcasts in the BAC, Iparralde, and Navarre. Thus, it contributes to the normalization of Euskara in the BAC, but it also fills the gap of accessing media in Basque in Iparralde and Navarre. Yet, the full coverage of the Basque Country by EITB is not without controversy, especially in Navarre.

EITB in Navarre: Between Arguments and Agreements

The story of EITB in Navarre is characterized by a series of arguments and agreements. The stormy relationship that the BAC and Navarre have had on this matter has deeply affected access to media in Euskara in Navarre.[17] The situation seemed completely blocked for decades, but recent events appear to have improved the right of Navarrese Basque speakers to access media in their language via EITB.

EITB in Navarre: A Short Introduction

Watching television in Basque in Navarre has been a challenge for years. For this analysis, we will focus on the example of EITB in Navarre. Even if one could watch EITB in Navarre, for many years this was done under legally precarious circumstances.[18] Controversy has always accompanied the presence of EITB television channels in

Navarre. Over the years, both administrations have tried to reach an agreement for cooperation that, often, included television in Basque. On June 14, 1996, the lehendakari, José Antonio Ardanza, and the president of Navarre, Javier Otano, agreed on the creation the Organ for Conjoint Collaboration. However, soon after this agreement, Otano had to quit, and Juan Cruz Alli was appointed president in his place. Alli wanted to endorse the agreement of June 14, 1996, but he did not get the backing of the Navarrese Parliament (despite holding the majority). The Parliament followed the opinion of Miguel Sanz, who clearly was opposed to the agreement. During the years of Ibarretxe (1999–2009, lehendakari of the BAC) and Sanz (1996–2011, president of Navarre), the relationship between the administrations was clearly cold, and no agreements were signed. In July 2009, Lehendakari Patxi López and President Sanz managed to reach a three-point agreement regarding the Basque language, infrastructure, and EITB. Finally, in 2016, following the change of government, Navarrese President Uxue Barkos and Lehendakari Iñigo Urkullu signed an agreement, trying to go beyond the previous ones. Over time, it seems there is a willingness to move from broadcasting illegality toward legalization for EITB in Navarre, as well as a clear demand of Navarrese citizens for their linguistic rights on accessing media in Euskara to be fulfilled. That said, this matter requires deeper analysis.

The Issue of EITB in Navarre Explained

The issue of EITB broadcasting in Navarre is extremely complex, but this section will provide the key elements, without focusing on the technical details, of what this issue entailed for broadcasting media in Euskara in Navarre.

Since the eighties, EITB has occupied some of the digital frequencies that are available. Given these circumstances, the Basque government was interested in regularizing EITB's broadcast in Navarre. However, the Basque government and the Navarrese government had some disagreements on this matter. Over the years, the Navarrese government used the lack of capacity for new channels as an argument for stopping the broadcast of EITB in Navarre. For instance, in 2004, Navarre exclusively granted its only regional slots to the private sector.[19]

Both autonomous communities eventually started collaborating, and, on July 3, 2009, they signed a collaboration protocol for broadcasting ETB1 and ETB2 channels in Navarre.[20] But disagreements persisted, mainly about two points: the distribution of costs relating to signal transport, broadcasting, and maintenance;[21] and the representation of the "institutional reality" of Navarre.[22] The latter refers to the Constitutional Tribunal's Ruling 94/1985 of July 29[23] that should result, according to the collaboration protocol, in Navarre being differentiated from the BAC in the news appearing in EITB, and the different political and ideological sensitivities of Navarre being included and respected. This Collaboration Protocol was approved two months later. However, an issue regarding a weather map including Navarre together with the other two Basque administrations on the EITB news derailed the collaboration between the BAC and Navarre. In fact, it is clear the economic and political disagreements between the Navarrese and the Basque governments were "hampering [. . .] any chance of reaching an agreement to permit ETB broadcasts within Navarrese territory."[24] This led the positions of both governments to be increasingly distanced, and the government of Navarre ended up marking three conditions for broadcasting EITB in Navarre: legal compliance, respect of the institutional reality of Navarre, and zero cost for Navarre.

Finally, the agreement of 2016 helped things move forward. The Nafar Telebista television channel had not been broadcasting on its channel 26 since October 2016. The permit to broadcast Nafar Telebista was therefore revoked. Following this revocation, the regional channel was adjudicated to the ETB1 channel, starting later that autumn. Following the agreement of 2016, starting September 6, 2018, Iruñea (Pamplona) and its surrounding areas were able to watch the television channels ETB1, ETB2, and ETB3. The Navarrese government agreed to secure a regional channel to ETB2 and therefore, starting September 6, 2018, ETB2 arrived to the entire autonomous community. The adjudication of the regional channel to ETB2 freed local channel slots that until then had been used to broadcast ETB2. This allowed, in the case of Iruñea, to broadcast ETB3. This channel broadcasts mainly in Basque, and its content is mainly aimed at children. It is important to underscore that the BAC bears the cost of integrating EITB into the Navarrese channels and also pays for the broadcasting of EITB in Navarre.

Regarding the agreement between Navarre and the BAC for the broadcasting of EITB in Navarre, the government of Navarre underscored that reserving signals for channels of EITB had its legal base in the basic regulations that regulates audiovisual communication services. The General Audiovisual Law

7/2010, in its Article 40.4, establishes that "audiovisual communication's public service broadcasting by terrestrial Hertzian waves, of a community or autonomous city in another border and with linguistic and cultural affinities, may be carried out provided that it is agreed to by contract, and there is reciprocity."[25] In the same document, the Navarrese government highlighted that Navarre and the BAC maintain a framework of relationships, which are included in the Protocol of Collaboration renewed by both parties on May 10, 2016. For the development of this protocol, both governments subscribed on July 15, 2016, to an agreement for the broadcasting of EITB in the terms of the above-mentioned Article 40.4 of Law 7/2010. By this agreement, the government of Navarre undertook arbitrating the most appropriate technical solutions for the broadcasting of EITB, depending on the available digital channels. In developing this agreement, the Navarrese government agreed to facilitate a better reception of the EITB television channels in Navarre, on August 29, 2018. This facilitates the fulfillment of the right to receive information in Basque for the territory of Navarre (coinciding with the positive linguistic right of freedom of expression).

The Euskalerria Irratia Case

Euskalerria Irratia is a radio station in Navarre. Its main studios and headquarters are in Iruñea (Pamplona). It is the first radio station to broadcast fully in Basque in Navarre since its opening in 1988. When this station is not broadcasting its local programming, it connects with the radio station Euskadi Irratia (which belongs to EITB).

Euskalerria Irratia: A Short Introduction

During the late seventies, there were some radio programs in Basque in Navarre, but they slowly started to disappear. Worried about the future of Basque-language media in Navarre, a group of forty people decided to propel the presence of radio programs in Basque by founding a company called Iruñeko Komunikabideak S.A. Each one of them brought capital of 100,000 pesetas.[26] Journalist Mikel Bujanda (from Radio Pamplona Cadena SER) was named the director. Since it did not get broadcasting authorization, it started to air without a license on November 7, 1988, to meet the needs of the Basque speakers of the area of Iruñea who wanted to listen to the radio in Basque.

The founding principles of this company stipulated the station's ideological, political, and economic independence. The founders also created an association whose members contribute every month to the station's funding. Since the station did not get permits, it could not access institutional funding. This radio station has struggled from its birth to obtain a permit despite the efforts of the company, the station, and its collaborators.

Judicial and Administrative (Counter) Mobilization and Euskalerria Irratia

In 1990, Euskalerria Irratia competed for the call of broadcasting frequency permits in the Iruñea area from the government of Navarre (PSN). Law 31/1987 of December 18, on the management of telecommunications, created a legal regime giving power to the autonomous community of Navarre to grant licenses for broadcasting. Thus, the Navarrese government called public tender for the granting of broadcasting stations, with Foral Order 6/1990, of February 28. However, despite being the first call for broadcasting licenses under a newly created co-official linguistic regime, it did not guarantee the presence of a radio station broadcast in Basque.[27] This contrasts with the approach undertaken by the BAC in similar times, in which, from the beginning, the presence of Basque was considered. This call resulted in granting the licenses to Radio Blanca and Compañía Navarra de Radiodifusión. Meanwhile, Euskalerria Irratia did not obtain a broadcasting license, because a claim was made that it was not economically viable.[28]

Following up on this issue, the biggest "derision"—as Agirreazkuenaga puts it[29]—was formulated by Navarre's Superior Tribunal of Justice, in its decision of December 19, 1994. In this decision, the tribunal ruled that programming only in Euskara can be considered "detrimental to general cultural development and to the generality of the people."[30] The tribunal added that granting a license to this radio station would "discriminate against the majority of citizens" who do not speak Basque, adding data on the Basque speakers of the area of Pamplona that did not correspond to reality. The source of this data was not disclosed.[31] This highly questionable decision sets the tone of the issues that Euskalerria Irratia was about to endure.

In 1998, a new broadcast licensing procedure was developed, in which, for the area of Iruñea, only two frequencies were delivered. This call resulted in granting permits to Medios de Comunicación 21 SL (with the brand Net 21 Radio 105.6 FM) and to Radio Universidad de Navarra (89.3 FM). Once again, Euskalerria Irratia appealed the licensing procedure before the courts in 1999, and the Parliament of Navarre investigated the case. After the investigation, the Parliament discredited the adviser of the call and asked for his removal. This removal, however, did not happen.

In December 2005, the Superior Tribunal of Justice of Navarre ruled on those broadcasting permits.[32] The Superior Tribunal decided to invalidate the concession of broadcasting permits since these concessions were unlawful, and it ordered the retroaction of the administrative file.

The back-and-forth between the Superior Tribunal of Justice of Navarre annulling the unlawful procedures and the administration perpetuating unlawful procedures[33] continued until reaching the Spanish Supreme Court in 2013.[34] The government of Navarre and the University of Navarre challenged the 2009 decision of the Superior Tribunal of Justice of Navarre, annulling once again the procedure of granting radio licenses. The Supreme Court agreed with the Superior Tribunal of Justice of Navarre. The Navarrese government realized that it needed to obey administrative procedure and grant the broadcasting permits to the stations with the highest scores. Finally, in 2015, Iruñeko Komunikabideak S.A. obtained a broadcasting license, having received the second-highest score in the administrative process. In 2015, the process that started in 1997 finally came to an end. It is worth noting that a change of government occurred in Navarre in 2015, with policies now more in favor of the Basque language.

All these procedural incidents and court actions show the unwillingness of the Navarrese government to grant a broadcasting license to the only radio station fully broadcasting in Basque in the Mixed area for years. Yet, these court actions navigated the issue without expressly addressing the question of whether the Navarrese government should consider the linguistic diversity of the autonomous community when allocating the scarce resource of licenses for private radio stations. It is true that what needed to be challenged was the unlawfulness of the administrative procedures. However, we must bear in mind that the government of Navarre during those years was held by a party that was known for publicly showing contempt toward the Basque language.

The actions of the regional government had skirted the law for years. Thus, even if norms would have required positive actions toward the Basque language from the very beginning, it is reasonable to assume that not much would have gone differently. The issue might not be in the origin (the drafting on the norm that did not include the need for a Basque radio station) but rather in the constant avoidance of the law by the Navarrese administration. Similarly, Agirreazkuenaga believes the example of Euskalerria Irratia highlights how administrative procedures can mock an "ethereal interpretation" of the legal system claiming to protect linguistic pluralism.[35] Luckily, in this case, the systematic mobilization of the courts was shown to be the right path, despite the resistance of the government of Navarre. To sum up, in Arzoz's words:

> The "Euskalerria Irratia" case demonstrates that linguistic pluralism is a constitutional value that cannot remain a rhetorical proclamation but rather requires the articulation of minimum legal guarantees for it to display some legal effectiveness. [. . .] The guarantee of linguistic pluralism involves articulating a reservation of frequencies for broadcasts in the co-official languages of the autonomous Community or, alternatively, by the preferential assessment of the use of the co-official language in the granting of the concession.[36]

This reflection by Arzoz should be applied to any area of social life regarding linguistic pluralism: Any linguistic right, especially in the case of minorities, requires a minimum legal guarantee.

The Navarrese government's mobilization against Basque media is shown in the case of Euskalerria Irratia (as well as EITB, discussed earlier). These cases show a systematic limitation of media in Basque in Navarre. The issue of accessing media in Euskara was raised multiple times during the monitoring mechanisms of the Language Charter.[37] Basque being an official language together with Spanish in Navarre (with the nuance of territories, explained in part I) does not guarantee access to media in Euskara. Yet, the Law of 1986 foresees and supposedly protects media in Basque. The Euskalerria Irratia case shows a clear division between law in books and law in action. Law in books in this case would be law protecting Basque in media in Navarre, and the

Language Charter would help this area to be developed. But law in action was achieving the opposite. Law in action, in this case, would be the Navarrese government acting against the presence of Basque radio stations in Iruñea (Mixed area), which is unlawful. The unlawfulness of this action was pushed further by the Navarrese government not complying with the judicial decisions on the matter until the change of the government in 2015.

The importance of achieving a broadcasting license for Euskalerria Irratia is not only in the recognition of the radio station as officially established, and the recognition of a need for radio stations in Basque in Navarre, but also in the fact that it gave the entity the opportunity to apply for public funding. The importance of public funding is not negligible, notably in the case of media in minority languages. Therefore, it is another element to consider when exploring the context of media and the Basque language.

Public Funding of Private Media in Basque

Public funding is an important way for a government to support a minority language. In the BAC and Navarre, where Basque is co-official, public funding is necessary because of the size of the community of Basque speakers, still in the minority. Thus, media in Euskara often needs help from this funding to survive and to develop.

Considering the limited audience and the limitations in terms of profit, the key battle of media in Basque (bilingual or monolingual) is accessing public funding. One could imagine that accessing public funding for the creation of a newspaper in Euskara would be relatively easy when approaching the Basque government. Yet, it is quite a task. Díaz Noci offers the example of *Deia* and *Egin* in 1983, which asked for monetary help to launch both newspapers in Basque, but the funding was denied.[38] The same happened to *Argia*.[39] It must be said that the Normalization Law was already adopted by 1983, and this law shows a clear strategy from the Basque government to invest in public media.[40] As explained by Joxerra Garzia during a semi-structured interview,[41] the dichotomy between public and private is very present in the history of media in Basque. As a matter of fact, there is an almost systematic action-reaction situation, where, when a private media outlet in Basque is created, a mirroring public media outlet in Basque is created. Sometimes—and especially because of the funding behind it—the public media overtakes the market (like in the case of EITB), whereas, in other cases, private media wins the battle (like in the case of *Berria*).[42] Yet, for the private sector, public funding remains a main source of revenue. Indeed, even among Basque speakers, consumption of media in Basque is not automatically the first option. Since Basque speakers are also Spanish or French speakers at minimum, the variety of media they can access is wider, and so is the competition. For the case of the BAC especially, efforts are made to provide financial support for media in Basque.[43]

According to the data provided by Spain in the 2018 report submitted for the evaluation of the Committee of Experts of the Language Charter,[44] for the year 2016 the Basque government allocated 4,875,000 euros for grants for media in Basque. This substantial budget shows the commitment of the Basque government of the BAC to give media in Basque a chance in a setting dominated by Spanish (and increasingly by foreign languages such as English). In Navarre, however, the economic efforts made by the Navarrese government are significantly smaller than in the BAC. According to the same report of 2018,[45] in 2014 and 2015 no grant calls were made for media (media in Basque included). In 2016, Navarre allocated 290,000 euros for grants for media in Basque. The report also notes that for the year 2017, the grant call for media entirely in Euskara was improved and attained 580,000 euros. This indicates that the change of government in Navarre in 2015, as already mentioned, constituted a step forward when it comes to public funding of media in Basque.

Another element to consider when exploring public funding of media in the Basque language is the cross-border dimension. The Basque government and the POBL have also covered media in their agreement. The POBL lists media among its objectives for the linguistic project.[46] Indeed, regarding media, the POBL says the major challenge is "relying on the media to make Basque live in society and raise the level of language."[47] The 2018 agreement not only foresees funds for education,[48] but also for media. More precisely, from the total funds of 1,930,000 euros,[49] the sum of 310,000 euros is devoted to media. This sum is allocated to *Euskal Irratiak* (the federation of local radio stations who broadcast in Basque) to support, among other things, local or joint programming, to strengthen and to consolidate the radio network, and to structure and consolidate the new Donapaleu (Saint-Palais) radio station.[50] An additional 380,000 euros budgeted to a call for funding projects related to the Basque language goes to:

1. Subsidies for operators that have structured a permanent service in Basque, which are Aldudarrak bideo (web TV), Euskal Komunikabideak (*Iparraldeko Hitza* magazine), Iparla Baigura Komunikazioa (*Kazeta* website), Herria (weekly newspaper), and Errobi Promotions (bilingual web radio).[51]
2. Support for operators that integrate Basque into their activities: Iparla Baigura Komunikazioa (Mediabask), TVPI, Xibero telebista, and Mendililia irratia.[52]

Looking at the cross-border agreement of 2023,[53] 529,500 euros are budgeted to directly funding media in Basque. In line with the idea of improving the social use and social presence of Euskara, the funding of media has (in 2023) increased. From this overall budget of 529,500 euros, 310,000 euros are geared toward funding radio stations in Basque (Euskal Irratiak scores 235,000 euros, and local radio stations score the remaining 75,000 euros). The remaining 219,500 euros are distributed as follows: 80,000 euros for Aldudarrak bideo; 48,500 for Herria; 28,000 euros for Euskal Komunikabideak; 33,000 euros for Iparla Baigura Komunikazioa; and 30,000 euros for Errobi promotions. In line with the previous agreements, other projects regarding media have also received funding: Iparla Baigura Komunikazioa receives 5,000 euros; TVPI receives 32,000 euros; Lapurdi irratia radio-station receives 3,000 euros; and Gaztekom (new content on social media in Basque language) receives 8,000 euros. Media holds, therefore, some importance in the subsidies offered by the cooperation agreement between the two administrations. As seen previously, despite education trumping media when it comes to funds in this project, the latter receives a good amount of public funding.[54]

2deo: The Basque Audiovisual Lab

In an era when new technologies are increasingly more present in our lives, it is inevitable they become part of our media landscape as well. To answer the challenge of new information and communications technology (ICT) and the Basque media, a project has been developed in the BAC called 2deo.[55] An excellent example of how the BAC is trying to promote audiovisual production in Euskara, 2deo is an audiovisual lab in the Tabakalera building—a center devoted to contemporary culture in the city of Donostia-San Sebastián.

As explained by Iban Arantzabal during his interview,[56] 2deo was created from a gap. The project originated from asking the following question:

If the Basque language moves forward, is it suitable to have media in Euskara? In Arantzabal's view, the answer was an obvious "yes." Once his group started building the project, their research showed that children and teenagers consume less and less "traditional" media in Basque and spend more time on the internet or on their smartphones than watching television. Before putting the 2deo audiovisual lab into practice, Arantzabal and his group created successful pilot projects. One key example was creating an app for the *Go!azen* television program on channel ETB1. Via this app, they managed to have 25,000 people consuming and using an app entirely in Basque, a large number for the Basque speakers' community.

To fill the gap in the Basque audiovisual community, 2deo was created with experimentation in mind—mainly by providing the Basque audiovisual sector a place to experiment and observe what happens in the lab. One of the project's key elements is the Basque language, and the working language of 2deo is "almost 100 percent Basque," Arantzabal explained. The idea behind 2deo is to create new products to add to the products already available in the Basque media arena. According to Arantzabal, "2deo's natural framework is in internet and in the land of smartphones."[57] One successful result that could be mentioned is the *Zut* app, explained later.

It is worth noting that 2deo's definition of media and audiovisual media is broad: It includes video games, apps, websites, and so on. Its approach to media favors ICTs, the internet, and innovation—always taking Euskara as a starting point. The Basque language was in the project from the beginning. Arantzabal emphasizes how the name itself—2deo—can only be read in Euskara.[58] The name 2deo has the distinction of the Basque language, and they want to hold on to that. In fact, Arantzabal says, "creating in Euskara does not mean it will not be successful on the internet." Creating a good product in a regional or minority language does not hinder its popularity or spread. He mentions, for instance, the success of the Basque film *Handia* streaming on Netflix, underscoring that if there is a good story, it will work internationally—even if it is in Basque.

The 2deo audiovisual lab is a clear example of how the Basque media industry and the public institutions from the BAC are taking the production of media in Euskara seriously and trying to propel it toward the future by betting on innovation and adapting language normalization policies to new media platforms.

Public actors have a serious impact on the reality of the media landscape in the Basque language. From administrations and their streams of funding to courts and public media outlets, public actors shape media in Euskara. Yet, private actors also affect media in Euskara and are worth analyzing.

Private Actors

Media does not belong merely in the hands of public actors or institutions. In fact, private media is more the norm than the exception. In the realm of private media in Basque, we will explore the "proto-media" in Basque with *Bertsolaritza*, followed up by key actors *Egunkaria* and *Berria*. Finally, we will elaborate on "new" technologies and media in Euskara.

Exploring Bertsolaritza as Proto-media in Basque

For the following analysis, a broad definition of media is required: media as a means of communication that reaches or influences people widely. Starting from this definition, we will explore Bertsolaritza as a Basque proto-media.[59]

Explaining Bertsolaritza can be difficult. This essential part of Basque culture and identity is often described as an improvised popular poetry in Euskara. Key in Bertsolaritza is the communication between the poet/singer and the receiver. Therefore, it is difficult to understand Bertsolaritza without the Basque language, or the Basque culture without Bertsolaritza. For centuries, Euskara and Bertsolaritza have been present in the lives of Basques.

Despite the first book in Basque being published in 1545, the Basque-speaking population "has largely been illiterate in their native tongue, since teaching was always done in one of the dominant languages (Spanish or French)."[60] This led to the important use of oral genres by Basque speakers. As Garzia underscored, the vitality of these genres is remarkable:

> Voltaire described the Basques as "a people who sing and dance at the feet of the Pyrenees," and it is no coincidence that Basque improvised contest poetry [. . .] is one of the best-known examples of sung improvisation in the world, in regard to both the quality of the compositions and its social roots.[61]

Bertsolaritza was a medium used by Basques (illiterate in their language) to express themselves, to entertain, and to inform—coinciding with the role of media. As a matter of fact, some intellectuals saw the potential of this popular poetry and decided to analyze it. Already in 1919, Father Donostia expressed his admiration for this popular art.[62] Resurrección María de Azkue also worked on Bertsolaritza. Garzia emphasizes how using María de Azkue's *Euskalerriaren Yakintza* book, Anjel Lertxundi analyzed the different oral genres, focusing on the communicative needs of our modern era.[63]

For those who have never heard or read Bertsolartitza, the variety of the subjects with which it deals is astonishing: sporting exploits, events from distant wars, whale-hunting, love affairs, mythological genealogies, and more.[64] Among the Basques, "everything that concerned or mattered to the community was reviewed in the written bertsos."[65] Written *bertsos* can be seen as written media. In fact, they were even sold like newspapers, with the "seller" singing them out loud. Interestingly, many of those who listened to the *bertsos*, despite being illiterate in Euskara, ended up buying *bertso-paperak* (small collections of written *bertsos*). Written *bertsos* were a functional vehicle for communication. They could be understood as the first rudimentary media in Basque or as the predecessor of media in the Basque language.

Bertsos, just like media, faced censorship. During the Franco era, *bertso* singers (*Bertsolariak*) were often arrested because of the content of what they had just sang.[66] The censorship of the Basque language was extended to singing improvisation in Basque (because of the content of some of the *bertsos*). One aspect of Bertsolaritza which helps to explain its survival is cross-border cooperation. Indeed, Garzia explains how "soon bertsolaris from both sides of the River Bidasoa [. . .] began performing together, both in festivals held in the northern zone and those organized in the zone subjugated under the military boot of Franco's regime."[67] It is worth noting that Bertsolaritza covered then, and covers today, the three Basque administrations—including for the big competition (*Txapelketa Nagusia*) that occurs every four years.

Today, however, written *bertsos* are no longer a functional tool for communication as such[68] and thus would not be categorized as media. Bertsolaritza currently falls under the label of culture. Nevertheless, Bertsolaritza appears constantly in the media (in written form, on radio, on TV, on children's cartoons, and so on) and *bertso* singers are well respected intellectuals who are often writers or journalists too. *Bertso* singers are often invited to debates, to interviews on radio or television programs, to write opinion columns in newspapers, and so forth. Therefore, one might ask if Bertsolaritza can now be seen as the extension of the job of a writer or journalist. In any case, *bertso* singers are still key cultural actors of Basque society.

We could categorize Bertsolaritza as fulfilling the role of the media in the past, especially in the rural Basque Country. Bertsolaritza's evolution over time, paired with the growth of media in Basque and the rise of literacy, has relegated it to the domain of culture. Yet, Bertsolaritza maintains significant importance, still reaching a wide audience.[69] Understanding Bertsolaritza as being part of Basque "proto-media" can help us understand current tonalities or sensibilities of the reality of media in Euskara.

Having looked at Bertsolaritza as private media of the past, we should now look at private media in more contemporary terms.

Private Media in Basque

Before exploring further the landscape of private actors and media in Basque, we must start with a key element that has marked not only media in Basque but also the community of Basque speakers. The two examples that will be discussed marked a "before" and an "after" in the context of media in Euskara, via the written press. The spirit of *Egunkaria* still resonates in Basque media and the community of Basque speakers, while its successor, *Berria*,[70] managed to become the leading newspaper in Basque, distributed in the entire Basque Country.

Egunkaria: A Case of Freedom of Expression

Focusing on the rights of Basque speakers and analyzing them from the freedom of expression perspective, one should mention the case of *Egunkaria*. It is no secret that other (non-linguistic) political issues affect the regulation of Basque-language media. Relating back to the reflections on freedom of expression in the previous chapter, this example showcases an example of "anxiety logic" described by Schmalz[71] in relation to a newspaper in Euskara. Despite the *Egunkaria* case being focused on criminal law (explained below), we will undertake an alternative reading, exploring the importance of this case for media in Basque from a freedom-of-expression perspective. Analyzing the context of the closure of this newspaper will enable us to contextualize the reality of media in Basque through the years, as well as the attachment of the community of speakers to this newspaper.

The Basque newspaper *Egunkaria* was founded in 1989. Basque journalists wanted to establish an independent newspaper in Euskara. To initiate this project, they relied on civil society and their willingness to finance the project. Eventually, this bottom-up project managed to attract enough people to invest in the newspaper and, on December 6, 1990, the first issue was released. In 2003, the instruction by judge Del Olmo ordered the closure of the newspaper as a precautionary measure since he considered the newspaper to be in a relationship with the ETA terrorist group, and the Guardia Civil arrested ten people involved with the newspaper on February 20, 2003.

After a long procedure that started in 2003, the National High Criminal Court—the *Audiencia Nacional*—reached a decision about the *Egunkaria* case in 2010.[72] In this decision, the Court acquitted the accused and abolished the precautionary measures that had been taken since 2003. This decision emphasized the importance of a newspaper for an effective right to freedom of expression and information, especially in the case of a linguistic minority. Indeed, this decision strongly repudiated the steps taken by the Guardia Civil and Judge Del Olmo from the very beginning.

In the decision, the court confirmed there was no sign of illegal financing of the newspaper and that there was no sign of sending any kind of funds to the ETA terrorist group.[73] The decision also underscored how the provisional closing of a newspaper as a precautionary measure is a very delicate matter.[74] The provisional suspension has no basis in the Spanish Constitution, which only regulates the exceptions to the rights to freedom of expression and information (Articles 20.5 and 20.2) in the case of state of exception or siege (Article 55.1 and the organic law 4/1981 of June 1). But even in these situations, the Constitution does not allow closing a newspaper for terrorist crimes explicitly. This was already expressed by the Constitutional Tribunal in Decision 199/1987.

Regarding the importance of the right to information, the High Criminal Court highlighted in this decision how the right to communicate and receive truthful information is exercised in the paradigm of the press. This right is double, meaning that any interference or limitation on transmitting information will affect the right of all citizens to receive it. Additionally, this right has two different subjects: on the one hand, the citizens—collectively and individually—who receive the news and the information; and on the other hand, the journalists who are concerned with the search for the information for its diffusion to contribute to the public opinion in a democratic state. This also justifies a greater level of protection of the freedom of information for professionals.[75]

The judges of the court emphasized that there is no norm that expressly and directly allows the provisional suspension of any media activity. In addition, the judges believed the justification to use Article 129 of the Criminal Code to close down *Egunkaria* was insufficient. Furthermore, the court ruled that the media undertake an essential activity in a democratic society, since they are linked to "the exercise of basic human rights of the citizen."[76] This led the judges of the *Audiencia Nacional* to decide that the closing of the newspaper posed a "collective dimension added to the case of *Egunkaria* since it affects the readers in Basque . . . which makes its valuation more intense from the perspective of pluralism,"[77] pluralism being a value that appears together with freedom in Article 1 of the Constitution. This decision showcases the "anxiety logic" behind closing a newspaper publishing entirely in Basque. Limiting the right to freedom of expression, inspired by an "anxiety logic" of a newspaper written in Basque, underscores the importance of accessibility of media in a minority language. In a landscape where newspapers are under suspicion because of the minority language they use, freedom of expression should prevail.

Using the local example of the Basque language and media, with the case *Egunkaria*, we can understand the key place that freedom of expression occupies for linguistic minorities. In the case of linguistic minorities, languages being both a tool of communication and an identity mark, the necessity for freedom of expression to hold a linguistic dimension is undeniable.

Berria Newspaper

The *Berria* newspaper was founded after the closure of the *Egunkaria* newspaper. In addition to demonstrating the legal implications of closing a newspaper, the case of *Egunkaria* shows an awareness on the part of Basque speakers regarding the importance of preserving media outlets in their language. In fact, *Egunkaria* was the second Basque newspaper closed by judicial authorities.[78] In 2003, after the intervention of the instruction judge and the Guardia Civil, Basques went to the streets to demonstrate in favor of *Egunkaria*. This remains one of the largest demonstrations in the Basque Country to date. Building on this energy, civil society organized a fundraising campaign to found a new newspaper in Basque: *Berria*.[79] This newspaper was, again, created with a bottom-up dynamic, and once again succeeded. In fact, *Berria* is still operating and informing Basque readers.

Berria is currently published six days a week and has a daily circulation of 21,000 copies,[80] 150,000 readers, 13,580 subscribers, and 250 employees.[81] This newspaper is sold in the entire territory of the Basque Country (the BAC, Navarre, and Iparralde) and is published entirely in Basque. *Berria* was created to fill the gap of media in Euskara. Since the start of *Egunkaria* and *Berria*, the goal of these newspapers has been to provide information *in* Basque and to contribute to the normalization of the Basque language. Still today, *Berria* is the only daily newspaper published fully in Basque.

Basque civil society gathered 4,595,900 euros to establish *Berria*. Therefore, both *Egunkaria* and *Berria* showed the determination of the Basques to receive, access, and produce information in Euskara. Interestingly, the newspapers have been key for the survival and the use of the Basque language through the platform they offer to the Basque language (giving this language a "use" and showcasing it). But they have also been key actors in the development of Basque as a language (for the creation of vocabulary, for instance). The *estilo liburua*—a stylebook for writing—of *Egunkaria* marked a big step forward for the Basque language, and the stylebook of *Berria* is also a reference when it comes to producing texts in Euskara.[82] It is important to bear in mind that even if some earlier attempts were made to have a proper press in Basque, *Egunkaria* was the actor that standardized Basque for journalism. These documents were and are consulted as a reference for proper journalistic language and style in Basque. Since their beginnings, both newspapers paid close attention to the use of the Basque language, as well as the creation of vocabulary and its development.

Berria exemplifies the comprehensive language policy of the BAC: It acts through setting up and funding public media, and through financial support to private media. The newspaper currently relies heavily on public funding (even if it also receives streams of funding from subscriptions and advertising). According to a report submitted by Spain in 2018 to the Committee of Experts of the Language Charter,[83] via the call for grants for the consolidation, development, and normalization of media in Basque by the Department of Education, Language Policy, and Culture of the Government of the BAC,[84] *Berria* received a financial grant amounting to 5,379,245 euros between 2013 and 2016.[85]

Berria is considered the main printed daily newspaper in the entire territory of the Basque Country. Understanding that this private company fills the need for a written press in Euskara is key to defining the context of media in Basque. It shows the determination of the Basque community and the commitment of Basque journalism toward the Basque language in all three administrative areas (the BAC, Iparralde, and Navarre).

"New" Media and the Basque Language

Given that we live in the internet era, we must mention new information and communication technologies (ICT) and media in Basque. Basque speakers benefit enormously from the fever of technology and apps providing media content in Euskara: *Egunean Behin*[86] offering a daily trivia quiz in Basque; Netflix[87] broadcasting movies in Basque;[88] and Ttap[89] and Zut[90]—two innovative, Basque-only magazines exclusively in app form. Therefore, analyzing these technologies as they relate to Euskara is a must. After providing introductory remarks on the matter, we will explore the intersection of "new" (private) media and the Basque language.

Introductory Remarks on ICT, Regional or Minority Languages, and Media

When discussing regional or minority languages and ICT, it is often mentioned that this double-edged sword can be harmful or beneficial to these languages. Technology itself is not often harmful, but rather what we make of it. This translates also into the realm of regional or minority languages and ICT. The internet is often seen as a monolingual space, usually dominated by English as the *lingua franca*. However, technology can be used to the advantage or favor of regional or minority languages. Therefore, analyzing ICT's place in Basque media is crucial, notably in the current digitalization landscape.

Before moving forward, we must discuss a few points. First, since the Language Charter protects Euskara in Spain, the Committee of Experts increasingly considers the internet under its Article 11 on media.[91] Furthermore, McMonagle highlights that the reports and evaluations of the Committee of

Experts are highly instrumental in setting standards for regional or minority languages in Europe.[92] It is key to know that the Language Charter's interpretation of media evolves together with technology.

Second, we must keep in mind that ICT can only have a positive effect on regional or minority languages if minorities have access to it. If Basque speakers had no access to ICT, they would not be able to enjoy its benefits. Relatedly, there is a third point: ICT contributes to freedom of expression. This is even more important in the case of minorities and linguistic minorities. As discussed earlier in this chapter, expressing oneself on a platform in one's own language is fundamental. This is even more true in our information age, and ICT contributes to the fulfillment of this right.

In a nutshell, ICT in general, and the internet in particular, can be beneficial for regional or minority languages—if speakers have access to it—helping to fulfill minorities' right to freedom of expression, as well as being a powerful tool for communicating and sharing in one's own language(s). It is also a positive step that the Committee of Experts is increasingly adopting the internet within the scope of Article 11. Keeping these comments in mind, we will now turn to ICT and media in the Basque language.

Kanaldude: An Early Example of "New" Media, ICT, and Euskara

Looking at the landscape in Iparralde, the interesting example of Kanaldude should be mentioned.[93] The legal framework of Iparralde seems rather constraining when it comes to the inclusion of the Basque language in public media, but private media offers the freedom of creating media in any language. Thus, in the inner land of Iparralde, Kanaldude was born. Kanaldude, a private media station, belongs to Aldudarrak, a cooperative, and since 1997 has seen its project develop until becoming the web-television station that exists today. The Aldudarrak association was transformed in 2010 into a cooperative society of collective interests, under the name Aldudarrak Bideo, whose main activity is the web-television channel Kanaldude. This channel offers a weekly program in Euskara. Another important aspect of this channel is the focus on training and apprenticeship. Since its beginnings, Aldudarrak Bideo has worked with local audiovisual schools. This cooperative also works on other audiovisual projects, although their main activity is still the web-television channel.

The channel Kanaldude follows the following guidelines:[94]

1- It is a television channel in Euskara, aimed at Basque speakers and Basque learners, to promote the presence of Basque in the media, following the guidelines established by the POBL.
2- It is a local television channel that aims to show the local dynamics and seeks to foster the relationships between the local territories, offering local and social information.
3- It is participative television, where citizens have an important role in the creation of programs, based on the production system of the Participatory Audiovisual Federation.[95]
4- It is a television channel in Basque that promotes audiovisual creation supporting authors, scenographers, and producers, with the objective of energizing local audiovisual production.
5- It is television that constantly reflects on the connection between heritage and creation, following popular creations closely.

This television channel is a good example of the capacity of the Basque community to organize itself and fill the gaps left by the legal framework. Once again, with a restrictive legal landscape in Iparralde, notably in the realm of public institutions, a private entity was born to offset the extremely limited role given to Euskara in the media. Kanaldude has filled for many years the gap of accessing television in Euskara by using a "new" platform. Indeed, the internet has helped this project, making it more accessible. This television channel provides stories from Iparralde, with the dialects of Iparralde, which do not appear enough in EITB. In fact, EITB is often criticized for focusing its programming on the BAC and focusing their Euskara on the Basque dialect used in Gipuzkoa—despite its efforts to include a variety of territories and dialects. Kanaldude, however, is a weekly, online-based television channel and does not compare to EITB's reach, funding, or audience. Kanaldude should be seen for what it is: a local, successful dynamic outlet to promote Basque in the media in Iparralde, despite the harsh legal landscape that this language encounters in France.

Kanaldude is an example of the possibilities offered by private law in terms of linguistic minorities. In a legal environment where their officiality is not recognized, there is room for creativity using private law. Thus, the first step is to create, in this case, a private media platform in Basque. However, as in many cases, the viability of the project depends on the funding and the community. The latter, the community, needs to join the project so it can get traction. This also helps the economic viability of the project: As the community subscribes to the project, it will help to fund it.

Kanaldude was, from the beginning, a collaborative project, and has established itself as a web-television reference in Iparralde. This seems to be the pattern in the Basque case, where civil society is active in challenging the status quo (in this case, in the realm of media in Basque). Regarding funding, as we have noted earlier, this web-television media receives public funding from the collaboration agreement between the BAC and the POBL.[96] Here lies the connection between law in books and law in action. The co-officiality of Basque and Spanish in the BAC allows the regional government to undertake agreements to foster this language, even outside its borders. This is paired with the creation of an institution—with limited powers—dedicated to fostering the Basque language in Iparralde. While it is true that the POBL alone has made an impact, transborder cooperation covers even more ground. This legal and institutional framework allows for the law to be put into practice with funding policies benefiting projects such as Kanaldude, resulting in collaboration between norm users and norm givers. Another way to look at it would be to describe it as a synergy between top-down and bottom-up dynamics to foster the presence of Basque in media in Iparralde.

"New" ICT Media and Euskara

A great deal of evidence suggests that "users of lesser used languages are making use—often in very creative ways—of new communications technologies."[97] One cannot help but wonder how this creativity has translated into the Basque language.

In their research on European regional or minority language media and their digitalization, Ferré-Pavia and others have discovered among the regional or minority language media studied, that their presence on the internet was 90.8 percent for the year 2016.[98] Regarding the Basque case, the authors counted 123 media outlets, scoring an internet presence of 92.7 percent. Among those, nine outlets had no access to the internet, and six of these nine outlets were local, socially owned magazines while three were publicly owned local radio stations.[99]

These authors also discovered, for the case of Basque media outlets, that editors felt "comfortable with their online and social media performance" and that major media outlets "had even created tools, such as phone apps, to connect to their users."[100] Apps are a powerful tool for enabling regional or minority languages to reach their audience, notably their younger audience—an audience which respondents of these authors' research have mentioned having trouble reaching.[101]

Although we have not delved into the world of apps and the Basque language—a world that is quickly developing—two apps are worth mentioning regarding "new" media and Euskara. These two apps are Ttap and Zut. Both belong to the Goiena private media group and are exclusively in Basque. Ttap, created in 2018, is a weekly magazine, offering multimedia content on current issues. One year later, and following the same multimedia aspects, Zut was born: a magazine focused on younger readers, or as the magazine advertises, a magazine "for Generation Z." This app includes the innovative *IXA* series, a show only available on this platform.[102] Both these apps respond to the need for new ways of consuming media that are not foreign to Basque speakers. For the Basque language to survive in the realm of media, it must adapt itself to the new ways of consuming and spreading it. It is also interesting to note that both these apps are multimedia platforms, mixing written press with video content for instance. Innovation seems the way to go to perpetuate the use of media in Basque, by Basque speakers, notably considering the younger generations. These generations tend to spend more time on the internet or looking at their smartphones than reading printed newspapers or watching traditional television channels.

To cater to new trends, two new streaming platforms have entered the arena of media in Basque language: Primeran[103] and Makusi.[104] In September 2023,[105] Primeran went live to cater to new consumption trends of media. This way, Basque speakers can access a streaming platform in Basque language, instead of looking for the (minimal) content available in this language in other streaming platforms. To make it appealing, this streaming platform is free: Only registration is required. This streaming platform belongs to the EITB group. Following the same idea but catering toward children, the streaming platform Makusi was born[106] in April 2024. This offers content for children, making it extremely easy for parents to switch on content in Basque. This platform also belongs to the EITB media group and is also free. These two new platforms aim to provide a better chance for more people to access content in Basque. This will also hopefully help with consumption of media in Basque, leading to a growth in the use of the Basque language and an increase in the number of Basque speakers.

Concluding Remarks of Part III

The question of media and minority languages is complex. Taking the example of the Basque language, we have tried to understand what a legal framework on this matter can look like and how it can translate into society. This rich chapter has touched upon key elements when discussing media in the Basque language.

We have contextualized the world of media in Euskara by providing thoughts on its private actors, from its roots (with Bertsolaritza) to its recent evolution. Private projects have been key for the creation and offering of media in Basque. We have also discussed the impact of public institutions (from the BAC most importantly) on the development and improvement of the media landscape in Basque.

We touched on both the negative and the positive approaches toward the linguistic content of the right to freedom of expression. Recall that the negative side refers to the right to use one's language, while the positive side refers to the right to receive information in one's language. Throughout these chapters, we have seen examples that refer to both sides. The legal framework in France protects only the negative right, where, as we have seen, the presence of Basque in media is merely allowed. Yet, this contrasts with the positive approach taken by the BAC, where both the negative and positive rights are protected: The use of Basque is not only allowed in media, but, one could say, it is encouraged. The efforts put into place by the BAC for the creation and development of media in the BAC appear clearly with the example of EITB, and the determination for its broadcasting to be extended in Navarre and Iparralde.

We have also discussed the consideration of "new" media, or the efforts toward the creation of media formats that youth would want to consume, for example, 2deo. The topic of ICT or "new" media and the Basque language is essential to the future inclusion of this minority language. Euskara needs to evolve hand in hand with media. The case of Navarre on the spectrum of positive and negative sides of freedom of expression and Euskara, as always, is rather difficult to define. Once again, Basque speakers in Navarre face difficulties and contradictions that even translate into long battles in court as we have seen with the example of Euskalerria Irratia.

Media in the context of the Basque language showcases the importance of an active civil society. Bottom-up dynamics such as Kanaldude, *Egunkaria* (and later *Berria*), and Euskalerria Irratia have been crucial in creating the media landscape from which the Basque language now benefits. Interestingly, top-down dynamics usually help these examples, with EITB having been created with a similar mindset of wanting to develop and strengthen the Basque media, or by publicly financing media projects that broadcast in Basque. Despite the issues already raised in this chapter, the overall media landscape in Basque seems to be comprehensive, and gaps in the legal system tend to be filled by private initiatives.

Notes

1. We will also leave aside other important topics linked to media, such as advertising.
2. This role of EITB was mentioned by Garzia and Amonarriz during their respective interviews. See appendix 2.
3. EITB Media was created by Decree 285/2020of December 22. https://www.legegunea.euskadi.eus/webleg00-contfich/es/contenidos/decreto/bopv202100013/es_def/index.shtml (Accessed August 25, 2021).
4. Kike Amonarriz is a prominent Basque sociolinguist, humorist, and TV presenter. See appendix 2.
5. These documents are also available online: http://www.legebiltzarra.eus/ords/f?p=CTP:INICIATIVA_DETALLE:::::RESETBRCRMB,P18_ID:Y,58810&p_lang=eu (Accessed June 22, 2021).
6. Provided by Kike Amonarriz to the author. Report available at http://www.legebiltzarra.eus/ic2/restAPI/pvgune_descargar/default/43e79a51-4af0-4dbf-910a-2e25f4e71dfc (Accessed June 22, 2021).
7. For instance (to quote two examples among many others), with the TV series *Goenkale*, or the TV game *Mihiluze*.
8. Translated by the author: "EITBk mundua euskarari ireki dio, eta Euskara munduari."
9. See part II, chapter 5.
10. Places where the Basque language thrives even in public spaces, where mainly Basque was heard and spoken.
11. For more on the impact of the cuts because of the economic crisis, see: Casado Del Río, Guimerà i Orts, y Miguel De Bustos, "The impact of the cuts to

regional public service broadcasters on the audiovisual Industry: the Basque Country and Catalonia (2007–2014)."
12 The Basque public television was created with Law 5/1982 of May 20: https://www.eitb.eus/multimedia/corporativo/documentos/ley-5-1982-creacion-ente-eitb-sortze-legea.pdf (Accessed July 26, 2024). It was later slightly updated with two laws: (1) the Law 4/1996, of October 11, 1996: https://www.boe.es/buscar/doc.php?id=BOE-A-2012-867 (Accessed July 26, 2024), (2) the Law 8/1998, of March 27, 1998: https://www.boe.es/buscar/doc.php?id=BOE-A-2011-20041 (Accessed July 26, 2024).
13 http://www.euskadi.eus/contenidos/documentacion/sociometro_vasco_67/es_def/adjuntos/18sv67.pdf (Accessed March 18, 2019).
14 *Teknopolis* is a science and technology dissemination television program.
15 Navarre and Iparralde.
16 Sarasua, "Euskal Telebista eta euskal telebista. Berrantolatzeko oinarri batzuk."
17 This is an issue recurrently highlighted by the Language Charter's Committee of Experts' reports.
18 During the nineties, "pirate" repeaters were installed in Navarre and in Iparralde to access television in the Basque language, since television in Euskara was not easily available in either region. This has extended to recent times. For example, in 2012, ETB1 and ETB2 DTT signals could be picked up in the city and county of Pamplona, thanks to a private repeater installed by a group of activists.
19 Gutiérrez Montes y Espín, "Impact of the digital dividend release on regional digital terrestrial television in Spain: the cases of Andalusia, Catalonia, the Balearic Islands and Navarre."
20 General Collaboration Protocol between the autonomous community of the Basque Country and the chartered community of Navarre of July 3, 2009.
21 Gutiérrez Montes y Espín, "Impact of the digital dividend release on regional digital terrestrial television in Spain: the cases of Andalusia, Catalonia, the Balearic Islands and Navarre," 41.
22 Gutiérrez Montes y Espín., 41.
23 http://hj.tribunalconstitucional.es/es-ES/Resolucion/Show/474 (Accessed September 7, 2020).
24 Gutiérrez Montes y Espín, "Impact of the digital dividend release on regional digital terrestrial television in Spain: the cases of Andalusia, Catalonia, the

Balearic Islands and Navarre," 42.
25 Translated by the author.
26 Currently, 100,000 pesetas equal 601 euros. However, using any inflation calculator online, we can see that the actual value of 100,000 pesetas in the late eighties would more likely be closer to 1,460 euros in 2020.
27 Agirreazkuenaga, "La carta europea de lenguas regionales o minoritarias del Consejo de Europa como derecho interno," 132.
28 The issue of Euskalerria Irratia has reached the Committee of Experts of the Language Charter several times, notably during its evaluation of 2005 (para. 427-429), where they observed that "the granting of subsidies is the most obvious way to facilitate and/or encourage the creation of a radio station or to help maintain an existing one [. . .] since "Euskalerria Irratia" is the only private radio station broadcasting entirely in Basque [. . .] and since it does not appear that the Navarre authorities have taken any steps to encourage and/or facilitate the creation of another radio station broadcasting essentially in Basque, the Committee of Experts considers that the present undertaking is not fulfilled," 69. See the report: https://rm.coe.int/CoERMPublicCommonSearchServices/DisplayDCTMContent?documentId=09000016806dba65 (Accessed July 31, 2024).
29 Agirreazkuenaga, "La carta europea de lenguas regionales o minoritarias del Consejo de Europa como derecho interno," 133.
30 F.J.6, as it appears in Agirreazkuenaga, 133. Translated by the author.
31 Agirreazkuenaga, 134.
32 Superior Tribunal of Justice of Navarre, 1381/2005: http://www.poderjudicial.es/search/contenidos.action?action=contentpdf&databasematch=AN&reference=975724&links=&optimize=20060209&publicinterface=true (Accessed February 21, 2019).
33 Superior Tribunal of Justice of Navarre, 1019/2009: http://www.poderjudicial.es/search/contenidos.action?action=contentpdf&databasematch=AN&reference=5594955&links=&optimize=20100520&publicinterface=true (Accessed February 21, 2019).
34 Spanish Supreme Court, Decision STS 6289/2013: http://www.poderjudicial.es/search/contenidos.action?action=contentpdf&databasematch=TS&ref-

erence=6931669&links=&optimize=20140117&publicinterface=true (Accessed February 21, 2019).
35 Agirreazkuenaga, "La carta europea de lenguas regionales o minoritarias del Consejo de Europa como derecho interno," 137.
36 Translated by the author. Arzoz, "Estatuto jurídico del Euskera en Navarra," 415.
37 See chapter 6.
38 Díaz Noci, "Los medios de comunicación y la normalización del euskera: balance de dieciséis años."
39 Díaz Noci., ibid., 447.
40 Law 10/1982. See chapter 3 (part I) and chapter 6.
41 Joxerra Garzia is a Basque journalist, writer, translator, and university professor at the UPV-EHU Basque public university. He is also a *bertsolari* (see below). He has conducted extensive research on *Bertsolaritza*. As a journalist, he has notably worked in Euskadi Irratia (Basque public radio) and EITB (where he hosted the TV show *Hitzetik Hortzera*). See appendix 2.
42 The newspaper *Berria* receives some public funding now. We will analyze the newspaper *Berria* later in this chapter.
43 See, for instance, the call for funding for media in Basque (2024): https://www.legegunea.euskadi.eus/orden/orden-26-abril-2024-del-consejero-cultura-y-politica-linguistica-que-se-regula-y-se-convoca-concesion-subvenciones-promocion-difusion-yo-normalizacion-del-euskera-vida-social-ano-2024-convocatoria-/euskalgintza/webleg00-contfich/es/ (Accessed July 26, 2024).
44 https://rm.coe.int/spainpr5-en/16808de6fc (Accessed November 4, 2020).
45 Ibid.
46 http://www.mintzaira.fr/fileadmin/documents/Documents_OPLB/Hizkuntza_Politika_Proiektua/2006_eep_oplb_hizkuntza_politika_proiektua.pdf (Accessed January 25, 2018). Media is mentioned on page 42.
47 Translated by the author. Ibid., 42.
48 See part II, chapter 5.
49 https://www.irekia.euskadi.eus/uploads/attachments/12068/AkordioaEEP.pdf?1531503353 (Accessed March 31, 2019).
50 Ibid., 5.
51 Ibid., 6.
52 Ibid.

53 https://www.mintzaira.fr/fr/outils/les-actualites/actualite/article/decisions-relatives-au-soutien-des-operateurs-de-laction-linguistique-2023.html (Accessed July 31, 2024).

54 It should be mentioned that, over the years, other EU funding of media in Basque could be found indirectly. An example of this is the Euroregion NAEN (Nouvelle-Aquitaine Euskadi Navarra), which has founded projects such as *Zubiak* ("Bridges" in English)—a joint radio program between Euskadi Irratia (from the BAC) and France Bleu Pays Basque (Iparralde). The NAEN Euroregion budgeted 40,000 euros in 2016, 50,000 euros in 2018, and 40,000 euros in 2019 to this project (https://www.euroregion-naen.eu/es/proyectos/los-partenariados-estrategicos/) (Accessed October 6, 2020). However, if we do not focus on the cultural side of media (films and their distribution, for instance), funding for Basque media is almost impossible to find from useful programs such as Creative Europe. It is true Creative Europe does finance some television programming, for example, but the author has not found recent support from this funding scheme that concerns Basque language media.

55 https://www.tabakalera.eus/es/laboratorio-audiovisual (Accessed October 6, 2020).

56 Iban Arantzabal is a Basque blogger, philologist, and journalist. He has mainly worked in management in the field of media, notably in the *Goiena* media group (where he was the director) or, most recently, in *2deo* audiovisual lab. Among other things, he is also a member of the board of directors of *Tokikom* (the largest network of local media in Basque).

57 From the interview, translated by the author: "Gure joko-esparru naturala internet izango da eta nik esango nuke esku-telefonoa dela esparruetako bat."

58 The number two in Basque is "bi." 2deo is pronounced "bee-day-oh" (and the Basque word for *video* is "bideo"—pronounced just like "2deo"—hence the play on words.)

59 The documentary "What is bertsolaritza?" provides more insight. https://www.mintzola.eus/es/kulturartea/el-audiovisual-what-is-bertsolaritza (Accessed April 17, 2019).

60 Garzia, "Basque oral ecology," 47.

61 Garzia., 47-48.

62 Garzia., 53-54.

63 Garzia., 54. Anjel Lertxundi is a Basque writer, journalist, literary critic, and

screenwriter.
64   These are some examples mentioned by Joxerra Garzia in his article. This list is not comprehensive. The topics now have developed to include any contemporary event or topic.
65   Garzia, "Basque oral ecology," 57. A "*bertso*" is a stanza.
66   It is interesting to note that under Franco, before any public show, the singers were asked to provide a list of songs they were going to perform. Since Bertsolaritza is an improvised action, they could not provide before the show what exactly they were going to sing, and therefore gave false lists of songs.
67   Garzia, "History of Improvised Bertsolaritza: A Proposal," 93.
68   Garzia, "Basque oral ecology," 58.
69   The National Bertsolari Championship of 2017 gathered forty-three *bertso* singers, performing in front of an audience of 14,600 people. See the official website of the 2017 Championship: https://www.bertsozale.eus/eu/bertsolari-txapelketa-nagusia (Accessed October 14, 2020).
70   *Berria* is not the only private newspaper in the Basque language, but it is the main newspaper consumed in Basque. Because of time and space constraints of this thesis, we are going to focus mainly on this newspaper.
71   Schmalz, "Beyond an Anxiety Logic: A Critical Examination of Language Rights Cases before the European Court of Human Rights."
72   Audiencia Nacional, Sala de lo Penal, Sección Primera, Sentencia Número 27/2010: http://www.poderjudicial.es/search/contenidos.action?action=contentpdf&databasematch=AN&reference=5554836&links=%2227%2F2010%22&optimize=20100422&publicinterface=true (Accessed September 21, 2018).
73   Ibid. Hechos Probados, point III.
74   Ibid. In Fundamentos Derecho.
75   Translated by the author: "The right to communicate and receive truthful information, whose paradigm is the press, is a double right, in such a way that any interference or limitation in the free power to issue information will affect the right of all to receive it. And it has a different subject, on the one hand, as receivers of news and messages the community and each citizen in particular, on the other hand, the journalist, who stands as a privileged instrument of the right to the extent that he is concerned with the search for information for its dissemination in order to contribute to the formation of public opinion in a

democratic state—in this sense, STC 105/1983-. That is why the professional exercise of freedom of information by the media and by journalists, guarantee of a free public opinion, has greater consideration and a maximum level of protection, as stated in STC 165/1987."

76   Translated by the author.
77   Translated by the author.
78   *Egin*, a bilingual newspaper that closed in 1998, also accused of being linked to ETA. In 2009, the Supreme Court acquitted the newspaper, confirming the unlawfulness of the closure of this newspaper.
79   Hence the name. *Berria* means "new" as well as "the news" in the Basque language.
80   Apart from its presence online, or via its app, *Berria*, according to the MIDAS (Minority Dailies Association) media document. https://www.berria.eus/publizitatea/MIDAS_Media_2018.pdf (Accessed April 27, 2019).
81   According to the data provided by the *Berria* website. https://www.berria.eus/berrialaguna/berriataldea (Accessed October 28, 2020).
82   https://www.berria.eus/estiloliburua/ (Accessed April 27, 2019).
83   https://rm.coe.int/spainpr5-en/16808de6fc (Accessed October 28, 2020).
84   For 2022–2024, for instance, see the call:
     https://www.euskadi.eus/ayuda_subvencion/2016/hedabideak-2016-grupo-a/web01-tramite/es/ (Accessed July 31, 2024).
85   See the Report of the Committee of Experts of 2018, ibid.,192.
86   In English, "once a day." This app is developed by the company Codesyntax and is a big success among Basques. https://www.codesyntax.com/es/proyectos/egunean-behin (Accessed October 14, 2020).
87   There are (as of June 2021) petitions asking Netflix and Disney+ to provide more content dubbed or subtitled in Basque. Similarly, streamers on the Twitch platform are asking the Basque language (alongside other regional or minority languages) to be included as a streaming language tag, following the success of the #CatalanLoveTwitch campaign.
88   One can find movies such as *Loreak*, *Errementari*, *Handia*, and *Black is Beltza* in Basque on this platform.
89   This magazine app was awarded the 2019 Rikardo Arregi Prize for journalism. https://ttap.eus/ (Accessed October 14, 2020).

90 https://www.zut.eus/ (Accessed November 4, 2020).
91 McMonagle provides an extensive analysis of this topic in McMonagle, "The European Charter for Regional or Minority Languages: Still Relevant in the Information Age?"
92 McMonagle, 13.
93 https://kanaldude.eus/ (Accessed April 27, 2019).
94 Ibid. Translated by the author.
95 http://www.audiovisuel-participatif.org/ (Accessed April 27, 2019).
96 If we look at Kanaldude's website, we can see other regional public institutions also fund this project: Région Nouvelle-Aquitaine and the Communauté d'Agglomération Pays Basque.
97 Ó Riagáin, "Some Reflections on the New Media and Lesser Used Languages," 39.
98 Ferré-Pavia et al., "Internet and Social Media in European Minority Languages: Analysis of the Digitalization Process."
99 Ferré-Pavia et al., 1072.
100 Ferré-Pavia et al., 1079.
101 Ferré-Pavia et al., 1080.
102 This project was elaborated with 2deo, an audio-visual lab which is a collaboration between a private media group and a public institution.
103 https://primeran.eus/ (Accessed July 31, 2024).
104 https://makusi.eus/ (Accessed July 31, 2024).
105 https://www.eitb.eus/es/grupo-eitb/detalle/9305507/primeran-nueva-plataforma-de-streaming-en-euskera-y-de-contenidos-vascos--desde-15-de-septiembre-de-2023/ (Accessed July 31, 2024).
106 https://www.eitb.eus/es/grupo-eitb/detalle/9480701/arranca-makusi-primera-plataforma-digital-en-euskera-para-publico-infantil-y-juvenil-26-de-abril/#:~:text=Al%20igual%20que%20el%20resto,haciendo%-20cast%20desde%20tu%20dispositivo (Accessed July 31, 2024).

Conclusion

The questions this research has tried to answer are, first, how Euskara is regulated by law in the three Basque administrations and, second, what the nature of the relationship is between this legal framework and Basque society. To answer these questions, this book has provided a comparative analysis between France and Spain, and it has showcased how the legal framework of a minority language changes the outcome of its policies of protection, and how civil society and the community of speakers respond to this framework. For instance, when focusing on the regional regulation of the Basque language in Spain, by looking at both Navarre and the BAC, we have seen how, despite being under the same national normative framework, the local or regional regulations on the official status of a language can result in drastic differences among the practical implications for speakers. Linguistic rights in Navarre vary from area to area, whereas linguistic rights remain the same in the entire territory of the BAC. A comparative analysis of the legal framework of the Basque language answered the first research question.

Throughout this book, we have seen the pivotal role played by norm users in the Basque case. Via the examples of education and media, we identified cooperation and friction between the norm users and the norm givers: the partnership between the community of speakers and institutions, as well as roadblocks and disputes. An examination and understanding of these dynamics helped us to answer the second research question.

The author believes this study has shown the importance of examining law in context. In fact, by merely focusing on the black-letter law, one could not have seen beyond the non-recognition of officiality to the Basque language in Iparralde or in some areas of Navarre and could not have understood the reality of the Basque speakers there. The sociolegal approach in this research has enabled us to tell the story of the Basque linguistic minority, who, as a minority, is often not fully portrayed in the field of law. This is where the strength of the sociolegal methodology lies.

Within the sociolegal approach, we have used the contrast between "norm user" and "norm giver" to obtain a theoretical explanatory framework of the Euskara landscape. This dichotomy is relevant for describing the reality of the

Basque language. Tension or teamwork between the norm users and the norm givers in the case of Euskara results in a constellation of continuously evolving language rights protection. Additionally, as minorities are underrepresented or set aside in the norm giver scene, focusing on norm users is essential. Therefore, norms alone do not describe the entire picture.

The following discussion will provide a critical summary of the research to provide some recommendations *de lege ferenda*, as well as implications for future research.

Summary

This research on the legal framework of the Basque language has shown the importance of analyzing law within its context. By examining the legal framework of the Basque language, we better understand the reality of Basque speakers, their claims, and the different practices and dynamics they put into place. At the same time, by looking into the context, we better grasp the implementation of the legal system on the Basque language and the different outcomes it can have among the community of speakers. The Basque language is regulated in different ways: The BAC offers a comprehensive legal corpus with the aim of providing full co-officiality to the language alongside Spanish, whereas Navarre has compartmentalized co-officiality into linguistic areas, and France has barely provided for a legal framework of regional language and has rather focused on regulating the superiority of French.

This research has focused on the relationship between the legal framework of the Basque language and society. Because Euskara, the Basque language, is a minority language both in France and in Spain, we have analyzed its rich and heterogeneous legal framework from both national as well as regional systems. Even in Spain, we noted the disparities between the legal regime of the Basque language in the BAC and in Navarre. Thus, under the same constitutional regime, two different approaches toward the protection of the Basque language have been undertaken.

Article 3 of the Spanish Constitution recognizes and protects the multilinguistic realities of Spain but relies on the autonomous communities for their recognition and protection. Therefore, the Basque language is protected in the two autonomous communities that categorize this language as co-official. This "territorial" thinking of language protection has been paired with the central state becoming the guardian of the Spanish language. Sadly, this has led to some controversies, notably in the realm of state administration or the judicial systems, which have been systemically posing difficulties for the implementation of the Language Charter. In fact, the monitoring mechanism of the Language Charter has raised the need to tackle the issue of the non-inclusion of co-official languages in state administration and their lack of use and limited access in the judicial system. These issues remain of utmost importance even in the latest report of 2018.

The analysis of the legal framework of the Basque language has shown the constant tension that still exists between Spanish and regional languages, and between the central state and the autonomous communities. The sharing of competences is not an easy task, and the linguistic zoning of Navarre does not help. Such zoning seems to strengthen divisions in Navarre and adds a layer of complication to linguistic rights. As we have seen in this research, scholars, Language Charter experts and the Committee of Ministers have insisted on the difficulties this language zoning poses for effective protection of the Basque language in Navarre. Indeed, working with linguistic rights in Navarre looks a lot like juggling. Notably, by focusing on the example of education and media, we have discovered what linguistic zoning entails for the everyday life of Basque speakers and their access to education and media in Basque.

With the example of media, we have seen the stubbornness of the Navarrese administration to follow a lawful procedure to admit a radio broadcasting station fully in Basque in Pamplona, a refusal that even extends to court challenges. The right to access education in Basque in Navarre is heavily influenced by linguistic zoning. Luckily, civil society has intervened to fill the gap, with the creation of Ikastola schools, for instance. However, despite the offering of education in Basque on paper, Model D is still not as available as it should be. Furthermore, during this research we have uncovered other factors besides the legal system and its (non)application that are essential to understanding education in Basque. The diversity of Navarrese society is not merely linguistic. Factors such as economic background or political beliefs are essential when contextualizing this issue. In fact, the shift of power in 2015 clearly marked a positive turn in favor of language rights in Navarre, showing the importance of politics for language rights in this administrative territory.

We have also dived into the autonomous community of the BAC, which aspires to fully grant co-officiality to the Basque language.[1] And, throughout the book, what stands out is the militant approach in favor of Euskara by the BAC, which multiplies cooperation with Navarre and Iparralde, even with pecuniary help. From the educational system, in which the Basque language is included in all the three major systems of public schooling, to the commitment for a bilingual offer in higher education, the BAC has the most inclusive offering in education in Euskara. Regarding media, the BAC has put into place EITB, which broadcasts also in Navarre and Iparralde, covering the three Basque administrative territories, and taking a proactive role for the normalization of the Basque language. Despite the issues EITB still has, and the need for a reform, as we have already analyzed, it remains the media of reference when it comes to television broadcasting in Basque. Apart from public media, the BAC also takes a proactive approach toward funding private media in Basque, and newspapers such as *Berria* benefit from this funding. Indeed, the BAC dedicates energy and budget money toward the normalization of the Basque language in all aspects of social life. The idea of linguistic normalization is entrenched in the BAC.

In this book we have elaborated on the rights of the Basque language in all the administrations where it is spoken. Therefore, we have also researched the legal framework of the Basque language in France and in Iparralde. In France, we have seen the tradition of a monolingual state, symbolized by the proclamation of the French language as the language of the nation in Article 2 of the Constitution. Yet, the constitutional amendment of 2008 included a mention of the regional languages. Despite the hope that speakers of regional languages of France had placed in this article, we have seen it did not result in many changes. It has also been interesting to analyze the legal framework of the Basque language in a new setting, since in 2017 the region of Iparralde gained administrative recognition for the first time in France, with the creation of the *Communauté d'Agglomération Pays Basque*. Notwithstanding France not granting the same level of devolution of powers to Iparralde as Spain does with the autonomous communities, we identified small steps taken in favor of the Basque language, notably in education with the existence of bilingual education or the inclusion of immersive schooling in early stages. However, as the 2021 decision[2] of the Constitutional Council on the newly adopted Molac law[3] clearly showed, France is far from adopting immersive schooling in public schools any time soon.

What seems to define the context of the Basque language in Iparralde are bottom-up dynamics. Civil society, or the community of speakers, is very active in creating projects, filling the gap left by the legal framework. Basque speakers in Iparralde have expectations for their linguistic rights to be fulfilled, and the legal system seems to constantly fail them. Yet, by using private law, they manage to create immersive schooling with Ikastola schools or web-television channels with Kanaldude. Also, the POBL, in transborder collaboration with the BAC, offers a funding opportunity for schooling and media broadcasting in Basque.

This book sought to define the legal framework of the Basque language and to define the interconnections between it and society, and it has clearly shown that norm users have a way of influencing the law in books. The example of education has shown, for instance, since the offer of schooling models depends on the enrollment of children in Model A, B, or D, that parents have a say in the educational system's offering in Euskara. This provokes a ripple effect, wherein more parents choosing to send their children to Model D makes Model D more available, thus inviting more children to be enrolled in Model D (because the nearest school offers Model D, for instance). Also, the demand created by civil society or the community of speakers pushes the normative order to evolve. To illustrate this, we have seen how Ikastola schools were created when schooling in the Basque language was not available. That ended up creating the expectation for the Basque government in the BAC to create a school system where Euskara was taught and was used as a means to teach. Other times, norm users do not see their needs met by the legal framework and thus, work to fill the gap. This is the case of Ikastola schools, Kanaldude, Euskalerria Irratia, or Egunkaria, for instance.

We have seen that norm users—the speakers in this case—have a way of influencing the law. Yet, the normative framework is extremely important for achieving such a goal. In other words, norm users might want to include immersive schooling in Iparralde, but the normative framework conditions and shapes the way they can do this. Over time, by mobilization, civil society has managed to make changes and improve the reality of immersive schooling in France. However, since the Constitutional Council has decided on the unconstitutionality of the inclusion of immersive schooling in public schools, the only way to do so remains private law.

Additionally, this research revealed that norm givers are also norm users. Norm givers create policies to put norms into practice. This is illustrated in media by the creation of EITB by the government of the BAC. The BAC included the co-officiality of the Basque language together with Spanish in its Statute of Autonomy but did not stop there. To fully proceed to the "normalization" of the language, it also created a Basque public media where speakers (and even non-speakers) could turn to receive information and entertainment in Euskara. In education, we could mention the creation of immersive and bilingual schooling in Basque, and all the support that this needs to be implemented: education of teachers, funding, infrastructures, and more. This extends to the cooperation agreements signed between the POBL and the BAC for funding projects participating in the development of the Basque language.

This book also contributes to the discussion on the linguistic side of the right to freedom of expression. We have discussed both the positive and negative aspects of this right. France portrays the negative aspect (the right to use one's language) while the BAC embodies both the positive and the negative aspects by its proactive attitude toward the Basque language. Navarre lies somewhere in between, as the situation in Navarre is always more complicated because of the political division on language matters and the linguistic zoning. The negative right sets the bare minimum for the fulfillment of freedom of expression of linguistic-minority speakers, whereas the positive right involves a comprehensive approach to the rights of the speaker. In other words, it goes a step further, guaranteeing that minority language speakers can receive information in their language, for the better achievement of linguistic rights.

The gap between the expectation of norm users and norm givers is also apparent in this research. Navarrese norm givers and the social demand of the Basque speakers in Navarre do not correspond. This results in the Basque-speaker community pushing for change. In Iparralde, the normative framework of the Basque language falls short compared to the expectations of the Basque speakers (norm users), who actively try to challenge it. Yet, by adopting governance practices they manage to fill in the blanks left by the legal framework.

Finally, it is worth noting this research gives an account of the transborder cooperation between institutions concerning the Basque language. Despite not being a comprehensive account of all the transborder cooperation dynamics, by transversally working on the legal framework, education, and media, this research offers an understanding of the key elements of transborder cooperation in the realm of Basque language rights.

Recommendations

Based on the research conducted, one clear issue that this book has highlighted is the difficulties posed by the linguistic zoning in Navarre. This zoning hinders the rights of Basque speakers in Navarre, and even more so those who are in the so-called "non-Basque-speaking area." Additionally, linguistic zoning makes the application of any linguistic policy much more complicated than it needs to be. For a better implementation of linguistic rights in Navarre, the abolition of linguistic zoning would be advisable in favor of a co-official regime like the one in place in the BAC. Moreover, because the main administrative institutions, educational institutions, and media broadcasting are in Iruñea (in the Mixed area), there is already some co-officiality that must already be installed—in theory. And yet, as we have seen, the practice of the law in books shows there is still work to do for the fulfillment of these rights. Therefore, this would not involve too great a logistical effort from the Navarrese government to put into place. However, as we have seen on multiple occasions in this book, the biggest obstacle toward the implementation of the current linguistic rights, and by extension future general co-officiality in all of Navarre, is politics and not law. The division over linguistic rights seems extremely important, sometimes unsurmountable, in Navarre. Therefore, even though fully extending the co-official regime to the entire territory seems to be the most beneficial scenario for Basque speakers in Navarre, with the implementation of a real choice for citizens to use, instruct, study, or access media in either of the official languages, the social and political reality of Navarre does not allow for that in the foreseeable future. Discourses of "anxiety logic" over the so-called "imposition" of the Basque language are an everyday matter.

Another takeaway from this research is the need for a more comprehensive legal framework toward granting rights to linguistic minorities in France, and not a mere declaration for the protection of regional languages. Such a declaration, first, does not guarantee any concrete rights for these minorities, as decided by the Constitutional Council in 2011,[4] and second, does not cover all linguistic minorities in France (only "regional" languages). In addition, the social expectation of strengthening minority language rights is shown by the constant attempts to adopt laws protecting regional languages (the most recent being the Molac law)[5] or to adopt the Language Charter; this expectation is also displayed by civil society's and communities of speakers' efforts to fill the gaps left by the legal framework. It would be advisable, therefore, not only to strengthen the legal protection of regional or minority languages in France to meet the expectations of the community of speakers, but also to strengthen the presence of these languages where they are already limitedly included—places such as public television and radio broadcasting, public education, and public institutions such as the POBL—so that these languages are not relegated to the private sphere.

On a positive note, transborder cooperation seems to be an effective method for the improvement of the Basque language overall. Transborder cooperation shows that uniting forces—notably between Hegoalde and Iparralde—help the Basque language. Resources go further when cooperation is the order of the day.

It is important for the central state in Spain to honor the articles of the Language Charter that require from it efforts, namely regarding the inclusion of regional or minority languages protected under this text both in the central administration system and the judicial system. Although this book did not examine these two areas of social life, this issue has been repeatedly emphasized in numerous monitoring mechanism reports of the Language Charter.

Considering the teachers' interviews and the trend of increasing immigration, policymakers ought to acknowledge that the shape of Basque society is changing, and, therefore, the educational system needs to change with it. Another layer to this is that many immigrants who join Navarre or the BAC come from Spanish-speaking countries of origin and thus, the study and use Basque needs to be emphasized. In Iparralde, society is still mostly French-speaking, and the immigrants are also mainly French-speaking. This poses a problem in a reality where Basque speakers already have difficulties learning, using, and accessing media in Basque. It is rare for the "monolingual" French-speaking community to feel a connection toward the Basque language or a need to learn or use it. This adds to the decline of the language.

Additionally, a common issue in all three administrations is the (lack of) social use of the Basque language. Even in the BAC, where studying, accessing media, working, and interacting with the local and regional administration is possible in Euskara, there seems to be a significant concern about the decrease of the social use of Basque. In Iparralde, even in immersive schools, the use of the Basque language among students during the breaks or outside of school is a challenge. In Navarre, the same issue is apparent, even among the students enrolled in Model D. This research did not study the social use of the Basque language, but one area that could help it might be media. However, to be relevant for the younger generations, media must evolve, notably from the television to the smartphone and the internet. Media can help create vocabulary that younger generations would use, but it needs to consider the new consumption of media. Luckily, 2deo is already working with this new generation in mind, but a greater number of similar projects or with a similar idea in mind are needed to bring Euskara to media platforms that these generations would use.

Implications for Future Research

This research has contributed, first, critical information on the legal framework of the Basque language throughout the entire Basque Country. It did so by carrying out a comparative analysis on the regulation of the Basque language both in France and in Spain and in all three administrative regions where Basque is spoken. Comprehensive research needed to be conducted on this matter, so that the entire community of Basque speakers is represented, and not only the members in Spain. As shown in the literature review, scholarly work on the Basque language tends to focus on the Spanish side, and little research analyzes the Basque Country in its entirety because of the difficulties in exploring two national regulations as well as three administrative legal systems. This research has successfully managed to provide the whole spectrum of the regulation of the Basque language, as well as its regulation on education and media specifically, all three administrative regions included. The comparative analysis provided in this book has the potential to encourage similar projects about other regional or minority languages. Moreover, it is hoped that it will inspire further research focusing on the entire legal system of the Basque Country, including both the French and the Spanish sides.

Second, this book has provided a sociolegal view on the subject, which adds a layer of explanation as well as context to the normative dimension of the Basque language. Interviews and examples in the areas of education and media give a more accurate view on the law in action surrounding the Basque language. The current research has some limitations, notably since it covers only two areas of social life. Indeed, the book elaborates on two areas—education and media—which are nevertheless fundamental when talking about regional or minority languages, but future studies could address more examples. For instance, further research could elaborate on areas such as social, economic, and cultural lives; administration; and judicial institutions. Nevertheless, by focusing on these two examples, the book has already provided an accurate portrait of the context of the legal framework of the Basque language.

Third, this book confirms the linguistic content of the right of freedom of expression. Additionally, we have elaborated on the negative and positive aspects of this right. Hence, this research offers evidence of the importance of freedom of expression for minority language speakers. This right includes both the right to use one's language and the right to receive information in one's language. The example of the *Egunkaria* newspaper shows the importance of taking into consideration the linguistic content when discussing the closure of a media outlet writing or broadcasting in a minority language. The "anxiety logic" behind its closure was discriminatory and affected both the right of Basque journalists to publish a newspaper entirely in Basque, and the right of Basque speakers to access a daily newspaper in Euskara. Thus, by focusing on this example, the case law from the European Court of Human Rights helped us to analyze the linguistic aspect of freedom of expression.

This argument on the linguistic content of freedom of expression ties back to the claim of language rights not being only a group right but also being an individual right. Language rights are often only conceived in a collective fashion, yet, by focusing on the speaker, the norm user, the individual, we understand one's right to use their mother tongue or the language of one's choice, as well as one's right to receive information in their mother tongue or their language of choice. Further research, notably comparative research on other linguistic minorities, would provide more empirical examples on the linguistic side of the freedom of expression.

Additionally, this book has found that future research could usefully examine how this normative framework on the Basque language will respond to new challenges, such as the recent increase in immigration (notably for schooling) and the topic of new media and new generations accessing them (2deo is already considering this new generation). The current book could be a stepping stone for such research.

Overall, this book has shown the richness of the Basque language, its legal framework, and its social context, and it has highlighted the added value of undertaking a sociolegal study approach. Despite the challenge of analyzing the legal framework of the entire Basque Country, it has provided a much-needed comprehensive view of the normative dimension of the Basque language. Moreover, by taking a sociolegal approach to the Basque language and analyzing the examples of education and media, the author has been able to present the whole story of the normative dimension of the Basque language. It is hoped that this research will inspire further study on Euskara, other regional or minority languages, or even stake a claim for the added value provided by the sociolegal approach.

Notes

1 Yet recently (as of 2024), we can observe a trend of backsliding on granting co-officiality in accessing the administration in the BAC because of recent judicial decisions. See Arzoz, "Las consecuencias de la confusa doctrina constitucional sobre el "equilibrio inexcusable" entre las lenguas oficiales: a propósito de la STC 85/2023, de 5 de julio."
2 Decision of the Constitutional Council no. 2021-818, May 21, 2021.
3 Law no. 2021-641 on the heritage protection of regional languages and their promotion.
4 Decision of the Constitutional Council no. 2011-130, May 20, 2011.
5 It must be said, optimistically, a recent (as of 2024) decision of the Council of the State in 2022 accepted the inclusion of regional languages when outside the scope of the Toubon law of 1994. For further explanation, see Gaillard, "L'arrêt du Conseil d'Etat, collectif pour la défense des loisirs verts: les petits pas des langues régionales."

Bibliography

Adrey, Jean-Bernard. *Discourse and struggle in minority language policy formation: Corsican language policy in the EU context of governance.* Palgrave studies in minority languages and communities. Basingstoke [England]; New York: Palgrave Macmillan, 2009.

———. "Language, Nation and State in French Linguistic Nationalism: History, Developments and Perspectives." En *Discourse and struggle in minority language policy formation: Corsican language policy in the EU context of governance*, 107-41. Palgrave studies in minority languages and communities. Palgrave Macmillan, 2009.

Agirreazkuenaga, Iñaki. "Euskararen Araubide Juridikoa Autonomia Erkidegoan, Nafarroan eta Ipar Euskal Herrian." *Bat Soziolinguistika Aldizkaria* n° 70 (2009): 15-40.

———. "La carta europea de lenguas regionales o minoritarias del Consejo de Europa como derecho interno." En *Estudios sobre el estatuto jurídico de las lenguas en España*, 105-46. Atelier Editorial, 2006.

Agirreazkuenaga, Irati. "The role of the media in empowering minority identities: Basque-language radio during the Franco dictatorship (1960s–1976) and their influence as identity catalysts." *Media, Culture & Society* 34 (4) (2012): 498-509.

Aldasoro Lecea, Eduardo. "La evolución de la enseñanza en euskera en Navarra: una perspectiva pedagógica." *Revista internacional de estudios vascos* 46, 2 (2001): 593-624.

Aragón Reyes, Manuel. "Las competencias del Estado y las Comunidades Autónomas sobre Educación." *Revista Española de Derecho Constitucional* núm.98 (2013): 191-99.

Arzoz, Xabier. Bilingual Higher Education in the Legal Context. Group Rights, State Policies and Globalisation. Volume 2. Studies in International Minority and Group Rights, 2012.

———. "Estatuto jurídico del Euskera en Navarra." En *Estudios sobre el estatuto jurídico de las lenguas en España*, 1a Edición. Atelier Editorial, 2006.

———. "Las consecuencias de la confusa doctrina constitucional sobre el "equilibrio inexcusable" entre las lenguas oficiales: a propósito de la STC 85/2023, de 5 de julio." *Revista de Llengua i Dret-Journal of Language and Law* (blog), 16 de mayo de 2024.

———. "Legal Mobilisation at the Subnational Level: The Case of Language Rights in the Spanish Autonomous Community of Navarre." En *Dia Anagnostou (ed.), Rights and Courts in pursuit of social change : Legal mobilisation in the multilevel European system?*, Oñati international series in law and Society, 53-77. Oxford: Hart Publishing, 2014.

———. "New Developments in Spanish Federalism." *L'Europe en Formation*, n.º nº363 (2012): 179-88.

———. "The implementation of the European Charter for Regional or Minority Languages in Spain." En *The European Charter for Regional or Minority Languages: Legal Challenges and Opportunities*, Council of Europe, 2008.

———. "The protection of linguistic diversity through Article 22 of the Charter of Fundamental Rights." En *Respecting linguistic diversity in the European Union*, editado por Xabier Arzoz, 145-173, 2008.

Ayerbe, Mª Rosa. "Las fuentes del Derecho territorial vasco y navarro." En *Identitateak Eta Euskal Zuzenbideak. Indagaciones Sobre Identidades y Derecho Vasco. Les Identités et Les Droits Basques En Questions.* Enquiries into Basque Identities and Laws, 77-106, 2018.

Azurmendi, M. J., E Bachoc, y F Zabaleta. "Reversing Language Shift: The Case of Basque." En *Can threatened languages be saved?*, 234-59, 2001.

Baztarrika Galparsoro, Patxi. "A Look at the European Charter for Regional or Minority Languages from the Point of View of the Basque Language and the Basque Country." *Revista de Llengua i Dret*, n.º 69 (2018): 52-77.

Bengoetxea, Joxerramon. "Legal theory and sociology of law." En *Research Handbook on the Sociology of Law*, 7-18. Edward Elgar Publishing, 2020.

———. Neil MacCormick y la razón práctica institucional, 2015.

———. "The Formal and the Ideal Euskal Herria: Plural Identities and Laws." *En Identitateak Eta Euskal Zuzenbideak. Indagaciones Sobre Identidades y Derecho Vasco. Les Identités et Les Droits Basques En Questions.* Enquiries into Basque Identities and Laws, 340-48, 2018.

Benoit-Rohmer, Florence. "Les langues officieuses de la France." *Revue française de droit constitutionnel*, n.º 2001/1 (nº45) (2001): 3-29. https://doi.org/10.3917/rfdc.045.0003.

Bertile, Véronique. *Langues régionales ou minoritaires et constitution: France, Espagne et Italie*. Collection de Droit public comparé et européen 2. Bruxelles: Bruylant, 2008.

Bullain, Iñigo. "Esparterismo berria eta eskubide historikoak." En *Identitateak Eta Euskal Zuzenbideak. Indagaciones Sobre Identidades y Derecho Vasco. Les*

Identités et Les Droits Basques En Questions. Enquiries into Basque Identities and Laws, 127-30, 2018.

———. "Identidad vasca en tránsito." En *Identitateak Eta Euskal Zuzenbideak. Indagaciones Sobre Identidades y Derecho Vasco. Les Identités et Les Droits Basques En Questions.* Enquiries into Basque Identities and Laws, 107-26, 2018.

Carcassonne, Guy. "Les interdits et la liberté d'expression." *Les Nouveaux Cahiers du Conseil constitutionnel* 36, n.º 3 (2012): 55. https://doi.org/10.3917/nccc.036.0055.

Casado Del Río, Miguel Ángel, Josep Ángel Guimerà i Orts, y Juan Carlos Miguel De Bustos. "The impact of the cuts to regional public service broadcasters on the audiovisual Industry: the Basque Country and Catalonia (2007–2014)." *Communication & Society* 29, n.º 4 (2016): 9-27.

Chicot, Pierre-Yves. "L'autochtonie sur les territoires du Canada et de la France : analyse juridique comparée du droit des minorités culturelles." *Revue internationale de droit comparé* 63, n.º 1 (2011): 109-28. https://doi.org/10.3406/ridc.2011.20134.

Cobreros Mendazona, Eduardo, y Alessandro Pizzorusso. *El régimen jurídico de la oficialidad del euskara.* Oñati: Instituto Vasco de Administración Pública, 1989.

Cormack, Mike. "Minority Language Media in Western Europe." *European Journal of Communication* 13, n.º 1 (1998): 33-52.

———. "Problems of Minority Language Broadcasting: Gaelic in Scotland." *European Journal of Communication* Vol. 8 (1993): 101-17.

De Beco, Gauthier, ed. *Human rights monitoring mechanisms of the Council of Europe.* Routledge research in human rights law. Milton Park, Abingdon, Oxon; New York: Routledge, 2012.

De Varennes, Fernand. "Language protection and the European Charter for Regional or Minority Languages: quo vadis?" En *The European Charter for Regional or Minority Languages: Legal Challenges and Opportunities*, Council of Europe Publ., 2008.

De Witte, Bruno. "Introduction: Exploring a Central Pillar of the European Minority Rights System." En *The Framework Convention for the Protection of National Minorities: a Useful Pan-European Instrument?*, Eds. Verstichel, A., Alen, A., De Witte, B., Lemmens, P., 2008.

———. "Language Rights and the Work of the European Union." En *Language Rights and Conflict Prevention*, 221-30, 2018.

———. "Linguistic minorities in Western Europe : expansion of rights without (much) litigation ?" En *Dia Anagnostou (ed.), Rights and Courts in pursuit of social change : legal mobilisation in the multi-level European system ?*, Oñati international series in law and Society., 27-52. Oxford: Hart Publishing, 2014.

———. "The Constitutional Resources for an EU Minority Protection Policy." En *Minority protection and the enlarged European Union: the way forward*, 107-24, 2004.

———. "The protection of linguistic diversity through provisions of the EU Charter other than Article 22," En *Respecting linguistic diversity in the European Union*, editado por Xabier Arzoz, 177-90, 2008.

Debbasch, Roland. "La République indivisible, la langue française et la nation." En *Langue(s) et Constitution(s)*, Presses universitaires d'Aix-Marseille., 56-74, 2004.

Díaz Noci, Javier. "La langue basque dans les médias de la Communauté Autonome Basque." *Cahiers internationaux de sociolinguistique* 1/11 (2017): 107-29. https://doi.org/DOI 10.3917/cisl.1701.0107.

———. "Los medios de comunicación y la normalización del euskera: balance de dieciséis años." *Revista internacional de estudios vascos* 43 (2) (1998): 441-59.

Dunbar, Robert. "6. The Committee of Experts of the European Charter for Regional or Minority Languages (the CECL)." En *Human Rights Monitoring Mechanisms of the Council of Europe*, editado por Gauthier De Beco, 2012.

———. "Article 7. Objectives and principles." En *Shaping language rights: commentary on the European Charter for Regional or Minority Languages in light of the Committee of Experts' evaluation*, Council of Europe, 2012.

Fernández Alonso, Isabel, y José Joaquín Blasco Gil. "Press subsidy policies in Spain in the context of financial crisis (2008–2012): An analysis of the Catalan case." *European Journal of Communication* Vol. 29, n.º 2 (2014): 171-87.

Ferré-Pavia, Carme, Iñaki Zabaleta, Arantza Gutierrez, Itxaso Fernandez, y Nicolás Xamardo. "Internet and Social Media in European Minority Languages: Analysis of the Digitalization Process." *Journal of Communication Systems* 12 (2019): 1065-86. https://doi.org/1932–8036/20180005.

Ferreres Comella, Víctor. *Constitution of Spain: a contextual analysis*. Constitutional systems of the world. Oxford: Portland, OR: Hart Publishing, 2013.

Fishman, Joshua A., ed., *Can Threatened Languages Be Saved? Reversing Language Shift, Revisited; a 21st Century Perspective*. Multilingual Matters 116. Clevedon: Multilingual Matters, 2001.

Flors-Mas, Avel·lí, y Ibon Manterola. "Els models lingüístics de l'educació obligatòria a la Comunitat Autònoma Basca i a Catalunya: una visió comparada." *Revista de Llengua i Dret*, n.º 75 (2021): 27-45. https://doi.org/10.2436/rld. i75.2021.3590.

Gaillard, Florian. "L'arrêt du Conseil d'Etat, collectif pour la défense des loisirs verts: les petits pas des langues regionals." *Revista de Llengua i Dret*, n.º 80 (s. f.): 206-16. http://dx.doi.org/10.58992/rld.i80.2023.4013.

Garat, Maialen, y Xan Aire. *Seaska 40 urte euskararen alde*. Donostia; Baiona: Elkar, 2009.

Garcia, Nuria. "Tensions between cultural and utilitarian dimensions of language: a comparative analysis of "multilingual" education policies in France and Germany." *Current Issues in Language Planning* 16:1-2 (2015): 43-59.

Garzia, Joxerra. "Basque oral ecology." *Oral Tradition Journal* 22, n.º 2 (2007): 47-64.

———. "History of Improvised Bertsolaritza: A Proposal." *Oral Tradition Journal* 22, n.º 2 (2007): 77-115.

Guset, Victor. "Le volet linguistique de la liberté d'expression selon la Cour européenne des droits de l'homme: le long chemin d'une consécration encore inachevée." *Revue Trimestrielle des Droits de l'Homme* n° 2013/96 (2013): 811 828.

Gutiérrez Montes, Eladio, y Marc Espín. "Impact of the digital dividend release on regional digital terrestrial television in Spain: the cases of Andalusia, Catalonia, the Balearic Islands and Navarre." *Communication & Society* 29, n.º 4 (2016): 29-44.

Harguindeguy, J. B., y X. Itçaina. "Towards a Consistent Language Policy for the French Basque Country? Actors, Processes and Outcomes." *European Urban and Regional Studies* 19(4) (2012): 434-47.

Heidemann, Kai A. "In the Name of Language: School-Based Language Revitalization, Strategic Solidarities, and State Power in the French Basque Country." *Journal of Language, Identity & Education* 13:1 (2014): 53-69.

Henrard, Kristin. "A patchwork of "successful" and "missed" synergies in the jurisprudence of the ECHR." En *Synergies in Minority Protection: European and International Law Perspectives*, 314-64. Cambridge University Press, 2008.

Hofmann, R. "The Framework Convention for the Protection of National Minorities: An Introduction." En *The Rights of Minorities. A Commnetary on the European Framework Convention for the Protection of National Minorities.*, Ed. Weller, M., s. f.

Irujo, Xabier, y Iñigo Urrutia. "Basque in the Foral Community of Navarre(CFN)." En *The Legal Status of the Basque Language today: one language, three administra-*

tions, seven geographies and a diaspora, 197-220, 2008.

J. Gilbert, D. Keane. "Equality versus Fraternity? Rethinking France and its Minorities." *International Journal of Constitutional Law* Vol. 14, n.º No.4 (2016): 883-905.

Kasares, Paula. "Hikuntz eskubideak Euskal Herrian: zer eskubidez ari garen eta zertan diren." *Giza Eskubideei buruzko Deustu Koadernoak* 31.Zenb (2004).

Kelly-Holmes, Helen, Máiréad Moriarty, y Sari Pietikäinen. "Convergence and divergence in Basque, Irish and Sámi media language policing." *Language Policy* 8(3) (2009): 227-42. https://doi.org/10.1007/s10993-009-9126-y.

Lacasta Estaun, Gartzen. "El Euskera en el alto Aragón." *Cuadernos de Sección. Hizkuntza eta Literatura*, Donostia. Eusko Ikaskuntza, 12 (1994): 141-278.

Levade, Anne. "Discrimination positive et principe d'égalité en droit français." *Pouvoirs* 4, n.º nº111 (2004): 55-71. https://doi.org/DOI 10.3917/pouv.111.0055.

López-Goñi, Irene. "Basque Schools in Navarre: The Early Stages, 1931-1936. *History of Education Quarterly* Vol. 45, n.º No.4 (2005): 565-592.

MacCormick, Neil. "Institutional Normative Order: A Conception of Law." *Cornell Law Review* 82, n.º 5 (1997): 1051-70.

———. *Institutions of law: an essay in legal theory*. New York: Oxford University Press, 2007.

Malo, Laurent. "Les langues régionales dans la Constitution française : à nouvelles donnes, nouvelle réponse ?" *Revue française de droit constitutionnel* 2011/1 (nº 85) (2011): 69-98. https://doi.org/10.3917/rfdc.085.0069.

Marko, J. "Constitutional recognition of ethnic difference—towards an emerging European minimum standard?" En *The Framework Convention for the Protection of National Minorities: a Useful Pan-European Instrument?*, Verstichel, A., Alen, A., De Witte, B., Lemmens, P., 19-31, 2008.

Masa, M. "Ikastolas as a Social Innovation Phenomenon: a case study." En *Implications of current research on social innovation in the Basque Country*. Current Research Series, nº4, 2011.

McMonagle, Sarah. "The European Charter for Regional or Minority Languages: Still Relevant in the Information Age?" *Journal on Ethnopolitics and Minority Issues in Europe* 11, n.º No2 (2012): 1-24.

Mezo, Josu. El palo y la zanahoria: política lingüística y educación en Irlanda (1922–1939) y el País Vasco (1980–1998). Estudios políticos. Madrid: Centro de Estudios Políticos y Constitucionales, 2008.

Milian i Massana, Antoni. *Más sobre derechos lingüísticos: reflexiones sobre los límites consti-*

tucionales y su interpretación por el Tribunal Constitucional. Estudios autonómicos y federales 5. Valencia: Tirant lo Blanch, 2016.

———. "Recognition of the Basque language in EU law: A Pending issue?" En *The Legal Status of The Basque Language Today: one language, three administrations, seven different geographies and a diaspora*, 93-114, 2008.

Monreal Zia, Gregorio. "Origen de la Ley del Vascuence de Navarra." *Revista internacional de estudios vascos* 46, n.º 2 (2001): 517-43.

Moseley, Christopher, ed. *Atlas of the World's Languages in Danger.* 3rd ed. entirely revised, Enlarged and Updated. Paris: Unesco, 2010.

Nicolau, Ingrid, y Raluca Lupu. "The Child's right to education and culture in French legislation." *Contemporary Readings in Law and Social Justice* 5(2) (2013): 255-60.

Ó Riagáin, Dónall. "Some Reflections on the New Media and Lesser Used Languages." *Journal on Ethnopolitics and Minority Issues in Europe* 11, n.º No2 (2012): 37-41.

Oroz Bretón, Nekane, y Pablo Sotés Ruiz. "Bilingual Education in Navarre: Achievements and Challenges." *Language, Culture and Curriculum* 21:1 (2008): 21-38.

Palacin Mariscal, Ihintza. "Ikastolen Elkartea, example of effective transfrontier cooperation under the European Language Charter." *Oñati Socio-Legal Series* 7, n.º n.6 (2015): 1343-70.

Parry, R. G. "History, Human Rights and Multilingual Citizenship: Conceptualising the European Charter for Regional or Minority Languages." *Northern Ireland Legal Quarterly, 61(4),* 2010, 329-348.

Pérez Fernández, José Manuel, Iñaki Agirreazkuenaga, Xabier Arzoz, y Ramón d'Andrés, eds. *Estudios sobre el estatuto jurídico de las lenguas en España.* Colección Atelier administrativo. Barcelona: Atelier Libros Jurídicos, 2006.

Pérez Medina, J.M. "The case of Spain." En *Minority Language Protection in Europe: Into a New Decade*, Council of Europe, 2010.

Poggeschi, Giovanni. Le nazioni linguistiche della Spagna autonómica: universalità della lingua castigliana e vitalità delle lingue regionali. Ius publicum Europaeum 4. Verona: CEDAM, 2002.

Pons Parera, Eva. "International Legislation and the Basque Language." En *The Legal Status of the Basque Language today: one language, three administrations, seven different geographies and a diaspora*, 74-91, 2008.

Razquin Lizarraga, Martín María. "La organización territorial interna de los territorios forales." *Documentación Administrativa, Nueva Época* n°3 (2016).

Rigoni, Isabelle, Laura Navarro, y Eugénie Saitta. "Les médias des minorités culturelles et linguistiques en Espagne, en France et en Italie." En *Les médias de la diversité culturelle dans les pays latins d'Europe*, 55-70. Bruylant, 2011.

Rosenfeld, Michel. "Constitutional Identity." En *The Oxford Handbook of Comparative Constitutional Law*, 756-77, 2012.

Rosenfeld, Michel, y András Sajó, eds. *The Oxford handbook of comparative constitutional law*. 1st ed. Oxford: Oxford University Press, 2012.

Rouland, Norbert. "La tradition juridique française et la diversité culturelle." *Droit et société* Production de la norme juridique, n.º n°27 (1994): 381-419. https://doi.org/10.3406/dreso.1994.1283.

Rouland, Norbert, Stéphane Pierré-Caps, y Jacques Poumarède. *Droit des minorités et des peuples autochtones*. 1. éd. Droit politique et teorique. Paris: Presses Universitaires de France, 1996.

Ruiz Vieytez, Eduardo J. "Minorías, nacionalidades y minorías nacionales. La problemática aplicación en España del Convenio marco para la protección de las minorías Nacionales del Consejo de Europa." *Revista Vasca de Administración Pública / Herri-Arduralaritzarako Euskal Aldizkaria*, n.º 82 (1 de diciembre de 2008): 187-225. https://doi.org/10.47623/ivap-rvap.82.2008.1.06.

Sarasua, Jon. "Euskal Telebista eta euskal telebista. Berrantolatzeko oinarri batzuk." *Jakin*, 2013.

Schmalz, Dana. "Beyond an Anxiety Logic: A Critical Examination of Language Rights Cases before the European Court of Human Rights." *Human Rights Law Review* 20 (2020): 101-19. https://doi.org/doi: 10.1093/hrlr/ngaa003.

Sieyès, Emmanuel Joseph. *Qu'est-ce que le Tiers-Etat?*, 1789.

Thornberry, Patrick, y María Amor Martín Estébanez. *Minority Rights in Europe: A Review of the Work and Standards of the Council of Europe*. Repr. Strasbourg: Council of Europe, 2006.

Torrealdai, Joan Mari. *El libro negro del euskera*. 6. ed. Temas vascos 6. Donostia: Ttarttalo, 2000.

Trifunovska, Snežana. "The case of the Baltic states." En *Minority language protection in Europe: into a new decade*, Council of Europe, 2010.

Tudela Aranda, José. "Small Worlds in the Spanish Autonomous State." *L'Europe en Formation*, n.º n°369 (marzo de 2013): 138-50. https://doi.org/DOI 10.3917/eufor.369.0138.

Urrutia, Iñigo, y Xabier Irujo. "The Basque Language in the Basque Autonomous Community (BAC)." En *The Legal Status of the Basque Language Today: one language, three administrations, seven different geographies and a diaspora*, 165-95, 2008.

Urrutia Libarona, Iñigo. "Estatuto jurídico del euskera en el País Vasco." En *Estudios sobre el estatuto jurídico de las lenguas en España*, 1a Edición. Atelier Editorial, 2006.

———. "Hizkuntza eskubideak eta euskara hezkuntza sisteman." *Ikastaria* 16 (2008): 171-90.

Verpeaux, Michel. "La révision constitutionnelle à l'arrachée." *La semaine juridique-édition générale*, n.º num 31-35 (2008): 170-178.

———. "L'unité et la diversité dans la République." *Cahiers du Conseil constitutionnel Le Conseil constitutionnel et les collectivités territoriales*, n.º nº42 (2014).

Weller, M., ed. *The rights of minorities in Europe: a commentary on the European Framework Convention for the Protection of National Minorities*. Oxford commentaries on international law. Oxford; New York: Oxford University Press, 2005.

Woehrling, Jean-Marie. "Droit des personnes, droit des minorités, droit des langues: les différentes techniques juridiques de protection de l'expression linguistique." En *Gestion des minorités linguistiques dans l'Europe du XXIe siècle*, Éd. Carmen Alén Garabato., 217-29, 2013.

———. "Introduction." En *Shaping language rights: commentary on the European Charter for Regional or Minority Languages in light of the Committee of Experts' evaluation*, 11-34, 2012.

———. "Le droit constitutionnel français à l'épreuve des langues régionales." *Revista de llengua i dret*, n.º nu. 35 (2001): 79-88.

———. The European Charter for Regional or Minority Languages: A Critical Commentary. Strasbourg: Council of Europe, 2005.

Ysàs, Pere. "La Transición española. Luces y sombras." *Ayer* 79 (2010): 31-57.

Zabaleta Apaolaza, Eneritz. "Inmersión lingüística y Constitución: una perspectiva francesa." *Revista de llengua i dret*, n.º 73 (2020): 94-112. https://doi.org/10.2436/rld.i73.2020.3440.

———. "Le ñ de la discorde : retour sur le contentieux Fañch et la transcription des noms et prénoms non français dans l'état-civil français—Eneritz Zabaleta." *Revista de Llengua i Dret-Journal of Language and Law* (blog), 30 de enero de 2020. https://eapc-rld.blog.gencat.cat/2020/01/30/le-n-de-la-discorde-retour-sur-le-contentieux-fanch-et-la-transcription-des-noms-et-prenoms-non-francais-dans-letat-civil-francais-eneritz-zabaleta/.

———. "Principios constitucionales sobre las lenguas en Francia." *Revista de llengua i dret* num.63 (2015): 92-112.

Zabaleta, Iñaki, Carme Ferré-Pavia, Arantza Gutierrez, Itxaso Fernandez, y Nikolas Xamardo. "European minority language media and journalism: Framing their marginal reality." *The International Communication Gazette* 76 (3) (2014): 275-95.

Zalbide, Mikel, y Jasone Cenoz. "Bilingual Education in the Basque Autonomous Community: Achievements and Challenges." *Language, Culture and Curriculum* 21, n.º 1 (agosto de 2008): 5-20. https://doi.org/10.2167/lcc339.0.

Appendix 1: Legal Documents

International and European Legal Documents:
- International Covenant on Civil and Political Rights (ICCPR): https://www.ohchr.org/sites/default/files/ccpr.pdf.
- Convention on the Rights of the Child: https://www.ohchr.org/en/instruments-mechanisms/instruments/convention-rights-child.
- Treaty on the Functioning of the European Union (TFEU): https://eur-lex.europa.eu/legal-content/EN/TXT/?uri=celex%3A12012E%2FTXT.
- European Convention on Human Rights (ECHR): https://prd-echr.coe.int/documents/d/echr/convention_eng.
- European Charter for Regional or Minority Languages (Language Charter): https://www.coe.int/en/web/european-charter-regional-or-minority-languages/text-of-the-charter.
- Framework Convention for the Protection of National Minorities (FCPNM): https://rm.coe.int/16800c10cf.

Spanish Constitution of 1978:
https://www.boe.es/legislacion/documentos/ConstitucionINGLES.pdf.

French Constitution of 1958:
https://www.conseil-constitutionnel.fr/en/constitution-of-4-october-1958#:~:text=France%20shall%20be%20an%20indivisible,organised%20on%20a%20decentralised%20basis.

French Laws on Education:
- Law no. 2013-595, of orientation and programming for the refoundation of the school of the Republic, July 8, 2013: https://www.legifrance.gouv.fr/loda/id/JORFTEXT000027677984/.
- Article L.123-3, Code of Education: https://www.legifrance.gouv.fr/codes/article_lc/LEGIARTI000027747739.

The Basque Autonomous Community:
- Normalization Law 10/1982: https://www.boe.es/buscar/act.php?id=BOE-A-2012-5539#:~:text=Se%20reconoce%20a%20todos%20los,la%20lengua%20oficial%20que%20elijan.

o Decree 231/2011 on Audiovisual Communication: https://www.legegunea.euskadi.eus/eli/es-pv/d/2011/11/08/231/dof/spa/html/webleg00-contfich/es/#:~:text=De%20conformidad%20con%20la%20citada,previa%20otorgada%20mediante%20concurso%20p%C3%BAblico.

Appendix 2: Interviews

- **AIRE, Xan (December 18, 2019)**
Xan Aire is the coordinator of the linguistic project of Seaska.

- **AMONARRIZ, Kike (February 8, 2019)**
Kike Amonarriz is a prominent Basque sociolinguist, humorist, and television presenter. He is currently the president of the *Euskalzaleen Topagunea* (the federation of the Basque language and Basque media associations of Hegoalde). Among other things, he has also worked as a Basque technician in the municipality of Tolosa, and as a sociolinguist, with publications relating to the Basque language. He has worked for *Argia* magazine, as well as Basque public television (EITB), where he has contributed as an actor, script writer, and presenter.

- **ARANTZABAL, Iban (July 4, 2019)**
Iban Arantzabal is a Basque blogger, philologist, and journalist. He has mainly worked in management in media, notably with the Goiena media group (where he was the director) or, most recently, in the 2deo audiovisual lab. He is also a member of the board of directors of Tokikom (the largest network of local media in Basque).

- **ARRESE, Susana (April 21, 2020)**
Susana Arrese is a parent of two daughters who went to Txantxiku Ikastola in Oñati. She belonged to the parent committee of this Ikastola. As we know, the role of parents is extremely important in the functioning of Ikastolas. Therefore, she actively participated in the functioning and decision-making of this Ikastola school.

- **GARZIA, Joxerra (January 17, 2019)**
Joxerra Garzia is a Basque journalist, writer, translator, and professor at the UPV-EHU Basque public university. He is also a *bertsolari*. As a journalist,

he has notably worked in Euskadi Irratia (Basque public radio) and EITB (where he hosted the *Hitzetik Hortzera* TV show), and he has published articles in several magazines and newspapers.

- **HARIGNORDOQUY, Eztitxu (April 20, 2020)**

Teacher of the Basque language in secondary schools of Miarritze/Biarritz and Angelu/Anglet, Eztitxu Harignordoquy is a young teacher in the French public bilingual system in Iparralde.

- **MANTEROLA, Edurne (November 17, 2019)**

In 2019, Edurne Manterola was the director of the secondary school Piarres Larzabal (in the town of Ziburu in Iparralde) and has been teaching in Seaska since 1986. She is currently still a teacher.

- **OIHARTZABAL, Lontxo (January 9, 2018)**

Lontxo Oihartzabal was among the drafters of the bilingual schooling models. He taught in the pedagogy department at the University of the Basque Country, where he notably focused on bilingualism and multilingualism, as well as helped develop educational research lexicon.

- **SILVO, Amaia (April 30, 2020)**

Amaia Silvo is a public school teacher who has taught both in the non-Basque-speaking area and in the Mixed area of Navarre.

- **TEACHER 1 (April 21, 2020)**

Teacher 1, in the town of Hondarribia in Gipuzkoa, has been teaching for more than thirty-five years. Her first years were in the private Catholic schools, and she soon moved to teaching in an Ikastola. Later, this Ikastola joined with the town's public school to become a public school (*eskola*) in 1994.

Index

Note: Figures and tables are indicated by *f* or *t* following the page number. End note information is indicated by n and note number following the page number.

2deo, 240–42, 258n58, 261n102, 271, 272

ABCM Zweisprächigkeit schools, 126
AEK (Alfabetatze Euskalduntze Koordinakuntza), xxin11, 134–35, 173n30, 174n41
age, Basque speakers by, xiii–xiv, xivf, 160, 161t, 164–65, 164f
Agglomeration Community of the Basque Country (France), 45–47, 46f, 54–55nn80,87,89, 265
Aguirre, Jose Antonio, 185, 187n12
Aire, Xan, 162–63, 181n21, 287
Aldudarrak Bideo, 240, 249
Alfabetatze Euskalduntze Koordinakuntza (AEK), xxin11, 134–35, 173n30, 174n41
Alli, Juan Cruz, 232
Amonarriz, Kike, 227–31, 254n4, 287
apps, 241, 248, 252, 260nn86,89
Araba, 66–67, 140, 226
Arantzabal, Iban, 240–41, 258n56, 287
Ardanza, José Antonio, 232
Arenaza y Segorbe, Javier Pérez de, 142
Argentina, x
Argia, 185, 238
Arias-Salgado, Fernando, 195
Arrese, Susana, 151, 180n102, 287
Arslan v. Turkey (1999), 207
Association Ekin v. France (2001), 209–10

Association of Ikastola schools (Ikastolen Elkartea), 133, 140
Audiovisual Communication Decree (2011, Spain), 196, 217n48
Audiovisual Communication Law (Law 2009-258, France), 200–201
Audiovisual Media Services Directive (Directive 2010/13/EU), 204

BAC. *See* Basque Autonomous Community
Baleraic Islands, 16, 63, 111n3
Ballantyne, Davidson, and McIntyre v. Canada (1993), 184, 206
Barkos, Uxue, 232
Bas-Lauriol Law (1975, France), 53n64
Basque Autonomous Community (BAC)
   2deo in, 240–42
   autonomy for, 60, 61, 65–68, 78n44 (*see also* Statute of Autonomy *subentry*)
   Berria in, 247–48
   as bilingual territory, 63
   Constitution stance in, 61
   demographics of, 112n21, 113–14n37
   education in Basque language in, 85, 92, 94–97, 99–100, 111n3, 112n21, 130–36, 136f, 139–51, 165–66, 169–70, 173n30, 175nn45–46, 177n68, 266, 268
   EITB in, 226–31, 233–34, 250, 267–68
   Ikastola schools in, 139–44, 145, 151, 165, 169–70

Language Charter in, 16, 19, 205–6
Law of Local Institutions of, 67
legal status of Basque language in, ix,
  x–xi, 16, 18–19, 48, 63, 65–68, 74,
  78–79n49 (*see also under* educational
  legal framework; media legal
  framework; Spanish law)
media in Basque language in, 184–86,
  193–97, 205–6, 225–31, 233–34,
  238–42, 247–48, 250–51, 253, 266,
  267–68
Normalization Law 10/1982 in, 67–68, 95
parental choice in, 145–51, 145*f*–50*f*
regional collaboration with, 134–35,
  233–34, 239–40, 251
statistical data on Basque in, xii–xvi, xiii*f*–
  xv*f,* 113–14n37
statistical data on school enrollment in,
  145–51, 145*f*–50*f*
Statute of Autonomy for, 60, 66–67, 68,
  78–79nn44,49, 95, 140–41, 194–95
teachers in, 94–96, 130–31, 165–66
territory of, ix, xxn6, 67, 77–78n38 (*see
  also* Araba; Bizkaia; Gipuzkoa)
universities in, 99–100, 135–36, 136*f,* 139,
  175nn45–46, 177n68, 230
Basque Country (Euskal Herria)
  Agglomeration Community of, 45–47, 46*f,*
    54–55nn80,87,89, 265
  Basque language in (*see* Basque language)
  cultural heterogeneity and cooperation in,
    ix–x
  diasporic communities of, x, xxin14
  territories in, ix, xxn6 (*see also* Basque
    Autonomous Community; Iparralde;
    Navarre)
  transnational support in, 133–35, 239–40,
    251, 268, 270
Basque language (Euskara)
  context for (*see* context for Basque language)

education and (*see* education)
future research on, 271–73
history of, ix, x–xi
legal framework of (*see* legal framework)
media and (*see* media)
oral transmission of (*see* oral traditions)
prohibition on use of, x–xi, 66–67
recommendations for strengthening,
  269–71
research methodology and findings on, xvi–
  xix, 263–68
statistical data on, xii–xvi, xiii*f*–xv*f,*
  113–14n37, 160, 160*f,* 161*t,* 163–65,
  163*f*–64*f,* 203
Basque nationalist party. *See* Partido Nacionalista
  Vasco-Euzko Alderdi Jeltzalea
Basque University Law (Law 3/2004, Spain),
  99–100
Belgian linguistic case, 7–8, 208
Berria, 239, 244–48, 257n42, 259–60nn70,79
Bertsolaritza, xxn4, 242–44, 259nn66,69
Bertsularien Lagunak, 174n41
Biga bai, 134–35, 174n41
Bildu coalition, 132
bilingualism
  educational requirements for, 86, 95–97,
    103, 108–9, 122n130, 130, 138
  media and, 195, 225, 229
  non-Basque languages and, xxiin30
  parental choice for, 159–60, 159*t,* 161*f,*
    162–63, 165
  Spanish Constitution support for, 63–64
  statistics on, xiv–xv, xv*f*
  teachers and, 165–66, 168–69
Bizkaia, 66–67, 140
Bressola schools, 126
Breton language, 47, 56n94. *See also* Diwan
  schools
Brouard, Santiago, 142
Bujanda, Mikel, 234

Index

Calandreta schools, 126
Canada, 23n23, 183–84, 206
Carrero Blanco, Luis, 60
Casas Vila, Enrique, 142
Catalonia
   autonomy for, 60, 61–62, 75n2
   as bilingual territory, 63
   education in, 92–93, 113n33, 126, 170n1
   Language Charter in, 16
Chaho, Joseph Augustin, 184, 186n9
Chapman v. United Kingdom (2001), 7, 25n46
Charter for the Environment (2004, France), 34
Charter of Fundamental Rights, EU, 20–21, 30n111
circulaires (regulatory acts, France), 107–9, 121n115, 128
Collaboration Protocol (BAC-Navarre), 233–34
commercial signage, language on, 23n23, 53n64, 57n100, 73
Communauté d'Agglomération Pays Basque. *See* Agglomeration Community of the Basque Country; Iparralde
Compañía Navarra de Radiodifusión, 235
context for Basque language
   education as (*see* educational context for Basque language)
   future research on, 271–73
   media as (*see* media context for Basque language)
   norm users in (*see* norm users)
   recommendations for improving, 269–71
   research methodology and findings on, xvi–xix, 263–68
Convention on the Protection and Promotion of the Diversity of Cultural Expressions (2005), 45, 199
Convention on the Rights of the Child (1989), 6, 106–7

Corsica, 34–35, 41, 55n83, 103, 120n100
Council of Europe. *See* European legal framework
court
   education regulation by, 125–29, 170n1
   European Court of Human Rights as, 6–8, 24n29, 206–13, 223n127
Creative Europe, 258n54
criminal procedure rights, 6, 19, 27n68
Cyprus v. Turkey (2001), 208

Declaration of the Rights of Man and of the Citizen (1789, France), 34, 35, 198–99
Declaration on the Rights of Persons Belonging to National or Ethnic, Religious and Linguistic Minorities, 6
Decree 5/2012 (Spain), 198
Decree 231/2011 (Spain), 196, 216–17nn44,46
Deia, 238
Deixonne Law (1951, France), 101–2, 107
diacritic marks, 47, 56n94
diasporic communities, x, xxin14
disabilities, people with, 231
discrimination, prohibiting, 4–5, 19, 30n111, 199, 201
Disney+, 260n87
Diwan schools, 38, 50n34, 103–5, 109, 126–29
Dorronsoro, Argi, 195
Durango, market of, x

EA (Eusko Alkartasuna), 178n85
ECHR (European Convention of Human Rights), 6–8, 206–13
ECtHR (European Court of Human Rights), 6–8, 24n29, 206–13, 223n127
education
   context for Basque language in (*see* educational context for Basque language)

future research on, 271–73
higher (*see* universities)
importance of, xviii
legal framework of Basque language in (*see* educational legal framework)
overview of, 85–87
research methodology and findings on, xvii–xviii, 265–68
educational context for Basque language, 125–70
  in BAC, 130–36, 139–51, 165–66, 169–70, 173n30, 175nn45–46, 177n68, 266, 268
  court role in, 125–29, 170n1
  French, 86, 125–29, 132–35, 137–40, 142, 144, 157–65, 168–70, 173n30, 174–75nn41,45, 176–77nn58,68, 266–67
  funding in, 127, 129–35, 143
  higher education as, 135–39, 136*f*, 175nn45–46, 176–77nn58,62,68
  Ikastola schools as, 126, 129, 132–34, 139–44, 145, 151, 159, 162–63, 165, 169–70, 265, 267
  immersive schooling in, 125–29, 132–34, 139–44 (*see also* Diwan schools; Ikastola schools)
  in Iparralde, 132–35, 137–40, 142, 144, 157–65, 168–70, 173n30, 174–75nn41,45, 176–77nn58,68, 266–67
  in Navarre, 131, 135, 136–37, 139, 143–44, 151–57, 166–68, 169–70, 173n30, 265
  overview of, 125, 169–70
  parental choice in, 145–65, 145*f*–50*f*, 151*t*–52*t*, 152*f*–55*f*, 158*t*–59*t*, 160*f*–61*f*, 161*t*, 163*f*–64*f*, 267
  private actors in, 139–69
  public actors in, 125–39
  recommendations for strengthening, 270–71
  regional and transnational collaboration and, 132–35, 174n41
  Spanish, 85–86, 126, 130–37, 139–57, 165–68, 169–70, 170n1, 173n30, 175nn45–46, 177n68, 265–66, 268
  teachers in, 127–28, 130–31, 137–38, 165–69
  Xalbador School as, 132–34
educational legal framework, 89–110
  in BAC, 85, 92, 94–97, 99–100, 111n3, 112n21, 130–31, 140–44
  Constitution and Constitutional Council (French) guiding, 101, 103–7, 119–20nn99–100, 127–28
  Constitution and Constitutional Tribunal (Spanish) guiding, 89–94
  French, 38, 42, 44, 47–48, 52nn61–62, 56n99, 86, 101–10, 118–23nn76,99–100,115,130–131, 127–28, 144
  higher education in, 98–101, 110, 112n22, 115n50
  human rights in, 6
  immersive schooling in, x, 96, 98, 102, 103–6, 108–9, 111n3, 115n49, 118n76, 140–44 (*see also* Diwan schools; Ikastola schools)
  in Iparralde, 86, 109–10, 122n130, 144
  Language Charter and international law in, 24n35, 89, 106–7, 111n3, 133, 135
  multimodal system in, 95–96, 97–98, 109, 112n25, 114n45
  in Navarre, 73, 85–86, 97–98, 100–101, 115n49, 143–44
  overview of, 89
  parental choice in, 95–96, 98, 102
  regulatory acts or *circulaires* in, 107–9, 121n115, 128
  Spanish, x, 73, 85–86, 89–101, 111n3, 112nn21,25, 113–15nn33,36–37,45,49–50, 130–31, 140–44

teachers in, 94–96, 102
Education Law (1881, France), 86
Egin, 238, 260n78
Egitim ve Bilim Emekçileri Sendikasi v. Turkey (2012), 210
Eguna, 185
Egunean Behin, 248, 260n86
Egunkaria, x, 185, 244–47
EITB (Euskal Irrati Telebista)
  funding for, 228, 233, 239
  as media context, 185–86, 195, 202, 203, 205, 226–34, 239, 250, 252, 253–54, 267–68
  in Navarre, 226, 231–34
  overview of, 226–27
  positive impacts of, 227–28
  reform of, 227–31
EITB Basque, 226
EITB Euskal Kantak, 226
EITB Irratia, 226
EITB Musika, 226
EITBNET, 226
equality, principle of, 21, 35–36, 39–40, 128
Errobi Promotions, 240
Eskola futura, 138
Eskualduna, 185
ETA (Euskadi Ta Askatasuna), 60, 75n7, 142, 245
ETB1, 202, 226, 229–30, 232–33, 241, 255n18
ETB2, 226, 229, 232–33, 255n18
ETB3, 226, 229–30, 233
ETB4, 226
European Charter for Regional or Minority Languages (Language Charter)
  Basque language under, generally, xii, 9, 15–16, 19
  definition of regional or minority language in, 12
  in educational legal framework, 24n35, 89, 111n3, 133, 135
  French law and, 9, 11, 16, 19, 22, 38–40, 49n23, 50–51nn39,43,47, 269–70
  as linguistic rights treaty, 11–12, 27n68
  media under, 205–6, 237–38, 248–49
  minority and minority language protections under, 9–16, 18–19
  monitoring mechanism in, 14–15, 27–28n81,83, 237, 265
  obligations under, 10
  overview of, 9–11, 74
  recommendations for strengthening, 269–70
  research methodology and findings on, xvii, 265
  Spanish law and, 9, 15–16, 19, 22, 28n88, 65, 89, 111n3, 205–6, 237–38, 248–49, 265, 270
  structure of, 13–14
European Convention of Human Rights (ECHR), 6–8, 206–13
European Court of Human Rights (ECtHR), 6–8, 24n29, 206–13, 223n127
European legal framework, 3–22
  Basque language legal status in, xii, 3–4, 8, 9, 15–16, 18–22, 74, 203–13
  Framework Convention in, 6, 16–19, 22
  freedom of expression in, 5–6, 23n22, 206–13, 223n125
  human rights language protections in, 3, 4–8, 19, 21, 23–24nn22–23,29–30, 206–13
  Language Charter in (*see* European Charter for Regional or Minority Languages)
  linguistic diversity in, 4, 10–11, 20–21, 30n117, 222n100
  linguistic rights in, 4, 11–12, 19–22, 27n68, 206
  media in, 203–13, 221–23nn98,100,125,127, 237–38, 248–49

minority and minority language protections
in, 4–19, 20–22, 23–24nn2229–30,
207–13
official and working languages in, 19–20
overview of, 3–4
recommendations for strengthening,
269–70
references for, 285
research methodology and findings on, xvii,
265
European Union Charter of Fundamental
Rights, 20–21, 30n111
European Year of Languages (2001), 204,
222n100
Euroregion NAEN (Nouvelle-Aquitaine
Euskadi Navarra), 258n54
Euskadi at War, 209–10
Euskadi Irratia, 226, 229, 234, 258n54
Euskadi Ta Askatasuna (ETA), 60, 75n7, 142,
245
Euskaldunon Egunkaria. See *Egunkaria*
Euskalerria Irratia, 225, 234–38, 253–54,
256n28
Euskal Haziak, 134–35, 174n41
Euskal Herria. See Basque Country
Euskal Ikastolen Erakundea, 140–41
Euskal Irratiak, 174n41, 203, 239–40
Euskal Irrati Telebista. See EITB
Euskal Komunikabideak, 240
Euskaltegi schools, 130, 173n30
Euskal Telebista, 195, 226
Euskaltzaindia, 186–87n11
Euskara. See Basque language
Euskarabidea, 197–98, 218n56
Euskaraldia, x, xxin10, 113n36
Eusko Alkartasuna (EA), 178n85
Eusko Irratia, 226
Euzkadi'ko Agintzaritzaren Egunerokoa
(Euzkadi's Daily Newspaper), 185

Fañch, 47, 56n94
Ferry laws (1880s, France), 86
Finland, 24n29
foral (statutory) system, 65, 78n39, 97
Framework Convention for the Protection of
National Minorities (1995), 6, 16–19,
22
France Bleu Pays Basque, 203, 258n54
France Télévisions, 201–3, 202*f*
Franco, Francisco and Franco regime
autonomy revoked by, 60, 65–67
Basque language prohibitions under, x–xi,
66–67
education under, 85–86, 94–95
media control in, 185, 243, 259n66
name selection under, 24n30
transition after death of, 59, 94
freedom of expression
context for, 244–46, 253, 259–60n75
EU law and legal decisions on, 5–6, 23n22,
206–13, 223n125
French, 198–200, 209–10, 253, 268
future research on, 272
human rights and, 5–6, 23n22, 206–8
media and, generally, 183–84, 253, 268
(*see also* media)
Spanish, 190, 244–46, 253, 268
French education
adult Basque language, 134–35, 173n30
context for Basque language in, 86,
125–29, 132–35, 137–40, 142, 144,
157–65, 168–70, 173n30, 174–
75nn41,45, 176–77nn58,68, 266–67
court role in regulating, 125–29
funding for, 127, 132–35
immersive schooling in, 108–9, 118n76,
125–29, 132–34, 139–40, 142, 144 (*see
also* Diwan schools; Ikastola schools)
in Iparralde, 86, 109–10, 122n130,
132–35, 137–40, 142, 144, 157–65,

Index

168–70, 173n30, 174–75nn41,45, 176–77nn58,68, 266–67
legal framework for, 38, 42, 44, 47–48, 52nn61–62, 56n99, 86, 101–10, 118–23nn76,99–100,115,130–131, 127–28, 144
parental choice in, 102, 157–65
regional collaboration in, 134–35, 174n41
teachers in, 102, 127–28, 137–38, 168–69
transnational political activism in, 132–34
universities for, 110, 135, 137–39, 175n45, 176–77nn58,68
French law, 33–48
   Agglomeration Community and Iparralde under, 45–47, 46f, 54–55nn80,87,89, 265 (*see also* Iparralde)
   Article 2 of Constitution influencing, 26n56, 37–40, 41, 43, 50n27
   Article 75-1 of Constitution influencing, 40–43
   Bas-Lauriol Law as, 53n64
   Basque language under, x, xi–xii, 9, 16, 18–19, 21–22, 33–48, 74, 269–70 (*see also* education *and* media *subentries*)
   Constitution guiding, xi–xii, 26n56, 33–43, 50n27, 52nn54,58, 54n75, 101, 103–7, 127–28, 199
   decentralization and, 45, 54n75, 55n83
   Declaration of the Rights of Man and of the Citizen (1789) in, 34, 35, 198–99
   education under, 38, 42, 44, 47–48, 52nn61–62, 56n99, 86, 101–10, 118–23nn76,99–100,115,130–131, 127–28, 144 (*see also* French education)
   equality in, 35–36, 39–40, 128
   Framework Convention and, 18–19, 22
   French language under, xi, 33, 35–40, 43–44, 50n27, 53n64, 57n100, 86, 101–3, 200
   General Code of the Territorial Collectivities as, 45
   human rights in, 19, 21
   ICCPR and, 9, 26n56
   Language Charter and, 9, 11, 16, 19, 22, 38–40, 49n23, 50–51nn39,43,47, 269–70
   media under, 44, 186, 198–203, 209–10, 219n69, 253
   minority and minority language protections under, 9, 16, 21–22 (*see also* Basque language *subentry*)
   Molac Law as, 47–48, 51n47, 53nn62,71, 105–6, 266, 269
   name selection under, 6, 47, 56n94
   NOTRe Law as, 44–45, 46, 199–200
   overview of, 33, 74
   recommendations for changes to, 269–70
   references on, 285
   regulatory acts or *circulaires* in, 107–9, 121n115, 128
   research methodology and findings on, xvii, 263–68
   sovereignty in, 34, 35, 37, 41
   Toubon Law as, 43–44, 48, 50n27, 102–3
   unity or indivisibility of Republic under, 34–35, 39, 40
French media
   Berria as, 247–48
   context for, 184–86, 226, 230–31, 247–51, 253–54, 255n18, 267–68
   distribution of competences on, 199–200, 219n69
   EITB in, 226, 230–31
   freedom of expression in, 198–200, 209–10, 253, 268
   French language mandates in, 200–201
   funding of, 251
   in Iparralde, 184, 186, 201–3, 226, 231, 247–51, 254, 255n18, 267
   Kanaldude as, 249–51, 254

legal framework for, 44, 186, 198–203, 209–10, 219n69, 253
French Polynesia, 37–39, 50n37, 104, 120n100
French Revolution (1789), xi, 34, 45
fueros, 65–66

GAL (Grupos Antiterroristas de Liberación), 75n7, 142, 178n86
Galicia, 16, 60, 63–64, 75n5, 77n29, 111n3, 194
Garzia, Joxerra, 238, 242–43, 257n41, 287–88
Gayssot Law (1990, France), 199
Gaztea, 226, 229
Gaztekom, 240
General Audiovisual Law 7/2010 (Spain), 190, 191, 193, 233–34
General Code of the Territorial Collectivities (France), 45
General State Budget Act 37/1988 (Spain), 191
Gipuzkoa, 66–67, 132–34, 140, 143, 151, 165–66, 250
Go!azen, 241
Grégoire, Abbé, xi
Grupos Antiterroristas de Liberación (GAL), 75n7, 142, 178n86
Gypsies, 7, 25n46. *See also* Roma community

Haby Law (1975, France), 102, 108
Handia, 241
Handyside v. United Kingdom (1976), 207
Harignordoquy, Eztitxu, 162, 168–69, 181n119, 288
HB (Herri Batasuna), 142, 178n84
Hegoalde. *See* Basque Autonomous Community; Navarre
Herria, 185, 240
Herri Batasuna (HB), 142, 178n84

higher education. *See* universities
human rights
ECtHR for, 6–8, 24n29, 206–13, 223n127
freedom of expression and, 5–6, 23n22, 206–8
minority language protection through, 4–8, 19, 21, 23–24nn22–23,29–30, 207–8
minority rights vs., 3

Ibarretxe, Juan José, 232
ICCPR (International Covenant on Civil and Political Rights), 8–9, 23nn22–23, 26n56
Ikas-bi, 134–35, 174n41
Ikastola schools
as context for education, 126, 129, 132–34, 139–44, 145, 151, 159, 162–63, 165, 169–70, 265, 267
creation of, x, 144
legal standing of, 98, 109, 112n25, 115n49, 140–44
teachers in, 165
transnational funding and support for, 132–34
Ikastolen Elkartea (Association of Ikastola schools), 133, 140
IKER research center, 137–38
immigration, language and, 12, 182nn123,125, 231, 270
information communication technology. *See* internet and information communication technology
International Covenant on Civil and Political Rights (ICCPR), 8–9, 23nn22–23, 26n56
international legal framework, 3–22. *See also* European legal framework
Basque language legal status in, xii, 3–4, 8, 9, 15–16, 18–22
education in, 106–7 (*see also* European

Charter for Regional or Minority Languages)
human rights language protections in, 3, 4–8, 19, 21, 23–24nn22–23,29–30
minority and minority language protections in, 4–19, 20–22, 23–24nn22–23,29–30 (*see also* European Charter for Regional or Minority Languages)
overview of, 3–4
references for, 285
research methodology and findings on, xvii, 265
internet and information communication technology
as media context, 226, 240–41, 248–53, 271, 272
media legal framework applicable to, 199, 219n67, 248–49
Iparla Baigura Komunikazioa, 240
Iparralde
in Agglomeration Community, 45–47, 46*f*, 265
Berria in, 247–48
education in Basque language in, 86, 109–10, 122n130, 132–35, 137–40, 142, 144, 157–65, 168–70, 173n30, 174–75nn41,45, 176–77nn58,68, 266–67
Ikastola schools in, 109, 132–34, 139–40, 142, 144, 159, 162–63, 169–70
Kanaldude in, 249–51, 254
legal status of Basque language in, x, xi–xii, 46–47, 74 (*see also under* educational legal framework; French law; media legal framework)
media in Basque language in, 184, 186, 201–3, 226, 231, 247–51, 254, 255n18, 267
parental choice in, 157–65, 158*t*–59*t*, 160*f*–61*f*, 161*t*, 163*f*–64*f*

regional and transnational collaboration in, 132–35, 174n41
statistical data on Basque in, xii–xvi, xiii*f*–xv*f*, 160, 160*f*, 161*t*, 163–65, 163*f*–64*f*, 203
statistical data on school enrollment in, 157–65, 158*t*–59*t*, 160*f*–61*f*
teachers in, 102, 127–28, 137–38, 168–69
territory of, ix, xxn6, 54n81
universities in, 110, 135, 137–39, 175n45, 176–77nn58,68
Iparraldeko Hitza, 240
IRALE (Irakasleak Alfabetatu eta Euskalduntzea), 130–31
Iruñeko Komunikabideak S.A., 234–36
IXA series, 252

Johansson v. Finland (2007), 24n29
Jospin Law (1989, France), 102

Kanaldude, 249–51, 254
Kazeta website, 240
Korrika, x, xxin11

Labayen, Ramón, 195
Language Charter. *See* European Charter for Regional or Minority Languages
Lapurdi irratia, 240
Law for Political Reform (1976, Spain), 60
Law of Local Institutions of the BAC (2016, Spain), 67
Law on the Basque Language (Law 18/1986, Spain), 71–73, 97, 197
Law on the Basque Public School (Law 1/1993, Spain), 95, 112n25, 141–43
legal framework
context for application of (*see* context for Basque language)
educational (*see* educational legal framework)

European (*see* European legal framework)
French (*see* French law)
future research on, 271–73
international (*see* international legal framework)
media (*see* media legal framework)
as norm givers (*see* norm givers)
overview of, 1, 74–75
recommendations for improving, 269–71
references for, 285–86
research methodology and findings on, xvi–xix, 263–68
Spanish (*see* Spanish law)
Lertxundi, Anjel, 243, 258–59n63
linguistic diversity
    bilingualism and (*see* bilingualism)
    EU law on, 4, 10–11, 20–21, 30n117, 204, 222n100
    French law on, 201
    human rights for, 4
    Language Charter on, 10–11
    media legal framework on, 190, 201, 204
    Spanish law on, 190
linguistic rights. *See also* minority and minority language protections
    EU law on, 4, 11–12, 19–22, 27n68, 206
    human rights for, 4, 206
    Language Charter as treaty for, 11–12, 27n68
    recommendations for improving, 269–71
London Agreement, 38
López, Patxi, 232

Madame Cécile L. et autres (2011), 42, 104–5
Makusi, 252
Manterola, Edurne, 162, 181n120, 288
María de Azkue, Resurrección, 185, 186–87n11, 243
media
    context for Basque language in (*see* media context for Basque language)
    definition of, 242
    freedom of expression in (*see* freedom of expression)
    future research on, 271–73
    importance of, xviii, 183
    legal framework of Basque language in (*see* media legal framework)
    overview of, 183–86, 253–54
    research methodology and findings on, xviii, 265–68
Mediabask, 240
media context for Basque language, 225–54
    2deo as, 240–42, 258n58, 261n102, 271, 272
    in BAC, 184–86, 225–31, 233–34, 238–42, 247–48, 250–51, 253, 266, 267–68
    Berria as, 239, 244–48, 257n42, 259–60nn70,79
    Bertsolaritza as proto-media, 242–44, 259nn66,69
    Egunkaria as, 244–47
    EITB as, 185–86, 195, 202, 203, 205, 226–34, 239, 250, 252, 253–54, 267–68
    Euskalerria Irratia as, 225, 234–38, 253–54, 256n28
    freedom of expression and, 244–46, 253, 259–60n75, 268
    French, 184–86, 226, 230–31, 247–51, 253–54, 255n18, 267–68
    funding in, 226, 228, 233, 235, 238–40, 247–48, 251, 257–58nn42,54
    in Iparralde, 184, 186, 226, 231, 247–51, 254, 255n18, 267
    Kanaldude as, 249–51, 254
    in Navarre, 184, 186, 225–26, 231–40, 247–48, 253, 255–56nn18,28, 265, 268
    new information communication technology and, 226, 240–41, 248–53, 271, 272

overview of, 183–86, 225, 253–54
private actors in, 242–53
public actors in, 225–42
recommendations for strengthening, 271
Spanish, 184–86, 225–49, 250–51, 253–54, 255–56nn18,28, 265–68
media legal framework, 189–213
in BAC, 185–86, 193–97, 205–6, 253
European, 203–13, 221–23nn98,100,125,127, 237–38, 248–49
freedom of expression in, 190, 198–200, 206–13, 223n125, 244–46, 253
French, 44, 186, 198–203, 209–10, 219n69, 253
in Iparralde, 186, 201–3
in Navarre, 72, 73, 186, 193–94, 197–98, 205–6, 218nn52,55–57, 233–34, 237–38
overview of, 185–86, 189, 253–54
Spanish, 72, 73, 185–86, 189–98, 205–6, 216–17nn44,46,48, 218nn52,55–57, 233–34, 237–38, 244–46, 248–49, 253
Medios de Comunicación 21 SL, 236
Mendililia irratia, 240
Mentzen v. Latvia (2004), 208–9
minority and minority language protections
for Basque language (*see* Basque language)
European, 4–19, 20–22, 23–24nn22,29–30, 207–13 (*see also* European Charter for Regional or Minority Languages)
Framework Convention for, 6, 16–19, 22
freedom of expression and, 207–13, 223n125
human rights for, 4–8, 19, 21, 23–24nn22–23,29–30, 207–8
ICCPR for, 8–9, 23nn22–23
minority rights defined for, 3
new information communication technology and, 248–49
Mitterrand, François, 46, 126

Molac Law (2021, France), 47–48, 51n47, 53nn62,71, 105–6, 266, 269
Moyano Law (1857, Spain), 85

Nafarroako Euskara Elkargoa (Navarrese Society of Basque), 85–86
Nafar Telebista, 233
names, 6, 24nn29–30, 47, 56n94, 208–9
Navarre
autonomy for, 62, 65–66, 69–71, 78n44 (*see also* Statute of Autonomy *subentry*)
Berria in, 247–48
as bilingual territory, 63
education in Basque language in, 73, 85–86, 97–98, 100–101, 115n49, 131, 135, 136–37, 139, 143–44, 151–57, 166–68, 169–70, 173n30, 236, 265
EITB in, 226, 231–34
Euskalerria Irratia in, 225, 234–38, 253, 256n28
fueros in, 65–66
Ikastola schools in, 98, 115n49, 139, 143–44, 169–70, 265
Language Charter in, 16, 19, 205–6, 237–38, 265
Law 18/1986 in, 71–73, 97, 197
legal status of Basque language in, ix–xi, 16, 18–19, 48, 63, 65–66, 69–74, 80–81nn61–62,71, 74–75 (*see also under* educational legal framework; media legal framework; Spanish law)
linguistic zoning in, 69–73, 70*f*, 80–81nn61–62,71,74–75, 97–98, 143–44, 157, 265, 269
media in Basque language in, 72, 73, 184, 186, 193–94, 197–98, 205–6, 218nn52,55–57, 225–26, 231–40, 247–48, 253, 255–56nn18,28, 265, 268
parental choice in, 151–57, 151*t*–52*t*, 152*f*–55*f*

recommendations for Basque language in, 269
statistical data on Basque in, xii–xvi, xiii*f*–xv*f*
statistical data on school enrollment in, 151–57, 151*t*–52*t*, 152*f*–55*f*
Statute of Autonomy for, 66, 69–71, 78n44, 194, 197, 218n52
Strategic Plans of the Basque Language in, 197, 218n57
teachers in, 166–67
territory of, ix, xxn6, 79n57
universities in, 100–101, 135, 136–37, 139, 236
Navarrese Society of Basque (Nafarroako Euskara Elkargoa), 85–86
Netflix, 248, 260n87
new media. *See* internet and information communication technology
New Territorial Organization of the Republic (NOTRe Law, 2015, France), 44–45, 46, 199–200
NOLEGA (Development of the Law of Normalization/Normalizazio Legearen Garapena*)*, 130
nondiscrimination, principle of, 4–5, 19, 30n111
Normalization Law 3/1983 (Spain), 77n29
Normalization Law 10/1982 (Spain), 67–68, 95, 130–31, 194–95, 238
norm givers. *See also* legal framework
courts as, 126
definition of, xvi
research methodology and findings on, xvi–xviii, 263–64, 267–68
norm users. *See also* context for Basque language
definition of, xvi
function and role of, 75
Ikastola schools started by, 144

parents as, 145 (*see also* parents, educational choices by)
research methodology and findings on, xvi–xviii, 263–64, 267–68
teachers as (*see* teachers)
NOTRe Law (New Territorial Organization of the Republic, 2015, France), 44–45, 46, 199–200
Nouvelle-Aquitaine Euskadi Navarra (Euroregion NAEN), 258n54

Oihartzabal, Lontxo, 94–96, 144, 288
oral traditions, ix, xxn4, 184, 242–44, 259nn66,69
Ordinance of Villers Cotterêts (1539), xi
Ordóñez Fenollar, Gregorio, 142
Organic Law for the Improvement of Educational Quality (2013, Spain), 93–94
Organic Law of the Universities (Law 6/2001, Spain), 99, 100
Organic Law of the University System (2023, Spain), 98
Organization for Security and Cooperation in Europe (OSCE), 4
Otano, Javier, 232

PAI (Programa de Aprendizaje de Inglés), 182n124
parents, educational choices by
context for, 145–65, 145*f*–50*f*, 151*t*–52*t*, 152*f*–55*f*, 158*t*–59*t*, 160*f*–61*f*, 161*t*, 163*f*–64*f*, 267
legal framework for, 95–96, 98, 102
Parry, Gwynedd, 10
Participatory Audiovisual Federation, 250
Partido Nacionalista Vasco-Euzko Alderdi Jeltzalea (PNV-EAJ), 61, 142–43, 178n82, 227
Partido Popular (PP), 142, 178n85

Partido Socialista de Euskadi-Euskadiko Ezkerra (PSE-EE), 142, 178nn83,85, 227
Partido Socialista de Euskadi-Partido Socialista Obrero Español (PSE-PSOE), 142–43, 191
pastolara, xxn4
patents, 38
Pleven Law (1972, France), 199
POBL. *See* Public Office of the Basque Language
Pompidou, Georges, xi
Primeran, 252
Programa de Aprendizaje de Inglés (PAI), 182n124
Public Office of the Basque Language (POBL)
  Agglomeration Community and, 46–47, 55nn87,89
  description of, 55n87
  on media, 202–3, 239–40, 250, 251
  parental choice on education informed by, 158–59
  regional collaboration with, 134–35, 174n41, 239–40, 251
Public University of Navarre (UPNA), 100–101, 135, 136–37, 236

Radio 4, 195
Radio Blanca, 235
Radio Euskadi, 226, 229
Radio France, 203
Radio Popular, 186
Radio Universidad de Navarraa, 236
Radio Vitoria, 226
Radio y Televisión Española (RTVE), 190, 195
regulatory acts (*circulaires*, France), 107–9, 121n115, 128
Réveil Basque, Le, 184
Roma community, 18. *See also* Gypsies

RTVE (Radio y Televisión Española), 190, 195

Salazar Uriarte, Alfonso, 142
Sanz, Miguel, 232
Seaska, 122–23n131, 126, 134–35, 140, 174n41, 181n113. *See also* Ikastola schools
Sidiropoulos v. Greece (1998), 7
Sieyès, Emmanuel, 34
Silvo, Amaia, 166–68, 288
Sociolinguistic Survey (2016), xii–xvi, 113–14n37, 160, 163, 165
Spanish education
  adult Basque language, 130, 173n30
  in BAC, 85, 92, 94–97, 99–100, 111n3, 112n21, 130–36, 139–51, 165–66, 169–70, 173n30, 175nn45–46, 177n68, 266, 268
  context for Basque language in, 85–86, 126, 130–37, 139–57, 165–68, 169–70, 170n1, 173n30, 175nn45–46, 177n68, 265–66, 268
  court role in regulating, 126, 170n1
  funding for, 130–31, 134–35, 143
  immersive schooling in, x, 96, 98, 102, 103–6, 111n3, 115n49, 139–44 (*see also* Ikastola schools)
  legal framework for, x, 73, 85–86, 89–101, 111n3, 112nn21,25, 113–15nn33,36–37,45,49–50, 130–31, 140–44
  in Navarre, 73, 85–86, 97–98, 100–101, 115n49, 131, 135, 136–37, 139, 143–44, 151–57, 166–68, 169–70, 173n30, 236, 265
  parental choice in, 95–96, 98, 145–57
  regional collaboration in, 134–35
  teachers in, 94–96, 130–31, 165–68
  transnational political activism in, 132–34
  universities for, 98–101, 112n22, 115n50,

135–37, 136f, 139, 175nn45–46,
177n68, 230, 236
Spanish law, 59–73
Article 3 of Constitution influencing,
62–65
asymmetric model influencing, 62
BAC under (*see* Basque Autonomous
Community)
Basque language under, ix–xi, 9, 15–16,
18–19, 22, 48, 59–74 (*see also*
education *and* media *subentries*)
Castilian Spanish language in, 63–64,
77n29, 92–93, 95–98
Constitution guiding, xi, 15, 52n54,
59–65, 67, 77nn29–30, 89–94,
189–95, 245–46
education under, x, 73, 85–86, 89–101,
111n3, 112nn21,25, 113–15nn33,36–
37,45,49–50, 130–31, 140–44 (*see also*
Spanish education)
foral system in, 65, 78n39, 97
Framework Convention and, 18–19, 22
fueros and, 65–66
human rights under, 23n22
ICCPR and, 9
Language Charter and, 9, 15–16, 19, 22,
28n88, 65, 89, 111n3, 205–6, 237–38,
248–49, 265, 270
Law 18/1986 in, 71–73, 97, 197
Law for Political Reform as, 60
Law of Local Institutions of the BAC in, 67
media under, 72, 73, 185–86, 189–98,
205–6, 216–17nn44,46,48,
218nn52,55–57, 233–34, 237–38,
244–46, 248–49, 253
minority and minority language protections
under, 9, 11, 15–16, 18–19, 21–22 (*see
also* Basque language *subentry*)
name selection under, 6, 24n30
Navarre under (*see* Navarre)

Normalization Law 10/1982 in, 67–68, 95,
130–31, 194–95, 238
overview of, 59, 74
references on, 285–86
regional laws in, 65–66 (*see also under*
Basque Autonomous Community *and*
Navarre)
research methodology and findings on, xvii,
263–68
Second Republic and, 59–60, 66
State of Autonomies under, 61–62
Statute of Autonomy in (*see* Statute of
Autonomy (Spain))
unity under, 61
Spanish media
2deo as, 240–42, 258n58, 261n102, 271,
272
in BAC, 184–86, 193–97, 205–6, 225–31,
233–34, 238–42, 247–48, 250–51,
253, 266, 267–68
Berria as, 239, 244–48, 257n42,
259–60nn70,79
Bertsolaritza as proto-media, 242–44
context for, 184–86, 225–49, 250–51,
253–54, 255–56nn18,28, 265–68
distribution of competences on, 191–94
Egunkaria as, 244–47
EITB as, 185–86, 195, 202, 203, 205,
226–34, 239, 250, 253–54, 267–68
Euskalerria Irratia in, 225, 234–38,
253–54, 256n28
freedom of expression in, 190, 244–46,
253, 268
funding of, 190–91, 197–98, 226, 228,
233, 235, 238–40, 247–48
general rules on, 189–91
legal framework for, 72, 73, 185–86,
189–98, 205–6, 216–17nn44,46,48,
218nn52,55–57, 233–34, 237–38,
244–46, 248–49, 253

in Navarre, 72, 73, 184, 186, 193–94, 197–98, 205–6, 218nn52,55–57, 225–26, 231–40, 247–48, 253, 255–56nn18,28, 265, 268
new information communication technology and, 226, 240–41, 248–53
State of Autonomies (Spain), 61–62
Statute of Autonomy (Spain)
  for BAC, 60, 66–67, 68, 78–79nn44,49, 95, 140–41, 194–95
  Constitution and grants of, 62, 64, 77n30
  fueros and, 66
  Language Charter and, 16
  on media, 191, 194–95, 197, 218n52
  for Navarre, 66, 69–71, 78n44, 194, 197, 218n52
  Second Republic grants of, 60
Strasbourg Court. *See* European Court of Human Rights
streaming platforms, 252–53, 260n87
Sükran Aydin v. Turkey (2013), 210–12
Surio, Alberto, 227

teachers
  context for, 127–28, 130–31, 137–38, 165–69
  legal framework for, 94–96, 102
Teknopolis, 230, 255n14
Telenorte, 195
Televisión Española, 195
Torrealdai, Joan Mari, xi
Toubon Law (1994, France), 43–44, 48, 50n27, 102–3
Treaty on European Union (TEU), 20, 30n117
Treaty on the Functioning of the European Union (TFEU), 20, 29n110, 203–4, 221n98
Ttap, 248, 252, 260n89
Turkey, 18, 210–12

TVPI, 240
Twitch, 260n87
Txapelketa Nagusia, 243
Txirrita, 202

Uda-Leku, 174n41
ULIBARRI, 131
Unidad Alavesa, 178n85
United Nations (UN)
  Convention on the Protection and Promotion of the Diversity of Cultural Expressions, 45, 199
  Convention on the Rights of the Child, 6, 106–7
  Declaration on the Rights of Persons Belonging to National or Ethnic, Religious and Linguistic Minorities, 6
  Framework Convention for the Protection of National Minorities, 6, 16–19, 22
  human rights protections of, 4–6
United Nations Educational, Scientific and Cultural Organization (UNESCO), ix, 4, 70
United Nations Human Rights Committee, 4–5, 8–9
United States, x
Universidad del País Vasco-Euskal Herriko Unibertsitatea (University of the Basque Country), 135–36, 136f, 175n46, 177n68, 230
Universidad Pública de Navarra (UPNA, Public University of Navarre), 100–101, 135, 136–37, 236
universities
  as context for Basque language education, 135–39, 136f, 175nn45–46, 176–77nn58,62,68
  French, 110, 135, 137–39, 175n45, 176–77nn58,68
  legal framework for Basque in, 98–101,

110, 112n22, 115n50
media collaboration with, 230, 236
Spanish, 98–101, 112n22, 115n50, 135–37, 136*f*, 139, 175nn45–46, 177n68, 230, 236
University of Bordeaux Montaigne, 137–38, 176–77nn58,62,68
University of Pau and the Adour Region (UPPA), 137–39, 176–77nn58,68
Urkullu, Iñigo, 232

Uscal Herrico Gaseta, 184

Valencia, 16, 63, 111n3, 194
Vieuzac, Bertrand Barère de, xi

Xalbador School, 132–34
Xibero telebista, 240

Zut, 241, 248, 252

About the Author

Ihintza PALACIN MARISCAL studied law at the Université de Pau et des Pays de l'Adour (UPPA), in Bayonne, France, where she enrolled for a semester at the University of the Basque Country (UPV/EHU) with a cross-border grant. She then obtained an MA in sociology of law at the International Institute for the Sociology of Law in Oñati, Spain. There, she started exploring the Basque language and its cross-border dimension. After she graduated, she was admitted to the European University Institute, in Firenze, Italy, where, with the Salvador de Madariaga grant, she obtained an LLM on comparative European and International laws as well as a PhD in law. This book is based on that research.

After the completion of her PhD, she has been working to create a Cross-Border Cooperation Institute at the Franco-Spanish border, the Euro-Institut Pyrene. This project is a collaboration of three universities: UPPA via its Center of European Documentation and Research (CDRE), the University of the Basque Country (UPV/EHU), and the Public University of Navarre (UPNA). Since the project's funding was obtained by the Interreg POCTEFA program and the strategic partnership with the Euroregion Nouvelle-Aquitaine, Euskadi, Navarre, she has been part of the coordinating team.

While creating and coordinating the project, she also started teaching courses about European cohesion policy and legal tools for cross-border cooperation at the masters of cross-border collaboration of UPPA.

She is currently a lecturer on jurisprudence and philosophy of law at UPV/EHU, where she was recently appointed as a member of the Commission of the Basque Language of the Law faculty.

In addition, she is an active member of the Oñati Community, a network of alumni and students linked to the International Institute for the Sociology of Law, where she launched and coordinates the mentoring initiative.

www.ingramcontent.com/pod-product-compliance
Lightning Source LLC
Chambersburg PA
CBHW060943230426
43665CB00015B/2039